William Gilmore Simms

The Huguenots in Florida (1562-1570)

William Gilmore Simms

The Huguenots in Florida (1562-1570)

ISBN/EAN: 9783743377240

Manufactured in Europe, USA, Canada, Australia, Japa

Cover: Foto ©ninafisch / pixelio.de

Manufactured and distributed by brebook publishing software (www.brebook.com)

William Gilmore Simms

The Huguenots in Florida (1562-1570)

THE

LILY AND THE TOTEM;

OR,

THE HUGUENOTS IN FLORIDA.

A SERIES OF SKETCHES, PICTURESQUE AND HISTORICAL, OF THE
COLONIES OF COLIGNI, IN NORTH AMERICA.

1562—1570.

BY THE AUTHOR OF "THE YEMASSEE," "LIFE OF MARION,"
"LIFE OF BAYARD," ETC.

CHARLESTON, S. C.:
WALKER, EVANS & COGSWELL, PRINTERS,
Nos. 3 Broad and 109 East Bay Streets,
1871.

Entered according to Act of Congress, in the year 1850, by
W. GILMORE SIMMS, ESQ.,
In the Clerk's Office of the District Court of the United States for the Southern District of New York.

EPISTLE DEDICATORY.

TO THE

HON. JAMES H. HAMMOND,

OF

SOUTH CAROLINA.

My Dear Hammond:
I VERY well know the deep interest which you take in all researches which aim to devolope the early history of our State and country, and sympathize with you very sincerely in that local feeling which delights to trace, on your own grounds, and in your own neighborhood, the doubtful progresses of French and Spaniard, in their wild passion for adventure or eager appetite for gold. I have no doubt that the clues are in your hands which shall hereafter conduct you along a portion of the route pursued by that famous cavalier, Hernando de Soto; and I am almost satisfied that the region of Silver Bluff was that distinguished in the adventures of the Spanish Adelantado, by the presence of that dusky but lovely princess of Cofachiqui, who welcomed him with so much favor, and whom he treated with an ingratitude as unhandsome as unknightly. But I must not dwell on a subject so seductive; particularly, as I entertain the hope, in some future labor, to weave her legend into an appropriate, and I trust not unworthy history. For the present, inscribing these pages to you, as a memorial of a long and grateful intimacy, and of inquiries and conjectures, musings and meditations, enjoyed together,

which, it is my hope, have resulted no less profitably to you than to myself, I propose briefly to give you the plan of the volume in your hands.

The design of the narrative which follows, contemplates, in nearly equal degree, the picturesque and the historical. It belongs to a class of writings with which the world has been long since made familiar, through a collection of the greatest interest, the body of which continues to expand, and which has been entitled the "Romance of History." This name will justly apply to the present sketches, yet must not be construed to signify any large or important departure, in the narrative, from the absolute records of the Past. The romance here is not suffered to supersede the history. On the contrary, the design of the writer has been simply to supply the deficiencies of the record. Where the author, in this species of writing, has employed history, usually, as a mere loop, upon which to hang his lively fancies and audacious inventions, embodying in his narrative as small a portion of the chronicle as possible, I have been content to reverse the process, making the fiction simply tributary, and always subordinate to the fact. I have been studious to preserve all the vital details of the event, as embodied in the record, and have only ventured my own "graffings" upon it in those portions of the history which exhibited a certain baldness in their details, and seemed to demand the helping agency of art. In thus interweaving the history with the fiction, I have been solicitous always of those proprieties and of that *vraisemblance*, in the introduction of new details, which are essential to the chief characteristics of the history; seeking equally to preserve the general integrity of the record from which I draw my materials, and of that art which aims to present them in a costume the most picturesque. My labor has been not to make, but to perfect, a history; not to invent facts, but to trace them out to seemingly inevitable results;—to take the premise and work out the problem;—recognize the meagre record which affords simply a general outline; and endeavor, by a severe induction, to supply its details and processes. I have been at no. such pains to disguise the chronicle, as will prevent the reader from separating,—should he desire to do so,—the *certain* from the *conjectural*; and yet, I trust, that I have succeeded in so linking the two together, as to prevent the lines of junction from obtruding themselves offensively upon his consciousness. Upon the successful prosecution of this object, apart from the native interest which the subject itself possesses, depends all the merit of the performance. It is by raising the tone of the history, warming it with the hues of fancy, and making it dramatic by the continued exercise of art, rather than by any actual violation of its recorded facts, that I have endeavored to awaken interest. To bring out such portions of the event as demand elevation—to suppress those which are only cumbrous, and neither raise the imposing, nor relieve the unavoidable; and to supply, from the *probable*, the apparent deficiencies of the *actual*, have been the chief processes in the art which I have employed. What is wholly fictitious will appear rather as episodical matter, than as a part of the narrative; and a brief historical summary, even in regard to the episode, shall occasionally be employed to determine, for the reader, upon how much, or how little, he may properly rely as history.

The experiment of Coligny, in colonizing Florida, is one of those remarkable instances in the early settlement of this country, which deserve the particular attention of our people. Its wild and dark events, its startling tragedies, its picturesque and exciting incidents, long since impressed themselves upon my imagination, as offering suitable materials for employment in romantic fiction. In the preparation of the work which follows, I have rather yielded to the requisitions of publishers and the public, than followed the suggestions of my own taste and judgment. Originally, I commenced the treatment of this material, in the form of poetry; but the stimulus to a keen prosecution of the task was wanting: not so much, perhaps, in consequence of my own diminished interest in the subject, as because of the indifference of readers; who, in all periods have determined the usual direction of the writer. Hereafter, I may prosecute the experiment upon this history in still another fashion. I do not regard this work as precluding me from trying the malleability of its subject, and from seeking to force it into a mould more grateful to the dictates of my imagination. In abandoning the design, however, of shaping it to the form of narrative poetry, I may, at least, submit to the reader such portions of the verse as are already written. My purpose, as will be seen, by the fragmentary passages which follow, (in the *Appendix* at the close of the volume,) was to seize upon the strong points of the subject, and exhibit the whole progress of the action, in so many successive scenes; as in the plan adopted by Rogers in his "Columbus"— the one scene naturally forming the introduction to the other, and the whole, a complete and single history. To these fragments let me refer you. With these, my original design found its limit; the spirit which had urged me thus far, no longer quickening me with that impatient eagerness which can alone justify poetic labors. The plan is one which I am no longer likely to pursue. It will, no doubt, have a place of safe-keeping and harborage in some one of Astolpho's mansions. It need not be deplored on earth. I shall be but too happy if those who read the performance which follows, shall forbear the wish that it had shared the same destiny. To you, at least, I venture to commend it with a very different hope.

Very truly yours, as ever,

THE AUTHOR.

CHARLESTON, S. C.,
May 1, 1850.

CONTENTS.

I.
THE FIRST VOYAGE OF RIBAULT...................................1

II.
THE COLONY UNDER ALBERT......................................29

III.
THE LEGEND OF GUERNACHE, Chapter I........................37

IV.
THE LEGEND OF GUERNACHE, Chapter II.......................44

V.
THE LEGEND OF GUERNACHE, Chapter III......................59

VI.
THE LEGEND OF GUERNACHE, Chapter IV......................71

VII.
LACHANE, THE DELIVERER..81

VIII.
FLIGHT, FAMINE, AND THE BLOODY FEAST OF THE FUGITIVES..100

IX.
THE SECOND EXPEDITION OF THE HUGUENOTS TO FLORIDA....110

X.
HISTORICAL SUMMARY..123

XI.
THE CONSPIRACY OF LE GENRE—HISTORICAL SUMMARY.....131

XII.
THE CONSPIRACY OF LE GENRE..................................133

XIII.
HISTORICAL SUMMARY..164

XIV.
THE SEDITION AT LA CAROLINE..166

XV.
THE MUTINEERS AT SEA..185

XVI.
THE ADVENTURE OF D'ERLACH..193

XVII.
THE NARRATIVE OF LE BARBU..218

XVIII.
HISTORICAL SUMMARY...251

XIX.
CAPTIVITY OF THE GREAT PARACOUSSI................................263

XX.
IRACANA..294

XXI.
HISTORICAL SUMMARY...310

XXII.
THE FATE OF LA CAROLINE..321

XXIII.
THE FORTUNES OF RIBAULT..364

XXIV.
ALPHONSE D'ERLACH...387

XXV.
DOMINIQUE DE GOURGUES..414

APPENDIX..463

THE LILY AND THE TOTEM.

I.

THE FIRST VOYAGE OF RIBAULT.

Introduction—The Huguenots—Their Condition in France—First Expedition for the New World, under the auspices of the Admiral Coligny, Conducted by John Ribault—Colony Established in Florida, and confided to the charge of Captain Albert.

THE Huguenots, in plain terms, were the Protestants of France. They were a sect which rose very soon after the preaching of the Reformation had passed from Germany into the neighboring countries. In France, they first excited the apprehensions and provoked the hostility of the Roman Catholic priesthood, during the reign of Francis the First. This prince, unstable as water, and governed rather by his humors and caprices than by any fixed principles of conduct—wanting, perhaps, equally in head and heart—showed himself, in the outset of his career, rather friendly to the reformers. But they were soon destined to suffer, with more decided favorites, from the caprices of his despotism. He subsequently became one of their most cruel persecutors. The Huguenots were not originally known by this name. It does not appear to have been one of their own choosing. It was the name which distinguished them in the days of their persecution. Though frequently the subject of conjecture, its origin is very doubtful. Montluc, the Marshal, whose position at the time, and whose interests in the subject of religion were such as might have enabled him to know quite as well as any other person, confesses that the source and meaning of the appellation were unknown It is suggested that the name was taken from the tower of one Hugon, or Hugo, at Tours, where the Protestants were in the habit of assembling secretly for worship. This, by many, is assumed to be the true origin of the word. But there are numerous etymologies besides, from which the reader may make his selection,—all more or less plausibly contended for by the commentators. The commencement of a petition to the Cardinal Lorraine—" *Huc nos* venimus, serenissime princeps, &c.," furnishes a suggestion to one set of writers. Another finds in the words " *Heus quenaus,*" which, in the Swiss *patois*, signify " seditious fellows," conclusive evidence of the thing for which he seeks. Heghenen or Huguenen, a Flemish word, which means Puritans, or Cathari, is reasonably urged by Caseneuve, as the true authority; while Verdier tells us that they were so called from their being the *apes* or followers of John Hus—" *les guenons de Hus ;*"—*guenon* being a young ape. This is ingenious enough without being complimentary. The etymology most generally received, according to Mr. Browning, (History of the Huguenots,) is that which ascribes the origin of the name to " the word *Eignot,* derived from the German *Eidegenossen,* q. e. federati. A party thus designated existed at Geneva; and it is highly probable that the French Protestants would adopt a term so applicable to themselves." There are, however, sundry other etymologies, all of which seem equally plausible; but these will suffice, at least, to increase the difficulties of conjecture. Either will answer, since the name by which the child is christened is never expected to foreshadow his future character, or determine his career. The name of the Huguenots was probably bestowed by the enemies of the sect. It is in all likelihood a term of opprobrium or contempt. It will not materially concern us, in the scheme of the present performance, that we should reach any definite conclusion on this point. Their European history must be read in other volumes. Ours is but the American episode in their sad and protracted struggle with their foes and fortune. Unhappily, for present inquiry, this portion of their history attracted but too little the attention of the parent country. We are told of colonies in America, and of their disastrous termination, but the details are meagre, touched by the chronicler with a slight and careless hand; and, but for the striking outline of the narrative,—the leading and prominent events which compelled record,—it is one that we should pass without comment, and with no awakening curiosity. But the few terrible particulars which remain to us in the ancient summary, are of a kind to reward inquiry, and command the most active sympathies; and the melancholy outline of the Huguenots' progress, in the New World, exhibits features of trial, strength and suffering, which render their career equally unique in both countries;—a dark and bloody history, involving details of strife, of enterprise, and sorrow, which denied them the securities of home in the parent land, and even the most miserable refuge from persecution in the wildernesses of a savage empire. Their European fortunes are amply developed in all the European chronicles. Our narrative relates wholly to those portions of their history which belong to America.

It is not so generally known that the colonies of the Huguenots, in the new world, were almost coeval with those of the

Spaniards. They anticipated them in the northern portions of the continent. These settlements were projected by the active genius of the justly-celebrated French admiral, Gaspard de Coligny, one of the great leaders of the Huguenots in France. His persevering energies, impelled by his sagacious forethought, effected a beginning in the work of foreign colonization, which, unhappily for himself and party, he was not permitted to prosecute, with the proper vigor, to successful completion. His sagacity led him to apprehend, from an early experience of the character of the Queen-mother, in the bigoted and brutal reign of Charles the Ninth, that there would, in little time, be no safety in France for the dissenters from the established religion. The feebleness of the youthful Prince, the jealous and malignant character of Catharine—her utter faithlessness, and the hatred which she felt for the Protestants, which no pact could bind, and no concession mollify,—to say nothing of the controlling will of Pius the Fifth, who had ascended the Papal throne, sworn to the extermination of all heresies,—all combined to assure the Protestants of the dangers by which their cause was threatened. The danger was one of life as well as religion. It was in the destruction of the one, that the enemies of the Huguenots contemplated the overthrow of the other. Coligny was not the man to be deceived by the hollow compromises, the delusive promises, the false truces, which were all employed in turn to beguile him and his associates into confidence, and persuade them into the most treacherous snares. He combined a fair proportion of the cunning of the serpent with the dove's purity, and, maintaining strict watch upon his enemies, succeeded, for a long period, in eluding the artifices by which he was overcome at last. Availing himself of the influence of his position, and of a brief respite from that oper war which preceded the famous Edict of January, 1562, by which the Huguenots were admitted, with some restrictions, to the exercise of their religion, Coligny addressed himself to the task of establishing a colony of Protestants in America. He readily divined the future importance, to his sect, of such a place of refuge. The moment was favorable to his objects. The policy of the Queen-mother was not yet sufficiently matured, to render it proper that she should oppose herself to his desires. Perhaps, she also conceived the plan a good one, which should relieve the country of a race whom she equally loathed and dreaded.* It is possible that she did not fully conjecture the ultimate calculations of the admiral. The king, himself, was a minor, entirely in her hands, who could add nothing to her counsels, or, for the present, interfere with her authority; and, without seeking farther to inquire by what motives she was governed in according to Coligny the permission which he sought, it is enough that he obtained the necessary sanction. Of this he readily availed himself. It was not, by the way, his first attempt at colonization. Having in view the same objects by which he was governed in the present instance, he had, in 1555, sent out an expedition to Brazil under Villegagnon. This enterprise had failed through the perfidy of that commander. Its failure did not discourage the admiral. Though the full character of Catharine had not developed itself, in all its cruel and heartless characteristics, it was yet justly understood by

* Charlevoix expressly says, speaking, however, of Charles IX., "qu'il fut fort aise de voir que M. de Coligni n'employoit à cette expédition que des Calvinistes, parce que c'étoit autant d'ennemis, dont il purgeoit l'etat." Of Coligny's anxiety in regard to this expedition and his objects, the same writer says: " Coligny had the colony greatly at heart. It was, in fact, the first thing of which the admiral spoke to the king when he obtained permission to repair to the court."

him, and he never suffered himself to forget how necessary to the sect which he represented was the desired haven of security which he sought, in a region beyond her influence.

From Brazil he turned his eyes on Florida. This *terra incognita*, at the period of which we speak, was El Dorado to the European imagination. It was the New Empire, richer than Peru or Mexico, in which adventurers as daring as Cortes and Pizarro were to compass realms of as great magnificence and wealth. Already had the Spaniard traversed it with his iron-clad warriors, seeking vainly, and through numberless perils, for the treasure which he worshipped. Still other treasures had won the imagination of one of their noblest knights; and in exploring the wild realm of the Floridian for the magical fountain which was to restore youth to the heart of age, and a fresh bloom to its withered aspect, Ponce de Leon pursued one of the loveliest phantoms that ever deluded the fancy or the heart of man. To him had succeeded others; all seeking, in turn, the realization of those unfruitful visions which, like wandering lights of the swamp forest, only glitter to betray. Vasquez d'Ayllon, John Verazzani, Pamphilo de Narvaez, and the more brilliant cavalier than all, Hernando de Soto, had each penetrated this land of hopes and fancies, to deplore in turn its disappointments and delusions. With the wildest desires in their hearts, they had disdained the merely possible within their reach. They had sought for possessions such as few empires have been known to yield; and had failed to see, or had beheld with scorn, the simple treasures of fruit and flower which the country promised and proffered in abundance. This vast region, claimed equally by Spain, France, and England, still lay derelict. "Death," as one of our own writers very happily remarks, "seemed to guard the avenues of the country." None of the great realms which claimed it as their domain, regarded it in any light but as a territory which they might ravage. Yet, well might its delicious climate, the beauty of its groves and forests, the sweets of its flowers, which beguiled the senses of the ocean pilgrim a score of leagues from land—to say nothing of the supposed wealth of its mountains, and of the great cities hid among their far recesses—have persuaded the enterprise, and implored the prows of enterprise and adventure. To these attractions the previous adventurers had not wholly shown themselves insensible. Ponce de Leon, enraptured with its rich and exquisite vegetation, as seen in the spring season of the year, first conferred upon it the name of beauty, which it bears. Nor, had he not been distracted by baser objects, would he have failed utterly to discover the salubrious fountains which he sought. Here were met natives, who, quaffing at medicinal streams by which the country was everywhere watered, grew to years which almost rival those of the antediluvian fathers. Verazzani, the Florentine, unfolds a golden chronicle of the innocence and delight which distinguished the simple people by whom the territory was possessed, and whose character was derived from the gentle influences of their climate, and the exquisite delicacy, beauty, and variety of the productions of the soil. He, too, had visited the country in the season of spring, when all things in nature look lovely to the eye. But such verdure as blessed his vision on this occasion, constituted a new era in his life, and seemed to lift him to the crowning achievement of all his enterprises. The region, as far his eye could reach, was covered with " faire fields and plaines," " full of mightie great woodes," " replenished with divers sort of trees, as pleasant and delectable to behold as is possible to imagine ;—" Not," says the voyager, " like the woodes of Hercynia or the wilde deserts of Tartary, and the northerne coasts full of fruitlesse trees," but trees of sortes unknowen in Europe, which yeeld most sweete savours farre from the shoare." Nor did these constitute the only attractions. The appearance of the forests and the land " argued drugs and spicery," " and other riches of golde."

The woods were " full of many beastes, as stags, deere and hares, and likewise of lakes and pooles of fresh water, with great plentie of fowles, convenient for all kinde of pleasant game." The air was " goode and wholesome, temperate between hot and colde ;" " no vehement windes doe blowe in these regions, and those that do commonly reigne are the southwest and west windes in the summer season ;" " the skye cleare and faire, with very little raine ; and if, at any time, the ayre be cloudie and mistie with the southerne winde, immediately it is dissolved and waxeth cleare and faire againe. The sea is calme, not boisterous, and the waves gentle." And the people were like their climate. The nature which yielded to their wants, without exacting the toil of ever-straining sinews, left them unembittered by necessities which take the heart from youth, and the spirit from play and exercise. No carking cares interfered with their humanity to check hospitality in its first impulse, and teach avarice to withhold the voluntary tribute which the natural virtues would prompt, in obedience to a selfishness that finds its justification in serious toils which know no remission, and a forethought that is never permitted to forget the necessities of the coming day. Verazzani found the people as mild and grateful as their climate. They crowded to the shore as the stranger ships drew nigh, "making divers synes of friendship." They showed themselves " very courteous and gentle," and, in a single incident, won the hearts of the Europeans, who seldom, at that period, in their intercourse with the natives, were known to exhibit an instance so beautiful, of a humanity so Christian. A young sailor, attempting to swim on shore, had overrated his strength. Cast among the breakers, he was in danger of being drowned. This, when the Indians saw, they dashed into the surf, and dragged the fair-skinned voyager to land. Here, when he recovered from his stupor, he exhibited signs of the greatest apprehension, finding himself in the hands of the savages. But his lamentations, which were piteously loud, only provoked theirs. Their tears flowed at his weeping. In this way they strove to " cheere him, and to give him courage." Nor were they neglectful of other means. " They set him on the ground, at the foot of a little hill against the sunne, and began to behold him with great admiration, marveiling at the whitenesse of his fleshe;" " Putting off his clothes, they made him warme at a great fire, not without one great feare, by what remayned in the boate, that they would have rosted him at that fire and have eaten him." But the fear was idle. When they had warmed and revived the stranger, they reclothed him, and as he showed an anxiety to return to the ship, " they, with great love, clapping him fast about with many embracings," accompanied him to the shore, where they left him, retiring to a distance, whence they could witness his departure without awakening the apprehensions of his comrades. These people were of "middle stature, handsome visage and delicate limmes; of very little strength, but of prompt wit."

We need not pursue the details of these earlier historians. They suffice to direct attention to Florida, and to persuade adventure with fanciful ideas of its charming superiority over all unknown regions. But the adventurers, until Coligny's enterprise was conceived, meditated the invasion of the country, and the gathering of its hidden treasures, rather than the establishment of any European settlements in its glorious retreats. It was not till the eighteenth day of February, in the Year of Grace, one thousand five hundred and sixty-two, that the plan of the Admiral of France was sufficiently matured for execution. On that day he despatched two vessels from France, well manned and furnished, under the command of one John Ribault,* for the express purpose of making the first permanent European establishment in these regions of romance. The narrative of this enterprise is chiefly drawn from the writings of Rene Laudonniere, who himself went out as a lieutenant in the expedition. Laudonniere, in his narrative of their progress, says nothing of the secret objects of Coligny, of which he probably knew nothing. He ascribes to the King—the Queen-mother, rather—a nobler policy than either of them ever entertained. "My Lord of Chastillon," (Coligny) thus he writes,—" A nobleman more desirous of the publique than of his private benefits, understanding the pleasure of the King, his Prince, which was to discover new and strange countries, caused vessels for this purpose to be made ready with all diligence, and men to be levied meet for such an enterprise."

This is merely courtly language, wholly conventional, and which, spoken of Charles the Ninth,—a boy not yet in his teens—savors rather of the ridiculous. There is no question that the expedition originated wholly with Coligny ; as little is it questionable, though Laudonniere says nothing on this subject, that it was designed in consequence of that policy which showed him the ever present

* Charlevoix describes Ribault as "un ancien officier de marine," and speaks of him as a man of experience and "Zélé Huguenot." Of his vessels, on this expedition, he says that they belonged to the class called "Roberges, et qui differoient peu des Caravelles Espagnolles."

danger of the Huguenots. It does not militate against this policy that he made use of a pretext which was suggested by the passion for maritime discovery common in those days. By the assertion of this pretext, he was the more easily enabled to persuade the Queen-mother to a measure upon which she otherwise would never have suffered the ships of the Huguenots to weigh anchor.

But this question need not detain us. Laudonniere speaks of the armament as ample for the purpose for which it was designed—" so well furnished with gentlemen and with oulde souldiers that he (Ribault) had meanes to achieve some notable thing, and worthie of eternall memorie." This was an exaggeration, something Spanish in its tenor,—one of those flourishes of rhetoric among the voyagers of that day, which had already grown to be a sound without much signification. The vessels were small, as was the compliment of men dispatched. The objects of the expedition were limited, did not contemplate exploration but settlement, and, consequently, were not likely to find opportunity for great enterprises. The voyage occupied two months; the route pursued carefully avoided that usually taken by the Spaniards, whom already our adventurers had cause to fear. At the end of this period, land was made in the latitude of St. Augustine, to the cape of which they gave the name of St. François. From this point, coasting northwardly, they discovered "a very faire and great river"—the San Matheo of the Spaniards, now the St. John's, to which Ribault, as he discovered it on the first of May, gave the name of that month. This river he penetrated in his boats. He was met on the shore by many of the natives, men and women. These received him with gentleness and peace. Their chief man made an oration, and honored Ribault, at the close, with a present of "chamois skinnes." On the ensuing day, he "caused a pillar of hard stone to be planted within the sayde river, and not farre from the mouth of the same, upon a little sandie knappe," on which the arms of France were engraved Crossing to the opposite shores of this river, a religious service was performed in the presence of the Indians. There the redmen, perhaps for the first time, beheld the pure and simple rites of the genuine Christian. Prayers were said, and thanks given to the Deity, "for that, of his grace, hee had conducted the French nation into these strange places." This service being ended, the Indians conducted the strangers into the presence of their king,[*] who received them in a sitting posture, upon a couch made of bay leaves and palmetto. Speeches were made between the parties which were understood by neither. But their tenor was amicable, the savage chieftain giving to Ribault, at parting, a basket wrought very ingeniously of palm leaves, " and a great skinne painted and drawen throughout with the pictures of divers wilde beastes; so livly drawen and portrayed that nothing lacked life." Fish were taken for the Frenchmen by the hospitable natives, in weirs made of reeds, fashioned like a maze or labyrinth—" troutes, great mullets, plaise, turbots, and marvellous store of other sorts of fishes altogether different from ours." Another chief upon this river received them with like favors. Two of the sons of this chief are represented as " exceeding faire and strong." They were followed by troops of the natives, " having their bowes and arrowes, in marveilous good order."

[*] Laudonniere, in Hakluyt, gives the regal title among the Floridians as Paracoussi. Charlevoix writes the word Piraousti, or Piracousti; " et ausquels les Castillans donnent le titre général de Caciques." Mico, in subsequent periods, seems to have been the more popular title among the Florida Indians, signifying the same thing, or its equivalents, Chief, Prince, or Head Warrior.

From this river, still pursuing a northwardly course, Ribault came to another which he explored and named the Seine, (now the St. Mary's,) because it appeared to resemble the river of that name in France.* We pass over the minor details in this progress—how he communed with the natives—who, everywhere seemed to have entertained our Huguenots with equal grace and gentleness, and who are described as a goodly people, of lively wit and great stature. Ribault continued to plant columns, and to take possession of the country after the usual forms, conferring names upon its several streams, which he borrowed for the purpose from similar well-known rivers in France. Thus, for a time, the St. Mary's became the Seine; the Satilla, the Somme; the Altamaha, the Loire; the Ogechee, the Garonne; and the Savannah, the Gironde. The river to which his prows were especially directed, was that to which the name of Jordan had been given by Vasquez de Ayllon, some forty years before. This is our present Combahee. In sailing north, in this search, other smaller rivers were discovered, one of which was called the Belle-a-veoir. Separated by a furious tempest from his pinnaces, which had been kept in advance for the purpose of penetrating and exploring these streams, Ribault, with his ships, was compelled to stand out to sea. When he regained the coast and his pinnaces, he was advised of a "mightie river," in which they had found safe harborage from the tempest, a river which, "in beautie and bignesse" exceeded all the former. Delighted with this discovery, our Huguenots made sail to reach this noble stream.

The object of Ribault had been some safe and pleasant harborage, in which his people could refresh themselves for a

* " A quatorze lienes de la Riviere de Mai, il en trouva une troiséme qu'il noroma la Seine."—*Charlevoix's New France.* Liv. 1, p. 39.

season. His desires were soon gratified. He cast anchor at the mouth of a mighty river, to which, " because of the fairnesse and largenesse thereoff," he gave the name of Port Royale, the name which it still bears. The depth of this river is such, that, according to Laudonniere, " when the sea beginneth to flowe, the greatest shippes of France, yea, the argosies of Venice, may enter there." Ribault, at the head of his soldiers, was the first to land. Grateful, indeed, to the eye and fancy of our Frenchmen, was the scene around them. They had already passed through a fairy-like region, of islet upon islet, reposing upon the deep,— crowned with green forests, and arresting, as it were, the wild assaults of ocean upon the shores of which they appeared to keep watch and guard. And, passing between these islets and the main, over stillest waters, with a luxuriant shrubbery on either hand, and vines and flowers of starred luxuriance trailing about them to the very lips of this ocean, they had arrived at an imperial growth of forest. The mighty shafts that rose around them, heavy with giant limbs, and massed in their luxuriant wealth of leaves, particularly impressed the minds of our voyagers—" mightye high oakes and infinite store of cedars," and pines fitted for the masts of " such great ammirals " as had never yet floated in the European seas. Their senses were assailed with fresh and novel delights at every footstep. The superb magnolia, with its great and snow-white chalices; the flowering dogwood with its myriad blossoms, thick and richly gleaming as the starry host of heaven; the wandering jessamine, whose yellow trophies, mingling with grey mosses of the oak, stooped to the upward struggling billows of the deep, giving out odor at every rise and fall of the ambitious wavelet,—these, by their unwonted treasures of scent and beauty, compelled the silent but profound admiration of the strangers. " Exceeding pleasant " did the " very fragrant odour " make the place ; while other novelties interposed to complete the fascinations of a spot, the peculiarities of which were equally fresh and delightful. Their farther acquaintance with the country only served to increase its attractions. As they wandered through the woods, they " saw nothing but turkey cocks flying in the forests, partridges, gray and red, little different from ours, but chiefly in bignesse ;"—" we heard also within the woods the voices of stagges, of beares, of hyenas, of leopards, and divers other sorts of beasts unknown to us. Being delighted with this place, we set ourselves to fishing with nets, and caught such a number of fish that it was wonderful."

The same region is still renowned for its fish and game, for the monsters as well as the multitudes of the deep, and for the deer of its spacious swamps and forests, which still exercise the skill and enterprise of the angler and the hunter. This is the peculiar region also, of the " Devil fish," the " Vampire of the Ocean," described by naturalists as of the genus Ray, species Dio-don, a leviathan of the deep, whose monstrous antennæ are thrown about the skiff of the fisherman with an embrace as perilous as that wanton sweep of his mighty extremities with which the whale flings abroad the crowding boats of his hardy captors. Sea and land, in this lovely neighborhood, still gleam freshly and wondrously upon the eye of the visitor as in the days of our Huguenot adventurers ; and still do its forests, in spite of the *cordon* which civilization and society have everywhere drawn around them, harbor colonies of the bear which occasionally cross the path of the sportsman, and add to his various trophies of the chase.

With impressions of the scene and region such as realized to our Frenchmen the summer glories of an Arabian tale, it was easy to determine where to plant their colony. Modern conjecture, however, is still unsatisfied as to the site which was probably chosen by our voyagers. The language of Laudonniere is sufficiently vague and general to make the matter doubtful; and, unhappily, there are no remains which might tend to lessen the obscurity of the subject. The vessels had cast anchor at the mouth of Port Royal River. The pilots subsequently counselled that they should penetrate the stream, so as to secure a sheltered roadstead. They ascended the river accordingly, some three leagues from its mouth, when Ribault proceeded to make a closer examination of the country. The Port Royal "is divided into two great armes, whereof the one runneth toward the *west*, the other toward the *north*." Our Huguenot captain chose the *western* avenue, which he ascended in his pinnace. For more than twelve leagues he continued this progress, until he " found another arme of the river which ranne towards the *east*, up which the captain determined to sail and leave the greate current."

The red men whom they encounter on this progress are at first shy of the strangers and take flight at their approach, but they are soon encouraged by the gentleness and forbearance of the Frenchmen, who persuade them finally to confidence. An amiable understanding soon reconciles the parties, and the Floridian at length brings forward his gifts of maize, his palm baskets with fruits and flowers, his rudely-dressed skins of bear and beaver, and these are pledges of his amity which he does not violate. He, in turn, persuades the voyagers to draw near to the shore and finally to land. They are soon surrounded by the delighted and simple natives, whose gifts are multiplied duly in degree with the pleasure which they feel. Skins of the *chamois*—deer rather—and baskets of pearls, are offered to the chief among the whites, whom they proceed to entertain with shows of still greater courtesy. A bower of forest leaves and shrubs is soon built to shelter them "from the parching heate of the sunne," and our Frenchmen lingered long enough among this artless and hospitable people to get tidings of a "greate Indian Lorde which had pearles in great abundance and silver also, all of which should be given them at the king's arrival." They invited the strangers to their dwellings —proffering to show them a thousand pleasures in shooting, and seeing the death of the stag.

Our Huguenots, excellent Christians though they were, were by no means insensible to the tidings of pearl and gold. These glimpses of treasures, already familiar to their imaginations, greatly increase, in their sight, the natural beauties of the country. The narratives of the red men, imperfectly understood, and construed by the desires of the strangers, rather than their minds, were full of marvels of neighboring lands and nations,—great empires of wealth and strength,—cities in romantic solitudes,—high places among almost inaccessible mountains, in which the treasures are equally precious and abundant. Listening to such legends, our Frenchmen linger with the red men, until the approach of night counsels them to seek the security of their ships

But, with the dawning of the following day the explorations were resumed. Before leaving his vessel, however, Ribault provides himself with "a pillar of hard stone, fashioned like a column, whereon the armes of France were graven," with the purpose of planting "the same in the fairest place that he coulde finde." "This done, we embarked ourselves, and sayled three leagues towards the west; where we discovered a little river, up which wee sayled so long, that, in the ende, wee found it returned into the great current, and in his return, to make a little island separated from the firme lande, where wee went on shore, and by commandment of the captain, because it was exceeding faire and pleasant, there we planted the pillar upon a hillock open round about to the view and environed with a lake halfe a fathom deepe, of very good and sweete water."

We are particular in these details, in the hope that future explorers may be thus assisted in the work of identifying the places marked by our Huguenots. Everything which they see in the new world which surrounds them, is imposing to the eye and grateful to the sense. They wander among avenues of gigantic pines that remind them of the mighty colonnades in the great cathedrals of the old world. They are at once exhilarated by a sense of unwonted freshness and beauty in what they behold, and by aspects of grandeur and vastness which solemnize all their thoughts and fancies. With these feelings, when, in their wanderings, they arouse from the shady covers where they browsed " two stagges of exceeding bignesse, in respect of those which *they* had seene before," their captain forbids that they should shoot them, though they might easily have done so. The anecdote speaks well for Ribault's humanity. It was not wholly because he was " moved with the singular fairenesse and bignesse of them," as Laudonniere imagines, but because his soul was lifted with religious sentiment—filled with worship at that wondrous temple of nature in which the great Jehovah seemed visibly present, in love and mercy, as in the first sweet days of the creation.

To the little river which surrounded the islet, on which the pillar was raised, they gave the name of " Liborne." The island itself is supposed to be that which is now called Lemon Island.

The matter is one which still admits of doubt, though scarcely beyond the reach of certainty, in a close examination from the guide posts which we still possess. It is a question which may well provoke the diligence of the local antiquary. "Another isle, not far distant from" that of the pillar, next claimed the attention of the voyagers. Here they "found nothing but tall cedars, the fairest that were seene in this country. For this cause wee called it the Isle of Cedars."

This ended their exploration for the day A few days were consumed in farther researches, without leading to any new discoveries. In the meantime, Ribault prepared to execute the commands of his sovereign, in the performance of one of the tasks which civilization but too frequently sanctions at the expense of humanity. He was commanded by the Queen-mother to capture and carry home to France a couple of the natives. These, as we have seen, were a mild race, maintaining among themselves a gentle intercourse, and exercising towards strangers a grateful hospitality. It was with a doubtful propriety that our Frenchman determined to separate any of them from their homes and people. But it was not for Ribault to question the decrees of that sovereign whom it was the policy of the Huguenots, at present, to conciliate. Having selected a special and sufficient complement of soldiers, he determined " to returne once againe toward the Indians which inhabiteth that arme of the river which runneth toward the West." The pinnace was prepared for this purpose. The object of the voyage was successful. The Indians were again found where they had been at first encountered. The Frenchmen were received with hospitality. Ribault made his desires known to the king or chief of the tribe, who graciously gave his permission. Two of the Indians, who fancied that they were more favored than the rest of their brethren, by the choice of the Frenchmen, yielded very readily to the entreaties which beguiled them on board one of the vessels. They probably misunderstood the tenor of the application; or, in their savage simplicity, concluded that a voyage to the land of the pale-faces was only some such brief journey as they were wont to make, in their cypress canoes, from shore to shore along their rivers—or possibly as far down as the great frith in which their streams were lost. But it was not long before our savage voyagers were satisfied with the experiment. They soon ceased to be pleased or flattered with the novelty of their situation The very attentions bestowed upon them only provoked their apprehensions. The cruise wearied them; and, when they found that the vessels continued to keep away from the land, they became seriously uneasy. Born swimmers, they had no fear about making the shore when once in the water: and it required the utmost vigilance of the Frenchmen to keep them from darting overboard. It was in vain, for a long time, that they strove to appease and to soothe the unhappy captives. Their detention, against their desires, now made them indignant. Gifts were pressed upon them, such as they were known to crave and to esteem above all other possessions. But these they rejected with scorn. They would receive nothing in exchange for their liberty. The simple language in which the old chronicler describes the scene and their sorrows, has in it much that is highly touching, because of its very simplicity. They felt their captivity, and were not to be beguiled from this humiliating conviction by any trappings or soothings. Their freedom—the privilege of eager movements through billow and forest—sporting as wantonly as bird and fish in both—was too precious for any compensation. They sank down upon the deck, with clasped hands, sitting together apart from the crew, gazing upon the shores with mournful eyes, and chaunting a melancholy ditty, which seemed to the watchful and listening Frenchmen a strain of exile and lamentation—" agreeing so sweetly together, that, in hearing their song, it seemed that they lamented the absence of their friendes." And thus they continued all night to sing without ceasing

The pinnace, meanwhile, lay at anchor, the tide being against them; with the dawn of day the voyage was resumed, and the ships were reached in safety where they lay in the roadstead. Transferred to these, the two captives continued to deplore their fate. Every effort was made to reconcile them to their situation, and nothing was withheld which experience had shown to be especially grateful to the savage fancy. But they rejected everything; even the food which had now become necessary to their condition. They held out till nearly sunset, in their rejection of the courtesies, which, with a show of kindness, deprived them of the most precious enjoyment and passion of their lives. But the inferior nature at length insisted upon its rights. " In the end they were constrained to forget their superstitions," and to eat the meat which was set before them. They even received the gifts which they had formerly rejected ; and, as if reconciled to a condition from which they found it impossible to escape, they put on a more cheerful countenance. " They became, therefore, more jocunde ; every houre made us a thousand discourses, being marveillous sorry that we could not understand them." Laudonniere set himself to work to acquire their language. He strove still more to conciliate their favor ; engaged them in frequent conversation ; and, by showing them the objects for which he sought their names, picked up numerous words which he carefully put on paper. In a few days he was enabled to make himself understood by them, in ordinary matters, and to comprehend much that they said to him. They flattered him, in turn. They told him of their feats and sports, and what pleasures they could give him in the chase. They would take food from no hands but his ; and succeeded in blinding the vigilance of the Frenchmen. They were not more reconciled to their prison-bonds than before. They had simply changed their policy; and, when, after several days' detention, they had succeeded in lulling to sleep the suspicions of their captors, they stole away at midnight from the ship, leaving behind them all the gifts which had been forced upon them, as if, to have retained them, would have established, in the pale-faces, a right to their liberties—thus showing, according to Laudonniere, "that they were not void of reason."

Ribault was not dissatisfied with this result of his endeavor to comply with the commands of the Queen-mother. His sense of justice probably revolted at the proceeding ; and the escape of the Indians, who would report only the kindness of their treatment, would, in all likelihood, have an effect favorable to his main enterprise,—the establishment of a colony. This design he now broached to his people in an elaborate speech. He enlarged upon the importance of the object, drawing numerous examples from ancient and modern history, in favor of those virtues in the individual which such enterprise must develope. There is but one passage in this speech which deserves our special attention. It is that in which he speaks to his followers of their inferior birth and condition. He speaks to them as "known neither to the king nor to the princes of the realme, and, besides, descending from so poore a stock, that few or none of your parents, *having ever made profession of armes*, have beene knowne unto the great estates." This is in seeming conflict with what Laudonniere has

already told us touching the character and condition in society of
the persons employed in the expedition. He has been careful to
say, at the opening of the narrative, that the two ships were "*well
furnished with gentlemen* (of whose number I was one) and old
soldiers."* The apparent contradiction may be reconciled by a
reference to the distinction, which, until a late period, was made
in France, between the noblesse and mere gentlemen. The word
gentleman had no such signification, in France, at that period, as
it bears to-day. To apply it to a nobleman, indeed, would have
been, at one time, to have given a mortal affront, and a curious
anecdote is on record, to this effect in the case of the Princess de
la Roche Sur Yon, who, using the epithet "gentilhomme" to a
nobleman, was insulted by him; and, on demanding redress of
the monarch, was told that she deserved the indignity, having
been guilty of the first offence.

But Ribault's speech suggested to his followers that their inferior condition made nothing against their heroism. He, himself,
though a soldier by profession, from his tenderest years, had never
yet been able to compass the favor of the nobility. Yet he had
applied himself with all industry, and hazarded his life in many
dangers. It was his misfortune that "more regard is had to birth
than virtue." But this need not discourage *them*, as it has never
discouraged him from the performance of his duties. The great
examples of history are in *his* eyes, and should be in *theirs*

* Charlevoix seems to afford a sufficient sanction for the claim of Laudonniere, in behalf of the gentle blood among the followers of Ribault.
He says " Il avoit des esquipages choisis, et plusieurs volontaries, parmi
lesquels il y avoit *quelques gentilshommes.*" And yet Ribault should
have known better than anybody else the quality of his armament. Certainly, the good leaven, as the result showed, was in too small a proportion to leaven the whole colony

"Howe much then ought so many worthy examples move you to plant here? Considering, also, that hereby you shall be registered forever as the first that inhabited this strange country. I pray you, therefore, all to advise yourselves thereof, and to declare your mindes freely unto me, protesting that I will so well imprint your names in the King's eares, and the other princes, that your renowne shall hereafter shine unquenchable through our realm of France."

Ribault was evidently not insensible to fame. Had his thoughts been those of his sovereign, also, how different would have been the history! His soldiers responded in the proper spirit, and declared their readiness to establish a colony in the wild empire, the grandeur and beauty of which had already commended it to their affections. Delighted with the readiness and enthusiasm of his men, he weighed anchor the very next day, in order to seek out the place most fit and convenient for his settlement. "*Having sayled up the great river on the north side, in coasting an isle which ended with a sharpe point toward the mouth of the river;— having sailed awhile he discovered a small river which entered into the islande, which hee would not faile to search out, which done, he found the same deep enough to harbour therein gallies and galliots in good number. Proceeding farther, he found an open place joyning upon the brinke thereof, where he went on land, and seeing the place fit to build a fortresse in, and commodious for them that were willing to plant there, he resolved incontinently to cause the bignesse of the fortification to be measured out.*" The colony was to be a small one. Twenty-six persons had volunteered to establish it; as many, perhaps, as had been called for. The dimensions of the fort were small accordingly. They were taken by Laudonniere, and one Captain Salles, under

Ribault's directions. The fort was at once begun. Its length was sixteen fathoms, its breadth thirteen, " with flanks according to the proportion thereof." Then, for the first time, the European axe was laid to the great shafts of the forest trees of America, waking sounds, at every stroke, whose echoes have been heard for three hundred years, sounding, and destined to resound, from the Atlantic to the Pacific seas; leaving no waste of wood and wild, unawakened by this first music of civilization.

The site thus chosen by Ribault for his colony, though no traces have been left of the labor of his hands, is scarcely doubtful to the present possessors of the country. All the proofs concur in placing Fort Charles somewhere between North Edisto and Broad River, and circumstances determine this situation to be that of the beautiful little town of Beaufort, in South Carolina. The *Grande Riviere* of the French is our Broad River.* It was at the mouth of this river, in an island with a safe and commodious port, that the fort was established; and of the numerous islands which rise everywhere along the coast in this region, as a fortress to defend the verdant shores from the assaults of ocean, there is none which answers so well as this all the requisitions of this description. Besides, it is actually in the very latitude of the site, as given by Laudonniere; and the tradition of the Indians, as preserved by our own people, seems to confirm and to conclude the conjectures on this subject. They state that the first place in which they saw the pale faces of the Europeans

* Charlevoix, in his " Fastes Chronologiques," preparatory to his work on New France, locates Charles Fort, under Ribault, " near to the site of the present city of Charleston. In his " Histoire Generale," and in the map which illustrates this narrative, however, he concurs in the statement of the text. He also names the North Edisto the St. Croix.

was at Coosawhatchie, in South Carolina. Now, the Coosawhatchie is the principal stream that forms the *Grande Riviere* of the Frenchmen; and was, questionless, the first of the streams that was penetrated by the pinnace of Ribault. It is highly probable that it bore the name of Coosawhatchie through its entire course, until it emptied itself into the ocean. The testimony of the Indians, based simply upon their tradition, is of quite as much value as that of any other people. It is well known with what tenacity they preserve the recollection of important events, and with what singular adherence to general truthfulness. The island upon which Beaufort now stands was most probably that which yielded the first American asylum to the Huguenots of France!

Our Frenchmen travailed so diligently that, in a short space, the fortress was in some sort prepared for the colonists. It was soon in a defensible condition. "Victuals and warlike munition" were transferred from the shipping to the shore, and the garrison were furnished with all things necessary for the maintenance of their fortress and themselves. The fort was christened by the name of Charles, the King of France; while the small river upon which it was built received the name of Chenonceau. All things being provided, the colonists marched into their little and lovely place of refuge. They were confided to the charge of one Captain Albert, to whom, and to whose followers, Ribault made a speech at parting. His injunctions were of a parental and salutary character. He exhorted their Captain to justice, firmness and moderation in his rule, and his people to obedience; promising to return with supplies from France, and reinforcements before their present resources should fail them. But these exhortations do not seem to have been much regarded by either party. It will be for us, in future chapters, to pursue their fortunes, and to pluck, if possible, from the unwritten history, the detailed events of their melancholy destiny. Sad enough will it have been, even if no positive evil shall befall them,— that severance from their ancient comrades—that separation from the old homes of their fathers in *La Belle France*—that lonesome abode, on the verge of " ocean's gray and melancholy waste," on the one hand, and the dense, dark, repelling forests of Apalachia on the other;—doubtful of all they see,—in spite of all that is fresh and charming in their sight;—apprehensive of every sound that reaches them from the wilderness,—and filled with no better hope than that which springs up in the human bosom when assured that all hope is cut off—that one hope excepted, which is born of necessity, and which blossoms amid the nettles of despair. The isolation was the more oppressive and likely to be grievous, as we have reason to doubt that, though founding a colony for the refuge of a religious and persecuted people, they brought any becoming sense of religion with them Our progress thus far with the adventurers has shown us but few proofs of the presence among them of any feelings of devotion Ribault himself was but a soldier, and his ambition was of an earthly complexion. Had they been elevated duly by religion, they would have been counselled and strengthened in the solitude by God. Unhappily, they were men only, rude, untaught, and full of selfish passions,—badly ruled and often ill-treated, and probably giving frequent provocation to the pride and passions of those who had them under rule. But they began their career in the New World with sufficient cheerfulness. Its climate was delicious, like that of their own country. Its woods and forests were of a majesty and splendor beyond any of which their wildest fancies had ever dreamed and the security which the remoteness of the region promised them, and the novelty which invested every object in their eyes made the parting from their comrades a tolerably easy one. They heard with lively spirits the farewell shouts of their companions, and answered them with cheers of confidence and pride. The simple paragraph which records the leave-taking of the parties, is at once pleasing and full of pathos. "Having ended his (Ribault's) exhortations, we took our leaves of *each* of them, and sayled toward our shippes. We hoysed our sayles about ten of the clocke in the morning. After wee were ready to depart, Captain Ribault commanded to shoote off our ordnance, to give a farewell unto our Frenchmen; which fayled not to do the like on their part. This being done, wee sayled toward the north." That last shout, that last sullen roar of their mutual cannon, and the great waves of the Atlantic rolled, unbroken by a sail, between our colonists and *La Belle France*.

II.

THE COLONY UNDER ALBERT.

THE Colonists, thus abandoned by their countrymen, proceeded to make themselves secure in their forest habitations. Day and night did they address themselves to the completion of their fortress. They have seen none of the natives in the immediate neighborhood of the spot in which they had pitched their tents; but, aware of the wandering habits of the red-men, they might naturally look for them at any moment. Their toils, quickened by their caution, enabled them to make rapid progress. While they labored, they felt nothing of their loneliness. The employments which accompanied their situation, and flowed from its necessities, might be said to exercise their fancies, and to subdue the tendency to melancholy which might naturally grow out of their isolation. Besides, the very novelty of the circumstances in which they found themselves had its attractions, particularly to a people so lively as the French. Our Huguenots, at the outset, were very sensible to the picturesque beauties of their forest habitation. For a season, bird, and beast, and tree, and flower, presented themselves to their delighted eyes, in guises of constantly-varying attraction. The solitude, itself, possessed its charm, most fascinating of all,—until it became monotonous—

to those who had been little favored of fortune in the crowded world of civilization; and, with the feeling of a first freshness in their hearts, and, while in the performance of duties which were equally necessary to their safety, and new to their experience, the whole prospect before them was beheld through that rose-colored atmosphere which the fancy so readily flings before the mind, beguiling the soberer thought into forgetfulness. During this period they toiled successfully upon their fortifications. They raised the parapet, they mounted the cannon for defence; built rude dwellings within the walls, and in their boundless contiguity of shade, with the feeling that they were in some sort " monarchs of all they beheld ;" they felt neither loneliness nor fear.

Their homes built, their fortifications complete, they proceeded, in small detachments to explore the neighboring streams and woods. They had, so far, finished all their tasks without meeting with the natives. They did not shrink from this meeting. They now desired it from motives of policy. They had no reason to believe, from the specimens of the red-men whom they had already encountered, that they should have any difficulty in soothing any of the tribes; and they were justified in supposing that the impression already made upon those whom they met, would operate favorably upon their future intercourse. Boldly, then, our Frenchmen darted into the adjacent forests, gathering their game and provisions in the same grounds with the proprietors. But the latter were never to be seen. They were shy of the strangers, or they had not yet discovered their settlement. One day, however, a fortunate chance enabled a party of the Huguenots to discover, and to circumvent an Indian hunter, upon whom they came suddenly in the forests. At first the poor fellow was exceedingly dismayed at the encounter; but, subduing his fears, he submitted with a good grace to the wishes of his captors, and was conducted to the fortress. Here he was treated with consideration, and made happy by several trifles which were given him. His confidence was finally won, and his mouth was opened. He became communicative, and described his people and their territories. He avowed himself the subject of a great monarch, whom he called Audusta,*—a name, in which, under the corruptions of a French pronunciation, we recognize the well-known modern name of Edisto. He described the boundaries of empire belonging to this forest chieftain; and gave a general and not incorrect idea of the whole surrounding country.

Captain Albert was exceedingly delighted with his acquisition. It was important that he should open an intercourse with the natives, to whose maize-fields and supplies of venison his necessities required he should look. He treated the hunter with liberality and courtesy, dismissing him at night-fall with many presents, of a kind most grateful to the savage taste. These hospitalities and gifts, it was not doubted, would pave the way for an intercourse equally profitable and pleasant to both the parties. Suffering a few days to elapse after the departure of the hunter, Albert prepared to follow his directions, and explore the settlements of King Audusta. He did so, and was received with great kindness by the stately savage. The Indian hunter had made a favorable report of the Frenchmen, and Audusta adopted them as his friends and allies. He promised them provisions and assistance, and the

* The name in Charlevoix is written Andusta, but this is most probably an error of the press. Laudonniere in Hackluyt uniformly uses the orthography which we adopt, and which furnishes a coincidence so really striking in the preservation of a name so nearly the same in sound, to this very day, in the same region.

friendship of four other chiefs or princes, his tributaries, whose names are given as Mayou, Hoya, Touppa, and Stalamè.* These were all, in turn,—except the last,—visited by Albert, who found a frank and generous welcome wherever he came. He consumed several days in these visits; and the intercourse, in a little while, between the French and red-men, grew so great, " that, in a manner, all things were soon common between them." Returning to Audusta, Albert prepared to visit Stalamè, whose country lay north of Fort Charles some fifteen leagues. This would make his abode somewhere on the Edisto, near Giyham's, perhaps; or, inclining still north, to the head of Ashley River. Sailing up the river, (the Edisto probably,) they encountered a great current, which they followed, to reach the abode of Stalamè. He, too, received the strangers with hospitality and friendship. The intercourse thus established between the party soon assumed the most endearing aspect. The Indian kings took counsel of Albert in all matters of importance. The Frenchmen were called to the conference in the round-house of the tribe, quite as frequently as their own recognized counsellors. In other words, the leaders of the Huguenots were adopted into the tribe, that being the usual mode of indicating trust and confidence. Albert was present at all the assemblages of state in the realm of Audusta; at all ceremonials, whether of business or pleasure; at his great hunts; and at the

* A remark of Charlevoix, which accords with the experience of all early travellers and explorers among the American Indians, is worthy to be kept in remembrance, as enabling us to account for that frequent contradiction which occurs in the naming of places and persons among the savages. He records distinctly that each canton or province of Florida bore, among the red-men, the name of the ruling chief. Now, as a matter of course where the tribes are nomadic, the names of places continually underwent change, according to that of the tribe by which the spot was temporarily occupied.

singular feasts of his religion. One of these feasts, that of TOYA,* which succeeded the visit of Albert to the territories of Audusta and the four tributary kings, will call for an elaborate description hereafter, when we narrate the legend of Guernache, upon whose fate that of the colony seems to have depended.

The intercourse of our Huguenots with Audusta was of vital importance to the former. In the form of gifts, he yielded them a regular tribute of maize and beans, (corn and peas, in modern parlance,) and was easily persuaded to do so by the simple trifles, of little value, which the colonists proffered in return. It is not difficult to win the affections of an inferior people, where the superior is indulgent. Kindness will disarm the hostility of the savage, and justice will finally subdue the jealousy of conscious ignorance. Sympathy in sports and amusements, above all things, will do much towards bringing together tribes who differ in their laws and language, and will make them forgetful of all their differences. The French have been usually much more successful than any other people in overcoming the prejudices of the red-men of America. The moral of their nation is much more flexible than that of the Englishman and Spaniard;—the former of whom has always subdued, and the latter usually debased or destroyed, the races with which they came in conflict.

The policy of Albert did not vary from that which usually distinguished his countrymen in like situations. The French Protestant was, by no means, of the faith and temper of the English Puritan. In simplifying his religion, he did not clothe his exterior in gloom; he did not deny that there should be sunshine and

* According to Charlevoix, Toya was the name of the Floridian god, and not that of the ceremonies simply. " Elle se célébroit en l'honneur d'une Divinité nommée *Toya.*"

blossoms in the land. Our colonists at Fort Charles did not perplex the Indians with doctrinal questions. It is greatly to be feared, indeed, that religion did not, in any way, disturb them in their solitudes. At all events, it was not of such a freezing temper as to deny them the indulgence of an intercourse with the natives, which, for a season, was very agreeable and very inspiriting to both the parties.

But smiles and sunshine cannot last forever. The granaries of the Indians began to fail under their own profligacy and the demands of the Frenchmen. The resources of the former, never abundant, were soon exhausted in providing for the additional hungry mouths which had come among them. Shrinking from labor, they addressed as little of it as they well could, to the cultivation of their petty maize fields. They planted them, as we do now, a couple of grains of corn to each hill, at intervals of three or four square feet, and as the corn grew to a sufficient height, peas were distributed among the roots, to twine about the stalks when the vines could no longer impair its growth. They cropped the same land twice in each summer. The supplies, thus procured, would have been totally inadequate to their wants, but for the abundant game, the masts of the forest, and such harsh but wholesome roots as they could pulverize and convert into breadstuffs. Their store was thus limited always, and adapted to their own wants simply. Any additional demand, however small, produced a scarcity in their granaries. The improvidence of Audusta, or his liberality, prevented him from considering this danger, until it began to be felt. He had supplied the Frenchmen until his stock was exhausted; no more being left in his possession than would suffice to sow his fields.

"For this reason,"—such was the language of the savage monarch—" we must retire to the forests, and live upon its mast and roots, until harvest time. We are sorry that we can supply you no longer; you must now seek the granaries of our neighbors. There is a king called COUEXIS, a prince of great might and renown in this country, whose province lies toward the south. His lands are very fertile. His stores are ample at all seasons. He alone can furnish you with food for a long time. Before you approach the territories of Couexis, there is his brother, king Ouade, who is scarcely less wealthy. He is a generous chief, who will be very joyful if he may but once behold you. Seek out these, and your wants shall be supplied."

The advice was taken. The Frenchmen had no alternative. They addressed themselves first to Ouade. His territories lay along the river Belle, some twenty-five leagues south of Port Royal. He received them with the greatest favor and filled their pinnace with maize and beans. He welcomed them to his abode with equal state and hospitality. His house is described as being hung with a tapestry richly wrought of feathers. The couch upon which he slept, was dressed with " white coverlettes, embroidered with devises of very wittie and fine workmanship, and fringed round about with a fringe dyed in the colour of scarlet." His gifts to our Frenchmen were not limited to the commodities they craved. He gave them six coverlets, and tapestry such as decorated his couch and dwelling; specimens of a domestic manufacture which declare for tastes and a degree of art which seems, in some degree, to prove their intimacy with the more polished and powerful nations of the south. In regard to food hereafter, king Ouade promised that his new acquaintance should never want.

Thus was the first intercourse maintained by our Huguenots

with their savage neighbors. It was during this intimacy, and while all things seemed to promise fair in regard to the colony, that the tragical events took place which furnish the materials for the legend which follows, the narrative of which requires that we should mingle events together, those which occurred in the periods already noted, and those which belong to our future chapters. Let it suffice, here, that, with his pinnace stored with abundance, the mil (meal), corn and peas, of Ouade, Albert returned in safety to Fort Charles.

III.

THE LEGEND OF GUERNACHE.—Chap. I.

Showing how Guernache, the Musician, a great favorite with our Frenchmen, lost the favor of Captain Albert, and how cruelly he was punished by the latter.

GUERNACHE, the drummer, was one of the finest fellows, and the handsomest of our little colony of Frenchmen. Though sprung of very humble origin, Guernache, with a little better education, might have been deemed to have had his training among the highest circles of the Court. He was of tall and erect figure, and of a carriage so noble and graceful that, even among his associates, he continued to be an object of admiration Besides, he was a fellow of the happiest humor. His kindness of heart was proverbial. His merriment was contagious. His eye flashed out in gayety, and his spirit was ever on the alert to seize upon the passing pleasure, and subject it to the enjoyment of his companions. Never was fellow so fortunate in finding occasion for merriment; and happy, indeed, was the Frenchman who could procure Guernache as a comrade in the performance of his daily tasks. The toil was unfelt in which he shared—the weight of the task was dissipated, and, where it wore heavily, he came to the succor of his drooping companion, and his superior expertness soon succeeded in doing that which his pleasantry had failed to effect. He was the best fisherman and hunter—was as brave as he was light-hearted—was, altogether, so perfect a character, in the estimation of the little band of Albert, that he found no enemy among his equals, and could always choose his companion for himself. His successes were not confined to his own countrymen. He found equal favor in the sight of the Indians. Among his other accomplishments, he possessed the most wonderful agility—had belonged, at one time, to a company of strolling players, and his skill on tight and slack rope—if we are to credit old stories—would put to the blush the modern performances of the Ravels and Herr Cline. It was through his means, and partly by his ingenuity, that the Indian hunter was entrapped and brought into the fort,—through whose agency the intimacy had been effected with the people of Audusta and the other chiefs; and, during this intimacy, Guernache had proved, in various ways, one of the principal instruments for confirming the favorable impressions which the Indian had received in his intercourse with the Frenchmen. He was everywhere popular with the red men. Nothing, indeed, could be done without him. Ignorant of his inferior social position among the whites, the simple savages sent for him to their feasts and frolics, without caring for the claims of any other person. He had but to carry his violin—for, among his other accomplishments, that of fiddling was not the smallest—to secure the smiles of the men and the favors of the women; and it was not long before he had formed, among the savages, a class for dancing, after the European fashion, upon the banks of the Edisto. Think of the red men of Apalachia, figuring under a Parisian teacher, by night, by torch-light, beneath the great oaks of the original forest! Such uncouth antics might well offend, with never-lessening wonder, the courtly nymphs of the Seine and the Loire. But the Indians suffered from no conventional apprehensions. They were not made to feel their deficiencies under the indulgent training of Guernache, and footed it away as merrily, as if each of their damsels sported on a toe as light and exquisite as that of Ellsler or Taglioni. King Audusta, himself, though well stricken in years, was yet seduced into the capricious mazes which he beheld with so much pleasure, and, for a season, the triumph of Guernache among the palms and pines of *Grande Riviere*, was sufficiently complete, to make him wonder at times how his countrymen ever suffered his departure from the shores of La Belle France!

At first, and when it was doubtful to what extent the favor of the red-men might be secured for the colony, Captain Albert readily countenanced the growing popularity of his fiddler among them. His permission was frequently given to Guernache, when king Audusta solicited his presence. His policy prompted him to regard it as highly fortunate that so excellent an agent for his purposes was to be found among his followers; and, for some months, it needed only a suggestion of Guernache, himself, to procure for him leave of absence. The worthy fellow never abused his privileges—never was unfaithful to his trust—never grew insolent upon indulgence. But Captain Albert, though claiming to be the cadet of a noble house, was yet a person of a mean and ignoble nature. Small and unimposing of person, effeminate of habit, and accustomed to low indulgences, he was not only deficient in the higher resources of intellect, but he was exceedingly querulous and tyrannical of temper. His aristocratical connexions alone had secured him the charge of the colony, for which nature and education had equally unfitted him.

His mind was contracted and full of bitter prejudices; and, as is the case commonly with very small persons, he was always tenacious to the very letter, of the nicest observances of etiquette After a little while, and when he no longer had reason to question the fidelity of the red men, he began to exhibit some share of dislike towards Guernache; and to withhold the privileges which he had hitherto permitted him to enjoy. He had become jealous of the degree of favor in which his musician was held among the savages, and betrayed this change in his temper, by instances of occasional severity and denial, the secret of which the companions of Guernache divined much sooner than himself. Though not prepared, absolutely, to withhold his consent, when king Audusta entreated that the fiddler might be spared him, he yet accorded it ungraciously; and Guernache was made to suffer, in some way, for these concessions, as if they had been so many favors granted to himself.

They were, indeed, favors to the musician, though, to what extent, Albert entertained no suspicion. It so happened that among his other conquests, Guernache had made that of a very lovely dark-eyed damsel, a niece of Audusta, and a resident of the king's own village. After the informal fashion of the country, into which our Frenchmen were apt readily to fall, he had made the damsel his wife. She was a beautiful creature, scarcely more than sixteen; tall and slender, and so naturally agile and graceful, that it needed but a moderate degree of instruction to make her a dancer whose airy movements would not greatly have misbeseemed the most courtly theatres of Paris. Monaletta,—for such was the sweet name of the Indian damsel,—was an apt pupil, because she was a loving one. She heartily responded to that sentiment of wonder—common among the savages—that the

Frenchmen should place themselves under the command of a chief, so mean of person as Albert, and so inferior in gifts, when they had among them a fellow of such noble presence as Guernache, whose qualities were so irresistible. The opinions of her head were but echoes from the feelings in her heart. Her preference for our musician was soon apparent and avowed; but, in taking her to wife, Guernache kept his secret from his best friend. No one in Fort Charles ever suspected that he had been wived in the depth of the great forests, through pagan ceremonies, by an Indian Iawa,* to the lovely Monaletta. Whatever may have been his motive for keeping the secret, whether he feared the ridicule of his comrades, or the hostility of his superior, or apprehended a difficulty with rivals among the red men, by a discovery of the fact, it is yet very certain that he succeeded in persuading Monaletta, herself, and those who were present at his wild betrothal, to keep the secret also. It did not lessen, perhaps, the pleasure of his visits to the settlements of Audusta, that the peculiar joys which he desired had all the relish of a stolen fruit. It was now, only in this manner that Monaletta could be seen. Captain Albert, with a rigid austerity, which contributed also to his evil odor among his people, had interdicted the visits of all Indian women at the fort. This interdict was one, however, which gave little annoyance to Guernache. A peculiar, but not unnatural jealousy, had already prompted him repeatedly to deny this privilege to Monaletta. The simple savage had frequently expressed her desire to see the fortress of the white man, to behold his foreign curiosities, and, in particular, to hearken to the roar of that

* Iawa was the title of the priest or prophet of the Floridian. The word is thus written by Laudonniere in Hakluyt. It is probably a misprint only which, in Charlevoix, writes it "Iona."

mimic thunder which he had always at command, and which, when heard, had so frequently shaken the very hearts of the men of her people.

In this relation stood the several parties, when, one day, a messenger came to Fort Charles from King Audusta, bearing a special invitation to Captain Albert to attend, with the savage tribes, the celebration of the great religious "feast of *Toya*." He was invited to bring as many of his men as he thought proper, but, in particular, not to forget their favorite Guernache. The feast of Toya, seems to have constituted the great religious ceremonial of the nation. It took place about the middle, or the close of summer, and seems to have been a sort of annual thanksgiving, after the laws of a natural religion, for the maturing of their little crops. Much of the solemnities were obvious and ostentatious in their character. Much more, however, was involved and mysterious, and held particularly sacred by the priesthood. The occasion was one, at all events, to which the Indians attached the greatest importance; and, naturally anxious to acquire as great a knowledge as possible of their laws, customs and sentiments, Captain Albert very readily acceded to the invitation,—preparing, with some state, to attend the rustic revels of Audusta. He took with him a fair proportion of his little garrison, and did not omit the inimitable Guernache. Ascending the river in his pinnace, he soon reached the territories of the Indian monarch. Audusta, with equal hospitality and dignity, anticipated his approach, and met him, with his followers, at the river landing. With a hearty welcome, he conducted him to his habitations, and gave him, at entrance, a draught of the cassina beverage, the famous tea of the country. Then came damsels who washed their hands in vessels of water over which floated the leaves of the odorous bay, and flowers of rare perfume; drying them after with branches of plumes, scarlet and white, which were made of the feathers of native birds of the most glorious variety of hue. Mats of reed, woven ingeniously together by delicate wythes of all colors, orange and green, and vermillion, dyed with roots of the forest, were then spread upon the rush-strewn floor of the royal wigwam; and, with a grace not unbecoming a sovereign born in the purple, Audusta invited our Frenchmen to place themselves at ease, each according to his rank and station. The king took his place among them, neither above the first, nor below the last, but like a friend within a favorite circle, in which some might stand more nearly than others to his affections. They were then attended with the profoundest deference, and served with the rarest delicacies of the Indian *cuisine*. As night came on, fresh rushes were strewed upon the floor, and they slept with the cheerful music of songs and laughter, which reached them at intervals, through the night, from the merry makers in the contiguous forests. With the dawning of the next day, preparations for the great festival were begun.

IV.

THE LEGEND OF GUERNACHE.—Chap. II.

THE FESTIVAL OF TOYA.

Being a continuation of the legend of Guernache; showing the superstitions of the Red-Men; how Guernache offended Captain Albert, and what followed from the secret efforts of the Frenchmen to penetrate the mysteries of Toya!

It would be difficult to say, from the imperfect narratives afforded us by the chroniclers, what were the precise objects of the present ceremonials;—what gods were to be invoked;—what evil beings implored;—what wrath and anger to be deprecated and diverted from the devoted tribes. As the Frenchmen received no explanation of their mystic preparations, so are we left unenlightened by their revelations. They do not even amuse us by their conjectures, and Laudonniere stops short in his narrative of what did happen, apologizing for having said so much on so trifling a matter. We certainly owe him no gratitude for his forbearance. What he tells us affords but little clue to the motive of their fantastic proceedings. The difficulty, which is at present ours, was not less that of Albert and his Frenchmen: They were compelled to behold the outlines of a foreign ritual whose mysteries they were not permitted to explore, and had their curiosity provoked by shows of a most exciting character, which only mocked their desires, and tantalized their appetites. On the first arrival of Albert, and after he had been rested and refreshed, Audusta himself had conducted him, with his followers, to the spot which had been selected for the ceremonies of the morrow. "This was a great circuit of ground with open prospect and round in figure." Here they saw "many women roundabout, which labored by all means to make the place cleane and neate." The ceremonies began early on the morning of the ensuing day. Hither they repaired in season, and found "all they which were chosen to celebrate the feast," already "painted and trimmed with rich feathers of divers colours." These led the way in a procession from the dwelling of Audusta to the "place of Toya." Here, when they had come, they set themselves in new order under the guidance of three Indians, who were distinguished by plumes, paint, and a costume entirely superior to the rest. Each of them carried a tabret, to the plaintive and lamenting music of which they sang in wild, strange, melancholy accents; and, in slow measures, dancing the while, they passed gradually into the very centre of the sacred circle. They were followed by successive groups, which answered to their strains, and to whose songs they, in turn, responded with like echoes. This continued for awhile, the music gradually rising and swelling from the slow to the swift, from the sad to the passionate, while the moods of the actors and the spectators, also varying, the character of the scene changed to one of the wildest excitement. Suddenly, the characters—those who were chief officiators in this apparent hymn of fate—broke from the enchanted circle—darted through the ranks of the spectators, and dashed, headlong, with frantic cries, into the depths of the neighboring thickets. Then followed another class of actors. As if a sudden and terrible doom overhung the nation, the Indian women set up cries of grief and lamentation. Their passion grew to madness. In their rage, the mothers seized upon the young virgins of the tribe, and, with the sharp edges of muscle shells, they lanced their arms, till the blood gushed forth in free streams, which they eagerly flung into the air, crying aloud at every moment, "He-to-yah! He-to-yah! He-to-yah!"*

These ceremonies, though not more meaningless, perhaps, in the eyes of the Christian, than would be our most solemn religious proceedings in those of the Indian, provoked the laughter of Albert and some of his Frenchmen. This circumstance awakened the indignation of their excellent friend, Audusta. His displeasure was now still farther increased by a proceeding of Captain Albert. It was an attempt upon their mysteries. That portion of the officiating priesthood—their Iawas—who fled from the sacred enclosure to deep recesses of the woods, sought there for the prosecution, in secret, of rites too holy for the vulgar eye. Here they maintained their *sanctum sanctorum*. This was the place consecrated to the communion of the god with his immediate servants—the holy of holies, which it was death to penetrate or pass. Albert suffered his curiosity to get the better of his discretion. Offended by the laughter of the Frenchmen, at what they had already beheld, and fearing lest their audacity should lead them farther, the king, Audusta, had gathered them again within the royal wigwam, where he sought, by marked kindness and distinction, to make them forgetful of what had been

* Adair likens the cry of the Southern Indians to the sacred name among the Jews—"Je-ho-vah." He writes the Indian syllables thus—"Yo-he-wah," and it constitutes one of his favorite arguments for deducing the origin of the North American red-men from the ancient Hebrews

denied. They had seen, as he told them, the more impressive portions of the ceremonial. There were others, but not of a kind to interest them. But the fact that there was something to conceal, stimulated the curiosity of Albert. In due degree with the king's anxiety to keep his secret, was that of the French captain's to fathom it. Holding a brief consultation with his men, accordingly, he declared his desire to this effect; and proposed, that one of their number should contrive to steal forth, and, finding his way to the forbidden spot, should place himself in such a position as would enable him to survey all the mysterious proceedings. To this course, Guernache frankly opposed his opinions. His greater intimacy with the red-men led him properly to conceive the danger which might ensue, from their discovery of the intrusion. He had been well taught by Monaletta, the degree of importance which they attached to the security of their mystic rites. Arguing with the honesty of his character, he warned his captain of the risk which such unbecoming curiosity would incur—the peril to the offender, himself, if detected; and the hazards to the colony from the loss of that friendship to which they had been already so largely indebted. But the counsels of Guernache were rejected with indignity. Prepared, already, to regard him with dislike and suspicion, Albert heard his suggestions only as so much impertinence; and rudely commanded him not to forget himself and place, nor to thrust his undesired opinions upon the consideration of gentlemen. The poor fellow was effectually silenced by this rebuke. He sank out of sight, and presumed no farther to advise. But the counsel was not wholly thrown away Disregarded by Albert, it was caught up, and insisted on, by others, who had better conventional claims to be heard, and the proposition might have been defeated but for the ready interposition of one Pierre Renaud, a young fellow, who, perceiving the captain's strong desire to seek out the mystery, and anxious to ingratiate himself with that person, boldly laughed at the fears of the objectors, and volunteered, himself, to defy the danger, in his own person, in order to gratify his chief. This silenced the controversy. Albert readily availed himself of the offer, and Pierre Renaud was commanded to try his fortune. This he did, and, notwithstanding the surveillance maintained over them by Audusta and his attendants, " he made such shift, that, by subtle meanes, he gotte out of the house of Audusta, and secretly went and hid himselfe behinde a very thick bush, where, at his pleasure, he might easily descry the ceremonies of the feaste."

We will leave Renaud thus busy in his espionage, while we rehearse the manner in which the venerable Audusta proceeded to treat his company. A substantial feast was provided for them, consisting of venison, wild fowl, and fruits. Their breadstuffs were maize, batatas, and certain roots sodden first in water, and then prepared in the sun. A drink was prepared from certain other roots, which, though bitter, was refreshing and slightly stimulant. Our Frenchmen, in the absence of the beverages of Italy and France, did not find it unpalatable. They ate and drank with a hearty relish, which gratified the red-men, who lavished on them a thousand caresses. The feast was followed by the dance. In a spacious area, surrounded by great ranks of oaks, cedars, pines, and other trees, they assembled, men and women, in their gayest caparison. The men were tatooed and painted, from head to foot, and not inartistically, in the most glowing colors. Birds and beasts were figured upon their breasts, and huge, strange reptiles were made to coil up and around their legs and arms. From their waists depended light garments of white cotton, the skirts being trimmed with a thick fringe of red or scarlet. Some of them wore head-dresses consisting of the skins of snakes, or eagles, the panther or the wild cat, which, stuffed ingeniously, were made to sit erect above the forehead, and to look abroad, from their novel place of perch, in a manner equally natural and frightful. The women were habited in a similarly wild but less offensive manner. The taste which presided in their decorations, was of a purer and a gentler fashion. Their cheeks were painted red, their arms, occasionally but slightly tattooed, and sometimes the figure of a bird, a flower or a star, might be seen engrained upon the breast. A rather scanty robe of white cotton concealed, in some degree, the bosom, and extended somewhat below the knees. Around the necks of several, were hung thick strands of native pearls, partially discolored by the action of fire which had been employed to extricate them from the shells. Pearls were also mingled ingeniously with the long tresses of their straight, black hair; trailing with it, in not unfrequent instances, even to the ground. Others, in place of this more valuable ornament, wore necklaces, anklets and tiaras, formed wholly of one or other of the numerous varieties of little sea shells, by which, after heavy storms, the low and sandy shores of the country were literally covered. Strings of the same shell encircled the legs, which were sometimes of a shape to gratify the nicest exactions of the civilized standard. The forms of our Indian damsels were generally symmetrical and erect, their movements at once agile and graceful—their foreheads high, their lips thin, and, with a soft, persuasive expression, inclining to melancholy; while their eyes, black and bright, always shone with a peculiar forest fire that seemed happily to consort with their dark, but not unpleasing complexions. Well, indeed, with a pardonable vanity, might their people call them the "Daughters of the Sun." He had made them his, by his warmest and fondest glances. These were the women, whose descendants, in after days, as Yemassees and Muscoghees and Seminoles, became the scourge of so large a portion of the Anglo-American race.

When the Frenchmen beheld this rude, but really brilliant assemblage, and saw what an attractive show the young damsels made, they were delighted beyond measure. Visions of the rout and revel, as enjoyed in *La Belle France*, glanced before their fancies; and the lively capering that followed among the young Huguenots, informed Captain Albert of the desire which was felt by all. In stern, compelling accents, he bade Guernache take his violin, and provide the music, while the rest prepared to dance. But Guernache excused himself, alleging the want of strings for his instrument. These were shown, in a broken state, to his commander. He had broken them, we may state *en passant*, for the occasion. His pride had been hurt by the treatment of his captain. He felt that the purpose of the latter was to degrade him. Such a performance as that required at his hands, was properly no part of his duty; and his proud spirit revolted at the idea of contributing, in any way, to the wishes of his superior, when the object of the latter was evidently his own degradation. Albert spoke to him testily, and with brows that did not seek to subdue or conceal their frowns. But Guernache was firm, and though he studiously forebore, by word or look, to increase the provocation which he had already given, he yet made no effort to pacify the imperious nature which he had offended. The excuse was such as could not but be taken. There was the violin, indeed, but there, also, were the broken strings. Albert turned from the musician with undisguised loathing; and the poor fellow sunk back with a secret presentiment of evil. He but too well knew the character of his superior.

Meanwhile, the red men had resort to their own primitive music. Their instruments consisted of simple reeds, which, bound together, were passed, to and fro, beneath the lips and discoursed very tolerable harmonies;—and a rude drum formed by stretching a raw deer.skin over the mouth of a monstrous calabash, enabled them, when the skin had been contracted in the sun, to extort from it a very tolerable substitute for the music of the tambourine. There were other instruments, susceptible of sound if not of sweetness. Numerous damsels, none over fifteen, lithe and graceful, carried in their hands little gourds, which were filled with shells and pebbles, and tied over with skins, dried also in the sun. With these, as they danced, they kept time so admirably as might have charmed the most practised European master. Thus, all provided, some with the drum, and others with flute-like reeds and hollow, tinkling gourds, they only awaited the summons of their partners to the area. Shaking their tinkling gourds, as if in pretty impatience at the delay, the girls each waited, with anxious looks, the signal from her favorite.

The Frenchmen were not slow in seeking out their partners. At the word and signal of their captain, they dashed in among the laughing group of dusky maidens, each seeking for the girl whose beauties had been most grateful to his tastes. Nor was Captain Albert, himself, with all his pride and asceticism, unwilling to forget his dignity for a season, and partake of the rude festivities of the occasion. When, indeed, did mirth and music fail to usurp dominion in the Frenchman's heart? Albert greedily cast his eyes about, seeking a partner, upon whom he might bestow his smiles. He was not slow in the selection. It so happened, that

Monaletta, the spouse of Guernache, was not only one of the loveliest damsels present, but she was well known as the niece of King Audusta. Her beauty and royal blood, equally commended her to the favor of our captain. She stood apart from all the rest, stately and graceful as the cedar, not seeming to care for the merriment in which all were now engaged. There was a dash of sadness in her countenance. Her thoughts were elsewhere—her eyes scarcely with the assembly, when the approach of Albert startled her from her reverie. He came as Cæsar did, to certain conquest; and was about to take her hand, as a matter of course, when he was equally astounded and enraged to find her draw it away from his grasp.

".You will not dance with *me*, Monaletta?"

"No," she answered him in broken French—"No dance with you—dance with *him!*" pointing to Guernache.

Speaking these words, she crossed the floor, with all the bold imprudence of a truly loving heart, to the place where stood our sorrowful and unhappy violinist. He had followed the movements of Albert, with looks of most serious apprehension, and his heart had sunk, with a sudden terror, when he saw that he approached Monaletta. The scene which followed, however grateful to his affections, was seriously calculated to arouse his fears. He feared for Monaletta, as he feared for himself. Nothing escaped him in the brief interview, and he saw, in the vindictive glances of Albert, the most evil auguries for the future. Yet how precious was her fondness to his heart! He half forgot his apprehensions as he felt her hand upon his shoulder, and beheld her eyes looking with appealing fondness up into his own. That glance was full of the sweetest consolation,—and said everything that was grateful to his terrified affections She, too, had seen the look of hate and anger in the face of Albert, and she joyed in the opportunity of rebuking the one with her disdain, and of consoling the other with her sympathies. It was an unhappy error. Bitter, indeed, was the look with which the aroused and mortified Albert regarded the couple as they stood apart from all the rest. Guernache beheld this look. He knew the meaning of that answering glance of his superior which encountered his own. His looks were those of entreaty, of deprecation. They seemed to say, "I feel that you are offended, but I had no purpose or part in the offence." His glance of humility met with-no answering indulgence. It seemed, indeed, still farther to provoke his tyrant, who, advancing midway across the room, addressed him in stern, hissing accents, through his closed and almost gnashing teeth.

"Away, sirrah, to the pinnace! See that you remain in her until I summon you! Away!"

The poor fellow turned off from Monaletta. He shook himself free from the grasp which she had taken of his hand. He prepared to obey the wanton and cruel order, but he could not forbear saying reproachfully as he retired—

"You push me too hard, Captain Albert."

"No words, sir! Away!" was the stern response. The submissive fellow instantly disappeared. With his disappearance, Albert again approached Monaletta, and renewed his application. But this time he met with a rejection even more decided than before. He looked to King Audusta; but an Indian princess, while she remains unmarried, enjoys a degree of social liberty which the same class of persons in Europe would sigh for and supplicate in vain. There were no answering sympathies in the king's face, to encourage Albert in the prosecution of his suit. Nay, he had the mortification to perceive, from the expression of his countenance, that his proceedings towards Guernache—who was a general favorite—had afforded not more satisfaction to him, than they had done to Monaletta. It was, therefore, in no very pleasant mood with himself and those around him, that our captain consoled himself in the dance with the hand of an inferior beauty. Jealous of temper and frivolous of mind—characteristics which are frequently found together—Albert was very fond of dancing, and enjoyed the sport quite as greatly as any of his companions. But, even while he capered, his soul, stung and dissatisfied, was brooding vexatiously over its petty hurts. His thoughts were busied in devising ways to revenge himself upon the humble offender by whom his mortification originally grew. Upon this sweet and bitter cud did he chew while the merry music sounded in his ears, and the gaily twinkling feet of the dusky maidens were whirling in promiscuous mazes beneath his eye. But these festivities, and his own evil meditations, were destined to have an interruption as startling as unexpected.

While the mirth was at its highest, and the merriment most contagious, the ears of the assembly were startled by screams, the most terrible, of fright and anguish. The Frenchmen felt a nameless terror seizing upon them. The cries and shrieks were from an European throat. Wild was the discord which accompanied them,—whoops of wrath and vengeance, which, as evidently issued. only from the throats of most infuriated savages. The music ceased in an instant. The dance was arrested. The Frenchmen rushed to their arms, fully believing that they were surrounded by treachery—that they had been beguiled to the feast only to become its victims. With desperate decision, they prepared themselves for the worst. While their suspense and fear were at their highest, the cause of the alarm and uproar soon became apparent to their eyes. Bursting, like a wounded deer, suddenly, from the woods by which the dwelling of Audusta was surrounded, a bloody figure, ghastly and spotted, appeared before the crowd. In another moment the Frenchmen recognized the spy, Pierre Renaud, who had volunteered to get at the heart of the Indian mysteries—to follow the priesthood to their sacred haunts, and gather all the secrets of their ceremonials.

We have already seen that he reached his place of watch in safety. But here his good fortune failed him: his place of espionage was not one of concealment. In the wild orgies of their religion,—for they seem to have practised rites not dissimilar to, and not less violent and terrible than those of the British Druids,—the priests darted over the crouching spy. Detected in the very act, where he lay, "squat like a toad," the Iawas fell upon him with the sharp instruments of flint with which they had been lancing and lacerating their own bodies. With these they contrived, in spite of all his struggles and entreaties, to inflict upon him some very severe wounds. Their rage was unmeasured; and the will to slay him was not wanting. But Renaud was a fellow equally vigorous and active. He baffled their blows as well as he could, and at length breaking from their folds, he took fairly to his heels. Howling with rage and fury, they darted upon his track, their wild shrieks ringing through the wood like those of so many demons suffering in mortal agony. They cried to all whom they saw, to stay and slay the offender. Others joined in the chase, as they heard this summons. But fortune favored the fugitive. His terror added wings to his flight. He was not, it seems, destined to such a death as they designed him. He outran his pursuers, and, dodging those whom he accidentally encountered, he made his way into the thick of the area, where his comrades, half bewildered by the uproar, were breaking up the dance. He sank down in the midst of them, exhausted by loss of blood and fatigue, only a moment before the appearance of his pursuers.

The French instantly closed around their companion. They had not put aside their weapons, and they now prepared themselves to encounter the worst. The aspect of the danger was threatening in the last degree. The Iawas were boiling with sacred fury. They were the true rulers of their people. Their will was sovereign over the popular moods. They demanded, with violent outcry, the blood of the individual by whom their sacred retreats had been violated, and their shekinah polluted by vulgar and profane presence. They demanded the blood of *all* the Frenchmen, as participating in the crime. They called upon Audusta to assert his own privileges and theirs. They appealed to the people in a style of phrenzied eloquence, the effects of which were soon visible in the inflamed features and wild action of the more youthful warriors. Already were these to be seen slapping their sides, tossing their hands in air, and, with loud shrieks, lashing themselves into a fury like that which enflamed their prophets. King Audusta looked confounded. The Frenchmen were his guests. He had invited them to partake of his hospitality, and to enjoy the rites of his religion. He was in some sort pledged for their safety, though one of them had violated the conditions of their coming. His own feelings revolted at giving any sanction for the assault, yet he appeared unable or unwilling to resist the clamors of the priesthood. But *he* also demanded, though with evident reluctance, the blood of the offender. He was not violent, though urgent, in this demand. He showed indignation rather than hostility; and he gave Albert to understand that in no way could the people or the priesthood be appeased, unless by the sacrifice of the guilty person.

But Albert could not yield the victim. The French were prepared to perish to a man before complying with any such demand. They were firm. They fenced him in with their weapons, and declared their readiness to brave every peril ere they would abandon their comrade. This resolution was the more honorable, as Pierre Renaud was no favorite among them. Though seriously disquieted by the event, and apprehensive of the issue, Albert was man enough to second their spirit. Besides, Renaud had been his own emissary in the adventure which threatened to terminate so fatally. His denial was inferred from his deportment; and the clamor of the Indians was increased. The rage of the Iawas was renewed with the conviction that no redress was to be given them. Already had the young warriors of Audusta procured their weapons. More than an hundred of them surrounded our little band of Frenchmen, who were only thirteen in number. Bows were bent, lances were set in rest, javelins were seen lifted, and ready to be thrown; and the drum which had been just made to sound, in lively tones, for the dance, now gave forth the most dismal din, significant of massacre and war. Already were to be seen, in the hands of some more daring Indian than the rest, the heavy war-club, or the many-teethed macana, waving aloft and threatening momently to descend upon the victim; and nothing was wanting but a first blow to bring on a general massacre. Suddenly, at this perilous moment, the fiddle of Guernache was heard without; followed, in a moment after, by the appearance of the brave fellow himself. Darting in between the opposing ranks, attended by the faithful Monaletta, with a grand crash upon his instrument, now newly-strung, followed by a rapid gush of the merriest music, he took both parties by the happiest surprise, and instantly produced a revulsion of feeling among the savages as complete as it was sudden.

"Ami! ami! ami!" was the only cry from an hundred voices, at the reappearance of Guernache among them. They had acquired this friendly epithet among the first words which they had learned at their coming, from the French; and their affection for our fiddler had made its application to himself, in particular, a thing of general usage. He *was* their friend. He had shown himself their friend, and they had a faith in *him* which they accorded to no other of his people. The people were with him, and the priesthood not unfriendly. Time was gained by this diversion; and, in such an outbreak as that which has been described, time is all that is needful, perhaps, to stay the arm of slaughter. Guernache played out his tune, and cut a few pleasant antics, in which the now happy Monaletta, though of the blood royal, readily joined him. The musician had probably saved the party from massacre. The subsequent work of treaty and pacification was comparatively easy. Pierre Renaud was permitted to depart for the pinnace, under the immediate care of Guernache and Monaletta. The Iawas received some presents of gaudy costume, bells, and other gew-gaws, while a liberal gift of knives and beads gratified their warriors and their women. The old ties of friendship were happily reunited, and the calumet went round, from mouth to mouth, in token of restored confidence and renewed faith. Before nightfall, happily relieved from his apprehensions, Albert, with his detachment, was rapidly making his way with his pinnace, down the waters of the swiftly-rolling Edisto.

V.

THE LEGEND OF GUERNACHE.—Chap. III

The Legend of Guernache is continued, showing how the Fortress of the Huguenots was destroyed, and what happened thereafter to Guernache the Musician.

THE fidelity which Guernache had shown in the recent difficulty with the Indians, did not appear to lessen in any degree the unfavorable impressions which Capt. Albert had received of that worthy fellow. Indeed, the recent and remarkable service which he had rendered, by which, in all probability, the whole party had been preserved from massacre, rather increased, if any thing, the hostile temper of his superior. The evil spirit still raged within the bosom of Capt. Albert, utterly baffling a judgment at no period of particular excellence, and blinding every honorable sentiment which might have distinguished him under other influences. He was now doubly mortified, that he should be supposed to owe his present safety to the person he had wronged—a mortification which found due increase as he remembered how much greater had been the respect and deference of the savages for his drummer than for himself. This recollection was a perpetual goad to that working malice in his heart, which was already busied in devising schemes of revenge, which were to salve his hurts of pride and vanity, by the sufferings as well as humiliation of his subordinate. It will scarcely be believed that, when fairly out of sight of the village of Audusta, he rebuked Guernache sharply, for leaving the pinnace against his orders, and even spoke of punishing him for this disobedience.* But the murmurs of some of his officers, and, perhaps, a little lurking sentiment of shame in his own bosom, prevented him from attempting any such disgraceful proceeding. But the feeling of hostility only rankled the more because of its suppression, and he soon contrived to show Guernache and, indeed, everybody besides, that from that hour he was his most bitter and unforgiving enemy, with a little and malignant spirit, he employed various petty arts, which a superior of a base nature may readily command on all occasions, by which to make the poor fellow feel how completely he was at his mercy; and each day exposed him to some little snare, or some stern caprice, by which Guernache became involuntarily an offender. His tyrant subjected him to duties the most troublesome and humiliating, while denying, or stinting him of all those privileges which were yet commonly accorded to his comrades. But all this would have been as nothing to Guernache, if he had not been denied permission to visit, as before, the hamlet of Audusta, where his princess dwelt. On the miserable pretext that the priesthood might revenge upon him the misconduct of Renaud, Albert insisted upon his abstaining wholly from the Indian territories. But this pretence deceived nobody, and nobody less than Guernache. Little did the

* Charlevoix thus describes Captain Albert: "Le Commandant de Charles-Fort étoit un homme de main, et qui ne manquoit pas absolument de conduite, mais il etoit brutal jusqu'à la férocité, et ne sçavoit pas meme garder les bienséances. . . . . Il punissoit les moindres fautes, and toujours avec excès, &c.—N. France, Liv. 1. p. 51.

petty tyrant of Fort Charles imagine that the object of his malice enjoyed a peculiar source of consolation for all these privations. His comrades were his friends. They treated him with a warmth and kindness, studiously proportioned to the ill-treatment of his superior. They assisted him in the severer tasks which were allotted him to fulfil—gave him their company whenever this was possible, while he was engaged in the execution of his most cheerless duties, and soothed his sorrows by the expression of their almost unanimous sympathies. Nor did they always withhold their bitter denunciations of the miserable despotism under which he suffered, and which they feared. Dark hints of remedy were spoken, brows frowned at the mention of the wrongs of their companion, and the head shaken ominously, when words of threatening significance were uttered—appealed gratefully to certain bitter desires which had taken root in the mind of the victim. But these sympathies, though grateful, were of small amount in comparison with another source of consolation, which contributed to sustain Guernache in his tribulation. This was found in the secret companionship of his young and beautiful Indian wife. Denied to see him at the village of Audusta, the fond and fearless woman determined to seek him at all hazards in his own domain. She stole away secretly to the fortress of the Huguenots. Long and earnest was the watch which she maintained upon its portals, from the thickets of the neighboring wood. Here, vigilant as the sentinel that momently expects his foe, she harbored close, in waiting for the beloved one. Her quick instincts had already taught her the true cause of his denial, and of her disappointment; and her Indian lessons had made that concealment, which she now believed to be necessary to her purpose, a part of the habitual policy of her people

She showed herself to none of the people of the fortress. She suspected them all; she had no faith but in the single one. And he, at length, came forth, unaccompanied, in the prosecution of an occasional labor—that of cutting and procuring wood. She suffered him to make his way into the forests—to lose sight of the fortress, and, with a weary spirit and a wounded soul, to begin his lonely labors with the axe. Then did she steal behind him, and beside him; and when he moaned aloud—supposing that he had no auditor—how startling fell upon his ear the sweet, soft whisper of that precious voice which he had so lovingly learned to distinguish from all others. He turned with a gush of rapturous delight, and, weeping, she rushed into his arms, pouring forth, in a wild cry, upon his breast, the whole full volume of her warm, devoted heart!

That moment, in spite of all his fears, was amply compensative to Guernache for all his troubles. He forgot them all in the intensity of his new delights. And when Monaletta led him off from his tasks to the umbrageous retreat in the deeper woods where her nights had been recently passed,—when she conducted him to the spot where her own hands had built a mystic bower for her own shelter—when she declared her purpose still to occupy this retreat, in the solitude alone,—that she might be ever near him, to behold him at a distance, herself unseen, when he came forth accompanied by others—to join him, to feel his embrace, hear his words of love, and assist him in his labors when he came forth unattended—when, speaking and promising thus, she lay upon the poor fellow's bosom, looking up with tearful and bright eyes in his wan and apprehensive countenance—then it was that he could forget his tyrant—could lose his fears and sorrows in his love, and in the enjoyment of moments the most precious to his heart, forget all the accompanying influences which might endanger his safety.

But necessity arose sternly between the two, and pointed to the exactions of duty. The tasks of Guernache were to be completed. His axe was required to sound among the trees of the forest, and a certain number of pieces of timber were required by sunset at his hands. It was surprising as it was sweet to behold the Indian woman as she assisted him in his tasks. Her strength did not suffice for the severer toils of the wood-cutter, but she contrived a thousand modes for contributing to his performances. Love lightens every labor, and invents a thousand arts by which to do so. Monaletta anticipated the wants of Guernache. She removed the branches as he smote them, she threw the impediments from his way,—helped him to lift and turn the logs as each successive side was to be hewn. She brought him water, when he thirsted, from the spring. She spoke and sung to him in the most encouraging voice when he was weary He was never weary when with her.

Guernache combatted her determination to remain in the neighborhood of the fortress; but his objections were feebly urged, and she soon overcame them. He had not the courage to insist upon his argument, as he had not the strength to resist the consolations which her presence brought him. She soon succeeded in assuring him that there was little or no danger of detection by their enemy. She laughed at the idea of the Frenchmen discovering her place of concealment, surprising her in her progress through the woods, or overtaking her in flight; and Guernache knew enough of Indian subtlety readily to believe that the white was no match for the dusky race in the exercise of all those arts which are taught by forest life. "But her loneliness and privation, exposed to the season's changes, and growing melancholy in the absence from old associates?" But how could she be lonely, was her argument, when near the spot where he dwelt—when she could see and hear and speak with him occasionally? She wished no other communion. As for the exposure of her present abode, was it greater than that to which the wandering life of the red-man subjects his people at all seasons? The Indian woman is quite as much at home in the forest as the Indian warrior. She acquires her resources of strength and dexterity in his company, and by the endurance of similar necessities and the employment of like exercises. She learns even in childhood to build her own green bower at night, to gather her own fuel, light her own fire, dress her own meat—nay, provide it; and, weaponed with bow, and javelin and arrow, bring down buck or doe bounding at full speed through the wildest forests. Her skill and spirit are only not equal to those of the master by whom she is taught, but she acquires his arts to a degree which makes her sometimes worthy to be lifted by the tribe from her own rank into his. Monaletta reminded Guernache of all these things. She had the most conclusive and convincing methods of argument. She reassured him on all his doubts, and, in truth, it was but too easy to do so. It was unhappy for them both, as we shall see hereafter, that the selfish passion of the poor musician too readily reconciled him to a self-devotion on the part of his wife, which subjected her to his own perils, and greatly tended to their increase. With the evil eye of Albert upon him, he should have known that safety was impossible for him in the event of error. And error was inevitable now, with the pleasant tempter so near his place of coventry. We must not wonder to discover now that Guernache seldom sleeps within the limits of the fortress. At midnight, when all is dark and quiet, he leaps over the walls, those nights excepted when it is his turn of duty to watch within. His secret is known to some of his comrades; but they are too entirely his friends to betray him to a despot who had, by this time, outraged the feelings of most of those who remained under his command. Guernache was now enabled to bear up more firmly than ever against the tyranny of Albert. His, indeed, were nights of happiness. How sweetly sped the weeks, in which, despite his persecutions, he felt that he enjoyed a life of luxurious pleasures, such as few enjoy in any situation. His were the honest excitements of a genuine passion, which, nourished by privation and solitude, and indulged in secresy, was of au intensity corresponding with the apparent denial, and the real embarrassments of such a condition. His pleasures were at once stolen and legitimate; the apprehension which attends their pursuit giving a wild zest to their enjoyment; though, in the case of Guernache, unlike that of most of those who indulge in stolen joys, they were honest, and left no cruel memories behind them.

It was the subject of a curious study and surprise to Captain Albert, that our musician was enabled to bear up against his tyranny with so much equal firmness and forbearance. He watched the countenance of Guernache, whenever they met, with a curious interest. By what secret resource of fortitude and hope was it that he could command so much elasticity, exhibit so much cheerfulness, bear with so much meekness, and utter no complaint. He wondered that the irksome duties which he studiously thrust upon him, and the frequently brutal language with which his performances were acknowledged, seemed to produce none of the cruel effects which he desired. His victim grew neither sad nor sullen. His violin still was heard resounding merrily at the instance of his comrades; and still his hearty, whole-souled laughter rang over the encampment, smiting ungraciously upon the senses of his basely-minded chief. In vain did this despot study how to increase and frame new annoyances for his subordinate. His tyranny contrived daily some new method to make the poor fellow unhappy. But, consoled by the peculiar secret which he possessed, of sympathy and comfort, the worthy drummer bore up cheerfully under his afflictions. He was resolved to wait patiently the return of Ribault with the promised supplies for the colony, and meanwhile to submit to his evil destiny without a murmur. It was always with a secret sense of triumph that he reminded himself of the near neighborhood of his joys, and he exulted in the success with which he could baffle nightly the malice of his superior. But, however docile, the patience and forbearance of Guernache availed him little. They did not tend to mitigate the annoyances which he was constantly compelled to endure. We are now to recall a portion of the preceding narrative, and to remind our reader of the visit which Captain Albert paid to the territories of Ouade, and the generous hospitalities of the King thereof. Guernache had been one of the party, and the absence of several days had been a serious loss to him in the delightful intercourse with his dusky bride. He might naturally hope, after his return from a journey so fatiguing, to be permitted a brief respite from his regular duties. But this was not according to the policy of his malignant superior. Some hours were consumed after arriving at the fort, in disposing of the provisions which had been obtained. In this labor Guernache had been compelled to partake with others of his companions. Whether it was that he betrayed an unusual degree of eagerness in getting through his task—showing an impatience to escape which his enemy detected and resolved to baffle, cannot now be said; but to his great annoyance and indignation, he was burdened with a portion of the watch for the night—a duty which was clearly incumbent only upon those who had not shared in the fatigues of the expedition. But to expostulate or repine was alike useless, and Guernache submitted to his destiny with the best possible grace. The provisions were stored, the gates closed, the watches set, and the garrison sunk to sleep, leaving our unhappy musician to pace, for several hours, the weary watch along the ramparts. How he looked forth into the dense forests which harbored his Monaletta! How he thought of the weary watch she kept! What were her fears, her anxieties? Did she know of his return? Did she look for his coming? The garrison slept—the woods were mysteriously silent! How delightful it would be to surprise her in the midst of her dreams, and answer to her murmurs of reproach—uttered in the sweetest fragmentary Gallic—"Monaletta! I am here! Here is your own Guernache!"

The temptation was perilously sweet! The suggestion was irresistible; and, in a moment of excited fancy and passion, Guernache laid down his piece, and leaped the walls of the fortress. He committed an unhappy error to enjoy a great happiness, for which the penalties were not slow to come. In the dead of midnight, the garrison, still in a deep sleep, they were suddenly aroused in terror by the appalling cry of "fire!" The fort, the tenements in which they slept, the granary, which had just been stored with their provisions, were all ablaze, and our Frenchmen woke in confusion and terror, unknowing where to turn, how to work, or what to apprehend. Their military stores were saved—their powder and munitions of war—but the "mils and beanes," so recently acquired from the granaries of King Ouade, with the building that contained them, were swept in ashes to the ground.

This disaster, full of evil in itself, was productive of others, as it led to the partial discovery of the secret of our drummer. Guernache was not within the fort when the alarm was given. It is not improbable that, had he not left his post, the conflagration would have been arrested in time to save the fort and its provisions. His absence was noted, and he was discovered, approaching from the forests, by those who bore forth the goods as they were rescued from the flames. These were mostly friends of Guernache, who would have maintained a generous silence; but, unhappily, Pierre Renaud was also one of the discoverers. This person not only bore him no good will,—though gratitude for the service rendered him at the feast of Toya should have bound him forever to the cause of Guernache,—but he was one who had become a gross sycophant and the mere creature of the governor. He knew the hatred which the latter bore to Guernache, and a sympathizing nature led him promptly to divine the cause. Overjoyed with the discovery which he had made, the base fellow immediately carried the secret to his master, and when the first confusion was over, which followed the disaster, Guernache was taken into custody, and a day assigned for his trial as a criminal. To him was ascribed the fire as well as desertion from his post. The latter fact was unquestionable—the former was inferred. It might naturally be assumed, indeed, that, if the watch had not been abandoned, the flames could not have made such fearful headway. It was fortunate for our Frenchmen that the intercourse maintained with the Indians had been of such friendly character. With the first intimation of their misfortune, the kings, Audusta and Maccou, bringing with them a numerous train of followers, came to assist them in the labor of restoration and repair. "They uttered unto their subjects the speedy diligence which they were to use in building another house, showing unto them that the Frenchmen were their loving friends and that they had made it evident unto them by the gifts and presents which they had received;—protesting that he whosoever put not his helping hand to the worke with all his might, should be esteemed as unprofitable." The entreaties and commands of the two kings were irresistible. But for this, our Huguenots, "being farre from all succours, and in such extremitie," would have been, in the language of their own chronicler, "quite and cleane out of all hope." The Indians went with such hearty good will to the work, and in such numbers, that, in less than twelve hours, the losses of the colonists were nearly all repaired. New houses were built; new granaries erected; and, among the fabrics of this busy period, it was not forgotten to construct a keep—a close, dark, heavy den of logs, designed as a prison, into which, as soon as his Indian friends had departed, our poor fiddler, Guernache, was thrust, neck and heels! The former were rewarded and went away well satisfied with what they had seen and done. They little conjectured the troubles which awaited their favorite. He was soon brought to trial under a number of charges—disobedience of orders, neglect of duty, desertion of his post, and treason! To all of these, the poor fellow pleaded "*not guilty;*" and, with one exception, with a good conscience. But he had not the courage to confess the truth, and to declare where he had been, and on what mission, when he left the fort, on the night of the fire. He had committed a great fault, the consequences of which were serious, and might have been still more so; and the pleas of invariable good conduct, in his behalf, and the assertion of his innocence of all evil intention, did not avail. His judges were not his friends; he was found guilty and remanded to his dungeon, to await the farther caprices and the judgment of his enemy.

VI.

THE LEGEND OF GUERNACHE.—Chap. IV.

THE DUNGEON AND THE SCOURGE.

Being the continuation of the melancholy Legend of Guernache.

THE absence of Guernache from his usual place of meeting with Monaletta, brought the most impatient apprehension to the heart of the devoted woman. As the time wore away—as night after night passed without his coming, she found the suspense unendurable, and gradually drew nigh to the fortress of the Huguenots. More than once had he cautioned her against incurring a peril equally great to them both. But her heart was already too full of fears to be restrained by such dangers as he alone could have foreseen; and she now lurked about the fort at nightfall, and continued to hover around long after dawn, keeping watch upon its walls and portal. So close and careful, however, was this watch, that she herself remained undetected. One day, however, to her great satisfaction, one of the inmates came forth whom she knew to be a friend and associate of Guernache. This was one Lachane, affectionately called *La Chere**

* The names are thus written by Laudonniere in Hakluyt. But in Charlevoix there is only one given to this personage, and that is "Lachau."

by the soldiery, by whom he was very much beloved. Lachane was a sergeant, a good soldier, brave as a lion, but with as tender a heart, when the case required it, as ever beat in human bosom. He had long since learned to sympathize with the fate of Guernache, and had made frequent attempts to mollify the hostile feelings of his captain, in behalf of his friend. To the latter he had given much good counsel; and, but for *his* earnest entreaties and injunctions, he would have revealed to Albert the true reason for the absence of Guernache from his post. But Guernache dreaded, as well he might, that the revelation would only increase the hate and rage of his superior, and, perhaps, draw down a portion of his vengeance upon the head of the unoffending woman. Lachane acquiesced in his reasoning, and was silent. But he was not the less active in bringing consolation, whenever he could, to the respective parties. He afforded to Monaletta, whose approach to the fort he suspected, an opportunity of meeting with him; and their interviews, once begun, were regularly continued. Day by day he contrived to convey to her the messages, and to inform her of the condition of the prisoner; to whom, in turn, he bore all necessary intelligence, and every fond avowal which was sent by Monaletta. But the loving and devoted wife was not satisfied with so frigid a mode of intercourse; and, in an evil hour, Lachane, whose own heart was too tender to resist the entreaties of one so fond, was persuaded to admit her within the fort, and into the dungeon of Guernache. We may censure his prudence and hers, but who shall venture to condemn either? The first visit led to a second, the second to a third, and, at length, the meetings between the lovers took place nightly. Lachane, often entreating, often exhorting, was yet always complying. Monaletta was admitted at midnight, and conducted forth by the dawn in safety; and thus meeting, Guernache soon forgot his own danger, and was readily persuaded by Monaletta to believe that she stood in none. The hours passed with them as with any other children, who, sitting on the shores of the sea, in the bright sunset, see not the rising of the waters, and feel not the falling of the night, until they are wholly overwhelmed. They were happy, and in their happiness but too easily forgot that there was such a person as Captain Albert in their little paradise.

But the pitcher which goes often to the well, is at last broken. They were soon destined to realize the proverb in their own experience. Something in the movements of Lachane, awakened the suspicions of Pierre Renaud, whose active hostility to Guernache has been shown already. This man now bore within the fortress the unenviable reputation of being the captain's spy upon the people. This miserable creature, his suspicion's once awakened, soon addressed all his abilities to the task of detecting the connection of Lachane with his prisoner; and it was not long before he had the malignant satisfaction of seeing him accompany another into the dungeon of Guernache. Though it was after midnight when the discovery was made, it was of a kind too precious to suffer delay in revealing it, and he hurried at once to the captain's quarters, well aware that, with such intelligence as he brought, he might safely venture to disturb him at any hour. But his eagerness did not lessen his caution, and every step was taken with the greatest deliberation and care. Albert was immediately aroused; but, unwilling, by a premature alarm, to afford the offenders an opportunity to escape, or to place themselves in any situation to defy scrutiny, some time was lost in making arrangements. The progress of Albert, and his satellites, going the rounds, was circuitous. The sentries were doubled with singular secrecy and skill. Such soldiers as were conceived to be most particularly bound to him, were awakened, and placed in positions most convenient for action and observation;—for Albert and Renaud, alike, conscious as it would seem of their own demerits, had come to suspect many of the soldiers of treachery and insurrection. These, perhaps, are always the fears most natural to a tyranny. Accordingly, with everything prepared for an explosion of the worst description, Captain Albert, in complete armor, made his appearance upon the scene.

Meantime, however, the proceedings of Renaud had not been carried on without, at length, commanding the attention and awakening the fears of so good a soldier as Lachane. Having discovered, on his rounds, that the guards were doubled, and that the sentinel at the sally-port had not only received a companion, but that the individual by whom Monaletta had been admitted was now removed to make way for another, he hurried away to the dungeon of Guernache. Here, whispering hurriedly his apprehensions, he endeavored to hasten the departure of the Indian woman. But his efforts were made too late. He was arrested, even while thus busied, by the Commandant himself, who, followed by Renaud and two other soldiers, suddenly came upon him from the rear of the building, where they had been harboring in ambush. Lachane was taken into immediate custody. An uproar followed, the alarm was given to the garrison, torches were brought, and Guernache, with the devoted Monaletta, were dragged forth together from the dungeon. She was wrapped up closely in the cloak of Lachane, but when Renaud waved a torch before her eyes, in order to discover who she was, she boldly threw aside the disguise, and stood revealed to the malignant scrutiny of the astonished but delighted despot. Upon beholding her, the fury of Albert knew no bounds. The secret of Guernache was now apparent; and the man whose vanity she had outraged, by preferring another in the dance, was now in full possession of the power to revenge himself upon both offenders. In that very moment, remembering his mortification, he formed a resolution of vengeance, which declared all the venom of a mean and malignant nature. He needed no art beyond his own to devise an ingenious torture for his victim. A few words sufficed to instruct the willing Renaud in the duty of the executioner. He commanded that the Indian woman should be scourged from the fort in the presence of the garrison. Then it was that the sullen soul of Guernache shuddered and succumbed beneath his tortures. With husky and trembling accents, he appealed to his tyrant in behalf of the woman of his heart.

"Oh! Captain Albert, as you are a man, do not this cruel thing. Monaletta is innocent of any crime but that of loving one so worthless as Guernache. She is my wife! Do with me as you will, but spare her—have mercy on the innocent woman!"

"Ah! you can humble yourself now, insolent. I have found the way, at last, to make you feel. You shall feel yet more. I will crush you to the dust. What, ho! there, Pierre Renaud! Have I not said? the lash! the lash! Wherefore do ye linger?"

"Do not, Captain Albert! I implore you, for your own sake, do not lay the accursed lash upon this young and innocent creature. Remember! She is a woman—a princess—a blood relation of our good friend, King Audusta. Upon me—upon my back bestow the punishment, but spare her—spare her, in mercy!"

But the prayers and supplications of the wretched man were

met only by denunciation and scorn. The base nature of Albert felt only his own mortification. His appetite for revenge darkened his vision wholly. He saw neither his policy nor humanity; and the creatures of his will were not permitted to hesitate in carrying out his brutal resolution. Armed with little hickories from the neighboring woods, they awaited but his command, and with its repeated utterance, the lash descended heavily upon the uncovered shoulders of the unhappy woman. With the first stroke, she bounded from the earth with a piercing shriek, at once of entreaty, of agony, and horror. Up to this moment, neither she, nor, indeed, any of the spectators, except Renaud, and possibly Guernache himself, had imagined that Albert would put in execution a purpose so equally impolitic and cruel. But when the blow fell upon the almost fair and naked shoulders of the woman—when her wild, girlish, almost childlike shriek rent the air, then the long suppressed agonies of Guernache broke forth in a passion of fury that looked more like the excess of the madman than the mere ebullition, however intense, of a simply desperate man. He had struggled long at endurance. He had borne, hitherto, without flinching, everything in the shape of penalty which his petty tyrant could fasten upon him—much more, indeed, than the ordinary nature, vexed with frequent injustice, is willing to endure. But, in the fury and agony of that humiliating moment, all restraints of prudence or fear were forgotten, or trampled under foot. He flung himself loose from the men who held him, and darting upon the individual by whom the merciless blow had been struck, he felled him to the earth by a single blow of his Herculean fist. But he was permitted to do no more. In another instant, grappled by a dozen powerful arms, he was borne to the earth, and secured with cords which not only bound his limbs but were drawn so tightly as to cut remorselessly into the flesh. Here he lay, and his agony may be far more easily conceived than described, thus compelled to behold the further tortures of the woman of his heart, without being able to struggle and to die in her defence. His own tortures were forgotten, as he witnessed hers. In vain would his ears have rejected the terrible sound, stroke upon stroke, which testified the continuance of this brutal outrage upon humanity. Without mercy was the punishment bestowed; and, bleeding at every blow from the biting scourge, the wretched innocent was at length tortured out of the garrison. But with that first shriek to which she gave utterance, and which declared rather the mental horror than the bodily pain which she suffered from such a cruel degradation, she ceased any longer to acknowledge her suffering. Oh! very powerful for endurance is the strength of a loving heart! The rest of the punishment she bore with the silence of one who suffers martyrdom in the approving eye of heaven; as if, beholding the insane agonies of Guernache, she had steeled herself to bear with any degree of torture rather than increase his sufferings by her complaints. In this manner, and thus silent under her own pains, she was expelled from the fortress. She was driven to the margin of the cleared space by which it was surrounded. She heard the shouts which drove her thence, and heard nothing farther. She had barely strength to totter forward, like the deer with a mortal hurt, to the secret cover of the forest, when she sank down in exhaustion;—nature kindly interposing with insensibility, to save her from those physical sufferings which she could no longer feel and live !

With the morning of the next day, Guernache was brought before the judgment-seat of Albert. The charges were sufficiently serious under which he was arraigned. He had neglected his duty—had permitted, if not caused, the destruction of the fort by fire—had violated the laws, resisted their execution, and used violence against the officer of justice! In this last proven offence all of these which had been alleged were assumed against him. He was convicted by the rapid action of his superior, as a traitor and a mutineer; and, to the horror of his friends, and the surprise of all his comrades, was condemned to expiate his faults by death upon the gallows. Few of the garrison had anticipated so sharp a judgment. They knew that Guernache had been faulty, but they also knew what had been his provocations. They felt that his faults had been the fruit of the injustice under which he suffered. But they dared not interpose. The prompt severity with which Captain Albert carried out his decisions—the merciless character of his vindictiveness—discouraged even remonstrance. Guernache, as we have shown, was greatly beloved, and had many true friends among his people; but they were taken by surprise; and, so much stunned and confounded by the rapidity with which events had taken place, that they could only look on the terrible proceedings with a mute and self-reproachful horror. The transition from the seat of judgment to the place of execution was instantaneous. Guernache appealed in vain to the justice of Ribault, whose coming from France was momently expected. This denied, he implored the less ignoble doom of the sword or the shot, in place of that upon the scaffold. But it did not suit the mean malice of Albert to omit any of his tortures. Short was the shrift allowed the victim;—ten minutes for prayer—and sure the cord which stifled it forever. In deep horror, in a hushed terror, which itself was full of horror, his gloomy comrades gathered at the place of execution, by the commands of their petty despot. There was no concert among them, by which the incipient indignation and fury in their bosoms might have declared itself in rescue and commotion. One groan, the involuntary expression of a terror that had almost ceased to breathe, answered the convulsive motion which indicated the last struggle of their beloved comrade.* Then it was that they began to feel that they could have died for him, and might have saved him. But it was now too late; and prudence timely interposed to prevent a rash explosion. The armed myrmidons of Albert were about them. He, himself, in complete armor, with his satellite, Pierre Renaud, also fully armed, standing beside him; and it was evident that every preparation had been made to quell insubordination, and punish the refractory with as sharp and sudden a judgment as that which had just descended upon their comrade.

The poor Monaletta, crouching in the cover of the woods recovered from her stupor in the cool air of the morning, but it was sunset before she could regain the necessary strength to move. Then it was, that, with the natural tendency of a loving heart, curious only about the fate of him for whom alone her heart desired life, she bent her steps towards that cruel fortress which had been the source of so much misery to both. Very feeble and slow was her progress, but it was still too rapid; it brought her too soon to a knowledge of that final blow which fell, with worse terrors than the scourge, upon the soul. She arrived

---

* Says Charlevoix:—"Il pendit lui-même un soldat, qui n'avoit point merité la mort, il en dégrada un autre des arms avec aussi peu de justice, puis il l'exila, et l'on crut que son dessein étoit de le laisser mourir de faim et de misere, etc." But we must not anticipate the revelations of the text.

in season to behold the form of the unfortunate Guernache, abandoned by all, and totally lifeless, waving in the wind from the branches of a perished oak, directly in front of the fortress. The deepest sorrows of the heart are those which are born dumb. There are some woes which the lip can never speak, nor the pen describe. There are some agonies over which we draw the veil without daring to look upon them, lest we freeze to stone in the terrible inspection. There is no record of that grief which seized upon the heart of the poor Indian woman, Monaletta, as she gazed upon the beloved but unconscious form of her husband. She approached it not, though watching it from sunset till the gray twilight lapsed away into the denser shadows of the night. But, with the dawn of day, when the Frenchmen looked forth from the fortress for the body of their comrade, it had disappeared. They searched for it in vain. From that day Monaletta disappeared also. She was neither to be found in the neighboring woods, nor among the people of her kindred. But, long afterwards they told, with shuddering and apprehension, of a voice upon the midnight air, which resembled that of their murdered comrade, followed always by the piercing shriek of a woman, which reminded them of the dreadful utterance of the Indian woman, when first smitten upon the shoulders by the lash of the ruffian. Thus endeth the legend of Guernache, and the Princess Monaletta.

VII.

LACHANE, THE DELIVERER.

But the sacrifice of Guernache brought no peace to the colony Our Huguenots were scarcely Christians. They were of a rude, wild temper, to which the constant civil wars prevailing in France had brought a prejudicial training. Our chronicler tells us nothing of their devotions. We hear sometimes that they prayed, but rather for the benefit of the savages than their own. Their public religious services were ostentatious ceremonials, designed to impress the red-men with an idea of their superior faith and worship. Laudonniere, who writes for them, and was one of their number, seldom deals in a religious phraseology, which he might reasonably be expected to have done as one of a people leaving their homes for the sake of conscience. But there is good reason to suppose that, with our Huguenots, as in the case of the New England Puritans, the idea of religion was more properly the idea of party. It was a struggle for political power that moved the Dissenters, as well in France as England, quite as much as any feeling of denial or privation on the score of their religion. This pretext was made to justify a cause which might have well found its sanction in its intrinsic merits; but which it was deemed politic to urge on the higher grounds of conscience and duty to God

Certain it is that we do not anywhere see, in the history of the colony established by Coligny, any proofs of that strong devotional sentiment which has been urged as the motive to its establishment. Doubtless, this was a prevailing motive, along with others, for Coligny himself; but the adventurers chosen to begin the settlement for the reception of the persecuted sect in Florida, were evidently not very deeply imbued with religion of any kind. They were a wild and reckless body of men, whose deeds were wholly in conflict with the pure and lovely profession of sentiment which has been made in their behalf. How far their deeds are to be justified by the provocations which they received, and the tyrannies which they endured, may be a question; but there can be no question with regard to the general temper which they exhibited—the tone of their minds—the feelings of their hearts—by all of which they are shown as stubborn, insubordinate and selfish. It is not denied that they had great provocation to violence; but Laudonniere himself admits that they were, in all probability, "not so obedient to their captain as they should have been." "Misfortune," he adds, " or rather the just judgment of God would have it that those which could not bee overcome by fire nor water, should be undone by their ownselves. This is the common fashion of men, which cannot continue in one state, and had rather to overthrow themselves, than not to attempt some new thing dayly."

Not only was no peace in the colony after the execution of Guernache, but the evil spirit, in the mood of Captain Albert, was very far from being laid. "His madness," in the language of the chronicler, "seemed to increase from day to day." He was not content to punish Guernache; he determined to extend his severities to the friends and associates of the unhappy victim.

Some of these he only frowned upon and threatened; but his threats were apt to be fulfilled. Others he brought up for punishment;—sympathy with his enemy, being a prime offence against the dignity and safety of our petty sovereign. Among those who had thus rendered themselves obnoxious, Lachane was necessarily a conspicuous object. In the same unwise and violent spirit in which he had pursued Guernache, Captain Albert was determined to proceed against this man, who was really equally inoffensive with Guernache, and quite as much beloved among the people. But the aspect of the two cases was not precisely the same. The friends of Lachane, warned by the fate of Guernache, were somewhat more upon their guard,—more watchful and suspicious,—and inclined to make the support and maintenance of the one, a tribute to the manes of the other. Besides, Pierre Renaud, who had some how been the deadly enemy of Guernache, had no hostility to Lachane. The latter, too, had not so singularly offended the *amour propre* of Captain Albert, by his successful rivalry among the damsels of Audusta. They had not so decidedly shown the preference for him as they had for the fiddler, over his superior. No doubt he was preferred, for he, too, like Guernache, was a person very superior in form and physiognomy to Albert. But, if they felt any preference for the former, they had not so offensively declared it, as the indiscreet Monaletta had done; and, with these qualifying circumstances, in his favor, Lachane was brought up for judgment. His offence, such as it was, did not admit of denial. Some palliation was attempted by a reference to the claims of Guernache, the excellence of his character, his usefulness, and the general favor he had found equally among the red-men and his own people. These suggestions were unwisely made. They censured equally the justice and the policy of the tyrant, and thus irritated anew his self-esteem. He thought himself exceedingly merciful, accordingly, in banishing the offender, whom it was just as easy and quite as agreeable to him, to hang. Lachane was accordingly sentenced to perpetual exile to a desert island along the sea. To this point he was conducted in melancholy state, by the trusted creatures of the despot.

It is not known to us at the present day, though the matter is still, probably, within the province of the antiquarian, to which of the numerous sea islands of the neighborhood the unhappy man was banished. It was one divided from the colony, and from the main, by an arm of the sea of such breadth, and so open to the most violent action of the waves, that any return of the exile by swimming, or without assistance from his comrades, was not apprehended or hoped for. His little desolate domain is described as about three leagues from Fort Charles, as almost entirely barren, a mere realm of sand, treeless and herbless, without foliage sufficient to shelter from sun and storm, or to provide against famine by its fruits. Should this island ever be identified with that of Lachane's place of exile, it should receive his name to the exclusion of every other.

Here, then, hopeless and companionless, was the unhappy victim destined to remain, until death should bring him that escape which the mercy of his fellows had denied. Yet he was not to be abandoned wholly; a certain pittance of provisions was allowed him that he might not absolutely die of famine. This allowance was calculated nicely against his merest necessities. It was to be brought him on the return of every eighth day, and this period was that, accordingly, on which, alone, could he be permitted to gaze upon the face of a fellow being and a countryman.

Certainly, a more cruel punishment, adopted in a mere wanton exercise of despotic power, could not have been devised for any victim by the ingenuity of any superior. Death, even the death by which Guernache had perished, had been a doom more merciful; for if, as was the case, the colonists at Fort Charles themselves had already begun to find their condition of solitude almost beyond endurance—if they, living as they did together, cheered by the exercise of old sports and homely converse, the ties and assurances of support and friendship, the consciousness of strength—duties which were necessary and not irksome, and the interchange of thoughts which enliven the desponding temper;—if, with all these resources in their favor, they had sunk into gloomy discontent, eager for change, and anxious for the returning vessels of Ribault, that they might abandon for their old, the new home which they found so desolate; what must have been the sufferings and agonies of him whom they had thus banished, even from such solace as they themselves possessed—uncheered even by the familiar faces and the well-known voices of his fellows, and deprived of all the resources whereby ingenuity might devise some methods of relief, and totally unblessed by any of those exercises which might furnish a substitute for habitual employments. No sentence, more than this, could have shown to our Frenchmen so completely the utter absence of sympathy between themselves and their commander; could have shown how slight was the value which he put upon their lives, and with what utter contempt he regarded their feelings and affections. Albert little dreamed how actively he was at work, while thus feeding his morbid passions, in arousing the avenging spirit by which they were to be scourged and punished.

These rash and cruel proceedings of their chief produced a

great and active sensation among the colonists—a sensation not the less deep and active, because a sense of their own danger kept them from its open expression. Had Albert pardoned Lachane, or let him off with some slight punishment, it is not improbable that the matter would have ended there; and the cruel proceedings against Guernache might have been forgiven if not forgotten. But these were kept alive by those which followed against their other favorite; and some of the boldest, feeling how desperate their condition threatened to become, now ventured to expostulate with their superior upon his wanton and unwise severities. But they were confounded to find that they themselves incurred the danger of Lachane, in the attempt to plead against it. It was one of the miserable weaknesses in the character of Captain Albert, to suppose his authority in danger whenever he was approached with the language of expostulation. To question his justice seemed to him to defy his power—to entreat for mercy, such a showing of hostility as to demand punishment also. He resented, as an impertinence to himself, all such approaches; and his answer to the prayers of his people was couched in the language of contumely and threat. They retired from his presence accordingly, with feelings of increased dislike and disgust, and with a discontent which was the more dangerous as they succeeded most effectually in controlling its exhibition.

But if such was the state of the relations between Albert and his people, how much worse did they become, when, at the close of the first eighth day after the banishment of Lachane, it was discovered that the orders for providing him with the allowance of food had been suspended, or countermanded. The captain was silent; and no one, unless at his bidding, could venture to carry the poor exile his allotted pittance. The eighth day passed. The men murmured among themselves, and their murmurs soon encouraged the utterance of a bolder voice. Nicholas Barré, a man of great firmness and intelligence, one of their number, at length presented himself before the captain. He boldly reminded him of the condition of Lachane, and urged him to hasten his supplies of food before he perished. But the self-esteem and consequence of Albert, under provocation, became a sort of madness. He answered the suggestion with indignity and insult.

"Begone!" he exclaimed, "and trouble me no more with your complaints. What is it to me if the scoundrel does perish? I mean that he shall perish! He deserves his fate! I shall be glad when ye can tell me that he no longer needs his allowance. Away! you deserve a like punishment. Let me hear another word on this subject, and the offender shall share his fate!"

The insulting answer was accompanied by all the tokens of brute anger and severity. The most furious oaths sufficed equally to show his insanity and earnestness. His, indeed, was now an insanity such as seizes usually upon those whom God is preparing for destruction. Barré deemed it only prudent to retire from the presence of a rage which it was no longer politic to provoke; but, in his soul, the purpose was already taking form and strength, which contemplated resistance to a tyranny so wild and reckless. He was not alone in this purpose. The sentiment of resistance and disaffection was growing all around him, and it only needed one who should embody it for successful exercise. But, for this, time was requisite. To decide for action, on the part of a conspiracy, it is first required that what is the common sentiment shall become the common necessity.

"Meanwhile," said Barré, "our poor comrade must not starve!"

This was said to certain of his associates when they met that night in secret. When two or three get together to complain of a tyranny, resistance is already begun. They echoed his sentiments, and arrangements were at once made for transmitting provisions to the exile. A canoe was procured for this purpose, and Barré, with one other comrade, set forth secretly at midnight on their generous and perilous mission.

The night was calm and beautiful—the sea, unruffled by a breeze, lay smooth as a mirror between the lonely island and the main. Though barren, and without shrub or tree, the island looked lovely also—a very realm of faery, in the silver smiling of the moon. With active and sinewy limbs, cheered by the sight, our adventurous comrades pulled towards it, reaching it with little effort, the current favoring their course. What, however, was their surprise and consternation, when, on reaching the islet, there was no answer to their summons. Drawing their boat upon the shore, they soon compassed the little empire with hasty footsteps; but they found nothing of the exile. The islet lay bare and bright in the unshadowed moonlight, so that, whether asleep or dead, his prostrate form must still have been perceptible. What bewildering imaginations seized upon the seekers? What had become of their comrade? Had he been carried off by the savages, by a foreign vessel, or, in his desperation, had he cast himself into the devouring sea? What more probable? Yet, as there was no answer to their questioning, there was no solution of their doubts. Hopeless of his fate, after a frequent and a weary search, and dreading the worst, they re-entered their canoe, and re-crossed the bay in safety—their hearts more than ever filled with disgust and indignation at the cruelty and malice of their commander.

But their quest was not wholly hopeless. When they had reached the main, and while approaching the garrison, they were greatly surprised by the sudden appearance of a human form between the fortress and the river. They remembered the poor Guernache, and, for a moment, a fearful superstition fastened upon their hearts. At first, the fugitive seemed to be approaching them; but, in an instant, wheeling about, as if in panic, he darted into the woods, and sought concealment in the thicket. This re-inspired them. They gave chase instantly. The efforts of the pursued were feebly made, and they soon overtook him. To their great relief and surprise, they found him to be the person they had been seeking—the banished and half-starved Lachane!

His story was soon told. He was nearly perished of hunger. Beyond the crude berries and bitter roots which he had gathered in the woods, he had not eaten for three days. The food which had been furnished him from the garrison had been partly carried from him by birds or beasts—he knew not which—while he slept; and, in the failure of his promised supplies, he had become desperate.

"For that matter," said the wretched exile, "I had become desperate before. Food was not my only or my chief want. I wanted shade from the desolating sun. I wanted rescue from the heavy hand of fire upon my brain; and, by day, I could scarcely keep from quenching the furnace that seemed boiling in my blood, by plunging deep down into the bowels of the sea. By night, when the fiery feeling passed away, then I yearned, above all, for the face and voice of man. It was this craving which made me resolve to brave the death which threatened me which ever way I turned—that, if I perished, it should still be in the struggle once more to behold the people of my love."

How closely did they press the poor fellow to their hearts!

"You should not have perished," said Nicholas Barré, boldly "I, for one, have become tired of this tyranny, under which we no longer breathe in safety. I am resolved to bear it no longer than I can. There are others who have resolved like me. But of this hereafter. Tell us, Lachane, how you contrived to swim across this great stretch of sea?"

"By the mercy of God which made me desperate—which made the seas calm—which gave me a favoring current, and which threw yon fragment of a ship's spar within my reach. But I nearly sunk. Twice did I feel the waters going over me; but I thought of France, and all, and the strength came back to me. I can say no more. I am weak—very weak. Give me to eat."

A flask of generous wine with which they had provided themselves, cheered and inspirited the sufferer. They laid him down at the foot of a broad palmetto, while one of them brought food from the canoe. Much it rejoiced them to see him eat. Ere he had satisfied his hunger, Lachane spoke again as follows:

"I rejoice to hear that you, and others, have resolved to submit no longer to this tyranny. It was not the desire of food, or friendship, only, that strengthened me to throw myself into the sea, in the desperate desire to see the garrison once more. But while my head flamed beneath the sun's downward blaze upon that waste of sand, while mine eyes burned like living coals fresh from the furnace, and my blood leaped and bounded like a mad thing about my temples and in all my veins, I saw all the terrible sufferings of our poor Guernache anew. I heard his voice—his bitter reproaches—and then the terrible scream of the poor Indian woman when the heavy rods descended upon her shoulder. Then I felt that I had not done what my soul commanded!—that I had abandoned my innocent comrade like a lamb to the butcher. I swore to do myself justice—to seek the garrison at Fort Charles, if, for no other purpose, to have revenge upon Albert. I verily believe, *mes amis*, that it was that oath that strengthened me in the sea—that lifted me when the waves went over me, and my heart was sinking with my body. I thought of the blows which might yet be struck for vengeance and freedom. I thought of Guernache and his murderer,—and I rose,—I struck out. I had no fear! I got a strength which I had not at the beginning; and I am here; the merciful God be praised forever more—ready to strike a fair blow at the tyrant, though I die the moment after!"

"That blow must now be struck very soon," said Nicholas Barré. "We are no longer safe. Albert rules us just as it pleases him, by his mere humor, and not according to the laws or usages of France. Every day witnesses against him. Some new tyranny—some new cruelty—adds hourly to our afflictions, and makes life, on such terms, endurable no longer. We are not men if we submit to it."

"Hear me," said Lachane; "you have not laid the plan for his overthrow?"

"Not yet! But we are ready for it. All's ripe. The proper spirit is at work."

"Let it work! All right; but look you, comrades, it is for this hand to strike the blow. I demand the right, because Guernache was my closest friend. I demand it in compensation for my own sufferings."

"It is yours, Lachane! You have the right!"

"Thanks, *mes amis!* And now for the plan. You have resolved on none yourselves. Hearken to mine."

They lent willing ears, and Lachane continued. His counsel was that Captain Albert should be advised of an unusual multitude of deer on one of the "hunting islands", in the neighborhood. These islands are remarkable—some of them—for the luxuriance and beauty of their forests. Here, the deer were accustomed to assemble in great numbers, particularly when pressed by clouds of Indian hunters along the main; nor were they loth to visit them at other seasons, when the tides were low and the seas smooth. Swimming across the dividing rivers, and arms of the sea, at such periods, in little groups of five or ten they found here an almost certain refuge and favorite browsing patches. To one of these islands, Barré, or some other less objectionable person, was to beguile Captain Albert. His fondness for the chase was known, and was gratified on all convenient occasions. He was to be advised of numerous herds upon the island, which passed to it the night before. They had been seen crossing in the moonlight from the main. Lachane, meanwhile, possessing himself of the canoe which his friends had just employed, armed with weapons which they were to provide, was to place himself in a convenient shelter upon the island, and take such a position as would enable him to seize upon the first safe opportunity for striking the blow. Numerous details, not necessary for our purpose, but essential to that of the conspirators, were suggested, discussed, and finally agreed upon, or rejected. Lachane simply concluded with repeating his demand for the privilege of the first blow—a claim farther insisted upon, as, in the event of failure, he who had already incurred the doom of outlawry, and had offended against hope, might thus save others harmless, who occupied a position of greater security. We need not follow the arrangement of the parties. Enough, that, when they were discussed fully, the three separated—Barré and his companion to regain the fort, and Lachane to embark in the canoe, ere day should dawn, for the destined islet where he was equally to find security and vengeance.

Everything succeeded to the wishes of the conspirators. Albert, who was passionately fond of the chase, was easily persuaded by the representations of Barré and his comrades. The pinnace was fitted out at an early hour, and, attended by the two conspirators, and some half dozen other persons, the greater number of whom were supposed to be as hostile to the tyrant as themselves, the Captain set forth, little dreaming that he should be the hunted instead of the hunter. Pierre Renaud, by whom he was also accompanied, was the only person of the party upon whom he could rely. But neither his creature nor himself had the slightest apprehension of the danger. The jealousies of the despot seemed for the moment entirely at rest, and, as if in the exercise of a pleasant novelty, Albert threw aside all the terrors of his authority. He could jest when the fit was on him. He, too, had his moments of play; a sort of feline faculty, in the exercise of which the cat and the tiger seem positively amiable. His jests were echoed by his men, and their laughter gratified him. But there was one exception to the general mirth, which arrested his attention. Nicholas Barré alone preserved a stern, unbroken composure, which the gay humor of his superior failed entirely to overcome. Nothing so much vexes superiority as that it should condescend in vain; and the silence and coldness of Barré, and the utter insensibility with which he heard the good things of his captain, and which occasioned the ready laughter of all the rest, finally extorted a comment from Albert, which gave full utterance to his spleen.

"By my life, Lieutenant Barré,"—such was the rank of this conspirator—"but that I know thee better, I should hold thee to be one of those unhappy wretches to whom all merriment is a hateful thing—to whom a clever jest gives offence only, and whom a cheerful laugh sends off sullenly to bed. Pray, if it be not too serious a humor, tell us the cause of thy present dullness."

"Verily, Captain Albert," replied the person addressed, fixing his eyes steadily upon him, and speaking in the most deliberate accents, "I was thinking of the deer that we shall strike to-day. Doubtless, he is even now making as merry as thyself among his comrades—little dreaming that the hunter hath his thoughts already fixed upon the choice morsels of his flanks, which, a few hours hence, shall be smoking above the fire. Truly, are we but little wiser than the thoughtless deer. The merriest of us may be struck as soon. The man hath as few securities from the morrow as the beast that runs."

Captain Albert was not the most sagacious tyrant in the world, or the moral reflections of our conspirator might have tended to his disquiet. He saw no peculiar significance in the remark, though the matter of it was all well remembered, when the subsequent events came to be known. Little, indeed, did the victim then dream of the fate which lay in wait for him. He laughed at the shallow reflection of Barré, which seemed so equally mistimed and unmeaning, and his merriment increased with every stroke of the oar which sent the pinnace towards the scene chosen for the tragedy. All his severities were thrown aside; never had he shown himself more gracious; and, though his good humor was rather the condescension of one who is secure in his authority, and can resume his functions at any moment, than the proof of any sympathy with his comrades, yet he seemed willing for once that it should not lose any of its pleasant quality by any frequent exhibition of his usual caprice. But for an occasional sarcasm in which he sometimes indulged, and by which he continued to keep alive the antipathies of the conspirators, the gentler mood in which he now suffered them to behold him, might have rendered them reluctant to prosecute their purpose. They might have relented, even at the last moment, had they been prepared to believe that his present good humor was the fruit of any sincere relentings in him. But he did not succeed to this extent, and, with a single significant look to his comrades, the stern Nicholas Barré showed to them that he, at least, was firm in the secret purpose which they had in view. His silence and gravity for a time served to amuse his superior, who exercised his wit at the expense of the sullen soldier, little dreaming, all the while, at what a price he should be required to pay for his temporary indulgence. But as Barré continued in his mood, the pride of the haughty superior was at length hurt; and, when they reached the shore, the insolence of Albert had resumed much of its old ascendancy.

Albert was the first to spring to land. He was impatient to begin the chase, of which he was passionately fond. The sport, as conducted in that day and region, was after a very simple fashion. It consisted rather in a judicious distribution of the hunters, at various places of watch, than in the possession of any particular skill of weapon or speed of foot. The island was small—the woods not very dense or intricate, and the only outlet of escape was across the little arm of the sea which separated the island from the main. The hunters were required to watch this passage, with a few other avenues from the forest. We need not observe their order or arrangement. It will be enough to note that Barré chose as the sentinel left in charge of the boat one of the firmest of the conspirators. This was a person named Lamotte—a small but fiery spirit—a man of equal passion and vindictiveness, who had suffered frequent indignities from Albert, which his own inferior position as a common soldier had compelled him to endure without complaint. But he was not the less sensible of his hurts, because not suffered to complain of them; and his hatred only assumed a more intense and unforgiving character, because it seemed cut off from all the outlets to revenge.

The arrangements of the hunters all completed, they began to skirt slowly the woody region by which the centre of the island was chiefly occupied. Gradually separating as they advanced, they finally, one by one, found their way into its recesses. A single dog which they carried with them, was now unleashed, and his eager tongue very soon gave notice to the hunters that their victim was afoot. As the bay of the hound became more frequent, the blood of Albert became more and more excited, and, pressing forward, in advance of all his companions, the sinuosities of the route pursued soon scattered the whole party. But this he did not heed. The one consciousness,—that which appealed to his love of sport,—led to a forgetfulness of all others; and it was no disquiet to our captain to find himself alone in forests where he had never trod before, particularly when his eager eye caught a glimpse of a fine herd of the sleek-skinned foresters, well-limbed, and nobly-headed, darting suddenly from cover into the occasional openings before him. A good shot was Captain Albert. He fired, and had the joy to see tumbled, headlong, sprawling, in his tracks, one of the largest bucks of the herd. He shouted his delight aloud;—shouted twice and clapped his hands!

His shouts were echoed, near at hand, by a voice at once strange and familiar! His instinct divined a sudden danger in this strange echo. He stopped short, even as he was about to bound forward to the spot in which the deer had fallen. Another shout!—but this was to his companions! He was now confounded at the new echo and the fearful vision which this summons conjured up. At his side, and in his very ears, rose another shout—a shriek rather—much louder than his own—a wild, indescribable yell,—which sent a thrill of horror through his soul. At the same instant, a gaunt, wild man—a half-naked, half-famished form—darted from the thicket and stood directly before him in his path!

"Ho! Ho! Ho!" howled the stranger.

"Guernache!" was the single word, forced from the guilty soul of the criminal!

"Guernache! Yes! Guernache, in his friend Lachane! Both are here! See you not? Look! Ho! Captain Albert,—look and see, and make yourself ready. Your time is short. You will hang and banish no longer!"

Wild with exulting fury was the face of the speaker—terrible the language of his eyes—threatening the action of the uplifted arm. A keen blade flashed in his grasp, and the discovery which Albert made, that, in the wild man before him, he saw the person whom he had so wantonly and cruelly decreed to perish, sufficed to make him nerveless. The surprise deprived him of resource, while his guilty conscience enfeebled his arm, and took all courage from his soul. His match-lock was already discharged. The *couteau de chasse* was at his side; but, before this could be drawn, he must be hewn down by the already uplifted weapon of his foe. Besides, even if drawn, what could he hope, by its employment, against the superior muscle and vigor of Lachane? These thoughts passed with a lightning-like rapidity through the brain of Albert. He felt that he had met his fate! He shrunk back from its encounter, and sent up a feeble but a painful cry for his creature,—" Pierre Renaud !"

" Ha! ha! you cry for him in vain!" was the mocking answer of Lachane. "Renaud, that miserable villain—that wretch after thy own heart and fashion—hath quite as much need of thee as thou of him! Ye will serve each other never more to the prejudice of better men. Hark! hear you not? Even now they are dealing with him!"

And, sure enough, even as he spoke, the screams of one in mortal terror, interrupted by several heavy blows in quick succession, seemed to confirm the truth of what Lachane had spoken. In that fearful moment Albert remembered the words, now full of meaning, which Nicholas Barré had spoken while they set forth. The hunter had indeed become the hunted. Lachane gave him little time for meditation.

" They have done with him! Prepare! To your knees, Captain Albert! I give you time to make your peace with God— such time as you gave my poor Guernache! Prepare!"

But, though Albert had not courage for combat, he yet found strength enough for flight. He was slight of form, small, and tolerably swift of foot. Flinging his now useless firelock to the ground, he suddenly darted off through the forests, with a degree of energy and spirit which it tasked all the efforts of the less wieldy frame of Lachane to approach. Life and death were on the event, and Albert succeeded in gaining the beach where the boat had been left before he was overtaken. But Lamotte, to whom the boat had been given in charge, pushed off, with a mocking yell of laughter, at his approach! His cries for succor were unheeded. Lamotte himself would have slain the fugitive but that he knew Lachane had claimed for himself this privilege. His spear had been uplifted as Albert drew nigh the water, but the shout of Lachane, emerging from the woods, warned him to desist. He used the weapon to push the pinnace into deep water, leaving Albert to his fate!

"Save me, Lamotte!" was the prayer, of the tyrant in his desperation, urged with every promise that he fancied might prove potent with the soldier. But few moments were allowed him for entreaty, and they were unavailing. Lamotte contented himself with looking on the event, ready to finish with his spear what Lachane might leave undone. Albert gazed around him, and as Lachane came, with one shriek of terror, darted into the sea. The avenger was close behind him. The water rose to the waist and finally to the neck of the fugitive. He turned in supplication, only to receive the stroke. The steel entered his shoulder, just below the neck. He staggered and fell forwards upon the slayer. The blade snapped in the fall, and the wounded man sunk down irretrievably beneath the waters. Lachane raised the fragment of his sword to Heaven, while, with something of a Roman fervor, he ejaculated—

"Guernache! dear friend, behold! the hand of Lachane hath avenged thee upon thy murderer!"

VIII.

FLIGHT, FAMINE, AND THE BLOODY FEAST OF THE FUGITIVES.

The assassination of Captain Albert restored peace, at least, to the little colony of Fort Charles. He had been the chief danger to the garrison, by reason of his vexatious tyranny, fomented ever by the miserable malice and espionage of Pierre Renaud Both of these had perished, and a sense of new security filled the hearts of the survivors. They had also gratified all revenges. The sequel of the narrative may be told, almost in the very words of the simple chronicle from which our facts are mostly drawn.

"When they (the conspirators) were come home againe, they assembled themselves together to choose one to be Governor over them." In this selection there was no difficulty. Jealousies and dissensions had ceased to exist, and the choice naturally fell upon Nicholas Barré,* whose former position, as Lieutenant under Albert, and whose recent connection with the party by which he

---

* " Il fallut songer ensuite à lui donner un successeur, et le choix que 'on fit, fut plus sage, qu'on ne devoit l'attendre de gens, dont les mains fumoient encore du sang de leur Chef. Ils mirent à leur tête un fort honnête homme, nommé Nicholas Barré, lequel par son adresse et sa prudence rétablit en peu de tems la paix et le bon ordre dans la colonie."—*Charlevoix, N. Fran., Liv. 1.*

was slain, had naturally given him a large influence among the colonists. He was equal to his new duties. He "knewe so well to quite himself of this charge that all rancour and dissention ceased among them, and they lived peaceably one with another." But, though harmony was restored among them, it was a harmony without hope. They had been abandoned by their countrymen. The supplies which Ribault had promised them had utterly failed. They had never, indeed, been levied. Ribault returned to France only to find it convulsed with a renewal of the civil war, under the auspices of that incarnate mischief, Catherine de Medicis, and her fatherless and cruel son, in whose name she swayed the country to its ruin. Coligny, the father of the colony, had enough to do in fighting the battles of the Huguenots at home. He could do nothing for those whom he had sent abroad. The peace of Longjumean had been of short duration, and there had been really no remission of hostilities on the part of the Catholics. In the space of three months more than two thousand of the former fell victims to the rage of the populace; and, though reluctantly, the Prince of Condé and Coligny were forced into a resumption of arms for the safety of their own persons. The immediate necessities of their situation were such as to defeat their efforts in behalf of the remote settlement at Fort Charles. They needed all their soldiers and Huguenots in France. Feeling themselves abandoned—they knew not why—the colonists in Florida ceased to behold a charm or solace in their solitary realm of refuge. Its securities were no longer sufficient to compensate for its loneliness. Better the strife, perhaps, than this unmeaning and unbroken silence. They were too few for adventure, and the discouragements resulting from their domestic grievances were enough to paralyze any such spirit

But for this there had been no lack of the necessary inducements In their second voyage to King Ouade, seeking "mil and beans," they had learned some of the secrets of the country which made their eyes brighten. They had discovered that there was gold in the land, and that the gold of the land was good. This prince had freely given them of his treasure. He had bestowed on them pearls of the native waters, stones of finest chrystal, and certain specimens of silver ore, which he described, in reply to their eager inquiries, as having been gathered at the foot of certain high mountains, the bowels of which contained it in greatest quantity. These were the mountains of Apalachia, and the truth of Ouade's revelations have been confirmed by subsequent discovery. The intelligence had greatly gladdened the hearts of our Frenchmen, and nothing but the feebleness of the garrison prevented Albert from prosecuting a search which promised so largely to gratify the lusts of avarice. His subsequent errors and fate put an end to the desire among his followers. They longed for nothing now so much as home. They had been temporarily abandoned by the Indians whose granaries they had emptied, and who had been compelled to wander off to remote forests in search of their own supplies. The gloom of the Frenchmen naturally increased in the absence of their allies, who had furnished them equally with food and recreation. Their provisions again began to fail them. Their resources in corn and peas were quite exhausted; and no more could be procured from the red-men, who had preserved a supply barely sufficient for the planting of their little fields. In this condition of want, with this feeling of destitution and abandonment, it was resolved among the Huguenots, to depart the colony. With a fond hope once more of recovering the shores of that country, still most beloved, which had so

unkindly cast them forth, they began to build themselves a
vessel sufficiently large to bear their little company. "And
though there were no men among them," says the chronicle,
"that had any skill, notwithstanding, necessitye, which is the
maistresse of all sciences, taught them the way to build it."
But how were they to provide the sails, the tackle and the
cordage? "Having no meanes to recover these things they were
in worse case than at the first, and almost ready to fall into
despayre." They were succored, when most desponding, by the
help of Providence. "That good God, which never forsaketh
the afflicted, did favor them in their necessitie." The Indians,
who had been for some time absent, seeking, by the chase, in
distant forests, to supply themselves with provisions in place of
those which they had yielded to the white men, now began to re-
appear; and, in the midst of their perplexities, they were visited
by the Caciques, Audusta and Maccou, with more than two
hundred of their followers. These, our Frenchmen went forth to
meet, with great show of satisfaction; and had they been sufficiently re-assured by the return of their red friends—had they
not been too much the victims of *nostalgia*, or homesickness, the
cloud might have passed from their fortunes, and the little colony
might have been re-established under favoring auspices. But
their only thought was of their native land. They declared their
wishes to the Indian chieftains, and, showing in what need of
cordage they stood, they were told that this would be provided
in the space of a few days. The Caciques kept their word, and,
in little time, brought an abundance of cordage. But other
things were wanted, and "our men sought all meanes to recover
roseñ in the woodes, wherein they cut the pine trees round about,
out of which they drew sufficient reasonable quantitie to bray the

vessel. Also they gathered a kind of mosse, which groweth on the trees of this countrie, to serve to caulke the same withall. There now wanted nothing but sayles, which they made of their own shirtes and of their sheetes." Thus provided with the things requisite, our Frenchmen hastened to finish their brigantine, and " used so speedie diligence " that they were soon ready to launch forth upon the great deep. They gave to their Indian friends all their surplus goods and chattels, leaving to them all the merchandise of the fort which they could not take away;—a liberality which gave the red-men the " greatest contentation in the worlde." But they re-embarked their forge, their artillery and other munitions of war. Unhappily, they were too impatient to begin their journey. In the too sanguine hope of reaching France, with a speed proportioned to their eager desires, they laid in no adequate provision for a long voyage. " In the meane season the wind came so fit for their purpose, that it seemed to invite them to put to sea. Being drunken with the too excessive joy which they had conceived for their returning into France, or rather deprived of all foresight and consideration:—without regarding the inconsistencie of the winds which change in a moment, they put themselves to sea, and, with so slender victuals, that the end of their enterprise became unlucky and unfortunate."

They had not sailed a third part of the distance, when they were surprised with calms, which so much hindered their progress that, during the space of three weeks, they had not advanced twenty-five leagues. In this period their provisions underwent daily diminution. In a short time their stock had sunk so low that it was necessary to limit the allowance to each man. We may conceive their destitution from this allowance. "Twelve grains of mill by the day, which may be in value as much as twelve peason!" But even this poor quantity was not long continued. It was "a felicity," in the language of the chronicle, which was of brief duration. Soon the "mill" failed them entirely—all at once—and they "had nothing for their more assured refuge, but their shoes and leather jerkins, which they did eate." But their misfortune was not confined to their food. Their supplies of fresh water failed them also. Never had adventurers set forth upon the seas with such wretched provision. Their beverage finally became the water of the ocean—the thirst-provoking brine. Such beverage as this increased their miseries —atrophy and madness followed—and death stretched himself out among them on every side. Nor were they suffered to escape from the most painful toils while thus contending against thirst and famine. Their wretched vessel sprang a-leak. The water grew upon them. Day and night were they kept busy in casting it forth, without cessation or repose. Each day added to their griefs and dangers. Their shoes and jerkins they had already devoured in their desperation, and where to look for other material to supply the materiel of distension, puzzled their thoughts. While thus distressed by their anxieties, with their comrades dying about them, a new danger assailed them, as if fortune was resolved to crush them at a blow, and thus conclude their miseries. The winds rose, the seas were lashed into fury by the storm. Their vessel, no longer buoyant, "in the turning of a hand" shipped a fearful sea, and was nearly swamped—" filled halfe full of water, and bruised in upon the one side." This was the las drop in the cup of misfortune which finally makes it overflow Then it was that the hearts of our Frenchmen sunk utterly within them. They no longer cared to contend for life. They gave themselves up to despair. "Being now more out of hope than ever to escape out of this extreme peril, they cared not for casting out of the water which now was almost ready to drown them; and as men resolved to die, everie one fell downe backwarde, and gave themselves over, altogether unto the will of the waves."

It was at this moment of extreme despondency, that Lachane tried to cheer them with new hope, and to new exertions. He encouraged them by various assurance, to hold out against fate, and struggle manfully to the last. He told them "how little way they had to sayle, assuring them that if the winde helde, they should see land within three dayes." "At worst," he added, "we can die when we can do no better. It will be always time enough for that. But this necessity is not now. We can surely put it off for some time longer. At present, let us live!"

Speaking thus, in the most cheerful manner, the brave fellow set them a proper example by which to dissipate their fears and to provide against them. He began to bail and cast out the water in which, in their extreme indifference to their fate, they either sat or lay. They took heart as they beheld him, and joined in the labor with new vigor, and that elastic spirit which is so characteristic of Frenchmen. But, when the three days had gone by, and still their eyes were unblessed with the sight of the promised land—when they had consumed every remnant of shoe and jerkin, and nothing more was left them to consume, they turned their eyes in bitter reproach upon the man who had persuaded them to live. He met their reproachful glances with a smile and instantly devised a remedy for their fears and weaknesses, through one of those terrible thoughts which, at any other period, would revolt, with extremest loathing, the humanity of the man, however little human.

"My comrades!" said the noble fellow, "you hunger—you

starve! You will perish unless you can get some food. I see it in your eyes. They have no lustre, and the courage seems to have gone out entirely from your hearts. You must not die! You must not lose your courage. You *shall* not. You shall drink life and courage out of my breast. I have enough there for all who thirst and faint. You shall feed upon my heart— you shall drink the blood of a brave man, and live for your friends and country. I have few friends, and my country can spare me. Better that one of us should die than that all should perish. I am ready to die for you! What! You shake your heads—you would not have it so—but it shall be so! You have loved me— you have suffered for me. Well, Lachane loves you in return— he will die for you. You shall remember him hereafter, when our own dear France receives you again in safety. You will bless his memory!"

A groan was the only reply of those around him. Lachane threw open his breast.

"There!" he cried; "Look! I am ready! I fear not death. Strike! See you not, my bosom is open to the knife. My hand is down—there!"—grasping the seat upon which he sate,— "There! it shall not be lifted to arrest the blow!"

The famished wretches looked with wolfish yearnings upon the white breast of the offered sacrifice; but there was still a human revolting in their hearts that kept them moveless and silent They longed for the horrible banquet, but still turned from it with a lingering human loathing. But Lachane was resolute.

"Ah!" said he, reproachfully; "you fear—you would not that I should die in this manner; but, *mes amis*, you know me not. You know not how it will glad my heart to know that its dying pulse shall add new life to yours Here, Lafourche, Genet—you are both beside me. You are the feeblest. You are dying fast You thirst; another day and you perish! You have a mother, Genet—a dear sister, Lafourche—why will you not live for them? Lo! you, now,—when I strike the blow,—do you both clap your mouths upon the wound. Drink freely—drink deep—that you may have strength—and let the rest drink after you. There!— my braves!—there."

With each of these last words, the brave fellow—thence called " Lachane, the Deliverer"—struck two fatal blows, one upon his heart, and one upon his throat. He leaned back between the two famished persons whom he had especially addressed, and, while the consciousness was yet in the eyes of the dying man, they sprang like thirsting tigers, and fastened their mouths upon each streaming orifice. The victim, smarting and conscious to the last, sunk in a few seconds, into the sacred slumber of death. This heroism saved the rest. He had struck with a firm hand and a resolute spirit. In his death they lived. Slow to accept his proffered sacrifice, he was scarcely cold, ere the survivors fastened upon his body; and, ere the last morsel of the victim was consumed, they had assurances of safety.*

It seemed as if expiation had been done; as if the sacrifice had purged their offences and made them acceptable to heaven. The land rose upon their vision,—a glimpse like that of salvation to

* Lest we should be suspected of exaggeration we quote a single sentence from the condensed account in Charlevoix;—" Lachau, celui là même, que la Capitaine Albert avoit exilé, après l'avoir dégradé des armes, déclara qu'il vouloit bien avancer sa mort, qu'il croyoit inévitable, pour reculer de quelques jours celle de ses compagnons. Il fut pris au mot, et on l'égorgea sur le champ, sans qu'il fît la moindre résistance. *Il ne fut pas perdu une goute de son sang, tous en burent avec avidité, le corps fut mis en pieces, et chacun en eut sa part.*"

the doomed one,—a sight " whereof they were so exceeding glad, that the pleasure caused them to remain a long time as men without sense; whereby they let the pinnesse floate this and that way without holding any right way or course." While thus wandering, in sight of France, but still at the mercy of the winds and waves, they were boarded by an English vessel. Here they were recognized by a Frenchman who happened to be one of the crew that had accompanied Ribault in his voyage. The most feeble were put upon the coast of France; the rest were taken to England, with the design that Queen Elizabeth, who meditated sending an expedition to Florida, might have the benefit of their report.

IX.

THE SECOND EXPEDITION OF THE HUGUENOTS TO FLORIDA.

The Fortress of La Caroline and the Colony of Landonniere.

THUS, unhappily, as we have seen, ended the first experiment of Coligny for the establishment of a Huguenot colony in the territory of the Floridian. The disasters which had attended the fortunes of the garrison at Fort Charles, were due, in some degree, to its seeming abandonment by their founder. But Coligny was blameless in this abandonment. When Ribault returned to France, from his first voyage, the civil wars had again begun, depriving the admiral of the means for succoring the colony, as had been promised. Nearly two years had now elapsed from that period, before he could recover the power which would enable him to send supplies or recruits for its maintenance. In all this time, with the exception of the small domain occupied by Fort Charles, the country lay wholly derelict, and in the keeping of the savages. But Coligny was now in a condition to resume his endeavors in behalf of his colony. He was again in possession of authority. The assassination of the Duke of Guise had restored to France the blessings of peace; and Coligny seized upon this interval of repose, to in-

quire after the settlement which had been made by Ribault
Three ships, and a considerable amount of money, were accorded
to his application; and the new armament was assigned to the
command of René Laudonniere—a man of intelligence, a good
seaman rather than a soldier, and one who had accompanied
Ribault on his first expedition, though he had not remained with
the colony.* Laudonniere found it easy enough to procure his
men, not only for the voyage but the colony. The civil wars had
produced vast numbers of restless and destitute spirits, who
longed for nothing so much as employment and excitement.
Besides, there was a vague attraction for the imagination, in the
tales which had reached the European world, of the wondrous
sweetness and beauty of the region to which they were invited.
Florida still continued, even at this period, to be the country
beyond all others in the new world, which appealed to the fancies
and the appetites of the romantic, the selfish, and the merely
adventurous. Ribault's own account of it had described the
wondrous sweetness of its climate, and the exquisite richness and
variety of its fruits and flowers. Then, there were the old dreams
which had beguiled the Spanish cavalier, Hernando de Soto, and
had filled with the desires and the hopes of youth, the aged
heart of Juan Ponce de Leon. It did not matter if death did
keep the portals of the country. This guardianship only seemed
the more certainly to denote the precious treasures which were
concealed within. In the absence of any certain knowledge,
men dreamed of spoils within its bowels, such as had been
yielded to Cortes and Pizarro, by the great cities and teeming
mountains of Tenochtitlan and Peru. They had heard true

* Charlevoix describes Laudonniere as " un gentilhomme de mérite—
bon officier de marine, et qui avoit même servi sur terre avec distinction

stories of its fruits and flowers; of its bland airs, so friendly to the invalid; of its delicious fountains, in which healing and joy lay together in sweet communion. It was the region in which, according to tradition, life enjoyed not only an exquisite, but an extended tenure, almost equalling that of the antediluvian ages. Its genial atmosphere was supposed to possess properties particularly favorable to the prolongation of human life. Laudonniere himself tells us of natives whom he had seen who were certainly more than two hundred and fifty years old, and yet, who entertained a reasonable hope of living fifty or a hundred years longer. These may have been exaggerations, but they are such as the human imagination loves to indulge in. But there was comparative truth in the assertion. Portions of the Floridian territory are, to this day, known to be favorable to health and longevity in a far greater degree than regions in other respects more favored; and, in the temperate habits, the hardy exercises, the simple lives of the red-men, unvexed by cares and anxieties, and unsubdued by toils, they probably realized many of the alleged blessings of a golden age. But the attractions of this region were not estimated only with respect to attractions such as these. The fountains of the marvellous which had been opened by the great discoverers, Columbus and Cortes, Balboa and Pizarro, were not to be quickly closed. The passion for adventure, in the exploration of new countries, made men easy of belief; and any number of emigrants were prepared to accompany our second Huguenot expedition. The armament of Laudonniere was ready for sea, and sailed from France on the 22d April, 1564.* A voyage of two months brought the voy-

* It was much superior to that originally sent out with Ribault. " On lui donna des ouvriers habiles dans tous les arts, &c.

agers to the shores of New France, which they reached the
25th of June, 1564. The land made was very nearly in the
same latitude as in the former expedition. It was a favorable
period for seeing the country in all its natural loveliness; and
the delight of the voyagers may be imagined, when, at May
River, they found themselves welcomed by the Indians, such of
the whites particularly as were recognized to have been of the
squadron of Ribault. The savages hailed them as personal
friends and old acquaintances. When they landed, they were
eagerly surrounded by the simple and delighted natives, men
and women, and conducted, with great ceremonials, to the spot
where Ribault had set up a stone column, with the arms of
France, " upon a little sandie knappe, not far from the mouth
of the said river." It was with a pleased surprise that Laudonniere
found the pillar encircled and crowned with wreaths of bay
and laurel, with which the affectionate red-men had dressed the
stone, in proof of the interest which they had taken in this imposing
memorial of their intercourse with the white strangers.
The foot of the pillar was surrounded by little baskets of maize
and beans; and these were brought in abundance, in token of
their welcome, and yielded by these generous sons of the forest
to their new visitors, at the foot of the pillar which they had thus
consecrated to their former friendship. They kissed the column,
and made the French do likewise. Their *Paracoussy*, or king,
was named Satouriova, the oldest of whose sons, named Athore,

que utilité dans une colonie naissante. Quantité de jeune gens de famille,
et plusieurs gentilshommes voulurent faire ce voyage *à leurs dépens*,
et on y joignoit des détachmens de soldats choisés dans de vieux
corps. *L'Admiral eut soin surtout qu'il n'y eût aucun catholique dans cet armament.*"

is described by Laudonniere as "perfect in beautie." Satouriova presented Laudonniere with a "wedge of silver"- one of those gifts which by no means lessened the importance of the giver, or of his country, in the eyes of our voyager. His natural inquiry was whence the silver came.

"Then he showed me by evident signes that all of it came from a place more within the river, by certain days journeyes from this place, and declared unto us that all that which they had thereof, they gat it by force of armes of the inhabitants of this place, named by them *Thimogoa*, their most ancient and natural enemies, as hee largely declared. Whereupon, when I saw with what affection and passion hee spake when hee pronounced *Thimogoa*, I understood what he would say; and to bring myself more into his favour, I promised him to accompany him with all my force, if hee would fight against them: which thing pleased him in such sorte, that, from thenceforth, hee promised himselfe the victorie of them, and assured mee that hee would make a voyage thither within a short space, and would commaund his men to make ready their bowes and furnish themselves with such store of arrows, that nothing should bee wanting to give battaile to Thimogoa. In fine, he prayed me very earnestly not to faile of my promise, and, in so doing, he hoped to procure me golde and silver, in such good quantitie, that mine affaires should take effect according to mine owne and his desire."

Here then we see cupidity beginning to plant in place of religion. Our Huguenot tells us of no prayers which he made, of no religious services which he ordered, in presence of the savages, for their benefit and his own. But his sole curiosity is to know where the gold grows, and to prompt the evil passions of the red-men to violence and strife with one another, in order that he may procure the object of his avarice.

With night, the parties separated, the French retiring to their ships and the Indians to the cover of their forests. But Laudonniere had something more to learn. The next day, "being allured with this good entertainment," the visit was renewed. "We found him, (the Paracoussy) under shadow of an arbor, accompanied with four-score Indians at the least, and apparelled, at that time, after the Indian fashion; to wit, with a great hart's skin dressed like chamois, and painted with divers colours, but of so lively a portraiture, and representing antiquity, with rules so justly compassed, that there is no painter so exquisite that coulde finde fault therewith. The natural disposition of this strange people is so perfect and well guided, that, without any ayd and favour of artes, they are able, by the help of nature oncly, to content the eye of artizans; yea, even of those which, by their industry, are able to aspire unto things most absolute."

What Laudonniere means by the paintings of the Indians, "representing antiquity," is not so clear. But it may be well, in this place, to mention that we do not rely here on the opinions of a mere sailor or soldier. In this expedition, Coligny had sent out a painter of considerable merit, named James Le Moyne, otherwise *de Morgues*, who was commissioned to execute colored drawings of all the objects which might be supposed likely to interest the European eye. To this painter are we indebted for numerous pictures of the people and the region, their modes of life, costume and exercises, which are now invaluable.

The Huguenots left their Indian friends with reluctance. As the ships coasted along the shores, pursuing their way up the river, the word "*ami*," one of the few French words which the simple red-men had retained, resounded, in varied accents, from men and women, who followed the progress of the strangers, running along the margin of the river, as long as the ships continued in sight. The French have not often abused the hospitality of the aborigines. In this respect, they rank much more humanly and honorably than either the English or the Spanish people. With a greater moral flexibility, which yields something to acquire more, they accommodated themselves to the race which they discovered, and, readily conforming to some of the habits of the red-men, acquired an influence over them which the people of no other nation have ever been able to obtain. It was with tears that the simple hunters along May River beheld the vessels of the Frenchmen gradually sinking from their eyes.

The vessels of Laudonniere passed up the river, himself and parties of his people landing occasionally, to examine particular spots of country. They are everywhere received with kindness. Two of the Indian words—"Antipola Bonassou,"—meaning "Friend and Brother,"—the French made use of to secure a favorable welcome everywhere.

Monsieur de Ottigny, a lieutenant of Laudonniere, with a small party, is conducted into the presence of a Cassique, whose great apparent age prompts him to inquire concerning it. "Whereunto he made answer, shewing that he was the first living originall from whence five generations were descended, as he shewed unto them by another olde man that sate directly over against him, which farre exceeded him in age. And this man was his father, which seemed to be rather a dead carkiss than a living body; for his sinewes, his veines, his arteries, his bones and other partes appeared so cleerely thorow his skinne, that a man might easily tell them and discerne them one from one another. Also his age was so great that the goode man had lost his sight, and could not speake one onely word but with exceeding great paine. Monsieur de Ottigni, having seene so strange a thing, turned to the younger of these two olde men, praying him to vouchsafe to answer to him that which he demanded touching his age. Then the olde man called a company of Indians, and striking twise upon his thigh, and laying his hand upon two of them, he shewed him by synes that these two were his sonnes; again smiting upon their thighes, he shewed him others not so olde which were the children of the two first, which he continued in the same manner until the fifth generation. But, though this olde man had his father alive, more olde than himselfe, and that bothe of them did weare their haire very long and as white as was possible, yet it was tolde them that they might yet live thirtie or fortie yeeres more by the course of nature: although the younger of them both was not lesse than two hundred and fiftie yeeres olde. After he had ended his communication he commanded two young eagles to be given to our men, which hee had bred up for his pleasure in his house."

A fitting gift at the close of such a narrative! Certainly, a patriarchal family; and, though we may doubt the correctness of this primitive mode of computing the progress of the sun, there can be no question that the Floridians were distinguished by a longevity wholly unparalleled in modern experience. It is claimed that the anglo-American races who have since occupied the same region, have shared, in some degree, in this prolonged duration of human life.

While the lieutenant of Laudonniere was thus held in discourse by the aged Indians, his commander was enjoying himself in more luxurious fashion. A particular eminence in the neighborhood of the river had fixed his eye, which he explored. Here he reposed himself for several hours. It is pleasant to hear our Frenchman's discourse of the beauty of the spot where his siesta was enjoyed.

"Upon the top thereof, we found nothing else but cedars, palms, and bay trees, of so sovereign odor, that balm smelleth nothing in comparison. The trees were environed round with vines, bearing grapes in such quantity that the number would suffice to make the place habitable. Touching the pleasure of the place, the sea may be seen plain and open from it; and more than five leagues off, near the river Belle, a man may behold the meadowes, divided asunder into isles and islets, interlacing one another. Briefly, the place is so pleasant, that those who are melancholie would be forced to change their humour."

There is no exaggeration in this. Such is the odor of the shrubs—such is the picturesqueness of the prospect.

Laudonniere departed with great reluctance from a region so favorable to health, so beautiful to the eye, and which promised so abundantly of fruits and mineral treasures. His course lay northwardly, in search of the colony of Captain Albert. He passes the river of Seine, four leagues distant from the May, and continues to the mouth of the Somme, some six leagues further. Here he casts anchor, lands, and is received with friendly welcome by the Paracoussy, or king of the place, whom he describes as "one of the tallest and best-proportioned men that may be found. His wife sate by him, which, besides her Indian beautie, wherewith she was greatly endued, had so virtuous a countenance and modest gravitie, that there was not one amongst us but did greatly commend her. She had in her traine five of her daughters, of so good grace and so well brought up, that I easily persuaded myself that their mother was their mistresse."

Here Laudonniere is again presented with specimens of the precious metals, and here we find him already in consultation with his men, touching the propriety of abandoning the settlement of Fort Charles, the fate of which he has heard in his progress from the Indians, for the more attractive regions of the river May. His arguments for this preference, may be given in his own language.

"If we passed farther to the north to seeke out Port Royall, it would be neither very profitable nor convenient, ... although the haven were one of the fairest of the West Indies : but that, in this case, the question was not so much of the beautie of the place as of things necessary to sustaine life. And that for our inhabiting, it was much more needful for us to plant in places plentiful of victuall, than in goodly havens, faire, deepe and pleasante to the view. In consideration whereof, I was of opinion, if it seemed goode unto them, to seate ourselves about the river of May: seeing also, that, in our first voyage, wee found the same onely, among all the rest, to abounde in maize and corn; *besides the golde and silver that was found there; a thing that put me in hope of some happie discoverie in time to come.*"

Doubtless the last was the conclusive suggestion. The views of Laudonniere were promptly agreed to by his followers; and, sailing back to the river of May, they reached it at daybreak on the 29th June. "Having cast anchor, I embarked all my stuffe and the souldiers of my company, (in the pinnace we may suppose,) to sayle right towards the opening of the river: wherein we entered a good way up, and found a creeke of a reasonable bignisse which invited us to refresh ourselves a little, while wee reposed ourselves there. Afterward, wee went on shore to seeke out a place, plaine, without trees, which wee perceived from the creeke."

But this spot, upon examination, does not prove commodious and it was determined to return to a point they had before discovered when sailing up the river. "This place is joyning to a mountaine (hill), and it seemed unto us more fit and commodious to build a fortresse ; . . . . . therefore we took our way towards the forests. . . . . Afterwards, we found a large plaine, covered with high pine trees, distant a little from the other ; under which we perceived an infinite number of stagges, which brayed amidst the plaine, athwart the which we passed : then we discovered a little hill adjoyning unto a great vale, very greene and in forme flat : wherein were the fairest meadows of the worlde, and grasse to feede cattel. Moreover, it is environed with a great number of brookes of fresh water, and high woodes which make the vale most delectable to the eye."

Laudonniere names this pleasant region after himself, the "*vale of Laudonniere.*" They pass through it, and, at length, after temporary exhaustion from fatigue and heat, they recover their spirits, and, penetrating a high wood, reach the brink of the river, and the spot which they have chosen for the settlement.

We have preferred, at the risk of being tedious, to quote these details, in order that the modern antiquarian may, if he pleases, seek for the traces of this ancient settlement. The foundation was not laid without due solemnity Laudonniere remembers that his people are Christians ; and, at the break of day, on the 30th June, 1564, the trumpets were sounded, and our Huguenots were called to prayer. The banks of the May, otherwise the St. Johns,[*] then

---

[*] "The evidence," says Johnson, however, in an appendix to his life of Greene, "is in favor of the St. Mary's, and would point to the first bluff

echoed, for the first time, with a hymn of lofty cheer from European voices.

"There we sang a psalme of thanksgiving unto God." Prayer was made, and, gathering courage from the exercise of their devotions, our Huguenots applied themselves to the duty of building themselves a fortress. In this work they were assisted by the Indians.* A few days sufficed, with this help, to give their fabric form. It was built in the shape of a triangle. "The side towarde the west, which was towarde the lande, was enclosed with a little trench and raised with towers made in forme of a battlement of nine foote high : the other side, which was towarde the river, was inclosed with a palisado of plankes of timber, after the manner that gabions are made. On the south side, there was a kinde of bastion, within which I caused an house for the munition to be built. It was all builded of fagots and sand, saving about two or three foote high with turfes, whereof the battlements were made. In the middest I caused a great court to be made of eighteen paces long and broad; in the middest whereof, on the one side, drawing toward the south, I built a *corps de garde*, and an house, on the other side, towarde the north." * * *

on the south side of that river." But this is certainly a mistake. The general conviction now is, that our St. John's was the May River of the French.

* Jacques de Moyne de Morgues represents the Indian Chief or Paracoussi of the neighborhood, Satouriova by name, as taking great umbrage at the erection of the fortress La Caroline within his dominions; thus differing from Laudonniere, who describes him and his subjects as cheerfully assisting in its erection. Charlevoix undertakes to reconcile the difference between them; but in a manner which would soon leave the chronicle and the historian at the mercy of the merest conjecture. The matter is scarcely of importance.

"One of the sides that enclosed my court, which I made very faire and large, reached unto the grange of my munitions: and, on the other side, towarde the river, was mine owne lodgings, round which were galleries all covered. The principal doore of my lodging was in the middest of the great place, and the other was towarde the river. A good distance from the fort, I built an oven."

It will be an employment of curious interest, whenever the people of Florida shall happen upon the true site of the settlement and structure of Laudonniere, to trace out, in detail, these several localities, and fix them for the benefit of posterity. The work is scarcely beyond the hammer and chisel of some Old Mortality, who has learned to place his affections, and fix his sympathies, upon the achievements of the Past

X.

HISTORICAL SUMMARY.

Thus, then, was founded the second European settlement on the Continent of America. The fortress was named LA CAROLINE, in honor of the French monarch, whom it was still the policy of the Huguenots to conciliate. The houses were of frail structure, and thatched with leaves of the palmetto. The domain was a narrow one, but it was probably sufficiently wide for the genius of Laudonniere. He soon shows himself sensible of all his dignities as the sole representative of his master in the New World. From his own account, he does not appear to have been the proper person for the conduct of so difficult, if not so great, an enterprise. There is no doubt that he was sufficiently brave ; but bravery, unsustained by judgment, is at best a doubtful virtue, and, in a situation of great responsibility, is apt to show itself at the expense of all discretion. The object of the colony of La Caroline was a permanent establishment—a place of refuge from persecution—where the seeds of a new empire might be planted on a basis which should ensure civil liberty to the citizen. The proper aim of such a settlement should have been security, self-maintenance, and peace with all men. These could only have been found in the economizing of their resources, in the application of all their skill and industry to the cultivation of the soil, and in the preservation of the most friendly relations among the Indians. These, unhappily, were not objects sufficiently appreciated by Laudonniere. His first error was that which arose from the universal passion of his time. He had seen the precious metals of the country—wedges of silver and scraps of gold—which declared the abundance of its treasures, and aroused all his passions for its acquisition. His whole energies were accordingly directed to the most delusive researches. He had scarcely built his fortress before he sent off his exploring expeditions. "I would not lose a minute of an hour," is his language, "without imploying the same in some *vertuous* exercise," and therefore he despatches his Lieutenant, Ottigny, in seeking for Thimogoa; that king, hostile to the Paracoussi Satouriova, whom he has pledged himself to the latter to make war upon. Satouriova gives the lieutenant a couple of warriors as guides, who were delighted at the mission,—" seeming to goe as unto a wedding, so desirous they were to fight with their enemies."

But Ottigny, whose real purpose is to obtain the gold of the people of Thimogoa, does not indulge his warlike guides in their desires. They encounter some of the people whom they seek, and make inquiries after the treasure. This is promised them hereafter. With the report of a king named Mayrra, who lives farther up the river, and abounds in gold and silver, Ottigny returns to La Caroline. Other adventurers follow, other kings and chiefs are brought to the knowledge of our Frenchmen. Plates of gold and silver are procured; large bars of the latter metal; and the lures are quite sufficient to keep the colonists employed in the one pursuit to the complete neglect of every other. Instead of planting, they rely for their provisions wholly upon the Indians ; and, for eighteeen months, the lieutenants of Laudonniere penetrated the forests in every possible direction. They appear not only to have explored the interior of Florida, Georgia and South Carolina, but to have prosecuted their insane search even to the Apalachian mountains. It is not improbable that our antiquarians frequently stumble upon the proofs of their progress, which they fondly ascribe to a much earlier period. We preserve, as subjects of proper comparison with aboriginal words still in use, and by which localities may yet be identified, the names of many of the chiefs with whom our Frenchmen maintained communion. From the Indians of King Mollova, Captain Vasseur obtains five or six pounds of silver. Mollova is the subject of a greater prince, named Olata Ovae Utina. The tributaries of this great chief are numerous;— Cadecha, Chilili, Eclavou, Enacappe, Calany, Anacharaqua, Omittaqua, Acquera, Moquoso, and many others. Satouriova is the chief sovereign along the waters of the May. He too hath numerous tributaries. He is the great rival monarch of Olata Utina. Potanou is one of his chiefs, "a manne cruel in warre, but pitiful in the execution of his furie." He usually took his prisoners to mercy, branding them upon the arm, and setting them free. Onatheaqua and Hostaqua are great chiefs, abounding in riches, that dwell near the mountains. According to the tales of the Indians of May River, the warriors of Olata Utina "armed their breasts, armes, thighes, legs and foreheads with large plates of gold and silver." Molona is a chief of the river of May, near the Frenchmen, and hostile also to the Thimogoans. Malicá is another of these chiefs of Satouriova, eager, like all the rest, to shed the blood of the hostile people whom the Frenchmen have unwisely promised to destroy. In order to win the favor of Molona, while that Paracoussi is entertaining them at his dwelling, Capt. Vasseur, returning from an expedition to the territories of Thimogoa, reports that nothing but their flight prevented him from utterly destroying that people. Improving upon his superior, one Francis La Caille, a sergeant, insisted that, with his sword, he has run two of the Thimogoans through the body. But this falsehood demands another for its security. The suspicious Indian insists upon handling the sword, "which the sergeant would not deny him, thinking that hee would have beheld the fashion of his weapon ; but hee soon perceived that it was to another ende ; for the old man, holding it in his hand, behelde it a long while on every place, to see if he could find any blood upon it which might show that any of their enemies had beene killed. Hee was on the point to say that he had killed none of the men of Thimogoa ; when La Vasseur preventing that which hee might object, showing, that, by reason of the two Indians which he had slain, his sword was so bloody, he was enforced to wash and make it cleane a long while in the river."

Another of the chiefs, dwelling near the Frenchmen, is Omoloa, an ally of Satouriova. These two summon Laudonniere to the expedition for which they have prepared themselves against the Thimogoans, and are offended that he now excuses himself. He was too busy with his explorations for any other object. But he sent to request two of his prisoners from Satouriova, which were denied him ; the old savage properly saying that he owed him no service, as he had taken no part in the expedition. This irritated the Frenchman, who, with twenty soldiers, suddenly appeared in the dwelling of the Paracoussi, and demanded and carried off the prisoners. His policy was, by freeing these prisoners, and sending them home to their sovereign, to conciliate his favor ;

but, in the meantime, he made an enemy of Satouriova An expedition was prepared to carry back the prisoners to Olata Utina. It was confided to Monsieur D'Erlach, one of Laudonniere's lieutenants, and consisted of ten soldiers. Their course lay up the river of May, more than fourscore leagues. They were received by the great Paracoussi Utina, with much favor, and were easily persuaded by him to take part in a war which he was even then waging with his hereditary enemy, Potanou. A surprise is attempted, and a battle ensues, in which the firearms of the French confound Potanou, and subject him to a sore defeat. One of his towns is captured, and all its men, women, and children, are made prisoners. Monsieur D'Erlach returns to *La Caroline*, with no inconsiderable spoil of gold and silver, skins painted, and other commodities of the Indians.

While thus engaged in the avaricious search for the precious metals, Laudonniere began to receive some intimations of the error into which he had fallen. The mistakes of his policy were beginning to appear in their consequences. His ships had long since departed for France. He had no present hope but in himself and his neighbors; and his garrison were about to suffer from the want of necessaries such as they should have relied upon their own industry to secure. The provisions furnished by the Indians were rapidly failing them. They had offended Satouriova, and thus forfeited the supplies which his favor might have furnished. In the always limited stores of the natives, there was a natural limit, beyond which they could neither sell nor give; since, to do so, would be to lose the grain necessary for sowing their fields at the approaching season. The exigencies of the colonies finally compelled them to seize upon the stores which the providence of the Indians compelled them to retain. These thus despoiled, withdrew promptly from the dangerous neighborhood, and, but for a fortunate, and seemingly providential circumstance, which afforded them succor for awhile, the distress of the garrison might have realized anew the misfortunes of the people of Fort Charles. We must let Laudonniere himself record the event, which had such beneficial consequences, in his own language:

"Thus," said he, "things passed on in this manner, and the hatred of Paracoussi Satouriova against mee did still continue, untill that, on the nine and twentieth of August, a lightning from heaven fell within halfe a league of our fort, more worthy, I believe, to be wondered at, and to be put in writing, than all the strange signes which have beene seene in times past. For, although the meadows were at that season all greene, and halfe covered over with water, nevertheless the lightning, in one instant, consumed above five hundred acres thereof, and burned, with the ardent heate thereof, all the foules which took their pastime in the meadowes—which thus continued for three dayes space—which caused us not a little to muse, not being able to judge whence this fire proceeded. One while we thought that the Indians had burnt their houses and abandoned their places for feare of us. Another while we thought that they had discovered some shippes in the sea, and that, according to their custome, they had kindled many fires here and there * * * I determined to sende to Paracoussi Serranay to knowe the truth. But, even as I was about to sende one by boate, sixe Indians came unto me from Paracoussi Allimicany, which, at their first entrie, made unto mee a long discourse, and a very large and ample oration (after they had presented mee with certain baskets full of maiz, of pompions, and of grapes), of the loving amity which Allinicany desired to continue with mee, and that he looked, from day to day, when it would please mee to employ him in my service. Therefore, considering the serviceable affection that hee bare unto mee, he found it very strange that I thus *discharged mine ordnance against his dwelling,* which had burnt up an infinite sight of greene meadowes, and consumed even downe unto the bottom of the water."

The simple message of the Paracoussi, suggested some advantages to Laudonniere, who did not now scruple to admit that all the mischief had been done by his wanton ordnance. He had shot, not really to injure his neighbor, but to let him form a proper idea of what he might do, in the way of mischief, should he have the provocation at any time. Since, however, the Paracoussi had come to the recollection of his duties, he, Laudonniere, would protect him hereafter. The red-man had only to continue faithful, and the white man would stifle his ordnance.

The sequel of this strange fire from heaven, may be given in few words. For three days it remained unextinguished, and, for two more days, the heat in the atmosphere was insupportable. The river suffered from a sympathetic heat, and seemed ready to seethe. The fish in it died in such abundance, of all sorts, *that enough were founde to have laden fiftie carts.* The air became putrid with the effluvia; the greater number of the garrison fell sick, and suffered nearly to death; while the poor savages removed to a distance from the region, which, since the settlement of the colonists, had been productive of little but mischief unto them. The distress of Laudonniere, under these events, was increased by discontents and mutinies among his people. They were not of a class so docile as their predecessors under Albert These, certainly, would not have borne so patiently with such a sway. The government of Laudonniere, if not a wise, was not a brutal or despotic one. But they threatened equally his peace and safety. They had cause for apprehension, if not for commotion. The promised supplies from France, which were to be brought by Ribault, had failed to arrive, and the discontent in the colony was beginning to assume an aspect the most serious. At this point, our narrative must enter somewhat more into details, and, for the sake of compactness, we must somewhat anticipate events.

XI.

THE CONSPIRACY OF LE GENRÉ.

HISTORICAL SUMMARY.

THE necessities of the colony now began to open the eyes of Laudonniere in respect to the errors of which he had been guilty. He found it important to discontinue his explorations among the Indian tribes, and to employ his garrison in domestic labors. They must either work or starve. Their tasks in the fields were assigned accordingly. This produced discontent among those who, having for some time, in Europe as well as recently in the new world, been chiefly employed as soldiers, regarded labor as degrading, and still flattered themselves with the more agreeable hope of achieving their fortunes by shorter processes. Their appetite for the precious metals had been sufficiently enlivened by the glimpses which had been given them, during their intercourse with the natives, of the unquestionable treasures of the country. It was still farther whetted by the influence of two persons of the garrison. One of these was named La Roquette, of the country of Perigort; the other was known as Le Genré, a lieutenant, and somewhat in the confidence of Laudonniere. Le Genré was the bold conspirator. La Roquette was perhaps quite as potential, though from art rather than audacity. He pretended to be a great magician, and acquired large influence over the more ignorant soldiers on the score of his supposed capacity to read the book of fate. Among his professed discoveries through this medium, were certain mines of gold and silver, far in the interior, the wealth of which was such—and he pledged his life upon it— that, upon a fair division, after awarding the king's portion, each soldier would receive not less than ten thousand crowns. The arguments and assurances of La Roquette persuaded Le Genré, among the rest. He was exceedingly covetous, and sought eagerly all royal roads for the acquisition of fortune. He was more easily beguiled into conspiracy, in consequence of the refusal of Laudonniere to give him the command of a packet returning into France. It was determined to depose and destroy the latter. Several schemes were tried for this purpose; by poison, by gunpowder, all of which failed, and resulted in the ruin only of the conspirators. With this introduction we introduce the reader more particularly to the parties of our history.

XII.

THE CONSPIRACY OF LE GENRÉ.—Chap. I.

Le Genré, one of the lieutenants of Laudonniere, was of fierce and intractable temper. His passions had been thwarted by his superior, whose preferences were clearly with another of his lieutenants, named D'Erlach.* This preference was quite sufficient to provoke the envy and enmity of Le Genré. His dislike was fully retorted, and with equal spirit by his brother officer. But the feelings of D'Erlach, who was the more noble and manly of the two, were restrained by his prudence and sense of duty. It had been the task of Laudonniere more than once to interfere between these persons, and prevent those outrages which he had every reason to apprehend from their mutual excitability; and it was partly with the view to keep the parties separate, that he had so frequently despatched D'Erlach upon his exploring expeditions. One of these appointments, however, which Le Genré had desired for himself, had given him no little mortification when he found that, as usual, D'Erlach had received

---

* Laudonniere, in Hakluyt, spells this name improperly. It is properly written D'Erlach. "Ce Gentilhomme," says Charlevoix, "étoit Suisse et il n'y a point de maison de Suisse plus connuë que celle d'Erlach."

the preference from his superior. It was no proper disparagement of the claims of others that D'Erlach had been thus preferred. That he was a favorite, was, perhaps, quite as much due to his own merits as to the blind partiality of his superior. In choosing him for the command of his most important expeditions, Laudonniere was, in fact, doing simple justice to the superior endowments of caution, prudence, moderation, and firmness, which the young officer confessedly possessed in very eminent degree. But Le Genré was not the person to recognize these arguments, or to acknowledge the superior fitness of his colleague. His discontents, fanned by the arts of others, and daily receiving provocation from new causes, finally wrought his blood into such a state of feverish irritation, as left but little wanting to goad him to actual insubordination and mutiny.

Laudonniere was not ignorant of the factious spirit of his discontented lieutenant. He had been warned by D'Erlach that he was a person to be watched, and his own observations had led him equally to this conviction. His eye, accordingly, was fixed keenly and suspiciously upon the offender, but cautiously, however, so as to avoid giving unnecessary pain or provocation. But Laudonniere's vigilance was partial only; and his suspicions were by no means so intense as those of D'Erlach. Besides, his attention was divided among his discontents. He had become painfully conscious that Le Genré was not alone in his factious feelings. He felt that the spirit of this officer was widely spreading in the garrison. The moods of others, sullen, peevish, and doubtful, had already startled his fears; and he too well knew the character of his *personnel*, and from what sources they had been drawn, not to be apprehensive of their tempers. Signs of insubordination had been shown already, on various occasions; and had not

Laudonniere been of that character which more easily frets with its doubts than provides against them, he might have legitimately employed a salutary punishment in anticipating worse offences. The looks of many had become habitually sullen, their words few and abrupt when addressed to their commander, while their tasks were performed coldly and with evident reluctance. Without exhibiting any positive or very decided conduct, by which to leave themselves open to rebuke, their deportment was such as to betray the impatience of bitter and resentful moods, which only forbore open utterance by reason of their fears. Laudonniere, without having absolute cause to punish, was equally wanting in the nice tact which can, adroitly, and without a fall from dignity, conciliate the inferior. Angry at the appearances which he could neither restrain nor chastise, he was not sufficiently the commander to descend happily to soothe. In this distracted condition of mind, he prepared to despatch his third and last vessel to France, to implore the long-expected supplies and assistance.

It was a fine evening, at the close of September, such an evening as we frequently experience during that month in the South, when a cool breeze, arising from the ocean, ascends to the shores and the forests, and compensates, by its exquisite and soothing freshness, for the burning heat and suffocating atmosphere of the day. Our Frenchmen at La Caroline were prepared to enjoy the embraces of this soothing minister. Some walked upon the parapets of the fortress, others lay at length along the bluff of the river, while others again, in the shade of trees farther inland, grouped together in pleasant communion, enjoyed the song or the story, with as much gaiety as if all their cares were about to be buried with the sun that now hung, shorn of his fiery locks, just above the horizon. Laudonniere passed among these groups with the look of one who did not sympathize with their enjoyments. He was feeble, dull, and only just recovering from a sickness which had nigh been fatal. His eye rested upon the river where lay the vessel, the last remaining to his command, which, in two days more, was to be despatched for France. He had just left her, and his course now lay for the deep woods, a mile or more inland. He was followed, or rather accompanied, by a youth, apparently about nineteen or twenty years of age—a younger brother of D'Erlach, his favorite lieutenant. This young man shared in the odium of his brother, as he also was supposed to enjoy too largely the favors of Laudonniere. The truth was, that he was much more the favorite than his brother. He was a youth of great intelligence and sagacity, observing mind, quick wit, and shrewd, capacious remark. The slower thought of his commander was quickened by his intelligence, and relied, much more than the latter would have been willing to allow, upon the insinuated, rather than expressed, suggestions of the youth. Alphonse D'Erlach, but for his breadth of shoulders and activity of muscle, would have seemed delicately made. He was certainly effeminately habited. He had a boyish love of ornament which was perhaps natural at his age, but it had been observed that his brother Achille, though thirty-five, displayed something of a like passion. Our youth wore his dagger and his pistols, the former hung about his neck by a scarf, and the latter were stuck in the belt about his waist. The dagger was richly hilted, and the pistols, though of excellent structure, were rather more remarkable for the beauty of their ornaments than for their size and seeming usefulness as weapons for conflict.

"And you think, Alphonse," said Laudonniere, when they had

entered the wood, "that Le Genré is really anxious to return to France in the Sylph."

"I say nothing about his return to France, but that he will apply to you for the command of the Sylph, I am very certain."

"Well! And you?——"

"Would let him have her."

"Indeed! I am sorry, Alphonse, to hear you say so. Le Genré is not fit for such a trust. He has no judgment, no discretion. It would be a hundred to one that he never reached France."

"That is just my opinion," said the youth, coolly.

"Well! And with this opinion, you would have me risk the vessel in his hands?"

"Yes, I would! The simple question is, not so much the safety of the vessel as our own. He is a dangerous person. His presence here is dangerous to us. If he stays, unless our force is increased, in another month he will have the fortress in his hands; he will be master here. You have no power even now to prevent him. You know not whom to trust. The very parties that you arm and send out for provisions, might, if they pleased, turn upon and rend us. If *he* were not the most suspicious person in the world—doubtful of the very men that serve him—he would soon bring the affair to an issue. Fortunately, he doubts rather more than we confide. He knows not his own strength, and your seeming composure leads him to overrate ours. But he is getting wiser. The conspiracy grows every day. I am clear that you should let him go, take his vessel, pick his crew, and disappear. He will not go to France, that 1 am certain. He will shape his course for the West Indies as soon as he is out of our sight, and be a famous picaroon before the year is over."

"Alphonse, you are an enemy of Le Genré."

"That is certain," replied the youth; "but if I am his enemy, that is no good reason why I should be the enemy of truth."

"True, but you suspect much of this. You know nothing."

"I *know* all that I have told you," replied the young man, warmly.

"Indeed! How?"

"That I cannot tell. Enough that I am free to swear upon the Holy Evangel, that all I say is true. Le Genré is at the head of a faction which is conspiring against you."

"Can you give me proof of this?"

"Yes, whenever you dare issue the order for his arrest and that of others. But this you cannot do. You must not. They are too strong for you. If Achille were here now!"

"Ay! Would he were!"

They now paused, as if the end of their walk had been reached. Laudonniere wheeled about, with the purpose of returning. They had not begun well to retrace their steps before the figure of a person was seen approaching them.

"Speak of the devil," said Alphonse, "and he thinks himself called; here comes Le Genré."

"Indeed!" said Laudonniere.

"See now if I am not right—he comes to solicit the command of the Sylph."

They were joined by the person of whom they had been speaking. His approach was respectful—his manner civil—his tones subdued. There was certainly a change for the better in his deportment. A slight smile might have been seen to turn the corner of the lips of young D'Erlach, as he heard the address of the new comer. Le Genré began by requesting a private interview with his commander. Upon the words, D'Erlach went aside and was soon out of hearing. His prediction was true. Le Genré respectfully, but earnestly, solicited the command of the vessel about to sail for France. He was civilly but positively denied. Laudonniere had not been impressed by the suggestion of his youthful counsellor; or, if he were, he was not prepared to yield a vessel of the king, with all its men and munitions, to the control of one who might abuse them to the worst purposes The face of Le Genré changed upon this refusal.

"You deny me all trust, Monsieur," he said. "You refused me the command when my claim was at least equal to that of Ottigny. You denied me that which you gave to D'Erlach, and now—Monsieur, do you hold me incompetent to this command?"

"Nay," said Laudonniere, "but I better prefer your services here—I cannot so well dispense with them."

A bitter smile crossed the lips of the applicant.

"I cannot complain of a refusal founded upon so gracious a compliment. But, enough, Monsieur, you refuse me! May I ask, who will be honored with this command?"

"Lenoir!"

"I thought so—another favorite! Well!—Monsieur, I wish you a good evening."

"You have refused him, I see," said Alphonse, returning as the other disappeared.

"Yes, I could do no less. The very suggestion that he might convert the vessel to piratical purposes, was enough to make me resolve against him."

And, still discussing that and other kindred subjects, Laudonnierre and his young companion followed in the steps of La Genré towards the fortress.

CHAPTER II.

THAT night the young Alphonse D'Erlach might have been seen stealing cautiously from the quarters of Laudonnierre, and winding along under cover of the palisades to one of the entrances of the fortress. He was wrapped in a huge and heavy cloak which effectually disguised his person. Here he was joined by another, whom he immediately addressed:

"Bon Pre?"

"The same: all's ready."

"Have they gone?"

"Yes!"

"Let us go."

They went together to the entrance. The person whom Alphonse called Bon Pre, was a short, thick-set person, fully fifty years of age. They approached the sentry at the gate.

"Let us out, my son," said Bon Pre; "we are late."

When they were without the walls, they stole along through the ditch, concealed in the deep shade of the place, cautiously avoiding all exposure to the star-light. On reaching a certain point, they ascended, and, taking the cover of bush and tree, made their way to the river, and getting into a boat which lay beneath the banks, pushed off, and suffered her to drop down the stream, the old man simply using the paddle to shape her course. A brief conversation, in whispers, followed between them.

"You told him all?" asked Bon Pre.

"No; but just enough for our purpose. As I told you, he believes nothing. He is too good a man himself to believe any body thoroughly bad."

"He will grow wiser before he is done. You did not suffer him to know where you got your information?"

"No—surely not. He would have been for having a court, and a trial, and all that sort of thing. You would have sworn to the truth in vain, and they would assassinate you. We must only do what we can to prevent, and leave the punishment for another season. If time is allowed us——"

"Ay, but that "if!" said the old man. "Time will not be allowed. Le Genré will be rather slow—but there are some persons not disposed to wait for the return of the parties under Ottigny and your brother."

"Enough!" said D'Erlach—"Here is the cypress."

With these words, the course of the canoe was arrested, the prow turned in towards the shore, and adroitly impelled, by the stroke of Bon Pre's paddle, directly into the cavernous opening of an ancient cypress which stood in the water, but close to the banks. This ancient tree stood, as it were, upon two massive abutments. The cavern into which the boat passed was open in like manner on the opposite side. The prow of the canoe ran in upon the land, while the stern rested within the body of the tree. Alphonse cautiously stepped ashore, and was followed by his older companion. They were now upon the same side of the river with the fortress. The course which they had taken had two objects. To avoid fatigue and detection in a progress by land, and to reach a given point in advance of the conspirators, who had taken that route. Of course, our two companions had timed their movements with reference to the previous progress of the former They advanced in the direction of the fort, which lay some three miles distant, but at the distance of fifty or sixty yards from the place where they landed, came to a knoll thickly overgrown with trees and shrubbery. A creek ran at its foot, in the bed of which stood numerous cypresses—amongst these Alphonse D'Erlach disappeared, while Bon Pre ascended the knoll, and seated himself in waiting upon a fallen cypress.

He had not long to wait. In less than twenty minutes, a whistle was heard—to which Bon Pre responded, in the notes of an owl. The sound of voices followed, and, after a little interval, one by one, seven persons ascended the knoll, and entered the area which was already partially occupied by Bon Pre. There were few preliminaries, and Le Genré opened the business. Bon Pre, it is seen, was one of the conspirators and in their fullest confidence. He had left the fort before them, or had pretended to do so. They had each left at different periods. We have seen his route. It is only necessary to add, that they had come together but a little while before their junction at the knoll. Of course, their several revelations had yet to be made. Le Genré commenced by relating his ill success in regard to the vessel.

"We must have it, at all hazards," said Stephen Le Genevois, "we can do nothing without it."

"I do not see that;" was the reply of Jean La Roquette. This person, it may be well to say, was one possessing large influence among the conspirators. He claimed to be a magician, dealt much in predictions, consulted the stars, and other signs, as well of earth as of heaven ; and, among other things, pretended, by reason of his art, to know where, at no great distance, was a mine of silver, the richest in the world. Almost his sole reason for linking himself with the conspirators, was the contempt with which his pretensions had been treated by his commander, in regard to the search after this mine.

"I do not see," he replied, "that this vessel is so necessary to us. A few canoes will serve us better."

"Canoes—for what?" was the demand of Le Genevois.

"Why, for ascending the rivers, for avoiding the fatigue of land travel, for bringing down our bullion."

"Pshaw! You are at your silver mine again; but that is slow work. I prefer that which the Spaniard has already gathered; which he has run into solid bars and made ready for the king's face. I prefer fighting for my silver, to digging for it."

Ay! fighting—no digging;" said Le Genré and he was echoed by other voices. But La Roquette was not to be silenced. His opinions were re-stated and insisted upon with no small vehemence, and the controversy grew warm as to the future course of the party—whether they should explore the land for silver ore, or the Spanish seas for bullion.

"*Messieurs*," said one named Fourneaux, "permit me to say that you are counting your chickens before they are out of the shell. Why cumber our discussion with unnecessary difficulties? The first thing to consider is how to get our freedom. We can determine hereafter what use we shall make of it. There are men enough, or will be enough, when we have got rid of Laudonniere, to undertake both objects. Some may take the seas, and some the land; some to digging. Each man to his taste. All may be satisfied—there need be no restraint. The only matter now to be adjusted, is to be able to choose at all. Let us not turn aside from the subject."

These sensible suggestions quieted the parties, and each proceeded to report progress. One made a return of the men he had got over, another of the arms in possession, and a third of ammunition. But the question finally settled down upon the fate of Laudonniere, and a few of his particular friends, the young D' Erlach being the first among them. On this subject, the conspirators not only all spoke, but they all spoke together. They were vehement enough, willing to destroy their enemy, but their words rather declared their anger, than any particular mode of effecting their object. At length Fourneaux again spoke.

"*Messieurs*," said he, "you all seem agreed upon two things; the first is, that, before we can do anything, Laudonniere and that young devil, D'Erlach, must be disposed of; the second, that this is rather a difficult matter. It is understood that they may rally a sufficient force to defeat us—that we are not in the majority yet, though we hope to be so; and that a great number who are now slow to join us, will be ready enough, if the blow were once struck successfully. In this, I think, you all perfectly agree."

"Ay—ay! There you are right—that's it;" was the response of Le Genré and Stephen Le Genevois.

"Very well; now, as it is doubtful who are certainly the friends of Laudonniere, it is agreed that we must move against him secretly. Is there any difficulty in this? There are several ways of getting rid of an enemy without lifting dagger or pistol. Is not the magician here—the chemist, La Roquette?—has he no knowledge of certain poisons, which, once mingled in the drink of a captain, can shut his eyes as effectually as if it were done with bullet or steel? And if this fails, are there not other modes of contriving an accident? I have a plan now, which, with your leave, I think the very thing for our purpose. Laudonniere's quarters, as you all know, stand apart from all the rest, with the exception of the little building occupied by the division of Le Genré, with which it is connected by the old bath-room. This bath-room is abandoned since Laudonniere has taken to the river. Suppose Le Genré here should, for safe-keeping, put a keg of gunpowder under the captain's quarters? and suppose farther, that, by the merest mischance, he should suffer a train of powder to follow his footsteps, as he crawls from one apartment to the other; and suppose again, that, while Laudonniere sleeps, some careless person should suffer a coal of fire to rest, only for a moment, upon the train in the bath-house. By my life, I think such an accident would spare us the necessity of attempting the life of our beloved captain. It would be a sort of providential interposition."

"Say no more! It shall be done!" said Le Genré. "I will do it!"

"Ay, should the other measure fail; but I am for trying the poison first;" said Fourneaux, "for such an explosion would send a few fragments of timber about other ears than those of the captain. He takes his coffee at sunrise. Can we not drug it?"

"Let that be my task;" said old Bon Pre, who had hitherto taken little part in this conference.

"You are the very man," said Fourneaux. "He takes his coffee from your hands. La Roquette will provide the poison."

"When shall this be done?" demanded Le Genré. "We can do nothing to-night. It will require time to-morrow to prepare the train."

"Ay, that is your part; but may not Bon Pre do his to-morrow? and should he fail——"

"Why should he fail?" demanded La Roquette. "Let him but dress his coffee with my spices, and he cannot fail."

"Yes," replied Bon Pre, "but it is not always that Laudonniere drinks his coffee. If he happens to be asleep when I bring it, I do not wake him, but put it on the table by his bedside, and, very frequently, if it is cold when he wakes, he leaves it untasted."

"Umph! but at all events, there is the other accident. That can be made to take effect at mid-night to-morrow—eh! what say you, Le Genré?"

"Without fail! It is sworn!"

Their plans being adjusted, the meeting was dissolved, and the parties separately dispersed, each to make his way back, as he best might, so as to avoid suspicion or detection, to Fort Caroline. They had scarcely disappeared when Alphonse D'Erlach emerged from the hollow of a cypress which stood upon the edge of the knoll where their conference had taken place.

CHAPTER III.

ALPHONSE D'ERLACH was one of those remarkable persons who seem, in periods of great excitement, to be entirely superior to its influence. He appeared to be entirely without emotions. Though a mere youth, not yet firm in physical manhood, he was, in morals, endowed with a strength, a hardihood and maturity, which do not often fall to the lot of middle age. In times of difficulty, he possessed a coolness which enabled him to contemplate deliberately the approach of danger, and he was utterly beyond surprises. His conference with old Bon Pre, when they met again that night was remarkably illustrative of these characteristics.

"What shall we do?" demanded the old man.

"Your part is easily done," was the reply—"you are simply to do nothing—to forbear doing. I understand your purpose in volunteering to do the poisoning. I will see Laudonniere in an hour. You will prepare the coffee—nay, let Fourneaux, or that fool of a magician himself, introduce the poison. Laudonniere will sleep, you understand."

"But, Le Genré—the gunpowder!"

"I will see to that."

"What will you do?"

"Nay, time must find the answer. I am not resolved; but, at all events, for the present, Laudonniere must know nothing. He must remain in ignorance."

"Why?"

"For the best reason in the world. Did he guess what we know, he would be for arming himself and all around him—creating a confusion under the name of law—attempting arrests, and so proceeding as to give opportunities to the conspirators to do that boldly, which they are now content to do basely. I think we shall thwart them with their own weapons. Let us separate now. I will see Laudonniere but a few moments before I sleep."

"*Can* you sleep to-night? I cannot! I shall hardly be able to sleep till the affair is over. I do not think, honestly speaking, that I have slept a good hour for the last week. I am certainly not conscious of having done so."

"Nature provides for all such cases. For my part I never want sleep—I always have it. I can sleep in a storm and enjoy it just as well. The uproar of winds and seas never troubles me. If it does, it is only to lull me into sleep again. I am a philosopher without knowing it, and by accident. But come—we must part."

The chamber of D'Erlach was in the same building with that of Laudonniere. They slept in adjoining apartments. D'Erlach purposely made some noise in approaching his, and Laudonniere cried out,

"Who is there ?—Alphonse ?"

"The same, sir."

"Come in—where have you been at this hour; is it not very late ?"

"Almost time for waking—an hour probably from dawn, though I know not exactly. But, suffer me to extinguish this light. We can talk as well in the dark."

"What have you to say ?" demanded Laudonniere, half rising at this preliminary.

"I have been getting some new lessons in chess from old Marchand."

"Ah! what new lesson ?" asked Laudonniere, whose passion for the game had prompted D'Erlach with the suggestion he made use of.

"Marchand, sir, is a most wonderful player. I have seen a great many persons skilled at the game, not to speak of yourself, and I am sure there is no one who can stand him. He absolutely laughs at my opposition. I wish you could play with him, sir."

"I should like it, Alphonse," replied the other, "but you know my position. This man, Marchand, is a turbulent person; scarcely respectful to me, and, if there be, as you think, a conspiracy on foot against me, he is at the head of it, be sure."

"Not so;" said the other, quietly, but decisively; "not so His bluntness is that of an honest man. His turbulence is that of self-esteem. He is above a base action, and, secure in his own character, he defies the scrutiny of superiority. I think you mistake him; at all events it is necessary that you should know him in chess. I am anxious to see you and him in conflict; and, if you will permit me, he shall bring his own men –for he will play with no other—he has his notions on the point—here, to-morrow night, when you will discover that he is not only a great player but a good fellow."

"You are a singular person, Alphonse;" said Laudonniere, smiling. "What should put chess into your head at such a time, particularly when you say there is such danger?"

"The man who can play chess when danger threatens is the very man to discover it; and the conspirator is never more likely to become resolved in his purpose than when he finds his destined victim in a state of anxiety. I should rather my enemy see me at chess—provided I can see him—than that he should find me putting my arms in readiness. They may be conveniently under the table, while the chess-board is upon it; and while I am moving my pawn with one hand, I can prepare my pistol with the other. But, sir, with your further permission, I will bring Challus and Le Moyne to see the match. They are both passionately fond of the game, and Le Moyne plays well, though nothing to compare either with yourself or Marchand."

"By the way, Alphonse, how is Le Moyne getting on with his pictures? It certainly was a strange idea of the Admiral, that of sending out, with such an expedition, painters of pictures and such persons. I can see the use of a mineralogist and botanist, but— these painters!"

"Le Moyne has made some very lovely pictures of the country. His landscapes are to the life, and he has that rare knowledge of the painter, which enables him to choose his point of view happily, and tells him how much to take in, and how much to leave out. The Admiral will be able to form a better idea of the country from the pictures of Le Moyne, than he will from the pebbles of Delille or the dried flowers and leaves of Serrier. Le Moyne shows him the rivers and the trees, the valleys and the hills; and, if his pictures get safely to France, the people there will envy us the paradise here which we are so little able to enjoy."

Laudonniere heard the youth with half-shut eyes, and the dialogue languished on the part of the former; but D'Erlach seemed resolute to keep him wakeful, and suggested continually new provocatives to conversation, until his superior, absolutely worn out with exhaustion, bade him go to sleep himself or suffer him to do so. Alphonse smiled, and left the room perfectly satisfied, as he beheld the faint streakings of daylight gliding through the interstices between the logs of which the building was composed. In less than an hour, hearing a sound as of one entering, he hastily went out of his chamber, for he had neither undressed himself nor slept, and met Bon Pre, with the salver of coffee, about to go into the chamber of Laudonniere.

"Well, is it spiced? Has La Roquette furnished the drug?"

"His own hands put it in."

"Very well; let us in together. Laudonniere is not likely to awaken soon, and I will remain with him 'till he does. If the coffee cools, and he offers not to drink, well. I will say nothing It is best that he should know nothing 'till all's over.

"But the rest!" said Bon Pre, in a whisper.

"We must manage that, also, quite as well as this."

"If you should want help?"

"We must find it. But the thing must go forward to the end. Remember *that!* This scoundrel must be suffered to burn his fingers."

"Can you contrive it—*you, alone?*"

"I think so; but, Bon Pre, you are here, and Challus, and Le Moyne, and Beauvais and Marchand, and, perhaps, one or two more—true men upon whom we can rely—and these, mark me, must be in readiness. Of this you shall learn hereafter."

They entered the chamber of Laudonniere. He still slept. Bon Pre placed the vessel of coffee beside him and disappeared. D'Erlach seated himself at a little distance from the couch. When Laudonniere wakened the liquor was cold. He laid it down again.

"What! you here, Alphonse; but you have been to bed?"

"I do not sleep as soundly as you. I left my chamber as old Bon Pre brought your coffee, and entered with him. You do not drink?"

"The coffee is cold."

"It spoils your breakfast, too, I imagine. You do not eat heartily at breakfast."

"No; dinner is my meal. But, Alphonse—did I dream, or did we not have some conversation about Marchand and chess-playing last night?"

"We did! This morning rather."

"Is he the great player you describe him?"

"He is. I can think of none better."

"Well—saucy as he is, I must meet him."

"You permitted me to arrange for it, to-night. I had your consent to bring some amateurs."

"Yes, I *do* recollect something of it—Le Moyne and—"

"Challus."

"Very well—let them come; but they must be patient. If Marchano is such a player, I must be cool and cautious. I must beat him."

"You will, but you will work for it. Marchand will keep you busy. And now, sir, there is another matter which I beg leave to bring to your remembrance. You remember the cypress canoe that lies upon the river banks, three miles or more above. It was claimed by the old chief Satouriova. We shall want it here for various, and, perhaps, important uses, when the ship sails. She will take most of your boats with her. Let me recommend that you send a detachment for this boat to-day. It should be an armed detachment, for the old chief is most certainly our enemy, and may be in the neighborhood. I would send Lieutenant Le Genré, as he lacks employment. I would give him his choice of six or eight companions, as, if he does not choose his own men, he might be apt to tyrannize over those who are friendly to you. Perhaps it would be better to give your orders early, that he should start at noon, as, at mid-day, the tide will serve for bringing the boat up without toil."

"Why, Alphonse, you are very nice in your details. But, you are right, and the arrangement is a good one."

"The sooner Le Genré receives his orders the more time for preparations;" said the youth indifferently.

"He shall have them as soon as I go below."

By this time Laudonniere was dressed and they descended the court together.

"Has he drunk," asked Le Genré anxiously, with Forneaux and La Roquette on each side, as they beheld Bon Pre descending from the chamber of Laudonniere with the vessel in his hand. The old man raised the silver lid of the coffee-pot, and showed the contents.

"Diable!" was the half-suppressed exclamation of La Roquette.

"Enough, comrade!" said Le Genré, in a whisper—"it remains for me."

They separated, and entered, from different points, the area where Laudonniere stood.

"Lieutenant;" said the latter, as Le Genré appeared in sight— "Take six men at noon and go up to the bluff of the old chief Satouriova and bring away the cypress canoe of which we took possession some time since. Launch her and bring her up. The tide will serve at that hour. Let your men be armed to the teeth, and keep on your guard, for you may meet the old savage on your way.

Le Genré touched his hat and retired.

"It is well, said he to Fourneaux, whom he had chosen as one of his companions, "that the commission did not send me off at once. I must make my preparation quickly and before I go."

Unseen and unsuspected, Alphonse D'Erlach was conscious all the while that the enemy was busy. But Laudonniere saw nothing to suspect, either in his countenance, or in the proceedings of the conspirator. At noon, Le Genré commenced his march, the only toils of which were over, when once the canoe was in their possession. The vessel was amply large to carry twenty soldiers as well as six, and the tide alone would bring them to the fortress in an hour or two.

The labors of Alphonse began as soon as Le Genré had disappeared with his party. The six men whom he had taken with him, were his confederates. The object of the youth was to operate in security, free from their *surveillance*. Still, his proceedings were conducted with great caution. Laudonniere neither suspected his industry nor its object. Arms and ammunition were accumulated in his chamber. Beauvais, and one or two brave and trusty friends, were placed there without the privity of any one, and the chess-party, including Marchand, Le Moyne and Challus, were properly apprized of the arrangements for the game between the former and Laudonniere. They were all amateurs, and there was good wine to be had on such occasions. They did not refuse. Alphonse took pains to noise about the expected meeting, and its object, and showed his own interest by betting freely upon his captain. He soon found those who were willing to risk their gold upon Marchand; and the lively Frenchmen of La Caroline, were very soon all agog for the approaching contest. But the labors of the youth did not cease here. He explored the cellar of the building in which he and Laudonniere slept, and there, as he expected, the arrangements had been already made for sending the Chief and himself by the shortest possible road to heaven. A keg of powder had been wedged in beneath the beams, with a train, following which, on hands and knees, Alphonse was conducted under the old bath-house, till he found himself beneath that of Le Genré. He did not disturb the train. He simply withdrew the keg of powder, carefully putting back, in the manner he found them, the old boxes and piles of wood, with which the incendiary had wedged it between the beams. This done, he rolled the keg before him over the path, by which it had evidently come, beneath the bath-house, and to that of Le Genré. Here he left it, still connected with the train of powder, but rather less distant from the match than Le Genré had ever contemplated. Perhaps, he sprinkled the train anew with fresh powder—it is certain that he went away secure and satisfied, long before Le Genré returned from his expedition, with the canoe of Satouriova.

CHAPTER IV.

At the hour appointed that night, for the contest between the chess players, Marchand, accompanied by Le Moyne and Challus, made his appearance in the apartments of René Laudonniere. Those of Alphonse D'Erlach were already occupied by four or five trusty fellows; and the arms which filled the apartment were ample for the defence of the party, while in the building, against any number assailing from without. The foresight of Alphonse had made all the necessary preparations, to encounter any foe, who might, after the explosion, attempt to carry their object in a bold way. He had no fear of this, but his habitual forethought led to the precautions. Meanwhile, of the designs against him and of the means taken for his safety, Laudonniere had not the slightest suspicion. His thoughts were occupied with one danger only—that of being beaten by Marchand. He valued himself upon his play—was one of those persons who never suffer themselves to be beaten when they can possibly help it—even by a lady. If our captain made any preparations, that day, it was for the supper that night, and the contest which was to follow it. His instruction, on the first matter, given to his cook, he retired to his chamber and exercised himself throughout the day in a series of studies in the game—planning new combinations to be brought into play, if possible, in the contest which was to follow His welcome to Marchand declared the opinion which he himself entertained of his studies.

"I shall beat you, Marchand."

"You can't—you shan't," was the ready answer; "you're not my match, captain."

This answer piqued Laudonniere.

"We shall see—we shall see; not your match! Well! we shall see."

We need not waste time upon the preliminaries of the contest. Enough that, about ten o'clock at night, we find the rival players placed at the table; the opposing pieces arrayed in proper order of battle, with Le Moyne and Challus, looking on with faces filled with expectation and curiosity. The face of Alphonse D'Erlach might also be perceptible, in a momentary glance over the shoulders of one or other of the parties; but his movements were capricious, and, passing frequently between his own and the chamber of Laudonniere, he only looked at intervals upon the progress of the game. Unhappily, the details of this great match, the several moves, and the final position of the remaining pieces, at the end of the contest, have not been preserved to us, though it is not improbable that the painter Le Moyne, as well as Challus, took notes of it. Enough, that Laudonniere put forth all his skill, exercised all his caution, played as slowly and heedfully as possible, and was—but we anticipate. Marchand, on the contrary, seemed never more indifferent. He scarcely seemed to look at the board—played promptly, even rapidly, and wore one of those cool, almost contemptuous, countenances which seemed to say, "I know myself and my enemy, and feel sure that I have no cause of fear." That his opinions were of this character is beyond all question; but, though his countenance expressed as much, Laudonniere reassured himself with the reflection that Marchand was well understood to be one of those fortunate persons who know admirably how to disguise their real emotions, however deeply they may be excited or anxious. Laudonniere's self-esteem was not deficient, in the absence of better virtues. He had his vanity at chess, and the game was so played, that the issue continued doubtful, except possibly to one of the spectators, almost to the last moment. Leaving the parties at the board, silent and studious, let us turn to the counsels of the conspirators, whom we must not suppose to be idle all this time.

They had assembled—half a dozen of them at least—and were in close conference at the quarters of La Roquette, at the opposite extremity of the fortress. They were all excited to the highest pitch of expectation. The hour was drawing nigh for the attempt, and all eyes were turned upon Le Genré.

"It is half past eleven," he exclaimed, "and the thing is to be done. But what is to be done, if those men whom we hold doubtful should take courage, and, in the moment of uproar take arms against us? We have made no preparations for this event. Now, this firing the train from my lodgings is but the work of a boy. It may be done by any body. It is more fitting that, with six or eight select men, well armed, I should be in reserve, ready to encounter resistance should there be any after the explosion."

Villemain, a youth of twenty-two, a dark, sinister-looking person, slight and short, promptly volunteered to fire the train. His offer was at once accepted.

"It is half-past eleven, you say? I will go at once," said Villemain.

"We will go with you," cried La Roquette and Stephen Le Genevois in the same breath.

"No! no! not so!" said Le Genré. "You have each duties to perform. You must scatter yourselves as much as possible, so as to increase the alarm at the proper moment. There will be little danger, I grant you, with Laudonniere, and that imp of the devil, D'Erlach, out of the way; but it must be prepared for. Once show the rest that these are done for, and we shall do as we think proper."

"What a fortunate thing for us is this game of chess. It disposes of the only persons we could not so easily have managed;" said Fourneaux. "Boxes them up, as one may say, so that they only need a mark upon them to be ready for shipment."

"And yet, somehow, I could wish," said Le Genevois, "that Marchand were not among them. I like that fellow. He is so bold, so blunt, and plays his game just as if it were his religion."

"I could wish to save the painter, if any," remarked La Roquette; "but at all events, we shall inherit his pictures."

"Bah! let the devil take him and them together! Why bother about such stuff; what's his pictures of the country to us, when the country itself is our own, to keep or to quit just as it pleases us? We are wasting time. Where's Villemain?"

"Here—ready!"

"Depart, then," said Le Genré; "the sooner you light the match after you reach my quarters, the better. We shall be ready for the blast."

"He is gone!" said Fourneaux.

"Let us follow, and each to his task;" cried Le Genré. "Each of you take care of the flying timbers; find you covers as you may. My men are mustered behind the old granary. *Adieu, my friends,*—the time has come!"

With these words, the company dispersed, each seeking his several position and duty. Let us adjourn our progress to the chamber of Laudonniere, where that meditative gamester still sits deliberate, with knotted brow, watching the movements of Marchand.

CHAPTER V.

THE game was still unfinished. The repeater of Alphonse D'Erlach was in his hand, as he entered from his own chamber, and threw a hasty glance across the chess-board. There Laudonnière sate, seeing nothing but the pieces before him. He was in the brownest of studies. His thoughts were wholly with the game, which had the power of contracting his forehead with a more serious anxiety than possibly all the cares of his colony had done. His opponent was the very personification of well-satisfied indifference. He leaned back in his seat, smiling grimly, and with a wink, now and then, to those who watched and waited upon the movements of Laudonniere.. Alphonse D'Erlach smiled also. The slightest shade of anxiety might be observed upon his brow, and his lips were more rigidly compressed than usual. He leaned quietly towards the board, and remarked indifferently—

"I see you are nearly at the close of your game."

"Indeed!" said Laudonniere, with some sharpness in his accents,—" and pray Monsieur Alphonse, how do you see that?"

"You will finish by twelve," was the reply. "I see that it now lacks but a few minutes of that hour."

"Pshaw, Monsieur!" exclaimed Laudonniere—"you talk illogically, you know nothing about it. Chess is one of those games——"

And he proceeded to expatiate upon the latent resources of the game, and how a good player might retrieve a bad situation in the last perilous extremity, by a lucky diversion.

"But there is no such extremity now," he continued to say, "and it is not improbable that we shall keep up the struggle till morning. The game cannot finish under an hour, let him do his best, even if he conquers in the end, which is very far from certain, though I confess he has some advantages."

"We shall see," was the reply, as Alphonse left the room, and returned in a few moments after. It was not observed by the parties, so intent were they on the game, that he now made his appearance in complete armor, nor did they hear the bustle in the adjoining apartment. Alphonse still held his watch in his grasp.

"The game is nearly finished. According to my notion, you have but two minutes for it."

"Two! how!" said Laudonniere, not lifting his head.

"But one!"

"There!" said Laudonniere, making the move that Marchand had anticipated. Marchand bent forward with extended finger to the white queen, when a shade of uneasiness might be traced by a nice observer in the countenance of D'Erlach. His lips were suddenly and closely compressed. The hand of the timepiece was upon the fatal minute. On a sudden, a hissing sound was heard, and, in the next instant, the house reeled and quivered as if torn from its foundation. A deep roar followed, as if the thunderbolt had just broke at their feet, and the whole was succeeded by a deafening ringing sound in all their ears.

"Jesus—mercy!" exclaimed Laudonniere—"The magazine!"

"Checkmate!" cried Marchand, as he set down the white queen in the final position which secured the game.

"Ay! it is checkmate to more games than one! Gentlemen, to arms, and follow me!" exclaimed Alphonse. "We are safe now!"

CHAPTER VI.

They rushed out, and were immediately joined by the select party from the chamber of D'Erlach, all armed to the teeth. Another party, under Bon Pre, of which none knew but the same person, encountered them when they emerged into the *Place D'Armes*. Alphonse led the way with confidence, and, while all was uproar and confusion below—while men were seen scattered throughout the area, uncertain where to turn, the sharp, stern voice of command was heard in their midst, in tones that forbade the idea of surprise. The drums rolled. The faithful were soon brought together, and presented such an orderly and strong array, that conspiracy would have been confounded by their appearance, even was there nothing else in the event to palsy their enterprise. But their engine had exploded in their own house. The dwelling of Laudonniere was only shaken by the explosion. It was that of Le Genré which was overthrown, and was now in flames. Its blazing timbers were soon scattered, and the flames extinguished, when the body of the conspirator was drawn forth, blackened and mangled, from the place where he had met his death ; still grasping between his fingers the fragment of match with which he had lighted the train to his own destruction. The conspirators, in an instant, felt all their feebleness. Already were the trusted soldiers of Laudonniere approaching them. Baffled in the scheme from which they had promised themselves so much, and apprehending worse dangers, they lost all confidence in themselves and one another ; and Le Genré, apprehending everything, seizing the moment of greatest confusion, leaped the walls of the fortress, and succeeded in escaping to the woods. The other leading conspirators, Le Genevois, La Fourneaux, and La Roquette, at first determined not to fly, not yet dreaming that they were the objects of suspicion; but when they beheld Bon Pre, late one of their associates, marshalling one of the squads of Laudonniere, they at once conjectured the mode and the extent of the discovery. They saw that they had been betrayed, and soon followed the example of Le Genré. In regard to the inferior persons concerned in the conspiracy, D'Erlach said nothing to Laudonniere, and counselled Bon Pre to silence also. He was better pleased that they should wholly escape than that the colony should lose their services, and easily persuaded himself that in driving Le Genré and his three associates from the field, he had effectually paralyzed the spirit of faction within the fortress. He had made one mistake, however, but for which he might not have been so easily content. Not anticipating the change in the plan of the conspirators, by which it had been confided to Villemain to fire the train instead of Le Genré, he had naturally come to the conclusion that the only victim was the chief conspirator. He was soon undeceived, and his chagrin and disappointment were great accordingly.

"Whose carcass is this?" demanded Laudonniere, as they threw out the mangled remains of the incendiary from the scene of ruin.

"That of your lieutenant, Le Genré," was the answer of D'Erlach, given without looking at the object.

"Not so!" was the immediate reply of more than one of the persons present. "This is quite too slight and short a person for Le Genré."

"Who can it be, then?" said D'Erlach, looking closely at the body, which was torn and blackened almost beyond identification. The face of the corpse was washed, and with some difficulty it was recognized as that of Philip Villemain, a thoughtless youth, whom levity rather than evil nature had thrown into the meshes of conspiracy.

"But what does it all mean, Alphonse?" demanded the bewildered Laudonniere, not yet recovered from his astonishment and alarm.

"Treason! as I told you!" was the reply. "There lies one of the traitors—the poor tool of a cunning which escapes. I had looked to make his principal perish by his own petard. But we must look to this hereafter. We must stir the woods to-morrow. They will shelter the arch traitor for a season only. Enough now, captain, that we are safe. Let us in to our fish Those trout were of the finest, and I somehow have a monstrous appetite for supper."

XIII.

HISTORICAL SUMMARY.

The policy of Laudonniere, influenced by the judgment of Alphonse D'Erlach suffered the proceedings of the conspiracy to pass without farther scrutiny. His chief care was to provide against future attempts of the same character. He had been for some time past engaged, among other labors, in putting the fortress in the best possible order, and he now strenuously addressed all his efforts to the completion of this work. A portion of his force was employed in sawing plank, and getting out timber; others were engaged in making brick for buildings, at or near an Indian village called Saravahi, which stood about a league and a half from the fort, upon an arm of the same river; others were employed in gathering food, and still other parties in exploring the Indian settlements for traffic. Le Genré, meanwhile, wrote to Laudonniere, in repentant language, from the neighboring forests. He had taken shelter among the red-men,—probably of the tribes of Satouriova, at present the enemy of the Frenchmen. He admitted that he deserved death, but declared his sorrow for his crime and entreated mercy. But his professions did not soothe or deceive his superior. About this time, a vessel with supplies arrived from France which enabled Laudonniere to send despatches home, containing a full narrative of the events which had passed. It was the misfortune of the garrison to have received an addition by the arrival of this vessel. Six or seven of the most refractory of the soldiers of the garrison were put on board ship, and others left in their place with our captain. These proved in the end, quite as mischievous as those which he had dismissed. They leagued with the old discontents of the colony. They stole the barks and boats of the garrison, ran away to sea, and became picaroons, seizing, among others, upon a Spanish vessel of the Island of Cuba, from which they gathered a quantity of gold and silver. Laudonniere proceeded to build other boats; which were seized when finished by the leaders of a new conspiracy, among whom were La Fourneaux, Stephen le Genevois, and others who were distinguished in this manner before. They finally seized Laudonniere in person, and extorted from him a privateer's commission. Then, compelling him to yield up artillery, guns, and the usual munitions of war, together with Trenchant, his most faithful pilot, they hurried away to sea under the command of one of his sergeants, Bertrand Conferrant, while La Croix became their ensign. Thus was the commandant of La Caroline stripped of every vessel of whatever sort, his stores plundered, and his garrison greatly lessened by desertions, while select detachments of his men, under favorite lieutenants, were engaged in new explorations among the red-men of the country. Our detailed narrative of these proceedings will employ the following chapters

XIV.

THE SEDITION AT LA CAROLINE.—Chap I.

MOUVEMENT.

There was bustle of no common sort in the fortress of La Caroline. The breezes of September had purged and relieved of its evil influences the stagnant atmosphere of summer. The sick of the garrison had crawled forth beneath the pleasant shadows of the palms, that grew between the fortress and the river banks, and there were signs of life and animation in the scene and among its occupants, which testified to the favorable change which healthier breezes and more encouraging moral influences, were about to produce among the sluggish inhabitants of our little colony. There were particular occasions for movement apart from the cheering aspects of the season. Enterprise was afoot with all its eagerness and hope. Men were to be seen, in armor, hurrying to and fro, busy in the work of preparation, while Monsieur Laudonniere himself, just recovered from a severe illness, conspicuous in the scene, appeared to have cast aside no small portion of his wonted apathy and inactivity. He was in the full enjoyment of his authority. He had baffled the disease which preyed upon him, and had defeated the conspiracy by which his life and power had been threatened. He was now disposed to think lightly of the dangers he had passed, though his having passed them, in safety, had tended greatly to encourage his hope and to stimulate his adventure. He now stood, in full uniform, at the great gate of the fortress, reading at intervals from a paper in his grasp, while extending his orders to his lieutenants. He was evidently preparing to make considerable use of his authority. It is, perhaps, permitted to a Gascon to do so, at all seasons, even when he owes his security to better wits than his own, and has achieved his successes in his own despite. Our worthy captain of the Huguenot garrison upon the river of May, was not the less disposed to insist upon his authority, because it had been saved to him without his own participation. It might have been difficult, under any circumstances, to persuade him of that, and certainly, the conviction, even if he had entertained it, would, at this juncture, have done nothing to dissipate or lessen the confident hope which prompted his present purposes. The present was no ordinary occasion. It was as an ally of sovereigns that Laudonniere was extending his orders. He had, already, on several occasions, permitted his lieutenants to take part in the warfare between the domestic chieftains, and he was now preparing to engage in a contest which threatened to be of more than common magnitude and duration. A warfare that seldom knew remission had been long waged between the rival warriors, whose several dominions embraced the western line of the great Apalachian chain. Already had the Huguenots fought on the side of the great potentate Olata Utina, commonly called Utina, against another formidable prince called Potanou. He was now preparing to second with arms the ambition of Kings Hostaqua and Onathaqua, who were preparing for the utter annihilation of the power of the formidable Potanou. Of the two former kings, such had been the account brought to Laudonniere, that he at first imagined them to be Spaniards. They were described as going to battle in complete armor, with their breasts, arms and thighs covered with plates of gold, and with a helmet or headpiece of the same metal. Their armor defied the arrows of the savages, and proved the possession of a degree of civilization very far superior to anything in the experience or customs of the red-men. Subsequently it was ascertained that they were Indians like the rest. differing from the rest, however, in this other remarkable trait, that, while all the other tribes painted their faces red, these warriors of Hostaqua and Onathaqua employed black only to increase the formidable appearance which they made in battle. The golden armor used by this people, and the excess of the precious metals which this habit implied, were sufficient inducements for our Huguenot leader to attempt his present enterprise. It had furnished the argument of the conspirators against him, that he done so little towards the discovery of the precious metals; having provoked that cupidity, which his necessities alone compelled him to refuse to gratify. His error, at the present moment was, in employing other than the discontents of his colony in making the discovery. But of this hereafter.

Laudonniere had not been wholly neglectful, even while he seemed to sleep upon his arms, of the reported treasures of the country. He had sent two of his men, La Roche Ferrière a clever young ensign, and another, to dwell in the dominions of King Utina, and these two had been absent all the summer, engaged in rambling about the country. Others, as we have seen, were sent in other directions. Lieutenant Achille D'Erlach, the brother of the favorite Alphonse, had been absent in this way, during all the period when Laudonniere was threatened by conspiracy; and it was now decreed that, even while his brother continued absent, Alphonse should depart also. The eagerness of Laudonniere would admit of no delay. His curiosity had just received a new impulse from a present which had been sent him by Hostaqua, consisting of a " Luzerne's skinne full of arrows, a couple of bowes, foure or five skinnes painted after their manner, and a chaine of silver weighing about a pounde weight." These came with overtures of friendship and alliance, which the Huguenot chief did not deem it polite to disregard. He sent to the savage king, " two whole sutes of apparell, with certain cutting hookes or hatchets," and prepared to follow up his gifts, by sending a small detachment of picked soldiers, under Alphonse d'Erlach, still more thoroughly to fathom the secrets of the country, but ostensibly to unite with Hostaqua and his ally against the potent savage Potanou, who was described as a man of boundless treasures, also.

The bearer of these presents from Hostaqua was an inferior chieftain named Oolenoe. This cunning savage, of whom we shall know more hereafter, did not fail to perceive that the ruling passion of our Huguenots was gold. It was only, therefore, to mumble the precious word in imperfect Gallic—to extend his hand vaguely in the direction of the Apalachian summits, and cry "gold—gold!" and the adroit orator of the Lower Cherokees, on behalf of his tribe or nation, readily commanded the attention of his gluttonous auditors. His auguments and entreaties proved irresistible, and the present earnestness of Laudonniere, at La Caroline, was in preparing for this expedition. To conquer Potanou, and to obtain from Hostaqua the clues to the precious region where the gold was reputed to grow, with almost a vegetable nature, was the motive for arming his European warriors. It was also his policy, borrowed from that of the Spaniards, to set the native tribes upon one another;—a fatal policy in the end, since they must invariably, having first destroyed the inferior, turn upon the superior, through the irresistible force of habit. But, even with the former object, we do not perceive that there was any necessity to take any undue pains in its attainment. Tribes that live by hunting only, must unavoidably come into constant collision. No doubt the natural tendency of the savage might be stimulated and made more inveterate and active, by European arts; and Laudonniere, however Huguenot, was too little the Christian to forbear them. With this policy he proposed to justify himself to those who were averse to the present enterprise. One of these was his favorite, Alphonse D'Erlach, the youth to whom he owed his life. This young man, on the present occasion, approached him where he stood, eager and excited with the business of draughting the proper officers and men for the present hopeful expedition. At a little distance, stood the stern old savage, Oolenoe, grimly looking on with a satisfaction at his heart, which was not suffered to appear on his immovable features. The artist of the *statuesque* might have found in his attitude and appearance, an admirable model. While his eye caught and noted every look and movement, and his ear every known and unknown sound and accent, the calm unvarying expression of his glance and muscles was that of the most perfect and cool indifference. They only did not sleep. He leaned against a sapling that stood some twenty paces removed from the entrance of the fort, a loose cotton tunic about his loins, and his bow and quiver suspended from his shoulders, in a richly-stained and shell-woven belt, the ground work of which was cotton also. A knife, the gift of Laudonniere, was the only other weapon which he bore; but this was one of those very precious acquisitions which the Indian had already purposed to bury with him.

As Alphonse D'Erlach approached his commander, a close observer might have seen in the eyes of Oolenoe, an increased brilliancy of expression. The sentiment which it conveyed was not that of love. It is with quick, intelligent natures to comprehend, as by an instinct of their own, in what quarter to find sympathies, and whence their antipathies are to follow. Oolenoe had soon discovered that D'Erlach was not friendly to his objects. With this conviction there arose another feeling, that of contempt, with which the extreme youth, and general effeminacy of the young man's appearance, had inspired him. He did not *seem* the warrior,—and the Indian is not apt to esteem the person of whose conduct in battle he has doubts. Besides, the costume of D'Erlach was that of dandyism; and, though the North American savage was no humble proficient in the arts of the toilet, yet these are never ventured upon until the reputation of the hunter and warrior have been acquired. Of the abilities of D'Erlach, in these respects, Oolenoe had no knowledge; and his doubts, therefore, and disrespects, were the natural result of his conviction that the youth was suspicious of, and hostile to, himself. Of these feelings, D'Erlach knew nothing, and perhaps cared as little. His features, as he drew nigh to Laudonniere, were marked with more gravity and earnestness than they usually expressed; and, touching the wrist of his commander, as he approached him, he beckoned him somewhat farther from his followers:

"It is not too late," said he, "to escape this arrangement."

"And why seek to escape it, Alphonse?" replied the other, with something like impatience in his tones.

"For the best of reasons. You can have no faith in this savage. If there be this abundance of gold in the country, why brings he so little. Where are his proofs? But this is not all But lately our enemy, jealous of our presence, and only respectful because of his fears, we can have no confidence in him, as an ally. He will lead the men whom you give him, into ambuscade —into remote lands, where provision will be found with difficulty, —require to be fought for at every step, and where the best valor in the world, and the best conduct will be unavailing for their extrication."

"To prevent this danger, Alphonse, you shall have command of the detachment," said Laudonniere, with a dry accent, and a satirical glance of the eye.

"I thank you, sir, for this proof of confidence," replied the other, no ways disquieted, "and shall do my best to avoid or prevent the evils that I apprehend from it; but ——"

"I have every confidence in your ability to do so, Alphonse," said the other, interrupting him in a tone which still betrayed the annoyance which he felt from the expostulations of his favorite. The latter proceeded, after a slight but respectful inclination of the head.

"But there is another consideration of still greater importance. Your security in La Caroline is still a matter of uncertainty. You know not the extent of the late conspiracy. You know not who are sound, and who doubtful, among your men. Le Genré, Fourneaux, Le Genevois, and La Roquette, are still in the woods. You are weakening yourself, lessening the resources of the fortress, and may, at any moment ——"

"Pshaw!" exclaimed Laudonniere, with renewed impatience. 'You are only too suspicious, Alphonse. You make too much of this conspiracy. It does not seem to me that it was ever so dangerous. At all events, the danger is over, the ringleaders banished and in the woods, and will rot there, if the wolves do not devour them. They, at least, shall not be made wolves of for me."

D'Erlach bowed in silence. His mouth was sealed against all further expostulation. He saw that it was hopeless—that his captain had got a fixed idea, and men of few ideas, making one of them a favorite, are generally as immovable as death. Besides, Alphonse saw that the obligations which he had so lately conferred upon his commander, in baffling the conspiracy of Le Genré, by his vigilance, had somewhat wounded his *amour propre*. It is a misfortune, sometimes, to have been too useful. The consciousness of a benefit received, is apt to be very burdensome to the feeble nature. The quick instinct of Alphonse D'Erlach readily perceived the condition of his captain's heart. A momentary pause ensued. Lifting his cap, he again addressed him, but with different suggestions.

"Am I to hope, sir, that you really design to honor me with this command?"

"Certainly, if you wish it, Alphonse."

"I certainly wish it, sir, if the expedition be resolved on."

"It is resolved on," said Laudonniere, with grave emphasis.

"I shall then feel myself honored with the command."

"Be it yours, lieutenant. In one hour be ready to receive your orders."

"One minute, sir, will suffice for all personal preparation;" and, with the formal customs of military etiquette, the two officers bowed, as the younger of them withdrew to his quarters. In one hour, he was on the march with twenty men, accompanied by Oolenoe and his dusky warriors.

CHAPTER II.—THE OUTLAWS.

The little battalion of Alphonse D'Erlach marched along the edge of a wood which skirted a pleasantly rising ground—one of those gentle undulations which serve to relieve the monotonous levels of the lower regions of Florida. Deep was the umbrage—dense in its depth of green, and dark in its voluminous foliage, the thicket which overlooked their march. Their eyes might not penetrate the enclosure, from which eyes of hate were yet looking forth upon them. The wood concealed the outlaws who had lately made their escape from La Caroline, after the exposure of their conspiracy. They had not ceased to be conspirators. Bold, bad men—sleepless discontents, yearning for plunder and power—the defeat of their schemes, and the necessity of their sudden flight from the scene of their operations, had not lessened the bitterness of their feelings, nor their propensity to evil. Fierce were the glances which they shot forth upon the small troop which D'Erlach conducted before their eyes on his purposes of doubtful policy. Little did he dream what eyes were looking upon him. Could they have blasted with a glance or curse, he had been transformed with all his followers where he passed. But the three conspirators had no power for more than curses. These, though "not loud, were deep." With clenched fists extended towards him on his progress, they devoted him to the wrath of a power which they did not themselves possess; and, watching his course through the parted foliage, until he was fairly out of sight, they delivered themselves, in muttered execrations, of the hate with which his very sight had inspired them. Stephen Le Genevois was the first to speak. He was a stalwart savage, of broad chest, black beard, and most dauntless expression.

"Death of my soul!" was his exclamation; "but that we have lost so much by the game, it were almost merry to laugh at the way in which that brat of a boy has outwitted us. We have been children in his hands."

"He is now in ours," said La Roquette, gloomily.

"Aye, if the Indian keeps his faith," was the desponding comment of Fourneaux.

"And why should he not keep faith," said Le Genevois. "He has good reason for it. When did the hope of plunder fail to secure the savage?"

'You must give him blood with it," responded Fourneaux.

"Aye, it must be seasoned. He must have blood," echoed La Roquette.

"Well, and why not? Do we not give him blood? will he not have this imp of Satan in his power? may he not feed on him if he will? Aye, and upon all his twenty!" exclaimed Le Genevois, fiercely.

"True—but ——"

"But, but, but—ever with your buts! You lack confidence, courage, heart, Fourneaux—you despair too easily! I wonder how you ever became a conspirator!"

"I sometimes wonder myself. Ask La Roquette, there. He can tell you. I owe it all to his magic."

"What says your magic now, Roquette—have you any signs for us?"

"Aye, good ones! We shall have what we desire. I have seen—I have said! Be satisfied." This was spoken with due solemnity by the person in whom the credulity of his companions had found sources of power unknown to their experience.

"But why not show us what you have seen? Speak plainly, man. Out with it, and leave that mysterious shaking of the head, which has really nothing in it."

Such was the language of the more manly and impetuous Le Genevois. It provoked only a fierce glance from the magician.

"All in good time," said the latter. "Be patient. We shall soon hear from Oolenoe."

"Good! and you have seen that we shall be successful?" demanded Fourneaux.

"We shall be successful."

"That will depend upon ourselves, rather than upon your visions, I'm thinking," said Le Genevois. "We must have courage, my friends. The signs are not good when we call for signs. If we despond, we are undone."

"Stay—hark!" said Fourneaux, interrupting him eagerly. "I hear sounds."

"The wind only."

"No!—hist."

They bent forward in the attitude of listeners, but heard nothing. They had begun again to speak, when an Indian, covered with leaves artfully glued upon his person, stood suddenly among them. They started to their feet and grasped their weapons.

"*Ami!*" was the single word of the intruder, at he stretched out his arms in signification of friendship.

"Said I not?" demanded the magician, confidently. "This is our man."

His assurance was confirmed by the savage, who spoke the French sufficiently to make himself understood. He came from Oolenoe, and a few sentences sufficed to place both parties in possession of their mutual plans. The outlaws were not without friends in La Caroline. They were to find their way once more into that fortress. They had no fears from the sagacity of Laudonniere, during the absence of the youthful but vigilant D'Erlach; and, for the latter, he was to be disposed of by Oolenoe. And now the question arose, who should venture to "bell the cat?" who should venture himself within the walls of La Caroline?

"Ah!" said one of the conspirators, "if we could only bring Le Genré to his senses. He would be the man."

"Speak nothing of him," cried Le Genevois, quickly; "he is no longer a man. He is a priest. That defeat has killed his courage. He repents, and is constantly writing to Laudonniere for mercy and pity, and all that sort of thing. He must not know what we design."

"Who has seen him lately?"

"I know not. He was crossed to the other side of the river by Captain Bourdet in his boats. He crossed to seek refuge with the people of Mollova."

"He is not far, be sure. He will linger close to the fort, in the hope to get back to it, and, finally, to France. He is not to be thought of in this expedition."

"Who then?" was the demand of Le Genevois. "Somebody must muzzle the cannon. Who? Who will take the peril and the glory of the enterprise, and in the character of an Indian, will put his head in the jaws of the danger?"

The question remained unanswered. Fourneaux excused himself on a variety of pleas, not one of which would be satisfactory with a brave man. La Roquette declared that his magical powers were always valueless when any restraint was set upon his person; in other words, he could better perform his incantations when the danger threatened everybody but himself. He certainly would not think of risking them within La Caroline, while Laudonniere was in power. Besides " he had no arts of imitation. He had no abilities as an actor." Stephen Le Genevois smiled as he listened to their pleas and excuses.

" My friends !" he exclaimed. " Did you think that I would suffer a good scheme to be spoiled by such as you? I but waited that you should speak. This adventure is mine, and I claim it. I will return to La Caroline. I will play the spy, and take the danger. Mark ye, now, comrade !"—addressing the Indian,— " prepare me for the business. Clothe me in copper, and make me what you please. I have no beauty that you need fear to spoil."

Thus saying, he threw off, with an air of scornful recklessness, the costume which he wore. Wild was the toilet, and wilder still the guise of our buoyant Frenchman. In an open space within the thicket, beneath a great moss-covered oak, which wore the beard of three centuries upon his breast, the chief conspirator yielded himself to the hands of the Indian. A keen knife shore from his head the thick black hair with which it was covered. A thin ridge alone was suffered to remain upon the coronal region, significant of the war-lock of that tribe of Apalachia, to which Oolenoe belonged. The small golden droplets which hung from the Frenchman's ears, were made to give way to a more massive ornament of shells, cunningly strung upon a hoop of copper wire.

His body, stripped to the buff, was then stained with the brown juices of a native plant, which, with other dye-stuffs, the Indian produced from his wallet. His brow was then dyed with deeper hues of red—his cheeks tinged with spots of the darkest crimson, while a heavy circlet of black, about his eyes, gave to his countenance the aspect of a demon rather than that of a man. This done, the savage displayed a small pocket mirror before the eyes of the metamorphosed outlaw. With an oath of no measured emphasis, the Frenchman bounded to his feet, his eyes flashing with a strange delight.

"It will do!" he shouted. "It likes me well! Were I now in France, there would be no wonder beside myself. I should stir the envy of the men—I should win the hearts of the women. I should be the loveliest monster. Ho! Ho! Would that my voice would suit my visage!"

A cotton tunic with which the Indian had provided himself, was wrapped round the loins of our new-made savage, his feet were cased with moccasins, and his legs with leggins made of deerskin—a bow and quiver at his shoulder—a knife in his girdle —a string of peag or shells about his neck;—and his toilet was complete. That very night, accompanied by his Indian comrade, Stephen Le Genevois entered the walls of La Caroline, bearing messages from Oolenoe and Alphonse D'Erlach—the latter of which, we need scarcely say, were wholly fraudulent. The credulous Laudonniere, delighted with assurances of success on the part of his lieutenant, was not particularly heedful of the nature of the evidence thus afforded him, and laid his head on an easy pillow, around which danger hovered in almost visible forms, while he, unconsciously, dreamed only of golden conquests, and discoveries which were equally to result in fame and fortune

His guardian angel was withdrawn. His mortified vanity had driven from his side the only person whose vigilance might have saved him. His own unregulated will had yielded him, bound, hand and foot, into the power of a relentless enemy.

CHAPTER III.—THE MIDNIGHT ARREST.

SWEET were the slumbers of Monsieur Laudonniere, commandant of the fortress of La Caroline. Anxious was the wakening of Stephen Le Genevois, the conspirator, who, in garbing himself after the fashion of the Indian, had not succeeded in clothing his mind in the stolid and stoic nature of his savage companion. The conspirators watched together in one of the inner chambers of the fortress. They had not restricted themselves to watching merely. Already had Le Genevois made his purpose known to one of his ancient comrades. The name of this person was La Croix. He was one of the trusted followers of Laudonniere, whose superior cunning alone had saved him from suspicion, even that of D'Erlach, at the detection of the former conspiracy. La Croix, in the absence of the latter, was prepared for more decisive measures He was one of those whose insane craving for gold had surrendered him, against all good policy, to the purposes of the conspirators. He was now in charge of the watch. As captain of the night, he led the way to the gates, which, at midnight, he cautiously threw open to the two companions of Le Genevois. Fourneaux and Roquette had been waiting for this moment. They were admitted promptly and in silence. Darkness was around them. The fortress slept,—none more soundly than its commander. In silence the outlaws led by La Croix, all armed to the teeth, made their way to his chamber. The sentinel who watched before it, joined himself to their number. They entered without obstruction and without noise; and, ere the eyes of the sleeper could unclose to his danger, or his lips cry aloud for succor, his voice was stifled in his throat by thick bandagings of silk, and his limbs fastened with cords which, at every movement of his writhing frame, cut into the springing flesh. He was a prisoner in the very fortress, where, but that day, he exulted in the consciousness of complete command. A light, held above his eyes, revealed to him the persons of his assailants;—the supposed Indians, in the outlaws whom he had banished, and others, whom, for the first time, he knew as enemies. When his eyes were suffered to take in the aspects of the whole group, he was addressed, in his own tongue, by the leading conspirator.

"René Laudonniere," said Stephen Le Genevois, in his bitter tones, "you are in our power. What prevents that we put you to death as you merit, and thus revenge our disgrace and banishment?"

The wretched man, thus addressed, had no power to answer. The big tears gathered in his eyes and rolled silently down his cheeks. He felt the pang of utter feebleness upon him.

"We will take the gag from your jaws, if you promise to make no outcry. Nod your head in token that you promise."

The prisoner had no alternative but to submit. He nodded, and the kerchief was taken from his jaws.

"You know us, René Laudonniere?" demanded the conspirator.

"Stephen Le Genevois, I know you!" was the answer.

"'Tis well! You see to what you have reduced me. You have held a trial upon me in my absence. You have sentenced me and my companions to banishment. You have made us outlaws, and we are here! You see around you none but those on whom you have exercised your tyranny. What hope have you at their hands and mine? Savage as you have made me in aspect, what should prevent that I show myself equally savage in performance. The knife is at your throat, and there is not one of us who is not willing to execute justice upon you. Are you prepared to do what we demand?"

"What is it?"

"Read this paper."

A light was held close to the eyes of the prisoner, and the paper placed near enough for perusal. The instrument was a commission of piracy—a sort of half-legal authority, common enough in that day, to the marine of all European countries, under maxims of morality such as made the deeds of Drake, and Hawkins, and other British admirals, worthy of all honor, which, in our less chivalric era, would consign them very generally to the gallows.

As Laudonniere perused the document, he strove to raise himself, as with a strong movement of aversion;—but the prompt grasp of Genevois fastened him down to the pillow.

"No movement, or this!"—showing the dagger. "Have you read?"

"I will not sign that paper!" said the prisoner, hoarsely.

"Will you not?"

"Never!"

"You have heard the alternative!"

Laudonniere was silent.

"You do not speak! Beware, René Laudonniere. We have no tender mercies! We are no children! We are ready for any crime. We have already incurred the worst penalties, and have nothing to fear. But you can serve us, living, quite as effectually as if dead. We do not want your miserable fortress. We are not for founding colonies. It is your ships that we will take, and your commission. We will spare your life for these. Beware! Let your answer square with your necessities."

"Genevois!" said the prisoner, "even this shall be pardoned —you shall all be pardoned—if you will forego your present purpose."

"Pshaw!" exclaimed the person addressed. "This to me! I scorn your pardon as I do your person! Speak to what concerns you, and what is left for you to do. Speak, and quickly, too, for the dawn must not find us here."

"I will not sign!" said the prisoner, doggedly.

"Then you die!" and the dagger was uplifted.

"Strike—why do you stop?" exclaimed Fourneaux; "we can slay him, and forge the paper."

His threatening looks and attitude, with the stern air which overspread the visage of Genevois, and, indeed, of all around him contributed to overcome the resolution of the wretched commander. Besides, a moment's reflection served to satisfy him, that the conspirators, having gone too far to recede, would not scruple at the further crime which they threatened.

"Will my life be spared if I sign? Have I *your* oath, Stephen Le Genevois? I trust none other."

"By G—d and the Blessed Saviour! as I hope to be saved, René Laudonniere, you shall have your life and freedom!"

"Undo my hands and give me the paper."

"The right hand only," said Fourneaux, with his accustomed timidity.

"Pshaw, unbind him!" exclaimed Genevois; "unbind him, wholly. There, René Laudonniere, you are free!"

"I cannot forgive you, Genevois; you have disgraced me forever," said the miserable man, as he dashed his signature upon the paper.

"You will survive it, *mon ami*," replied the other, with something like contempt upon his features. "You are not the man to fret yourself into fever, because of your hurts of honor. And now must you go with us to the ships. We will muffle your jaws once more."

"You will not carry me with you," demanded the commander, with something like trepidation in his accents.

"No! You were but an incumbrance. We will only take you to the ships, and keep you safe until we are ready to cast off. To your feet, men, and get your weapons ready. Softly, softly— we need rouse no other sleepers. Onward,—the night goes!— away!"

XV.

THE MUTINEERS AT SEA.

HISTORICAL SUMMARY.

For fifteen days was Laudonniere kept a close prisoner by the conspirators on board of one of his own vessels, attended by one of their own number, and denied all intercourse with his friends and people. One of the objects of this rigid *duresse*, was the coercion of the garrison. With its captain in their power, even were his followers better prepared, with the proper spirit and energy, to give them annoyance, they were thus able to put them at defiance; since any show of hostility on the part of the garrison might be visited upon the head of their prisoner. By this means they got possession of the armory, the magazines, the granaries; and, when ready to put to sea, and not before, did they release the unhappy commandant from his degrading durance.

It was at dawn on the morning of the 8th of December, that the two barks which the conspirators had prepared for sea, might have been seen dropping down the waters of May River, their white sails gleaming through the distant foliage. At the same moment, with head bowed upon his bosom, the unhappy Laudonniere, for the first time fully conscious of his weakness and his misfortune,—deeply sensible now to all his shame as he reflected upon the roving commission which had been extorted from him by the mutineers,—turned his footsteps from the banks of the river, and made his way slowly towards the fortress;—confident no longer in his strength—suspicious of the faith of all around him—and half tempted to sink his shame forever, with his dishonored person, in the waters of the river which had witnessed his disgrace. But he gathered courage to live when he thought of the revenge which fortune might yet proffer to his embrace.

We must now follow the progress of our maritime adventurers. They had, as we have seen, succeeded in fitting out two barks; one on which was confided to Bertrand Conferrant, one of Laudonniere's sergeants; the other to a soldier named D'Orange. La Croix was named the ensign to the former; Trenchant, the pilot of Laudonniere, was compelled, against his will, to assume this station on board the vessel of D'Orange. The original plan of the rovers was to pursue a common route, and mutually to support each other: but the plans of those who have given themselves up to excess, are always marked by caprices, and the two parties quarrelled before they had left the mouth of the river. They had arranged to descend together upon one of the Spanish islands of the Antilles, and on Christmas night, while the inhabitants were assembled at the midnight mass, at their church, to set upon and murder the inmates and sack the building and the town. Their dissentions affected this purpose; and when they emerged from the river May, they parted company;—one of the vessels keeping along the coast, in order the more easily to double the cape and make for Cuba;—the other boldly standing out to sea and making for the Lucayos. Both vessels proceeded with criminal celerity to the performance of those acts of piracy which had seduced them from their duties. The bark which took her way along the coast, was that of D'Orange. Near a place called Archaha, he took a brigantine laden with *cassavi*, the Indian breadstuff, and a small quantity of wine. Two men were slain, two taken in a sharp encounter with the people of Archaha. Transferring themselves and stores to the brigantine which they had captured, on account of its superiority, the pirates made sail for the cape of Santa Maria; and from thence, after repairing a leak in their vessel, to Baracou, a village of the island of Jamaica. Here they found an empty caravel which they preferred to their brigantine; and after a frolic among the people of Baracou, which lasted five days, they made a second transfer of their persons and material to the caravel. Dividing their force between their own and this vessel, which was of fifty or sixty tons burthen, they made for the Cape of Tiburon, where they met with a *patach*, to which chase was immediately given. A sharp encounter followed. The *patach* was well manned and provided, for her size. She had particular reasons for giving battle and for fighting bravely. Her cargo was very precious. It consisted of a large supply of gold and silver plate and bullion, merchandise, wines, provisions, and much besides to tempt the rovers, and quite as much to move the crew to a vigorous defence. But, over all, it had a-board the Governor of Jamaica himself, with two of his sons. This nobleman was equally fearless and skilful. He directed the resistance of his people, and gave them efficient example. But the force of our rovers was quite too great to be successfully resisted by one so small as that of the Governor, and he directed his people to yield the combat, as soon as he saw its hopelessness.

Greatly, indeed, were our free companions delighted with their successes. The treasure they had acquired was large, but they were not the persons to be content with it. They were apprised of another caravel laden with greater wealth and a more valuable merchandise, and they followed eagerly after this prey. But she escaped them, getting in safety into the port of Jamaica. The governor was a subtle politician. He soon discovered the character of the men with whom he had to deal, and he wrought successfully upon their cupidity. He proposed to ransom himself at an enormous price; and, with this object, they stood towards the mouth of the harbor in which the caravel had taken shelter. Blinded by their avarice, our rovers were persuaded to suffer the governor to despatch his two boys to their mother, his wife, in a boat which his captors were to furnish. The boys were to procure his ransom, and supplies were to be sent to the vessel also. But the secret counsel of the Governor to his sons, contemplated no such ransom as the free companions desired. They knew not that, in one of the contiguous havens, there lay two or more vessels, superior in burthen to their own, and manned and equipped for war. The Governor, with but a look and a word, beheld his sons depart. The lads knew the meaning of that look, and that single word; they felt all the ignominy of their father's position, and they knew their duty. A noble and courageous dame was the mother of those boys. With tears and tremors did she clasp her children to her breast; with horror did she hear of her lord's captivity; but she yielded to no feminine weaknesses which could retard her in the performance of her duty. Her movements were prompt and resolute. The Governor concealed his anxieties, and spoke fairly to his captors. Quite secure in their strength and position, eager with expectations of further gain, rioting in the rich wines they had already won, they entertained no apprehen sions of defeat or disappointment. They lay at the mouth of the haven, which stretched away for two leagues into the mainland. Here, suddenly, about the break of day, they saw emerging through a heavy fog, a couple of vessels of greater size than their own. Apprehending no danger, the pirates were taken by surprise The enemy was upon them before they could prepare for action, and they had scarcely an opportunity to attempt their flight. A volley of Spanish shot soon rang against their sides, and as the trumpets of D'Orange, from his brigantine, blew to announce their danger to those in charge of the captured vessels, he cut his cables and stood off for sea, closely pressed by his swift-footed enemies. Then it was that, watching his moment, the Governor of Jamaica seized upon the enemy nearest him and plunged him into the sea. His example was followed by his people, and the Spaniards coming up with the captured *patach* at the fortunate moment, the Frenchmen, with whom it was left in charge, threw down their arms, and yielded themselves at discretion to their enemies. Both vessels were recovered, while the brigantine of D'Orange, well navigated by Trenchant, succeeded in showing a clean pair of heels to her pursuers. The chase continued for several leagues without success ; and the brigantine, passing Cape des Aigrettes, and the Cape of St. Anthony, swept on to the Havanna. This was the desired destination of D'Orange; but his people were not wholly with him. Several of them, like Trenchant, the pilot, had been forced to accompany the expedition. These were anxious to escape from a connection which was not only against their desires, but was likely, by the crimes of their superiors, to result in the destruction of the innocent. Accordingly, under the guidance of Trenchant, a conspiracy was conceived against the conspirators. The wind serving, while D'Orange slept, Trenchant passed the channel of the Bahamas, and made over for the settlement on May River. The route taken was unsuspected, until the morning of the 25th of March, when they found themselves upon the coast of Florida. By this time, it was too late to prevent the determination of those who had resolved upon their return to La Caroline. The latter had grown strong by consultation together, and the true men urged the less guilty of the conspirators with promises of pardon at the hands of Laudonniere. This hope gradually extended to some of the most guilty; but the discussion which led to this conclusion, was productive of a scene which strikingly illustrates the profligacy of the human heart, particularly when it once throws off the restraints of social authority. The unhappy criminals, in nominal command of the roving brigantine were prepared to dance upon the brink of the precipice,—to sport with the dangers immediately before them, and convert into a farce the very tragedy whose denouêment they had every reason to dread. Well charged with wine, and quaffing full beakers to fortune, they suddenly conceived the idea of a mock court of justice, for the trial of their own offences. The idea was scarcely suggested than it was fastened upon by the wanton imaginations of this besotted crew. The court was convened, on the deck of the vessel, as it would have been at La Caroline. One of the parties personated the character of the judge: another counterfeited the costume and manner of Laudonniere, and appeared as the accuser. Counsel was heard on both sides. There were officers to wait upon and obey the decrees of the court. The cases were elaborately argued. Heavy accusations were made; ingenious pleas put in; and in the very excess of their recklessness, their ingenuity became triumphant. They showed themselves excellent actors, if not excellent men;

and caught from their own art, a momentary respite from the oppressive doubts which hung upon their destinies. It was somewhat ominous, however, that their judge—himself one of the most guilty—should say to them, when summing up for judgment—" Make your case as clear as you please—exert your ingenuity as you may, in finding excuses, yet, take my word for it, that, when you reach La Caroline, if Laudonniere causes you not to swing for it, then I will never take him for an honest man again."

This may have been intended as a mere jocularity. But fate frequently shapes our own words, as she does those of the oracle, in that double sense, which confounds the judgment while it ensures the doom. The counterfeit judge spoke prophetically. It was only when the offenders were fairly in the hands of Laudonniere, beyond escape or remedy, that they were taught to apprehend that they had too greatly exaggerated their sense of his mercy. He detached immediately from the rest four of the leading criminals, who were put in fetters. That was the judgment that prefigured their doom. They were sentenced to be hanged. They strove to question this judgment. The pleasant jest which they had enjoyed on ship-board was quite too recent, to suffer them to forego the hope that this summary decision upon their fate would turn out a jest also. But when they could doubt no longer, three of them took to their prayers with an appearance of much real contrition. The fourth,—a sturdy villain,—still had his faith in human agency. He appealed for protection to his friends and comrades.

"What," said he, "brethren and companions, will you suffer us to die so shamefully?"

"These are none of your companions," said Laudonniere;—

"they are no authors of seditions—no rebels unto the king's service. Ye appeal to them in vain."

A corps of thirty soldiers with their matchlocks ready, and under the command of Alphonse D'Erlach, who had returned from his Indian expedition, and who now stood ready and prompt to execute the orders of the chief, were, perhaps, more potent in silencing the appeal of the mutineer, and quieting the active sympathies of those to whom he prayed, than all the words of Laudonniere. But, at the entreaty of his people, the form of punishment was changed, and the criminals, instead of perishing by the rope, met their death from the matchlock. Among the victims of this necessary justice, were three of the original conspirators, and the ringleader, Stephen le Genevois. Thus ends the history of one of our roving vessels. The other, commanded by Bertrand Conferrent, which we parted with, on her progress towards the Lucayos, was never heard of after, and probably perished in the deeps, with all her besotted crew. Let us now leave the ocean, and follow, for a season, the progress of Alphonse D'Erlach upon the land, and into the territories of Paracoussi Hostaqua.

XVI.

THE ADVENTURE OF D'ERLACH.

It was in sullen and half resentful mood that Alphonse D'Arlach parted from his superior at the gates of *La Caroline*. Not that he felt any chagrin because of an outraged self-esteem, on account of his rejected counsels. His mortification and annoyance arose from his vexation at leaving a man in the hands of his enemies, whom he could not persuade of his danger, and who was, by this very proceeding, depriving himself of the only means with which he may have safely combated their hostility. It was probably with a justifiable sense of his own efficiency, that D'Erlach felt how necessary was his presence in the garrison at this juncture. He was quite familiar with the vanity of Laudonniere, his several weaknesses of character, and the facility with which he might be deluded by the selfish and the artful. But he had counselled him in vain; and it was with a feeling somewhat allied to scorn, that he was taught to see that his superior, having hitherto regarded him with something more than friendship—as a favorite indeed—had now, in consequence of the most important services, begun to look upon him somewhat in the light of a rival. We have witnessed the last interview between them. We are already in possession of the events which followed the absence of the lieutenant; events which positively would not have taken place, had not the scheme proved successful for procuring his absence from the fortress. Laudonniere's conscience smote him with a sense of his ingratitude, as the flowing plumes of D'Erlach disappeared amidst the distant umbrage; but he had no misgivings of that danger which the prescient thought of his lieutenant had described as already threatening. He had sufficient time allowed him to meditate equally upon his own blindness and the foresight of the youth, while his mutineers, for fifteen days kept him a close prisoner on board his own brigantine!

During this period, his young lieutenant, with his twenty Frenchmen, was making his way from forest to forest, under the somewhat capricious guidance of the subtle savage, Oolenoe. D'Erlach was more than once dissatisfied with this progress. He found himself frequently doubling, as it were, upon his own ground; not steadily ascending the country in the supposed direction of the Apatahhian Mountains, but rather inclining to the southwest, and scarcely seeming to leave those lower *steppes* which belonged wholly to the province of the sea. Without absolutely suspecting his dusky guide, D'Erlach was eminently watchful of him, and frequently pressed his inquiries in regard to the route they were pursuing,—when—noting the course of the sun, he found himself still turning away from those distant mountain summits which were said to await them in the north, with all their world of treasure. The plea of Oolenoe, while acknowledging a temporary departure from the proper path, alleged the difficulties of the country, the spread of extensive morasses, or the presence of nations of hostile Indians, which cut off all direct communication with the province which they sought.

To all this D'Erlach had nothing to oppose. The pretences

seemed sufficiently specious, and he continued to advance deep and deeper into the internal intricacies of the unbroken wild, making a progress, day by day, into regions which the European had never penetrated before. On this progress, each soldier had been provided with a certain allowance of food of a portable nature, which was calculated to last many days. The adoption of the Indian customs, in several respects, had made it easy to provide. The maize and beans of the country constituted the chief supply. The former, and sometimes both, crushed or ground, separately or together, and browned slightly before the fire, furnished a wholesome and literally palatable provision for such a journey. They were also to receive supplies from the contributions of Indian tribes through whose settlements they were to pass, and to traffic with other nations whom as yet they did not know. With this latter object the party was provided with a small stock of European trifles—knives, reaphooks, small mirrors, and things of this description.

Thus provided, they pressed forward for several days, on a journey which brought them no nearer to the province which they sought. Still the country through which they travelled was unbroken by a mountain. Gentle eminences saluted their eyes, and they sometimes toiled over hills which, even their exhaustion, which rendered irksome the ascent, did not venture to compare with those mighty ranges, scaling the clouds, of which the swelling narratives of the savage chiefs, and their own adventurers, had given such extravagant ideas. In this march they probably reached the Savannah, and crossed its waters to the rivers of Carolina. The scenery improved in loveliness, and to those who are accessible to the influences of mere external beauty, the progress at every step was productive of its own charm. Gentle valleys spread away before them in the embrace of guardian ranges of hill, and clear streams gushed out through banks that seemed to gladden in perpetual green. Enormous trees spread over them a grateful cover from the sun, and luscious berries of the wood, and unknown fruits, green and purple, were to be found lying in their path, which was everywhere traversed by the trailing vines which produced them. Birds of unknown plumage, and of wild and startling song, darted out from the brake to cheer them as they passed; and as they reached the steeps of sudden hills, they could catch glimpses of herds of sleek deer, that sped away with arrowy fleetness from the green valleys where they browsed, to the cover of umbrageous thickets where they lodged in safety.

The mind of the soldier, however, particularly the adventurer whom one passionate thirst alone impels, is scarcely ever sensible to the charms and attractions of the visible nature. Where they appeal simply to his sense of the beautiful, they are but wasted treasures, like gems that pave the great bed of ocean, and have no value to the finny tribes that glide below—each seeking the selfish object which marks his nature. The passion for the beautiful, with but few exceptions, is a passion that belongs to training and education; and even these seldom suffice, in the presence of more morbid desires, to wean the attention to the things of taste, unless these are recognized as accessories of the object of a more intense appetite. Even Alphonse D'Erlach, the *élève* of a superior class—one who had been benefitted by society and the schools, appreciated but imperfectly the loveliness of the landscape, and the fresh luxuriance of a vegetable life in a region that seemed so immediately from the hands of its Creator. His thoughts were of another nature. His anxieties were elsewhere. His eye was fixed upon his Indian guide, of whom his doubts had now become suspicions. Nightly had Oolenoe disappeared from the encampment. It was in vain that our lieutenant set spies upon his movements. He would disappear without giving the alarm and re-appear, when least expected, before the dawning. D'Erlach's vigilance was increased. He did not suffer his men to straggle; marching with care by day, his watches were equally divided by night, and his own eyes were kept open by intense anxiety, through hours when most were sleeping. Occasionally, glimpses of Indians were caught on distant hills, or on the edge of suddenly glancing waters. But any attempt to approach sent them into their canoes, or over the hill side—increasing the suspicions of D'Erlach, and awakening the apprehensions of his men. A something of insolence in the tone and manner of Oolenoe led our young lieutenant to suppose that the moment of trial was at hand; and he already began to meditate the seizure of his guide, as a security for the conduct of the Indians, when an incident occurred which the foresight of our lieutenant, great as it was, had never led him to anticipate.

It was at the close of a lovely evening in September, when the little detachment of Frenchmen were rounding a ravine. Oolenoe was advanced with D'Erlach some few paces before the rest. Both of them were silent; but they pressed forward stoutly, through a simple forest trail, over which the Frenchmen followed in Indian file. Suddenly, their march was arrested by a cry from the foot of the ravine, in the rear of the party, and along the path which they had recently traversed. The cry was human. It was that of a voice very familiar to the ears of the party. It was evidently meant to compel attention and arrest their progress At the instant, D'Erlach wheeled about and made for the rear.

A similar movement changed in like manner the faces of his followers; and, in a moment after, a strange, but human form darted out of the forest and made towards them.

The appearance of the stranger was wild beyond description. He had evidently once been white; but his face, hands, breast, and legs, for these were all uncovered, had been blackened by smoke, bronzed by the sun, and so affected by the weather, that it was with the greatest difficulty that his true complexion was discernible. But sure instincts and certain features soon enabled our Huguenots to see that he was a brother Frenchman. Of his original garments, nothing but tatters remained; but these tatters sufficed to declare his nation. His beard and hair, both black, long, and massive, were matted together, and hung upon neck and shoulders in flakes and bunches, rather than in shreds or tresses. His head was without covering, and the only weapon which he carried was a *couteau de chasse*, which, as it was of peculiar dimensions, silver-hilted, and altogether of curious shape, was probably the only means by which the Frenchmen identified the stranger.

The keen, quick eye of Alphonse D'Erlach seemed first, of the whites, to have discovered him. It is probable, from what took place at the moment, that Oolenoe had made him out in the same moment. The stranger was no other than Le Genré—the banished man who had headed the first conspiracy against Laudonniere. As he approached, rushing wildly forward, with his *couteau de chasse* grasped firmly in uplifted hand, D'Erlach raised his sword, prepared to cut him down as he drew nigh; when the words of his voice, shouted at the utmost of his strength, caused them to cast their eyes in another direction.

"Seize upon Oolenoe. Suffer him not to escape you."

At that moment, the keen, quick glance of the lieutenant beheld the rapid bounds of the savage, as he made for the cover of the neighboring thicket. His orders were instantly given. A dozen bodies instantly sprang forward in pursuit—a dozen matchlocks were lifted in deadly aim, but the lithe savage doubling like a hare, bounding forward, now squat, and seeming to fly along the surface of the ground like a lapwing, stealthy in every movement as a cat, as swift and agile,—succeeded in gaining the woods, though the carbines rang with their volley, and, throwing down their weapons, a score of the light-limbed Frenchmen started in the chase. A wild warwhoop followed the discharge of the pieces, declaring equally the defiance and disdain of the savage. The pursuit was idle, as a few seconds enabled him to find shelter in a morass, which the inexperienced Europeans knew not how to penetrate. Alphonse D'Erlach recalled his men from pursuit, fearing lest they might fall into an ambush, in which, wasting their ammunition against invisible enemies, they would only incur the risk of total destruction. He prepared to confront the stranger, whose first appearance had been productive of such a startling occurrence. Le Genré, meanwhile, had paused in his progress. He no longer rushed forward like a maniac ; but satisfied with having given the impulse to the pursuit of Oolenoe, and apparently conscious of how much was startling in his appearance, he now stood beside a pine which overhung the path, one hand resting against the mighty shaft, as if from fatigue, while from the other his *couteau de chasse* now drooped, its sharp extremity pointing to the ground.

His appearance thus indicated a pacific disposition ; but remembering his ancient treacheries only, and suspicious of his relations with Oolenoe, D'Erlach approached him with caution, as if to the encounter with an enemy. As he drew nigh, followed by his band, Le Genré addressed them with mournful accents.

"Is there no faith for me hereafter, *mes amis*? Am I forever cut off from the communion with my comrades? Shall there be no fellowship between us, D'Erlach? Shall we not forget the past—shall I not be forgiven for my crime, even when I repent it in bitterness and bloody tears. Behold, my brother—I proffer you the last assurance."

These words were accompanied by a sign, that of the mystic brotherhood—the ancient masons—which none but a few of the party beheld or comprehended. The weapon of Alphonse D'Erlach was dropped instantly, and his hand extended. He, too, belonged to the ancient order, and the security which was guaranteed by the exhibition of its token, on the part of the offender, served, when all other pleas would have failed, to secure him sympathy and protection.

"I have sinned, Alphonse—I know it—beyond forgiveness—sinned like a madman; but I have borne the penalty. Seldom has human sinner suffered from mental penalty, as I from mine. Behold me! look I longer human? I have taken up my covert with the wild beasts of the desert, and they fly from my presence as from a savage more fearful than any they know. In my own desperation I have had no fears. I have herded with beast and reptile, and longed for their hostility. I have lived through all, though I craved not to live, and the food which would have choked or poisoned the man not an outcast from communion with his fellows, has kept me strong, with a cruel vitality that has increased by suffering. The crude berries of the wood, the indigestible roots of the earth, I have devoured with a hideous craving; and, in the griefs and privations of my body, my mind has been purged of its impurities. I have seen my sin in its true colors—my folly, my vicious passions, the wretch that I was—the miserable outlaw and destitute that I am! That I repent of the crimes that I have done and sought to do, is the good fruit of this bitter on which I have rather preyed than fed. I wrote to Laudonniere of my sorrow and repentance, but he refused to hear me. Bourdet I sought, that he might take me once more to France; but he too dreaded communion with me; and when I rushed into his boat, he only bore me to the opposite shore of the river, and set me down to the exploration of new forests, and the endurance of new tortures. I blame them not, that they would not believe me—that they refused faith in one who had violated all faith before—that, equally due to his God and to his sovereign Oh! brother, do not *you* drive me from you also!"

And the miserable outlaw clasped his hands passionately together in entreaty, with a face wild with woe and despair, and would have fallen prostrate in humiliation before his comrades, if the arm of Alphonse D'Erlach had not sustained him.

"But what of this savage, Oolenoe!" demanded the lieutenant, when the first burst of grief had subsided from the lips of Le Genré.

"Ah! you know that I have been the prisoner to this savage, and to the very comrades of my sin. For this I have pursued you hither. While you march onward to snares such as the savages of Potanou have provided for you by means of this Oolenoe, treachery is busy and successful at La Caroline."

"Successful?"

"Ay! successful! But hear me. When I fled to the forest, I took sh..ter first with the people of Satouriova. I was found o.. and followed by Fourneaux, Stephen Le Genevois, and La

Roquette. To them, at times, came La Croix, whom Laudonniere still trusted, and whom even you did not suspect. They came to me with new plans. They were to contrive pretexts for sending you off to a distance, with the best men of the garrison. Oolenoe was a ready agent at once of Potanou, Satouriova, and the conspirators. In your absence, they were to get possession of the garrison and secure the person of Laudonniere."

"You mean not to say, Le Genré, that they have succeeded in this?"

"Ay, do I—the garrison is in their hands—the shipping; and Laudonniere is himself a close prisoner on board the unfinished brigantine."

"God of heaven! and I am here!"

"When the conspirators found that I no longer agreed to second them in their machinations, and when I threatened to expose them to Laudonniere, they employed Oolenoe to secure my person. Five of his people beset me at the same moment, and held me fast in one of their wigwams until their scheme had been carried into execution. With Laudonniere in their hands, I was abandoned by my keepers, and suffered to go forth. From them I learned the history of all that had taken place in the colony. I saw the danger, and felt that the only hope for Laudonniere lay in you. Fortunately, I had only to follow those who had held me captive, in order to find the route that you had taken. The people of Oolenoe were soon upon his tracks. I compassed theirs. It is one profit in the outlawed life which I have been doomed to endure, that it has taught me the arts of the savage—taught me the instincts of the beast,—his stealth, his endurance, his far-sight, and his eager and appreciating scent. Hark! dost hear! Put thy men in order. The subtle savage is about to gird thee in."

Scarcely had he spoken, when the forest was alive with cries of warfare. Wild whoops rang through the great avenues of wood, and sudden glimpses of the red-men, followed by flights of arrows, warned the Frenchmen still more emphatically to prepare against the danger. But the arrows, though discharged with skill and muscle, were sent from far;—the dread of the European firearms prompting a decent caution, which, in a great degree, lessened the superiority which the savages possessed in numbers. The woods were now filled with enemies. Tribe after tribe had collected, along their route, as the Frenchmen had advanced, and every forward step had served only to increase the great impediments in the way of their return. It was due wholly to the excellence of the watch nightly kept by D'Erlach, that they had not been butchered while they slept. It was in consequence of his admirable caution, and provision against attack while they marched, that they had not fallen into frequent ambush, as they moved by noonday. Nightly had the subtle chief, Oolenoe, stolen away to his comrades, arraying his numbers, and counselling their pursuit and progress. His schemes detected, the mask was thrown aside as no longer of use, and open warfare was the cry through the forests. The necessity was before our Frenchmen of fighting their way back. The effort of the red-men was to cut them off in detail, by frequent surprises, by incessant assaults and annoyances, and by straitening them in the search after water and provisions.

It would be a weary task to pursue, day by day, and hour by hour, the thousand details, by which each party endeavored to attain its object. The events of such a conflict must necessarily be monotonous Enough to say, that the whole genius of Alphonse D'Erlach was brought forth during the constant emergencies of his march and proved equal to them all. His first object was to pursue a new route on his return. This greatly shortened the distance, and increased the chances of food, since it was only from the route along which he came that Oolenoe had contrived the removal of all the provisions. The progress was thus varied on their return. It was enlivened by incessant attacks of the savages. Their arrows were continually showered upon our Frenchmen from every thicket that could afford an ambush; but, habited as they were with the *escaupil*, or stuffed cotton doublets, which the Spaniards had invented for protection in their warfare with the Indians, the damage from this source was comparatively small. Some few of the Frenchmen were galled by slight wounds, one or two were seriously hurt, and one of them suffered the loss of an eye. In all these conflicts, Le Genré fought with the greatest bravery—with a valor, indeed, that seemed to set at scorn every thought of danger or disaster. He was always the first to rush forward to the assault, and always the last to leave the pursuit, when the trumpets sounded the recal. He proved an admirable second to Alphonse D'Erlach, and materially contributed to the success of the various plans adopted by the latter for the safety of his people.

It was the ninth day from that on which they left La Caroline, when Le Genre made his appearance, and Oolenoe fled to the forests. Six days had they been engaged in their backward journey. In this route, diverging greatly from that which they had pursued before, and following the course indicated by the sun with a remarkable judgment, which tended still more to raise the reputation of Alphonse D'Erlach in the eyes of his followers, they suddenly struck into a path with which Le Genré himself was familiar. It proved to be one of those which he had pursued on a previous occasion, when, in the possession of the confidence of his chief, he had been permitted to lead forth a party for exploration. Our Frenchmen now knew where they were, and thirty-six hours of steady travelling would, they felt assured, bring them within sight of the fortress of La Caroline. But, as if the inveterate chieftain, Oolenoe, had made a like discovery at the same moment, his assaults became more desperate, and were urged with a singular increase of skill and fury. Now it was that the barbarian tribes of Florida seemed to gather into a host—such a host as encountered the famous Ponce de Leon and other Spanish chieftains when they sought to overrun the land. They no longer sped their arrows from a distance, which, in giving themselves security from the fire-arms of the Frenchmen, rendered their own shafts in great degree innocuous. But it was observed that, when they had succeeded in drawing the fire of the Frenchmen by two successive assaults, they usually grew bolder at a third, and came forward with an audacity which seemed to put at defiance equally the weapons and the spirit of their enemies. The inequality of numbers between the respective parties, made this subtle policy of Oolenoe particularly dangerous to the weaker Alphonse D'Erlach felt his danger, and the openly-expressed apprehensions of Le Genré declared it. The subject was one of great anxiety. The whole day had been spent in conflicts,—conflicts which were interrupted, it is true, by frequent intervals of rest, but which continued to increase in their violence as evening approached. Several of the Frenchmen were now wounded, two of them dangerously, and all of them were greatly wearied Le Genré urged D'Erlach to a night movement, in which they might leave their enemies behind them, and perhaps cause them to give up the pursuit, particularly as they would then be almost within striking distance of La Caroline ; but the coolness and judgment of D'Erlach had not deserted him, or been impaired by his increase of difficulties.

"And how," said he, "am I to know whether we shall find friends or foes in possession of La Caroline? This is not the least of my dangers. I must preserve my force against that doubt; but keep them fresh, certainly, and if possible without diminution, so that I may rescue Laudonniere or sustain myself. Besides, to attempt the night march I must leave these poor fellows, Mercœur and Dumain, to be scalped by the savages, or force them forward only that they may drop by the way. No! we must take rest ourselves, and give them all the rest we can. We must encamp as soon as possible, and the shelter of yon little bay, to which we are approaching, seems to offer an excellent cover. We will make for that."

He did as he said. His camp was formed on the edge of one of those basins which, in the southern country is usually termed a bay—so called in consequence of the dense forests of the shrub laurel that covers the region with the most glistening green, and fills the languid atmosphere with a most rich but oppressive perfume. Here he disposed his little command, so that the approaches were few and such as could be easily guarded. Here he was secure from those wild flights of arrows which, in a spot less thickly wooded, might have been made to annoy a company, discharged even in the darkness of the night. But Alphonse D'Erlach had another reason for selecting this as his present place of shelter. As soon as he had taken care of his wounded men, he examined the munitions of all. He had been sparing his powder,

and he was now rejoiced to find that the quantity was quite
sufficient, according to the exigencies of the warfare of that day,
to suffice for two or more days longer. This enabled him to devise
a project by which to ensnare the savages to their ruin. Hitherto
he had classed his men in three divisions. The first of these encountered the first onslaught of the enemy, and the second were
prepared for its renewal, while the third was a reserve for a
continuance of the struggle, giving time to the two first divisions
to reload. But it had been seen, during the day, that the savages
had made a corresponding division of their force;—that successive
attacks, followed up with great rapidity, drew the fires of his
several squads, and so well aware did the assailants now appear to
be of this practice, that, after the third fire, they boldly rushed
almost within striking distance of the Frenchmen, hurling their
stone hatchets with wonderful dexterity and precision. To provide
for this contingency—to convert it to profitable results—was the
study of D'Erlach. He felt that, but for some stratagem, it was
not improbable that the whole party would lose their scalps before
the closing of another day. He had observed that the bay in
which he harbored his men contained, interspersed with its laurels,
a perfect wilderness of *canes*, the fluted reeds of the swamp and
morass, common to the country, some of which grew to be nearly
twenty feet in height. These were still green in September, their
feathery tops waving to and fro in every breeze, while, under the
pressure of the sudden gust, their shafts, in seeming solid
phalanx, laid themselves almost to the earth, to recover, like an
artful and plumed warrior, when the danger had overblown.
Without declaring his plans, D'Erlach had a number of these
canes cut down in secresy, and divided into sections of four or five
feet. The extreme barrel of each of these sections was filled

tightly with gunpowder, and a fuse introduced at the orifice which received the powder. Strips from the shirts of his people were employed to bind the portion of the reed thus filled, and two of these shafts were lashed tightly to each matchlock, the charged portion protruding near the muzzle. He needed no words to explain his policy to his people. They understood the object in beholding the process, and admired the ingenuity which promised them hereafter the most signal advantages.

Rigid was the watch maintained that night in the camp of our Frenchmen. Fortunately, they had obtained that day a fresh supply of food while passing through a miserable hamlet, from which the occupants had fled at their approach. Their supper was eaten in silence and anxiety. The watches throughout the night were two, Le Genré taking the first, while D'Erlach, from twelve till daylight, maintained the last. There were no alarms. The Indians had retired, as was conjectured, to place themselves in some favorite place of ambush against the coming of the Frenchmen the next day. One of the two men who had been most severely wounded among the Frenchmen, died that night in great agony. The arrow of the savage had penetrated to his lungs. He had imprudently thrown off his coat of escaupil, in consequence of the great heat of the noonday, and a skirmish took place before he could reclothe himself, in which he received his hurt. D'Erlach had the body laid in the deepest portion of the bay, its only covering being a forest of canes, which were cut down and thrown over the corpse.

With the first rosy blush of the dawn, the little troop was in motion. At setting off D'Erlach gave ample directions for the anticipated conflict. His command was divided into three companies. From the first of these, three men were commissioned to deliver the fire of their pieces on the appearance of the Indians. The rest were to discharge one of the two loaded sections of cane attached to the matchlocks. The second and third were to do likewise. The effect of this arrangement would be to leave ten out of nineteen pieces undischarged, and ready for fatal use on the more daring approach of the savages. Their preparations, and the proposed *ruse* were soon put to proof. It was about nine o'clock in the morning, when the company was about to enter a defile which led to an extensive tract of pines. At the entrance, on each hand, stretched a morass that seemed interminable. The opening to the pine forest seemed a narrow gorge, the jaws of which were densely occupied with a tangled thicket that seemed to baffle approach. D'Erlach saw the dangers which awaited him in such a defile. His three bands were made to march separately as they approached it, and very slowly. A moderate interval lay between them, which would enable them, while an enemy could only attack them singly, in turn to support each other. The judgment of our young lieutenant did not deceive him. On each side of this gorge, Oolenoe had posted his warriors. They occupied the shelter of the thicket on both hands. Their eagerness and impatience, increased by the slow progress of the Frenchmen, whom they regarded as only marching to the slaughter, lost them some of the advantages of this position. They showed themselves too soon. With a horrid howl the young warriors discharged their arrows from the covert, and then boldly dashed out among the pines. The Frenchmen were nerved for the struggle. Forewarned, they had been forearmed. There was no surprise. Coolly, the three select men delivered the fire of their pieces, and each with fatal effect. In the same moment the charged barrels of the cane were ignited and torn asunder by an explosion which was sufficiently gun-like to deceive the unpractised ear of the Indian. The savages answered this fire by a cloud of arrows, and began to advance. It was now that the remaining section of the division, which had retained their fire, delivered it with great precision and an effect similar to the former; those who had emptied their pieces on the previous occasion, contenting themselves with discharging a cane. By this time, the two other divisions, under D'Erlach, had pushed through the gorge, and were spreading themselves right and left, among the pines, in a situation to practice the same game with their assailants, which had been played so well by the foremost party. We must not follow the caprices of the battle. It is enough to say that, deceived by the apparent discharge of all the pieces of the Frenchmen, the Indians, headed by Oolenoe himself, dashed desperately upon their enemies, and were received by the fatal fire from more than a dozen guns, which sent their foremost men headlong to the ground, the subtle chief, Oolenoe himself, among them. At this sight, the savages set up a howl of dismay, and fled in all directions; while Oolenoe, thrice staggering to his feet, at length sunk back upon the ground, writhing in an agony which did not, however, prevent him, on the approach of D'Erlach, from making a desperate effort to smite him with his stone hatchet. His whole form collapsed with the effort, and wrenching the rude but heavy implement from the dying savage, the lieutenant drove it into his brain and ended his agonies with a single stroke.

With this adventure, the difficulties of the party ceased. That night they reached the fortress, in season to confirm the authority of Laudonniere; and, as we have seen, to assist in the execution of the mutineers by whom he had been temporarily overthrown

XVI.

HISTORICAL SUMMARY.

SUSTAINED and reassured by the return of his lieutenant, Laudonniere, released from his bonds, proceeded to re-organize his garrison. He promoted those who had proved faithful when all threatened to be false, and deprived the doubtful, or the dangerous, of all their previous trusts. To improve and strengthen his forts, to build vessels, which were to supply the places of those which the mutineers had taken, and others of smaller burthen for the express navigation of the river, were his immediate cares, iu all of which his progress was considerable. During this period he lived on relations of tolerable amity with his Indian neighbors. Their little crops had, by this time, been harvested, and they were not unwilling to exchange their surplus productions for the objects of European manufacture which they coveted. The supplies brought by the red-men were "fish, deere, turki-cocks, leopards, little beares, and other things, according to the place of their habitation," for which they were recompensed with "certaine hatchets, knives, beades of glasse, combs, and looking-glasses." The "leopards and little beares" were probably wild cats and raccoons, or opossums, all of which furnished excellent feeding to our hungry Frenchmen in September. The wild-cat is usually a fat beast, differing very considerably from the more savage tribes to whom we liken him, the wolf and the panther; while the opossum is probably the fattest of all animals at seasons when the forest mast is abundant. Of the quality of the meat we will say nothing. To those with whom the appetite has been made properly subservient to the taste, and who suffer from no necessities, his flavor is scarcely such as legitimates his admission into the kitchen. But the case is far otherwise with those inferior tribes with whom the appetites are coarse and eager. The negro is seldom so well satisfied as when he feeds on 'possum. " 'Possum," is the common remark among this people, " 'possum heap better than pig !" To those who know how high is the estimate which the negro sets upon the pig family—an estimate which is the occasion of an epidemic under which a fat pig, straying into the woods in June and July, is sure to perish—the compliment is inappreciable.

Thus, feeding well, with his health and self-esteem gradually recovering, Laudonniere began to resume his explorations, and to cast his eyes about him with his old desire for precious discoveries It was about this time that he was visited by a couple of savages from the dominions of King Maracou. This potentate dwelt some forty leagues to the south of La Carolina. The Indians, among other matters, related to Laudonniere that, in the service of another native monarch named Onathaqua, there was a man whom they called " Barbu, or the bearded man," who was not of the people of the country. Another foreigner, whose name they knew not, was said to inhabit the house of King Mathiaca, a forest chieftain, whose tribes occupied a contiguous region. From the descriptions thus given him, Laudonniere readily conceived that these strange men were Christians. He accordingly opened a communication with the tribes by which the intermediate country was occupied, and under the stimulus of a liberal recompense, promised them in European goods, the two strangers were brought in safety to La Caroline. The conjecture of Laudonniere proved rightly founded. They were white men and Christians—Spaniards who had suffered shipwreck some fifteen years before, upon the flats called "The Martyrs," and over and against that region of the country, which at this period was called Calos—from a great native prince of that name.* This savage repaired to the wreck, and carried off into captivity its crew and passengers. Many of these were women, who became the wives of their conquerors. The king of Calos, whom a Spaniard described as the "goodliest and the tallest Indian of the country, a mighty man, a warrior, and having many subjects under his obedience," not only saved the Europeans from their wreck, but, by diligent and indefatigable perseverance, rescued most of the treasure that was in the vessel; the wealth which had been gleaned with unsparing cruelties from the bowels of the earth in Peru and Mexico. The treasures thus obtained by King Calos, were represented to be of almost limitless value. "He had great store of golde and silver, so farre forth that, in a certaine village, he had a pit full thereof, which was at the least as high as a man, and as large as a tunne." According to our Spaniards, it might be easy, "with an hundred shot," to obtain all this spoil; to say nothing of the scattered treasures which might be gleaned from the common people of the country. That the extent of their resources might not be under-valued, the captive Chris-

---

* "Ces Calos ou Carlos, sont anthropophages, et fort cruel, ils demeurent dans une Baye, qui porte également leur nom, et celui de Ponce de Leon."—CHARLEVOIX.

tians farther informed him, that the young women of the country, when engaged in their primitive dances, assembled to their festivities in a glorious costume, such as would be an irresistible charm in any European assembly. They were not only lovely in themselves, with their dark beauties partially unfolded to the gaze, and the tawny hues enlivened by the warm lustre of the sun, shining in crimson flushes through the prevailing hue of the complexion, but they wore, suspended from their girdles, plates of gold, large as a saucer, the number and weight of which would have totally impeded the action as well as agility of any but a people so exquisitely and vigorously proportioned. The men wore similar decorations, though not perhaps in such great profusion. This gold, according to their account, was derived chiefly from vessels cast away—the coasts of the territory of King Calos being particularly treacherous, and their secret, lurking shoals frequently rising up suddenly to rob the king of Spain of his hardly-won ingots. The residue of his wealth in the precious metals, King Calos derived from the kings and chiefs of the interior. Perhaps more of it was obtained in this way than our Spaniards knew. There can be no doubt but that the mines of the great Apalachian ranges were explored, however imperfectly, by the red-men of the country, following, in all probability, some superior races, who first taught them where to look, and of whom we have now but the most imperfect vestiges.

Among the articles of traffic, which the people of Calos sold to the interior tribes, was a domestic root, constituting a favorite bread-stuff which was particularly grateful to the palates of their people. This is described as forming a fine flour, than which it it is impossible to find better, and as supplying the wants of an immense tract of country. It was undoubtedly the breadstuff known as *coonti* in modern periods. This, and a species of date, taken from a sort of palm tree—the persimmon probably—were commodities in which they dealt to great extent. Of the root from which they made their favorite breadstuff, it is written, that the proprietors were very slow to part with, unless well paid for it. The people of King Calos are probably to be traced through a thousand fluctuations of place, character and fortune, to the Seminoles of recent periods—a like people, living in the same region, and rejoicing in the same fruits and freedom.

Of this King Calos, the narrative of our Spaniards goes farther, passing finally into the province of the miraculous. He is described as a prince held in special reverence by his subjects;—not simply for his valor as a soldier, or his wisdom as a ruler, but his wondrous powers as a magician. He seems to have combined the civil and the religious powers of the nation—to have been priest and prophet as well as Governor. The government of his country, like that of simple nations generally, was theocratic and patriarchal. His people were taught to believe that it was through his spells and incantations, that the earth brought forth her fruits. He resorted to various arts to perpetuate this faith, and various cruelties to subdue and punish that spirit of inquiry which might test too closely the propriety of his spiritual claims. Twice a year he retired from the sight of all his subjects, two or three of his friends alone excepted, and was supposed, at this season, to be busy with his mighty sorceries. Woe to the unlucky wretch who, whether purposely or by accident, intruded upon his mysteries. The dwelling to which he had resort was tabooed on every hand; and death, with the most fearful penalties, stood warningly at all the avenues by which it was approached. Each year a prisoner was sacrificed to the savage god he served; and this prisoner, so long as Barbu had been a captive, had been a Spaniard always—the supply being sufficient, from the frequency of wrecks upon the coast, by which an adequate number of captives was always to be had. The dominions of Calos are described as lying along a river, beyond the cape of Florida, forty or fifty leagues towards the southwest; while those of Onathaqua were nearer to La Caroline, on the northern side of the cape, "in a place which we call in the chart, Cannaverel, which is in 28 degreees."

When the two Spaniards were brought before Laudonniere they were entirely naked. Their hair hung below their loins, as did that of the savages; and so completely had they become accustomed to the habits of the red-men, that the resumption of the costume of civilization was not only strange but irksome. But Laudonniere was not disposed to permit their acquired habits to supersede those of their origin. He caused the hair of his newly-found Christians to be shorn, as heedless of the loss of strength which might follow as ever was Dalilah while docking the long locks of her giant lover. It was with great reluctance that the wild men submitted to this shearing. When the hair was finally taken off they insisted upon preserving it, and rolling it in linen put it away carefully, to be shown in Europe as a proof of their wild and cruel experience. In removing the shock from one of them, a little treasure of gold was found hidden in its masses to the value of five-and-twenty crowns, by which the Spaniard conclusively proved that one portion of his Spanish education had never deserted him. What a commentary upon the wisdom of civilization, that, in such a state, with such bonds, after such losses, of freedom, position, and the society of all the well-beloved and equal, his heart should still yearn for the keeping of a treasure which must, at every moment have only served to mock the possessor with the dearer treasures of home, country, friends, religion, of which his fortunes had made utter forfeit. But let us pass to the narrative of Barbu, himself—one of the recovered Spaniards—which we owe, in some degree to history, but mostly to tradition.

10

XVII.

THE NARRATIVE OF LE BARBU:

THE BEARDED MAN OF CALOS.

Now when Barbu, the bearded man, who had been dwelling among the people of Calos, had been shorn of the long and matted hair and beard, which had made him much more fearful to the eye than any among the savages themselves,—and when our right worthy captain had commanded that we should bathe and cleanse him, and had given him shirts of fine linen and clothes from his own wardrobe, so that he should once more appear like a Christian man among his kindred,—albeit he seemed to be greatly disquieted, and exceedingly awkward therein,—then did he conduct him into the *corps de garde*, where our people were all bidden to assemble. There, being seated all, Barbu, the Spaniard, being entreated thereto by our right worthy captain, proceeded to unfold the full relation of the grievous strait and peril by which he had fallen into the power of King Calos, and of what happened to him thereafter. And it was curious to see how that he, a Spaniard born, and not ill-educated in one of the goodly towns of old Spain, in all gentle learning, should, in the space of fifteen years sojourn among the savages, have so greatly suffered the loss of his native tongue. Slow was he of speech, and greatly minded to piece out with the

Indian language the many words in which the memory of his own had failed him. Well was it for our understanding of what he delivered, that so many of us had been dwelling among the red-men at other times,—to speak nothing of Monsieur D'Erlach, Monsieur Ottigny, both lieutenants in the garrison, and Monsieur La Roche Ferriere, who, with another, by special commandment of our captain, had dwelt for a matter of several months among the people of King Olata Utina. By means of the help brought by these, we were enabled to find the meaning of those words in which Barbu failed in his Spanish. So it was that we followed the fortunes of the bearded man, according to the narrative as here set down.

Then, at the repeated entreaty of Monsieur Laudonniere, Barbu arose and spoke:

"First, Señor Captain, I have to declare how much I thank you for the protection you have given me, the kindness which has clad me once more in Christian garments, and the cost and travail with which you have recovered me from my bonds among the heathen. Albeit, that I feel strangely in these new habits, and that my native tongue comes back to me slowly when I would speak from a full and overflowing heart, yet will I strive to make you sensible of all the facts in my sad history, and of the great gratitude which I feel for those by whose benevolence I may fondly hope that my troubles are about to end. I know not now the day or season when we left the port of Nombre de Dios, in an excellent ship, well filled with treasures of the mine, and a goodly company, on our return to the land of our fathers beyond the sea. My own share in the wealth of this vessel was considerable, and I had other treasures in the person of a dear brother, and a sister who accompanied us. Our sister was married to one who was with us also, and the united wealth of the three, such was our fond expectations, would enable us to retire to our native town of Burgos, and commend us to the favor of our people. But it was written that we should not realize these blessed expectations, and that I alone, of the four, should be again permitted to dwell among a Christian people. Yet I give not up the hope that I shall yet see my brother, who was carried away among the Indians of the far west, when we were scattered among the tribes, in the grand division of our captives. But this part of my story comes properly hereafter.

"We put to sea from the port of Nombre de Dios with very favoring winds; but these lasted us not long, ere they came out from all quarters of the heavens, and we ran before the storm under a rag of sail, without knowing in what course we sped. Thus, for three days, we were driven before the baffling winds; and when the storm lulled, the clouds still hung about us, and our pilot wot nothing of that part of the sea in which we went. Two days more followed, and still we were saddened by the clouds that kept evermore coming down from heaven, and brooding upon the deep like great fogs that gather in the morn among the mountains. Thus we sped, weary and desponding as we were, without any certainty as to the course we kept, or the region of space or country round about us. Meanwhile, the seams of our vessel began to yawn, and great was the labor which followed, to all hands, to keep her clear of water. This we did not wholly; and it was in vain that our carpenter sought for, in order to stop, the leak. Thus, weary and sad, we continued still sweeping forward slowly, looking anxiously, with many prayers, for the sun by day and the moon and stars by night. But the Blessed Virgin was implored in vain. We had offended. There was treasure on board the vessel, but it was stained with blood. You have not heard in your histories of the bloody Juan de Mores y Silva, who tortured the unhappy Mexicans by fire, even in the caverns where they resided, seeking the gold, which they gained not sufficiently soon, or in sufficient quantity, to satisfy his cruel lust for wealth. He was one of our companions on this voyage, bound homewards with an immense subsidy in ingots—huge chests of gold and silver—with which he aimed to swell into grandeur with new titles, when he arrived in Spain. But the just Providence willed it otherwise. He was, doubtless, the Jonah in our vessel, who fought against the prayers for mercy and protection which the true believers addressed to the Holy Virgin in our behalf."

Here our captain, Laudonniere, interrupted Barbu, and said—

"Verily, Señor Spaniard, had thy prayer been addressed to God himself, the Father, through the intervention and the mediation of the Blessed Saviour, his Son, whose blood was shed for sinners, it might have better profited thy case. Thy prayers to the Virgin were an unseemly elevation of a mortal woman over the divinity of the Godhead. But I will not vex thee with disputation. Thou art a Christian, though it is after a fashion which, to me seems scarcely more becoming than that of these poor savages of Calos, who yield faith, as thou tellest me, to the spells and enchantments of their bloody sovereign. But, proceed with thy story, which I shall be slow to break in upon again until thou art well ended."

With the permission thus vouchsafed him, Barbu, the bearded man, thus resumed his discourse:

"We plead for the interposition of the Virgin, Monsieur le

Capitaine, not as we deem her the source of power and of mercy, but as we hold it irreverent to rush even with our prayers to the feet of the awful Father himself; and rejoice to believe that she who was specially chosen, as one who should bear the burden of the Saviour-child, was of a spirit properly sanctified and pure for such purposes of interposition. But, as thou sayest, we will leave this matter. If we offend in our rites and offices, it is because we err in judgment, and not that our hearts wish to afflict the feelings or the thoughts of those who see with other eyes the truth. Besides, my long and outlandish abode among the red-men, might well excuse me many errors."

"And so, indeed, it might, Señor Spaniard," said Laudonniere graciously; then, as the latter remained silent, Barbu continued:

"Doubtless, Señor, as I said before, the bloody Juan de Mores y Silva, was the Jonah of our vessel, on whose account the Blessed Providence turned a deaf ear to our prayers and entreaties. It was not decreed that he should escape to rejoice in his ill-gotten treasure; and his fortunes were so mixed up with ours, that the overthrow of one was necessarily at the grievous loss and peril of us all. How many days we lay tossing on the tumultuous waves, or swept to and fro, beaten and sore distressed by the violent and changeful winds, I do not now remember, but it was in very sickness and hopelessness of heart, that we lay down at night as one lies down and submits to a power with which he feels himself wholly powerless to contend. Thus did we cast ourselves down—as the dreary shades of night came over us, with a deeper and drearier cloud than ever,—not seeking sleep, but seized upon by it, as it were, to save us from the suffering, akin to madness, which must haply follow upon our fearful waking thoughts. While we slept, our vessel struck upon the low flats of the Martyrs — those shoals which have laid bare the ribs of so many goodly and gold-laden ships of my countrymen, sucking down their brave hearts and all their treasures in the deep. We were lifted high by the surges, and rested, beyond recovery, upon the shoals, from which the remorseless seas refused again to lift us off. Our vessel lay upon one side, and the greedy waves rushed into her hold. We were stunned rather than awakened by the shock. We strove not for safety or repair. How many perished in the moment when the ship fell over I know not, but one of these was the husband of my sister. He was drowned in the first rush of the billows into the ship, though, as it was night, we knew it not. My sister had thrown herself beside my brother, and was sleeping upon his arm. She was the first to learn her misfortune, awaking, as she averred, to hear the faint cries of her lord for succor, though she knew not whence the sounds arose. When our eyes opened upon the scene, strange to say, the clouds had disappeared. The dark waves of the tempest had sped away to other regions. A gentle breeze from the land had arisen, full of sweet fragrance and a healing freshness, and, bright over head, in the blessed heavens, blossomed fresh the eternal host of the stars. Oh! the life and soothing in that smile of God. But we were not strong for the blessing, nor sufficiently grateful that life was still vouchsafed us. The day dawned upon us to increase our wretchedness. It left us without hope. Our food was ruined by the waves that filled the vessel, and though the land was spread before us in a lengthened stripe, bearing forests which were surely full of fragrance, we beheld not the means by which we should gain its pleasant shores with safety. Our boats had perished in the surf; one of them stove to pieces, and the other swept away. In our despondency and our sleep we had yielded our courage and our providence, and we lay now in the sight of heaven, amidst the equal realm of sea and sky, with the land spreading lovelily before us, yet could we do nothing for ourselves. We lay without food or drink all day, seeing nothing but the bare skies, the sea, and the shore, which only mocked our eyes. My sister sorrowed and sickened in my arms. She cried for water as one cries in the delirious agonies of fever. She would drink of the water of the deep, but this we denied her; and the day sunk again, and with it her hope and strength. With the increase of the winds that night, she grew delirious; and, when we knew not—and this was strange, for I cannot believe that I closed mine eyes that night—she disappeared. Once, it seemed that I heard her voice, in a wild scream, calling me by name, and I started forward to feel that she was gone. She left my arms while I lay insensible. It was not sleep. It was stupor. My consciousness was drowned in my great grief, and in the exhaustion of all my strength for lack of food.

"My brother and myself alone survived of all our family. With the knowledge that our sister was really gone—swallowed up, doubtless, in the remorseless deep, into which she had darted in her delirium—we came to a full consciousness. Then, when it was only misery to know, we were permitted to know all, and to feel the whole terrible truth pressing upon us, that we were alone in that dreary world of sea. Not alone of our company; only of our people. Many there were who still kept in life, watchful but hopeless. We could see their dusky forms by the faint light of the stars, crouching along the slanting plane of the vessel, upon which, by cord, and sail, and spar, we still contrived to maintain foothold; and, anon, our company would lessen. The solemn silence of all things, except the dash of the waves against us, rolling up with murmurs, and breaking away in wrath, was interrupted only by a sullen plunge, ever and anon, into the engulphing deep, as the hope went out utterly in the heart of the victim, and he yielded to death, rather than prolong the wretched endurance of a life so full of misery.

"Thus the night passed; not without other signs to cheer as well as startle us. Through the darkness we could see lights in the direction of the shore, as if borne by human hands. With the dawn of day, our eyes were turned eagerly in that direction. Nor did we look in vain. The shore swarmed with human forms. A hundred canoes were already darting along the margin of the great deep, and evident were the preparations of the people of this wild region, to visit our stranded vessel. In a little time they came. Their canoes were some of them large enough to carry forty warriors, though made from a single tree. They came to us in order of battle; a hundred boats, holding each from ten to fifty warriors. These carried spear and shield, huge lances, and well-curved bows, drawn with powerful sinews of the deer. Their arrows were long shafts of the feathery reed, such as flourish in all these forests. The feather from the eagle's wing gave it buoyancy, and the end of the shaft was barbed with a keen flint, wrought by art to an edge such as our best workmen give to steel. Many were the chief men among these warriors, who approached us in full panoply of barbaric pomp. Turbans of white and crimson-stained cotton, such as the Turk is shown to wear, though folded in a still nobler fashion, were wrapped about their heads, over which shook bunches of plumes taken from the paroquet, the crane, and the eagle. Robes of cotton, white, or crimson, or scarlet, colored with native dies of the forest, clothed their loins, and fell flowing from their shoulders;

and, ever and anon, as they came, they shook a thousand gourds which they had made to rattle with little pebbles, which, with their huge drum, wrought of the mammoth gourd, and covered with raw deer skin, made a clamor most astounding to our hapless ears. Thus they hailed our vessel, making it appear as if they intended to have fought us; but when they beheld how famishing we lay before them, with scarcely strength and courage enough to plead for mercy—speaking only through our dry and scalded eyes, and by clasping our hard and weary hands together—then it seemed as if they at once understood and felt for us; and they drew nigh with their canoes, and lowered their weapons, and darting with lithe sinews upon the sides of our leaning vessel, they held gourds of water to our lips, which cheered us while we swallowed, as with the sense of a fresh existence.

"Thus were we rescued from the yawning deep. The savages took us, with a rough kindness, from the wreck. They carried us in their canoes to the shore; and several were the survivors, as well women as men. They gave us food and nourishment, and when we were refreshed and strengthened, they separated us from our comrades, sharing us among our captors, each according to his rank, his power, or his favor with his sovereign. Seventeen of our poor Christians were thus scattered among the tribes and over the territories of the king of Calos. Some were kept in his household; but my hapless brother was not among them. He was given to a chief of the far tribes of the West, who made instant preparation to depart with him. When they would have borne us apart, with a swift bound and a common instinct, we buried ourselves in a mutual embrace. The chiefs looked on with a laugh that made us shudder; while he to whom my brother was given, with a savage growl, thrust his hands into the flowing locks of my brother, and hurled him away to the grasp of those who stood in waiting for the captive. He struggled once more to embrace me, and long after I could hear his cry—'Brother, brother, shall we see each other never more!' They heeded not his cries or struggles, or mine. They threw him to the ground with violence, bound him hand and foot, with gyves of the forest, and placing him in one of their great canoes, they sped away with him along the shores, as they treaded to the mighty West, where roll the great waters of the Mechachebe.

"Thus was I separated from my only surviving kinsman; and neither of us could tell the fate which was in waiting for the other. Verily, then did I look to find the worst. I no longer had a hope. It is my shame, as a Christian, that, in that desolate moment, I ceased to have a fear. I not only expected death, but I longed for it. I could have kissed the friendly hand that had driven the heavy stone hatchet of the savage into my brain. But, the Blessed Mother of God be praised, I thought not, in my despair, to do violence to my own self. That sin was spared me among my many sins, in that hour of despondency and woe; and all my crime consisted in the criminal indifference which made me too little heedful to preserve life. But this indifference lasted not long. I was the captive of the king of Calos himself. Nine others were kept by him including me, and among these was the cruel tyrant upon whose head lay the blood of so many of the wretched people of Mexico, Don Juan de Morés y Silva. He was the tyrant no longer. All his strength and courage had departed in his afflictions; and in the hour of our despair and terror, he was feebler than the meanest among us; feebler of soul than the girl whose heart beats with the dread that she cannot name, fearfully, as that of the little bird which you cover with your hand. We loathed him the worse for his miserable fear; and it made us all more resolute in courage to see one so cast down with his terrors, whom we had seen of late so insolent in his triumphs.

"When the lots were determined, the king of Calos drew nigh to examine us more heedfully. He had not before regarded us with any consideration. Verily, he was a noble savage to the eye. His person was tall, like one of the sons of Anak, and his carriage was that of a great warrior, born a prince, to whom it was natural equally to conquer and to rule. Rich were the garments of flowing cotton which he wore loosely, like a robe, mostly white, but with broad stains of crimson about the skirts and shoulders.

"A great baldrick hung suspended at his back, which bore a quiver, made of the skin of the rattle-snake, filled with arrows, each shaft better than a cloth-yard's length. The macana which he carried in his grasp, was a mighty club of hard wood, close in grain, and weighty as stone, which, save at the grasp or handle, was studded with sharp blades of flint, which resembled it to the mighty blade of the sword-fish. With this weapon mine eyes have seen him smite down two powerful enemies at a single stroke. Great was his forehead and high, and his cheek bones stood forth like knots upon his face, as if the cheeks were guarded by a shield. Black was his piercing eye, which grew red and fiery when he was angered; and, at such seasons, it was easier for him to smite than to speak. Unlike his people, he wore the natural growth of his hair, long and flowing straight adown his back, glossy with its original blackness, and with the oil of the bear, of which, like all his people, the lord of Calos made plentiful use. This king might be full forty years of age. Yet looked he neither young nor old—neither so young that you might not hold him the gravest and best counsellor of wisdom in the land, nor so old, but that he might better and more ingeniously lead in battle than any of his warriors. Certes, he was the most ready first to march when the invasion of the distant tribes had been resolved on; and, of a truth, never was statesman in the great courts of Europe—not the counsellors of the great Carlos himself—so cool in speculation, so just in judgment, so heedful to consider all the advantages and all the risks of an enterprise, before the first step was set down in the adoption of a policy. For seven years had I sufficient means, in the immediate service of his household, to watch the courses of his thoughts and character, and to know the virtues and the strength thereof. I saw him devise among his chiefs, and inform them with his own devices. I have seen him lead in battle, when all the plans were his own, and it was his equal teaching and valiancy by which the field was won. Verily, I say that this lord of Calos were a prince to mate with the best in Europe; and, but that we have in European warfare such engines of mischief as come not within the use or knowledge of his race, it were difficult to circumvent him in stratagem, or overcome his braves in battle. With an hundred shot—no less— and employing at the same time all the red-men as allies, who are hostile to this king of Calos—and they are many—and I doubt not Monsieur Laudonniere, but that you could penetrate his dominions and make the conquest thereof. But of him could you make no conquest. He is a warrior of the proudest stomach, who would rather perish than lose the victory; and who, most surely, would never survive the overthrow of his dominion.

" Me, did this great king examine with more curious eyes than he bestowed upon the other captives. I know not for what reason, unless because of the superior size and strength which I possess, and the extreme length and thickness of my beard and hair, of which, as a Christian man, I have always made too much account. All of us did he assign to labor; to the gathering of wood, and work in the maize fields, with the women. By-and-by, there came a preference for me beyond the others. I was brought into the king's household, and barbed his arrows, and wrought upon his great macanas, and strove, among the Indians, in hewing out his canoes from the cypress, first burning out the greater core with fire. But when harvest time came, a great festivity was held among the savages. Bitter roots were gathered in the woods, and great vessels of the beverage which was made thereof, was placed within the council or round-house of the nation. Thither did the chiefs resort and drink; and ever as they drank they danced, though the liquor wrought upon them like *aguardiente* with the European, and moved them even as the most violent of emetic medicines. Still danced they, and still they danced for the space of three whole days.—But the lord of Calos seemed not to mingle at this strange festival. He purposed rites still more strange—rites, which even now, I think upon with horror only. He had a dwelling to himself in the deep woods, whither he retired the night before the day when the great feast of the nation was to begin. Here he waited all the night, watching with reverence and patience the burning of a strange fire which had been wrought of many curious and fragrant herbs and roots. Three of the ancient people, the priests or Iawas, as they style themselves, retired with him to build this fire, which, when it began to burn, placing in store a sufficient supply of aromatic fuel that he might feed it still, they left him, with strange exorcising, to himself. And there he kept watch throughout the night. But early with the next morning he came forth, and he sprinkled the ashes of the fire upon the maize field, and he cried thrice, with a loud voice, of Yo-he-wah, which, I believe to mean the sacred name as known among the red-men. With each cry, as our poor Spaniards, myself among them, were gathering the green ears from the maize stalks, the priests who followed the king of Calos, seized bodily upon three of our brethren, taking us by surprise, and putting us all in a quaking fear. These three were all brought before the lord of Calos, who, not looking upon them as they lay bound at his feet, threw yet another vessel of sacred ashes into the air, and as these three Spaniards lay separate, with their faces looking up, I beheld the ashes sink immediately upon the breast of him whom I have already named to you—the Jonas by whom our vessel was doomed to wreck—the cruel Don Juan de Mores y Silva. Now, though the king surely looked not as he threw the ashes into the air, yet did it descend upon the breast of this said Spaniard, as certainly as if the eye and arm of this lord had been upon this particular person at the moment when he threw. Verily, though I know not well how it should be—being counselled by Holy Church against such belief—yet, verily, had this lord of Calos certain powers which did seem to justify the saying among his people, that he was a master of magic and of arts superior to those of common men.

"Now, when the Iawas, or priests, beheld where the ashes fell, they seized incontinently upon the Spaniard aforesaid. They bore him away from us, wondering and fearing all the while. But those who remained loosed the other two who had been bound, and they were set free with the rest, to pursue their labors in the corn-field. But we were not let to know the awful fate which befel the Spaniard who was taken. Verily, he saw his danger in the moment when the ashes lighted on his breast. His face was whiter than the blossom of the dogwood when it first opens to the spring. His eye glared, and his lip quivered like a leaf in the gusts of March, though nothing he spake at anything they did to him. But when they bore him away from our eyes, then a terrible fear and agony caused him to cry aloud—'Oh! my countrymen, will you not save me from the bloody savage!' I cannot soon forget that cry, which was clearly that of a person who beholds his doom. But of what avail? We had not the people, nor the strength, nor the weapons! A thousand savages danced wildly around the council-house, and the fields were full of these who came to drink and dance. Besides, we thought not of any danger but our own. We knew not how soon the fate was to befal us; for had it not seized upon Don Juan without a warning or a sign.

"They bore him to the secret tabernacle in the woods, where the lord of Calos watched alone. We saw not then, but afterwards we knew, what had been his fate. There they laid him upon a great mound of earth, with the sacred fire burning at his head in a large vessel of baked clay, formed with a nice art by the savages, and painted with the mystic figure of a bloody hand. The garments which he wore were taken off, and his limbs were fastened separately to great stakes driven in places about the mound. Thus were his hands and legs, his body and his very neck made fast, so that whatever might be the deed done upon him, he could oppose it not even in the smallest measure. But it was permitted him to cry aloud—and those of us who stole into the woods seeking to hear,—with a terrible curiosity which our very apprehensions fed,—we heard,—we heard,—and even as the awful scream of our late companion came piercing through the woods upon our ears,—we fled afar from the sound, which was that of a mortal agony and anguish. And, verily, the torture to which he was doomed was that which might well compel the poor outraged heart of humanity to cry aloud. With a keen knife, and the hand of one who had practised long at the cruel rite, the lord of Calos laid bare the breast of the victim, he not able to struggle even,—only to shriek,—he laid it bare as one peels the ripe fruit, and exposes the precious heart thereof! Even this did the lord of Calos. He stripped the skin from the breast of his victim, then, with sharp strokes, he smote away the flesh, until the quaking ribs lay bare to his point. With a sharp stone chisel he smote the breast-bone asunder, lifted the ribs, and tore away the smoking heart, which he cast, reeking red, into the burning fire of odorous woods and herbs, which then flamed up and brightened in the dark chamber, as if fed with some ichorous fuel. In that terrible agony, when the soul and the human life were thus rudely torn apart from the mutual embrace, it was told me by the lord of Calos, himself, that the victim burst one of the wythes that bound him, and freed his right hand, which he waved violently thrice, even while his murderer was plucking his heart away from its quivering fastenings! Oh! the horror, though for a moment only, of that awful consciousness! Verily, my friends, if the lord of Calos did possess a power of magic such as his people affirm, verily, I say, he paid a terrible price to the eternal hater of human souls, when he gat from him his perditious privilege!

"But the sufferings of that wretched victim, who then and thus perished, were they greater than those which followed our footsteps,—we, the survivors,—haunting us by night and day, with the mortal terrors of a fear that such must be our doom also? Every rustle of an approaching footstep among the maize-stalks where we toiled, breaking the stems and gathering the ripened ears, seemed to our woe-stricken souls, as the step of one who came as an executioner; while we labored in the gloomy thicket, gathering fuel for the winter fires, the same fear was hanging over us with a threat of the impending doom. We lived and slept in a continual dread of death, which made the hair whiten on every brow, even of the youngest, before that terrible winter was gone over.

"To us it was assigned to put away the body of our murdered comrade. But this was only after the three days of the feast was elapsed, and when the duty was tenfold distressing. Still, though all our senses revolted at the task, a fearful curiosity compelled a close examination of the victim. Then it was that we saw how the execution had been done, though we knew not then, nor until some time after, that the cell which enshrined and kept the heart had been torn open, and the sacred possession wrenched away with violent hands, even while the wretched victim had eyes to see, as well as sensibilities to feel, the sacrilegious and bloody theft. We bore the body far into the woods, wrapping it with leaves so as to hide it from our eyes, while we carried it in the bottom of an old canoe which we found for this purpose. Our burial was conducted after the fashion of the red-men. We laid the corse of our comrade upon a bed of leaves on the naked earth, and laid heavy fragments of pine and other combustible wood about him. With this we made a great pile, which we set on fire, and let to burn until everything was consumed. We then, with sad, sorrowing, and trembling hearts, returned, each one of us, in a mournful silence that wist not what to say, to our separate tasks, and the places which had been assigned us.

"Now, many months had passed in this manner, and still I was employed about the king's household. This lord of Calos distinguished me, as I have said, beyond my comrades. I had a great vigor of limb which is not common among this people, except in so much as it moves them to great agility. They are rather light, swift and expert, than powerful in war; and trust rather to great cunning than superior strength, in the meeting with their enemies. The king of Calos greatly admired to see me lift heavy logs of timber, such as would have borne down any among his people if laid upon his shoulders. But he himself had a strength superior to his people, and he wondered even more when, striving to lift the logs which I laid down, he found it beyond his mastery. Then, he put his bow into my hand, and giving me a cloth-yard shaft of reed, well tipped with a flinty barb, and dressed with an eagle's feather, he bade me draw it to the head, and send it as I would. Upon which, doing so, he greatly wondered to see how rapid and distant was the flight, for well he knew that the ability to shoot the arrow far comes rather from sleight than from strength, and is an art that only grows from practice. But this, perhaps, had not fully given me to the confidence of the king, had it not been for a service which I rendered on one occasion to his favorite son, a boy of but twelve years of age, whom I plucked from beneath the feet of a great stag, which the hunters had wounded in the forest. The red-men greatly delight to see their sons take part in the chase, even while their gristle is yet soft and their limbs feeble; for by this early practice they desired to make them strong and skilful. The son of the lord of Calos was a youth, tall and strong beyond his years; and because of the fondness of his father, exceedingly audacious in all manner of sports and strifes. Thus it was that, having seen a great stag wounded by the shaft of his sire, he had run in upon him with his slender spear. The staff of the spear broke, even as the barb penetrated the breast of the beast, and the boy fell forward at the mercy of his mighty antlers. Then was it that, seeing the lad's danger,—for I was at hand, bearing the victuals for the hunters—I threw down the basket, and rushing in, took the stag by his horns, in season for the lad to recover himself. The lord of Calos drew nigh and saw, but he offered no help, leaving it to his son to draw the keen knife which he carried, over the throat of the struggling beast. And, excepting what the boy said to me of thanks, nothing did I hear of the thing which I had done. But, three weeks after, the king made his preparations for a war party against the mountain Indians. Then he spoke to me, saying, in his own language,—which, by this time, I could understand,—Barbu,—this was the name which had been given me because of my beard—Barbu, it is not fit that one with such limbs and skill as thou hast, should labor still in the occupation of the women. Get thee a spear, such as will suit thy grasp, and there are bows and arrows for thy choice,—make thee satisfied with sufficient provision, and get thee ready to go against mine enemies. Thou shalt have to tear the flesh of a strong man!

"Verily, my friends, though it shames me to confess, that I, a Christian man, could lift weapon in behalf of one against another savage of the wilderness; yet such had been my sorrow, and so wretched did I feel at the base tasks to which I had been given, —so very unlike the valiant duties which had distinguished mine ancient service in the armies of Castile,—that I even rejoiced at the chance of putting on the armor of war,—and the meaner weapon of the red-men satisfied me then, who of old had carried, with great favor, the matchlock and the sword. But the weapon of the savage, as perchance thou knowest, is not greatly inferior, according to their usage, and in their country, to the superior im plements with which the Christian warrior takes the field. If the arquebuse is more fatal than the barbed arrow of the Indian, it is yet less frequently ready for the danger. While you shall have put your pieces in readiness for a second fire, the savage will deliver thirty javelins, each of which, if within bullet reach, shall inflict such an injury, short of death, as may disarm the wounded person. Their reeds are always ready at hand. To them every bay and river bank affords an armory, and the loss of their weapons, which were fatal to Frenchman or Spaniard, causes them but little mischief, since a single night will repair all their losses. Neither much time nor much cost is it to them to supply their munitions, of which they can always carry a more abundant provision than can we. The great superiority of the European, in his encounter with the red-man, is in his wisdom, the fruit of many ages of civilization, and not in the weapons which he wields in conflict. Let him exchange weapons with the savage, and he will still obtain the victory.

"It was because of this showing of superiority, together with the service which I had thus rendered to his son, that made the lord of Calos take me with him, armed as a warrior, on his expedition against the mountain Indians of Apalachy. I hastened to provide myself with weapons, as I was commanded, and I made for myself a great mace, such as that which the strongest warriors carried, which was a billet of hard wood, not more than four feet in length, with a handle easy to the grasp, while at each side ran down a great row of flinty teeth, each broad and sharpened like to a spear-head. It is a fatal weapon, with a well-delivered blow. In like manner did I imitate the practice of the red-men in dressing the head and breast for war. I put on the paints, red and black, which I beheld them use; but, instead of the unmeaning and rude figures which they scored upon the breast, I drew there the figure of a large cross, by which, though none but myself might know, I made anew my assurance to Holy Mother, of a faith unperishing, in Him who bore its burthen; and implored His protection against the perils which might lurk along the path. In the same manner, with a bloody cross, did I inscribe my forehead and each cheek, while I dipped my hands above the wrist in the black dyes which they also used as paints, and which they took from the walnut and other woods of the forest. Greatly did my Christian comrades wonder to behold me, painted after this fashion, with a bunch of turkey feathers tied about my head like the savage, and the strange weapons of the red-men in my grasp. These rejoiced exceedingly as they beheld me, and laughed and chatted among themselves, saying—' Yah-hee-wee! Yah-hee-wee!' with other words, by which they testified their satisfaction. But our Spaniards were in the same degree sorry, as it seemed to them that, in spite of the holy emblem upon my breast, I had delivered myself up to the enemy, and had put on, with the habit, all the superstitions of the Heathen. They had sorrow upon other grounds, since I was about to leave them, and, from the favor I had found with the lord of Calos, I had grown to be one to whom they began to look as to a mediator and protector.

"We set out thus for the country of the enemy, the lord of Calos leading the way upon the march, as is the custom with the Indians, while the foe is yet at a distance from the spot. But, as we drew nigh to the hills of the Apalachian, the young men were scattered on every hand, as so many light troops. They covered all the paths, they harbored in all places where they could maintain watch and find security, and nightly they sent in runners to the camp, reporting their discoveries. I entreated of the lord of Calos to be sent with these young men; but, whether he feared that I would seek an opportunity to fly and escape to the enemy, I know not. He refused, saying that it required scouts of experience,—men who knew the ways of the country, and that I could be of no use in such adventures. He was pleased to add that he wished me near him, as one of his own warriors—that is, the warriors of his family or tribe—that I might do battle at his side, and in his sight!

"We were not long in finding the enemy, who had received tidings of our approach. Several battles were fought, in which I did myself credit in the eyes of our warriors. The lord of Calos was greatly pleased. He took me with him into counsel, and it was fortunate that the advice which I gave, as to the conduct of the war, was adopted, and was greatly successful. Many were the warriors of the mountain whom we slew. Many scalps were taken, and more than a hundred captive boys and damsels. These, if young, are always spared, and taken into the conquering tribe. The former are newly marked with the totem of the people who take them, while the latter become the wives of the chiefs, who greatly value them. I confess to you, my brethren, that I was guilty of the sin of taking one of these same women into my cabin, who was to me as a wife, though no holy priest, with appointed ceremonials of the church, gave his sanction to our communion. She was a lovely and a loving creature, scarcely sixteen, but very fair. almost like a Spaniard, and of hair so long that she hath thrice wrapt it around her own neck and mine."

"Why didst thou not tell me of that woman?" said Laudonniere, interrupting the narrator. "Had we known, she should have been procured with thee. But, even now, it is not too late

We will bid the chief, Onathaqua, send her after thee, so that thou may'st wed her according to the rites of the church."

"Alas!" replied Barbu, "thou compellest me, Señor Laudonniere, to unravel sin after sin before thee. I have greatly erred and wandered from the paths of virtue, and from the laws of Holy Church, in my grievous sojourn among the savages. That woman filled no longer the place which she had at first in my affections. With increase of power and security, I grew wanton. I grew weary of her, and sold her to one of the chiefs for a damsel of his own house, which mine eyes coveted."

The Spaniard hung his head as he made this confession, while Laudonniere with severe aspect rated him for his lecheries. When the captain had ceased his rebuke, Le Barbu continued his story thus:

"We gained many battles in this war with the mountain Indians, who are neither so fierce, nor so subtle as those who dwell along the regions of the sea. Verily, the people of the lord of Calos are great dissemblers, treacherous beyond the serpent, valiant of their persons, and fight with excellent address. Great was the favor which I found with them because of my conduct in the war; and, in each succeeding war, for a space of six years, I became, in like manner, distinguished, until I became a most favorite chief with the lord of Calos, and a bosom friend and companion of his son—he whom I had rescued from the stag, and who had now grown up to manhood. Greatly did this lad favor his father. He was of a light olive complexion, scarcely more dark than the people of Spanish race, but superior in stature, well-limbed, and of admirable dexterity. With him I hunted from the fall of the leaf in autumn, to the budding of the leaf again in spring; and, when the summer time came, we sped away in our canoes, up the vast rivers of the country, through great lakes, many of which lie embadey in forests of mangrove and palm, where the forest swims upon the water. If it were possible for a Christian man— for one who has heard the sound of a great bell in the cities of the old world, and who has communed with the various good and wondrous things of civilization—to be content with a loss of these, and their utter exclusion from sight for ever, then might I have passed pleasantly the years of my captivity among the people of Calos. I had become a chief and was greatly honored. I had power and I was much feared. I had wealth—such wealth as the savage estimates—and I was loved; and the lord of Calos and his noble son, put in me a faith which never betrayed a doubt or a denial. But I had not power to shield my brother Christians, save in one case. Each year witnessed the sacrifice of a comrade. They were the victims to the Iawas. The priesthood was a power under which the kings themselves were made to tremble. With them was it to determine upon peace or war, life or death, bonds or freedom; and the strength of the king lay greatly in his alliance with the priesthood. But for this, the rule among the savage nations would be wholly with the people. Season after season, when came the harvest, one of our luckless Spaniards was taken away from the rest and doomed to the sacrifice. In this way the savages propitiate the unknown God, to whom they looked for victory over their enemies. Do not suppose that I beheld this cruelty without toiling against it. But I spoke in vain. I made angry the Iawas, until the lord of Calos himself addressed me, after this fashion—' Son of the stranger, art thou' not well thyself? Why wouldst thou be sick, being well? Art thou not thyself safe? Why, being so, put thy head under the macana? It is not wise in thee to *see* the things

11

over which the power is denied thee. Go then, with Mico Wa-ha-la,'—such was the name of his son—' go then with him into the great lake of the forest, and come not back for a season. Depart thou thus, always, when the maize is ready for the harvest.'

"I obeyed him; but not until I found that I was endangering my own safety to attempt further expostulation; and then it was that my companions perished, all save the one who now sits before thee with myself, and whom I saved because of a service which I rendered to the Iawa, and whom I persuaded to take my white brother into his wigwam. He went, even before myself, but through my means, into the service of Onathaqua."

Here Captain Laudonniere interrupted the speaker.

"For what reason," said he, "being such a favorite with the king of Calos and his son, didst thou at last leave his service for that of the King Onathaqua?"

"Alas, Señor Laudonniere, thy question shames me again, since it requires of me to lay bare another of the vices of my evil heart, and to confess how the bad passions thereof could lead me into follies which proved fatal to my better fortune. I had gained great honor among the savages by my prudence and my skill in war, my strength in battle, and the excellence of my counsel in the country of the enemy. I had gained the good will and protection of the great king of Calos, and the affection of his son, the noble young Mico Wa-ha-la! But these contented me nothing, though they brought plenty and security to my wigwam, and such delights as might satisfy the man, a dweller in the wilderness. I have said that I was greatly trusted by the king, the prince, and the head men of the country. These then, after I had been eight years in their service, confided to my charge a great and sacred commission. The time had come when it became proper that this Mico Wa-ha-la should take to himself a wife. Now, tidings had reached Calos of a creature, lovely as a daughter of the sun, who was the youngest child of the King Onathaqua. A treaty was agreed upon between the two kings for the marriage of their children; and I was dispatched, with a select body of warriors, to bring the maiden home to her new sovereign. It was not the custom for a chief desiring a wife, that he should seek her in person. Acccordingly I was dispatched, and I reached the territories of Onathaqua in safety. Here I beheld the maiden in pursuit of whom I came, and my froward heart instantly conceived the wildest affection for her beauty. Beautiful she was as any of our Castilian maidens, and as delicate and modestly proper in her bearing, as one may see in the gentlest damsel of a Christian country. Deeply was I smitten with this new flame, and greatly did I strive to please the maiden who had fired me with these fresh fancies. I spake with her in the Indian language, with charms of thought which had been taken from the Castilian, such as were vastly superior to those which belonged to Indian courtship. I sang to her many a glorious ballad of the sweet romance of my country, discoursing of the tender loves between the Castilian cavaliers and the dark-eyed and dark-tressed maidens of Grenada. Verily, the beauty of the delicate daughter of Onathaqua, the precious Istakalina—by which the people of Onathaqua understand the white lily of the lake before it opens—was no unbecoming representative of that choice dark beauty which made the charm of the Moorish damsel of my land, ere Boabdil gave up his sceptre into the hands of the holy Ferdinand. For Istakalina, I rendered the language of the Castilian romance into the dialect of her people; and with a sad fondness in her eyes, that drooped ever while looking upwards at the passionate gaze of mine, did she listen to the story of feelings and affections to which her own young and innocent nature did now tenderly incline. Thus was it that she was delivered into my keeping by her sire, that I should conduct her to the young Mico Wa-ha-la, my friend. And thus, with fond discourse of song and story, which grew more fond with every passing hour—with me to speak and she to listen—did we commence our journey homeward to the dominions of the lord of Calos. Alas! for me, and alas! for the hapless maiden, that, in the fondness of my passion, I forgot my trust; forgot preciously to guard and protect the precious treasure in my keeping; and, in the increase of my blind love, forgot all the lessons of war and wisdom, and all the necessary providence which these equally demand. Thus was it that I was dispossessed of my charge, at the very moment when it was most dear to my delight. Didst thou ask me for the hope which grew with this blind passion, verily, señor, I should have to say to thee that I had none. I thought not of the morrow; I dared not think of the time when Istakahna should fill the cabin of Wa-ha-la. I knew nothing but that she was with me, with her dark eyes ever glistening beneath their darker lids, as she met the burning speech of mine; that we thridded the sinuous paths of silent and shady forests, with none to reproach our speech or glances; our attendants, some of them going on before, and some following; and that, when she ascended the litter, which was borne by four stout savages, or sat in the canoe as we sped across lake or river—for both of these modes of travel did we at times pursue—I was still the nearest to her side, drunk with her sweet beauty, and the sad tenderness which dwelt in all her looks and actions

Nor was it less my madness that I fondly set to the account of her fondness for me, the very sadness with which she answered my looks, and the sweet sigh which rose so often to her softly parted lips. Verily, was never man and Christian so false and foolish as was I, in those bitter blessed moments. Thus was I blinded to all caution—thus was I heedless of all danger—thus was I caught in the snare, to the loss of all that was precious as well to my captor as myself.

"How was this? How happened it?" demanded Laudonniere as Le Barbu paused, and covered his face with his hands in silence, as if overcome with a great misery.

"Thou shalt hear, Señor. I will keep nothing from thee of this sad confession; for, verily, have I long since repented of the sin and folly which brought after them so much evil. Thou shalt know that, distant from the territories of the lord of Calos, a journey of some three days, and nearly that far distant also from the dwelling of Onathaqua, there lieth a great lake of fresh water, in the midst of which is an island named Sarropee. This island and the country which surrounds the lake, is kept by a very powerful nation, a fierce people, not so numerous as strong, because they have places of retreat and refuge, whither no enemy dare pursue them. On the firm land, and in open conflict, the lord of Calos had long before conquered this strange people; but in their secure harborage and vast water thickets, they mocked at the power of all the surrounding kings. These, accordingly, kept with them a general peace, which was seldom broken, except under circumstances such as those which I shall now unfold. The people of this lake and island are rich in the precious root called the *Coonti*, of which they have an abundance, of a quality far superior to that of all the neighboring country

Their dates, which give forth a delicious honey, are in great abundance also, and of these their traffic is large with all other nations. But that they are a most valiant people, and occupy a territory so troublesome to penetrate, they had been destroyed by other nations, all of whom are greedy for the rich productions which their watery realm bestows. Now, it was, that, in our journey homewards, we drew nigh to the great lake of the people of the isle of Sarropee. Here it was that my discretion failed me in my passion. Here it was that my footstep faltered, and the vision of mine eyes was completely shut. I knew that our people were at peace with the people of Sarropee, and I thought not of them. But had I not been counselled to vigilance in bringing home the daughter of Onathaqua, even as if the woods were thick with enemies? But I had forgotten this caution. I sent forth no spies; I sought for no wisdom from my young warriors; and, like an ignorant child that knows not of the deep gulf beneath, I stepped confidently into the little canoe which was to take Istakalina and myself across an arm of the lake which set inwards, while our warriors fetched a long compass around it. Alas! señor, I was beguiled to this folly by the fond desire that I might have the lovely maiden wholly to myself in the little canoe, for already did I begin to grieve with the thought that in a few days, the journey would be at an end, and I should then yield her unto the embraces of another. And thus we entered the canoe. I made for her a couch, in the bottom of the little boat, of leaves gathered from the scented myrtle. With the paddle in my hand, I began to urge the vessel, but very slowly, lest that we should too soon reach the shore, and find the warriors waiting for us. Sweetly did I strive to discourse in her listening ears; and with what dear delight did I behold her as she answered me only with her tears. But these were as the cherished drops of hope about mine heart, which gave it a life which it never knew before. While thus we sped, dreaming nothing of any danger, over the placid waters, with the dark green mangrove about us, and a soft breeze playing on the surface of the great lake, suddenly, from out the palm bushes, darted a cloud of boats, filled with painted warriors, that bore down upon us with shows of fury and a mighty shout of war. I answered them with a shout, not unlike their own, for already had I imbibed something of the Indian nature. I shouted the war-whoop of the lord of Calos, and tried to make myself heard by the distant warriors that formed my escort. And they did hear my clamors; for already had they rounded the bayou or arm of the lake which I had sought to cross, and were pressing down towards us upon the opposite banks. Then did I bestir the paddle in my grasp, making rapid progress for the shore, while the canoes of the Sarropee strove to dart between us and the place for which I bent. But what could my single paddle avail against their better equipment? Theirs were canoes of war, carrying each more than a score of powerful warriors armed for action, and prepared to peril their lives in the prosecution of their object. I, too, was armed as an Indian warrior, and with their approach, I betook me to my weapon. I had learned to throw the short lance, or the javelin of the savage, with a dexterity like his own; and, ere they could approach me, I had fatally struck with these darts two of their most valiant warriors. They strove not to return the arrows lest they should hurt the maiden, Istakalina, who had raised herself at the first danger, and now strove with the paddle which I had thrown down. As one of the canoes which threatened us drew nigh, I seized the great macana which I carried, and prepared myself to use it upon the most forward warriors; but when I expected that they would assail me with war-club and spear, the cunning savages thrust their great prow against our little boat, amidships, and even while my macana lighted on the head of one of the assailants, smiting him fatally, I fell over into the lake with the upsetting of our vessel. In a moment had they grasped Istakalina from the lake, and taken her to themselves in their own canoe, and as I raised my head from the water, beholding this mishap, a heavy stroke upon my shoulder, which narrowly missed my head, warned me of my danger. Then, seeing that I could no longer save the captive maiden, I dived deeply under, making my way like an otter, beneath the water, for the shore. A flight of arrows followed my rising to take the air, but they were hurriedly delivered, with little aim, and only one of them grazed my cheek. The mark is still here as thou seest. Again I dived beneath the water, still swimming shoreward, and when I next rose into the light and air, I was among the people of the lord of Calos. They were now assembled along the banks of the lake, as near as they could go to the enemy, some of them, indeed, having waded waist deep in their wild fury and desperate defiance. But of what avail were their weapons or their rage? The maiden, Istakalina, the princess and the betrothed of Wa-ha-la, was gone. The people of the Sarropee had borne her off, heeding me little even as they had taken her. She was already far off, moving towards the centre of the lake, and faint were the cries which now came from her, though it delighted my poor vain heart, in that desperate hour, to perceive that, in her last cries, it was my unhappy name that she uttered. They bore her away to the secret island where they dwelt, in secure fastnesses; and long and fruitless, though full of desperation, was the war that followed for her recovery. But, though I myself fought in this war, as I never have fought before, yet did I not dare to do battle under the eye, or among the warriors of the lord of Calos. I fled from his sight and from the reproaches of my friend, the Mico Wa-ha-la, for, in my soul, I felt how deep had been my guilt, and my conscience did not dare the encounter with their eyes. I took refuge with Onathaqua, the father of Istakalina; and when he knew of the valor with which I strove against the captivity of the maiden, he forgave me that I lost her through my own imprudence. Of the blind and selfish passion which prompted that imprudence, he did not dream, and he so forgave me. Under his lead, I took up arms against the tribes of Sarropee, and for two years did the war continue, with great slaughter and distress among the several nations. But, in all our battles, I kept ever on the northern side of the great lake, and never allowed myself to join with the warriors of Calos. They but too well conceived my guilt. The keen eyes of mine escort distinguished my passion, and saw that it was not ungracious in the sight of Istakalina. Too truly did they report us to the lord of Calos, and to my friend, the young Mico Wa-ha-la. Bitter was the reproach which he made me in a last gift which he sent me, while I dwelt with Onathaqua. It consisted of a single arrow, from which depended a snake skin, with the warning rattles still hanging thereto. 'Say to the bearded man,' said the Mico, 'when you give him this, that it comes from Wa-ha-la. Tell him that his friend sends him this, in token that he knows how much he hath been wronged. Say to the bearded man, that Wa-ha-la had but one flower of the forest, and that his friend hath gathered it. Let his friend beware the arrow of the warrior, and the deadly fang of the war-rattle, for the path between us is everywhere sown with the darts of death.'

Thus he spake, and I was silent. I was guilty. I could not excuse myself, and did not entreat. I felt the truth of his complaint and the justice of his anger. I felt how great had been my folly and my crime. Istakalina was lost to us both. Thus then, a fugitive, and an outlaw from Calos, dreading every moment the vengeance of Wa-ha-la and his warriors, I dwelt for seven years with Onathaqua, who hath ever treated me as a son. I have fought among his warriors, and shared the fortunes of his people, of which nothing more need be said. Tidings at length came to me, of a people in the country bearded like myself. Then came your messengers to Onathaqua, and you behold me here. I looked not for Frenchmen but for Spaniards I thank and praise the Blessed Mother of God, that I have found friends if not countrymen, and that I see, once more, the faces of a Christian people."

Thus ended the narrative of Le Barbu, or the Bearded Man of Calos.

XVIII.

HISTORICAL SUMMARY.

WE have already mentioned that, with the restoration of Laudonniere to power, and the complete subjection of his mutineers, he resumed by degrees his projects of exploration and discovery. Among other places to which he sent his barks, was the territory of King Audusta, occupying that region in which Fort Charles had been erected by Ribault, in the first attempt to colonize in the country. To Audusta, himself, were sent two suits of apparel, with knives, hatchets and other trifles; " the better," as Laudonniere says, " to insinuate myselfe into his friendship." To render this hope more plausible, " I sent in the barke, with Captaine Vasseur, a souldier called Aimon, which was one of those which returned home in the first voyage, hoping that King Audusta might remember him." This Aimon was instructed to inquire after another soldier named Rouffi, who, it appears, had preferred remaining in the country, when it had been abandoned by the colonists under Nicolas Barré.

Audusta received his visitors with great favor,—sent back to Laudonnicre a large supply of " mil, with a certaine quantity of beanes, two stagges, some skinnes painted after their manner, and certaine pearles of small value, because they were burnt." The old chief invited the Frenchmen once more to remove and plant in his territories. He proffered to give him a great country, and would always supply him with a sufficient quantity of grain. Audusta had known the Frenchmen almost entirely by benefits and good fellowship. The period of this visit to Audusta, which was probably in he month of December, is distinguished in the chronicle of Laudonniere, by expressions of delightful surprise at the number of stock doves (wild pigeons) which came about the garrison—" in so greate number, that, for the space of seven weekes together," they " killed with harquebush shot at least two hundred every day." This was good feeding. On the return of Capt. Vasseur from his visit to Audusta, he was sent with a present " unto the widow of Kinge Hiocaia, whose dwelling was distant from our fort about twelve leagues northward. She courteously received our men, sent me backe my barkes, full of mil and acornes, with certaine baskets full of the leaves of cassine, wherewith they make their drinke. And the place where this widow dwelleth, is the most plentifull of mil that is in all the coast, and the most pleasante. It is thought that the queene is the most beautifull of all the Indians, and of whom they make the most account: yea, and her subjects honour her so much that almost continually they beare her on their shoulders, and will not suffer her to go on foot."

The visit of Laudonniere, through his lieutenant, was returned, in a few days, by the beautiful widow, through her Hiatiqui, "which is as much as to say, her Interpreter."

Laudonniere continued his exploratious, still seeking provisions, and with the view to keeping his people from that idleness which hitherto had caused such injurious discontents in his garrison. His barks were sent up May River, to discover its sources, and make the acquaintance of the tribes by which its borders were occupied. Thirty leagues beyond the place called Mathiaqua, " th y discovered the entrance of a lake, upon the one side whereof no land can be seene, according to the report of the Indians, which had oftentimes climbed on the highest trees in the country to see land, and notwithstanding could not discerne any."

These few sentences may assist in enabling the present occupants of the St. John's to establish the location along that river, at the period of which we write. The ignorance of the Indians in regard to the country opposite, along the lake, indicates equally the presence of numerous tribes, and the absence of much adventure or enterprise among them—results that would seem equally to flow from the productive fertility of the soil, and the abundance of the game in the country. With this account of it as a *terra incognita*, the explorers ceased to advance. In returning, they paid a visit to the island of Edelano—one of those names of the Indians, which harbors in the ear with a musical sweetness which commends it to continued utterance. We should do well to employ it now in connection with some island spot of rare beauty in the same region.

This island of Edelano is " situated in the midst of the river ; as fair a place as any that may be seene thorow the world ; for, in the space of some three leagues that it may containe, in length and breadth, a man may see an exceedingly rich countrey and marvellously peopled. At the coming out of the village of Edelano, to goe unto the river side, a man must passe thorow an alley about three hundred paces long and fifty paces broad ; on both sides whereof great trees are planted, the boughes whereof are tied [blended ?] together like an arch, and meet together so artificially [as if done by art] that a man would thinke it were an arbour made of purpose, as faire, I say, as any in all Christendom, although it be altogether naturall."

Leaving the island of Edelano, thus equally famous for its beauties of nature and name, our voyagers proceeded "to Eneguape, then to Chilily, from thence to Patica, and lastly they came unto Coya." This place seems to have been, at this period, one of the habitations of the powerful king Olata Utina. In the name Olata, we find an affix such as is common to the Seminoles and Creeks of the present day. *Holata*, as we now write the word, is evidently the Olata of Laudonniere. It was probably a title rather than a name.* Olata Utina received his visitors with great favor, as he had always done before; and six of them were persuaded to remain with him, in order the better to see the country, while their companions returned to La Caroline. Some of these remained with the Indian monarch more than two months. One of them, named Groutald, a gentleman who had taken great pains in this exploration, reported to Laudonniere that he had never seen a fairer country. "Among other things, he reported to me that he had seene a place, named Hostaqua, and that the king thereof was so mighty, that he was able to bring three or four thousand savages into the field." Of this king we have heard before. It was the counsel of Monsieur Groutald to Laudonniere that he should unite in a league with this king, and by this means reduce the whole country into subjection. " Besides, that this king knew the passages unto the mountaine of Apalatci, which the Frenchmen desired so greatly to attaine unto, and where the enemy of Hostaqua made his abode, which was easie to be subdued, if so be wee would enter into league together." Hostaqua

* Holata Mico (or Blue King), and Holata Amathla, were distinguished leaders of the Seminoles in the late war in Florida.

sent to Laudonniere " a plate of a minerall that came out of this mountaine,—out of the foote whereof"—such was the glowing account given by the Indian monarch—" there runneth a streame of golde or copper." The process by which the red-men obtain the pure treasures of this golden stream was an exceedingly primitive one, and reminds us of the simple process of gathering golden sands in California. " They dig up the sand with an hollow and drie cane of reed, until the cane be full; afterward they shake it, and find that there are many small. graines of copper and silver among this sand; which giveth them to understand that some rich mine must needs be in the mountaine." Laudonniere is greatly impressed by this intelligence, " and because the mountaine was not past five or six days journey from our fort, lying towards the north-west, I determined, as soone as our supply should come out of France, to remove our habitation unto some river more towards the north, that I might be nearer thereunto."

An incident, which occurred about this time, still further increased the appetites of Laudonniere. He had suffered, and indeed sent, certain favorite soldiers to go into several parts of the country, among the savage tribes with whom he kept terms of amnesty and favor, in order that they should acquire as well a knowledge of the Indian language as of the country. One of these was named Peter Gambier. This man had rambled somewhat farther than his comrades. He had shared in all the more adventurous expeditions of the Indians, and had succeeded in gathering a considerable quantity of gold and silver, all of which was understood to have been directly or indirectly from the Indians, who dwelt at the foot of the Apalachian Mountains. These were tribes of the Cherokee nation, with whom the Indian nations along the sea-board were perpetually at war. Full of news, and burdened with his treasure, Peter Gambier prepared to return to La Caroline. He had made his way in safety until he reached the beautiful island with the beautiful name, Edelano, lying in the midst of but high up May River. On the same stream which was occupied by his countrymen, in force, the thoughtless soldier conceived himself to be quite safe. He was hospitably entertained by the chief or king of Edelano, and a canoe was accorded him, with two companions, with whom to descend the river to the fort. But the improvident Frenchman, allowed his precious treasures to glitter in the eyes of his host. He had not merely gold and silver, but he had been stocked with such European merchandises as were supposed most likely to tempt the savages to barter. A portion of this stock remained in his possession. The natural beauties of the island which they occupied had not softened the hearts of the savages with any just sense of humanity. They were as sensible to the *auri sacra fames* as were the Europeans, and just as little scrupulous, we shame to say it, in gratifying their appetites as their pale-faced visitors The possessions of the Frenchmen were sufficient to render the Mico of Edelano indifferent to all considerations of hospitality, and the two Indians whom he lent to Gambier were commissioned to take his life. Thus, accompanied by his assassins, he entered the canoe, and they were in progress down the river, when, as the Frenchman stooped over some fish which he was seething in the boat, the red-men seized the opportunity to brain him with their stone hatchets, and possess themselves of his treasures. When the tidings came to Laudonniere, he was not in a situation to revenge the crime; but the large acquisitions of gold and silver procured by his soldier, as reported to him, confirmed him in his anxiety to penetrate these tantalizing realms, in which the rivers ran with such glittering abundance from rocks whose caverns promised to outvie all that Arabian story had ever fabled of the magical treasures of Aladdin.

Scarcely had this event taken place, when the war was renewed between Olata Utina and Potanou. The former applied for assistance to Laudonniere, who, adopting the policy of the "Spaniards, when they were imployed in their conquests, who did alwayes enter into alliance with some one king to ruine another," readily sent him thirty arquebusiers, under Lieutenant Ottigny. These, with three hundred Indians, led by Utina, penetrated the territories of Potanou, and had a severe fight, which lasted for three hours, with the people of that potentate. "Without doubt, Utina had been defeated, unlesse our harquebusiers had borne the burthen and brunt of all the battell, and slaine a great number of the soldiers of Potanou, upon which occasion they were put to flight." The lieutenant of the French would have followed up the victory, but Utina, the Paracoussi, had gathered laurels quite enough for a single day, and was anxious to return home to show his scalps and enjoy his triumphs among his people. His tribes and villages were assembled at his return, and, for several days, nothing but feasts, songs and dances, employed the nation. Ottigny returned to the fort, after two days spent in this manner with Utina, and his return was followed by visits from numerous other chiefs, nearer neighbors than Utina, and enemies of that savage, who came to expostulate with Laudonniere against his lending succor to a prince who was equally faithless and selfish. They, on the other hand, entreated him to unite with them in the destruction of one who was a common enemy. This application had been made to him before but his policy had been rather to maintain terms of alliance, offensive and defensive, with a powerful chieftain, at some little distance, than to depend wholly upon others more near at hand. This policy was again drawn from that of the Spaniard. He was soon to be taught how little was the reliance which he could place in any of the forest tribes. He was about to suffer from those deficiencies and evils which were due to his anxious explorations of the country, when his people had been much better employed in the wholesome labors of the field, in the very eye of the garrison.

It was the custom of the Indian tribes, after the gathering and storing away of their harvests, to commence hunting with the first fall of the leaves, probably about the middle of September. The chase, during this period, was seldom such as to carry them far from the fields which they had watched during the summer. Near at hand, for a season at least, the game was in sufficient quantity to supply their wants. But, as the season advanced, and towards the months of January, February and March, they gradually passed into the deeper thickets, and disappeared from their temporary habitations. During this period, they build up new abodes, which are equally frail, in the regions to which they go, and which are contiguous to the hunting-grounds which they are about to penetrate. To these retreats the whole tribe retires; and hither they carry all the commodities which are valuable in their eyes. Their summer dwellings are thus as completely stripped as if the region were abandoned forever.

This removal, for which their previous experience should sufficiently have prepared our Frenchmen, was yet destined to have for them some very pernicious results. We have seen that certain subsidies of corn and beans had been procured from various tribes and nations; enough, according to Laudonniere, to serve them until the arrival of expected succors from France. But, calculating on these succors, and confident of their arrival during the month of April, our Frenchmen had become profligate of their stores. April found them straitened for provisions, and not an Indian could be seen. April passed slowly and brought no succor. With the month of May the Indians had returned to their former abodes; but, by this time, their remaining stock of grain had mostly found its way into the ground, in the setting of another crop. From the savages, accordingly, nothing but scanty supplies of fish could be procured, without which, says Laudonniere, "assuredly wee had perished from famine." Of the incompetence of this captain, and the wretched order which prevailed among his garrison, his incapacity and other incompetence, this statement affords sufficient proof. They neither tilled the earth for its grain, nor sounded the river for its finny tribes; though these realms were quite as much under their dominion as that of the savages; but they relied solely upon this capricious and inferior race, in the exploration of land and sea, for maintaining them against starvation.

May succeeded to April, and still in vain did our Frenchmen look forth upon the sea, for the ships of their distant countrymen. June came, and their wants increased. They fell finally into famine, of which Laudonniere himself affords us a sufficiently impressive picture.

" We were constrayned to eate rootes, which the most part of our men punned in the mortars which I had brought with me to beate gunnepowder in, and the graine which came to us from other places. Some tooke the wood of *esquine*, (?) beate it, and made meale thereof, which they boiled with water, and eate it

Others went with their harquebusies to seeke to kill some foule Yea, this miserie was so great, that that one was founde that had gathered up all the fish-bones that he could finde, which he dried and beate into powder to make bread thereof. The effects of this hidious famine appeared incontinently among us, for our bones eftsoones beganne to cleave so neare unto the skinne, that the most part of the souldiers had their skinnes pierced thorow with them in many partes of their bodies, in such sort that my greatest feare was, least the Indians would rise up against us, considering that it would have beene very harde for us to have defended ourselves in such extreme decay of all our forces, besides the scarsitie of all vittualls, which fayled us all at once. For the very river had not such plentie of fish as it was wont, and it seemed that the very land and water did fight against us." In this condition were they till the beginning of June. "During which time," says the chronicler, further—" the poore souldiers and handicraftsmen became as feeble as might be, and being not able to worke, did nothing but goe, one after another, as centinels, unto the clift of an hill, situate very neare unto the fort, to see if they might discover any French ship."

But their watchings still ended with disappointment. Thus was the hope with which the heart sickens, deferred too long. No ships greeted their famishing eyes, and they at length appealed to their commander, in a body, to take measures for returning to France, and abandoning the colony,—" considering that if wee let passe the season to embarke ourselves, wee were never like to see our country;" and alleging, plausibly enough, that new troubles had probably broken out in France, which was the reason that they had failed to receive the promised succors Laudonniere lent an easy ear to their demands. He, himself, was probably quite as sick of the duties, to which he was evidently unequal, as were his followers. It was, perhaps, prudent to submit to those for whom he could no longer provide. The bark "Breton" was fitted up, and given in charge to Captain Vasseur, and, as this vessel could carry but a small portion of the colony, it was determined to build a "faire ship," which the shipwrights affirmed could be made ready by the 8th of August. "Immediately I disposed of the time to worke upon it. I gave charge to Monsieur de Ottigny, my lieutenant, to cause timber necessary for the finishing of bothe the vessels to be brought, and to Monsieur D'Erlach, my standard-bearer, to goe with a barke a league off from the forte, to cut down trees fit to make plankes." Sixteen men, under the charge of a sergeant, were set "to labour in making coals; and to Master Hance, keeper of the artillery," was assigned the task of procuring rosin to bray the vessels. "There remained now but the principal, [object,] which was to recover vittualls, to sustain us while the worke endured" Laudonniere, himself, undertook to seek for this supply. He embarked with thirty men in the largest of his vessels, with the purpose of running along the coast for forty or fifty leagues. But his search was taken in vain. He procured no supplies. He returned to the fort only to defraud the expectations of his people, who now grew desperate with hunger and discontent. They assembled together, riotously, and, with one voice, insisted that the only process by which to extort supplies from the savages was to seize upon the person of their kings.

To this, at first, Laudonniere would not consent. The enterprise was a rash one. The consequences might be evil, in regard to any future attempts at settlement. He proposed one more trial among them, and sent despatches communicating his desire to traffic for food with the surrounding tribes. The Indians were not averse to listen. But they knew the distress under which the Frenchmen suffered, and were prepared to turn it to account. They came into the garrison with small supplies of grain and fish, enough to provoke appetite rather than to satisfy it. For these they demanded such enormous prices, as, if conceded, would have soon exhausted all the merchandise of the garrison. With one hand they extended their produce, while the other was stretched for the equivalent required. Knowing the desperation of the Frenchmen, they took care, while thus tantalizing their hopes and hunger, to keep out of reach of shot of arquebuse. In this way, they took the very shirts from the backs of the starving soldiers. When Laudonniere remonstrated against their prices, their answer was a bitter mockery.

"Very good," said the savages, "if thou make such great account of thy merchandise, let it stay thy hunger. Do thou eat of it and we will eat of our fish." This reply would be cheered with their open-throated laughter. The old ally of the French, the Paracoussi Utina, mocked them in like manner. His subjects followed his example; and, in the end, goaded to madness, Laudonniere resolved on adopting the course which his people had counselled; that, by which, taking one of their kings prisoner, food could be extorted for his ransom. The ingratitude of Utina, for past services, a recent attempt which he had made to employ the French soldiers in his own conquests, while professing to lead them only where they should find provisions, and the supposed extent of his resources, pointed him out to all parties as the proper person upon whom to try the experiment, on a small scale, which Cortez and Pizzarro had used, on a large one, in the conquest of Peru and Mexico.

XIX.

Of the captivity of the Great Paracoussi—Olata Ouvae Utina, and the war which followed between his people and the French.

CHAPTER I.

It being determined by Laudonniere, in the necessities of his people, to seize upon the person of the great Paracoussi, Olata Ouvae Utina, in order, by the ransom which he should extort, to relieve the famine which prevailed among the garrison, he proceeded to make his preparations for the event. Two of his barks were put in order for this purpose, and a select body of fifty men was chosen from his ranks to accompany him on the expedition. But this select body, though the very best men of the garrison, exhibited but few external proofs of their adequacy for the enterprise. So lean of flesh, so shrunk of sinew, so hollow-eyed were they, that their picture recals to us the description given by Shakspeare of the famished and skeleton regiments of Henry of Monmouth at the famous field of Agincourt—' A poor and starved band,' the very 'shales and husks of men,' with scarcely blood enough in all their veins, to stain the Indian hatchet, which they travel to provoke. But famine endows the sinews with a vigor of its own. Hunger enforced to the last extremities of nature, clothes the spirit of the man in the passions of the wolf and tiger. Lean and feeble as are our Frenchmen, they are desperate. They are in the mood to brave the forest chief in his fastnesses, and to seize upon his own heart, in the lack of other food. The very desperation of their case secures them against any misgivings.

The dominions of Holata Utina were distant from La Caroline, between forty and fifty leagues up the river. His chief town, where he dwelt, lay some six more leagues inland, a space over which our Frenchmen had to march. Leaving a sufficent guard in their vessels, Laudonniere and his company landed and proceeded in this quarter. He marched with caution, for he knew his enemy. His advance was conducted by Alphonse D'Erlach, his standard-bearer—one, whose experience and skill had been too frequently tried to leave it doubtful that his conduct would be a safe one. He had traversed the space before, and he knew the route thoroughly. The progress was urged with as much secrecy as caution. The cover of the woods was carefully maintained, the object of the party being a surprise. They well knew that Utina had but little expectation of seeing them, at this juncture, in his own abodes. None, so well as himself, knew how feeble was their condition, how little competent to any courageous enterprise. They succeeded in appearing at the village of the chief without provoking alarm. He himself was at home, sitting in state in the royal wigwam, with but few warriors about him. The fashion of the Indian, with less royal magnificence, in other words, with less art and civilization—is not greatly unlike that of the Turk. Olata Utina sat crossed legs upon a *dais* prepared of dressed skins of the deer, the bear and panther. The spotted hides hung over the raised portions of the seat which he kept, upon which also might be seen coverlets of cotton ingeniously manufactured, and richly stained with the bright crimson, scarlet, and yellow, of native dye-woods. This art of dyeing, the savages had brought to a comparatively high state of perfection. His house itself stood upon an artificial eminence of earth, raised in the very centre of his village, and overlooking it on every hand. It was an airy structure, with numerous openings, and the breeze played sweetly and capriciously among the coverlets which hung as curtains before the several places of egress and entrance. Utina himself was a savage of noble size and appearance. He carried himself with the ease and dignity of one born to the purple. His form, though an old man, was still unbending and tall. His countenance was one of great spirit and nobleness. With forehead equally large and high, with a dark eye that flashed with all the fires of youth, with lips that opened only to discourse in tones of a sweet but majestic eloquence, and with a shrewd sagacity, that made him, among a cunning people, a recognised master of all the arts of the serpent, he was necessarily a person to impress with respect and admiration those even who came with hostility.

It is probable that Utina knew nothing of the approach of the Frenchmen, until it was too late to escape them. But, before they entered the opened space assigned to the settlement, he was advised of their coming. Then it was that he threw aside his domestic habit and assumed his state. Then it was that he resumed his dignity and ascended the *dais* of stained cotton and flowing deer-skin. His turban of purple and yellow cotton was bound skilfully about his brow, his bow and quiver lay beside him, while at his feet was extended his huge macana, or war-club, which it scarcely seemed possible that his aged hands should now grasp with vigor sufficient for its formidable use. His hands, when the

Frenchmen entered the dwelling, held nothing more formidable than the earthen pipe, and the long tubulated reed which he busied himself in inserting within the bowl. Two of his attendant warriors retired at the same moment. These, Laudonniere did not think proper to arrest, though counselled to do so by D'Erlach. He knew not that they had been despatched by the wily Paracoussi for the purpose of gathering his powers for resistance.

Laudonniere appeared in the royal wigwam with but ten companions. Forty others had been dispersed by D'Erlach at proper points around the village. Of their proximity the king knew nothing. His eye took in, at a single glance, the persons of his visitors; and a slight smile, that looked derisive, was seen to overspread his visage. It was with something like good humor in his tones that he gave them welcome. A page at the same time brought forth a basket of wicker-work, which contained a large collection of pipes of all sorts and sizes. Another basket afforded a sufficient quantity of dried leaves of the tobacco and vanilla. The Paracoussi nodded to his guests as the boy presented both baskets, and Laudonniere, with two others of his company, helped themselves to pipes and weed. Thus far nothing had been said but " *Ami*," and " *Bonjour*." The welcome of the Indians was simple always, and a word sufficed among them as amply as the most studied and verbose compliment. The French had learned to imitate them in this respect, to be sparing of words, and to restrain the expression of their emotions, particularly when these indicated want or suffering.

But the necessities of our Frenchmen were too great and pressing, at the present time, to be silenced wholly by convention; and when, as if in mockery, a small trencher of parched corn was set before them, with a vessel of water, the impatience of Laudonniere broke into utterance.

"Paracoussi Utina," said he, "you have long known the want which has preyed upon our people,"

"My brother is hungry," replied Utina, with a smile more full of scorn than sweetness—"let my brother eat. Let his young men eat. There is never famine among the people of Utina."

"And if there be no want among the people of Utina, wherefore is it that he suffers the French to want? Why has he forgotten his allies? Did not my young men fight the battles of Utina against the warriors of the mighty Potanou? Did not many captives grace the triumph of Utina? Has the Paracoussi forgotten these services? Why does he turn away from his friends, and show himself cold to their necessities?"

"Why will my pale brother be talking?" said the other, with a most lordly air of indifference. "The people of Utina have fought against the warriors of Potanou for more than a hundred winters. My French brother is but a child in the land of the red-people. What does he know of the triumphs of my warriors? He saw them do battle once with the tribes of Potanou, and he makes account because he then fought on behalf of my people. My people have fought with the people of Potanou more than a hundred battles. Our triumphs have been witnessed by every bird that flies, every beast that runs, every fish that swims, between the villages of Potanou and the strong house of the Frenchman where he starves below. What more will our pale brother say, being thus a child among the red-men?"

"Why parley with the savage?" said Alphonse D'Erlach, "if you mean to take him? I care not for his insolence which chafes me nothing; but we lose time. You have suffered some of his warriors to depart. They are gone, doubtless, to gather the host together. We shall need all the time to carry our captive safely to the boats."

These words were spoken aloud, directly in the rear of Utina, D'Erlach having taken a place behind him in the conference. The Paracoussi was startled by the language. Some of it was beyond his comprehension. But he could not misunderstand the tone and manner of the speaker. D'Erlach was standing above him, with his hand stretched over him, and ready to grasp his victim the moment the word should be spoken. His slight form and youthful features, contrasted with the cold, inflexible expression of his eyes and face, very forcibly impressed the imagination of the Indian monarch, as, turning at the interruption, he looked up at the person of the speaker. But, beyond the first single start which followed the interruption, Utina gave no sign of surprise or apprehension.

"Awhile, awhile, Alphonse—be not too hasty, my son;" was the reply of Laudonniere. He continued, addressing himself to the Paracoussi:

"My red brother thinks he understands the French. He is mistaken. He will grow wiser before he grows much older. But it will be time then that I should teach him. It matters now only, that I should say to the Paracoussi Utina, *we want, and you have plenty*. We have fought your battles. We are your friends. We will trade with you for mil and beanes. Give us of these, according to our need, and you shall have of the merchandize of the French in just proportion. Let it be so, brother that peace may still flourish between our people."

"There is mil and beanes before my white brother. Let him take and divide among his people."

"But this will not suffice for a single meal. Does the Paracoussi laugh to scorn the sufferings of my people?"

"The Paracoussi laughs because the granaries of the red-men are full. There is no famine among *his* people. Hath the Great Spirit written that the red-man shall gather food in the proper season that the white man may sleep like the drowsy buffalo in the green pasture? Let my white brother drive from his ear the lying bird that sings to him: 'Sleep—take thy slumber under the pleasant shade tree, while the people of Utina get thee food!'"

"Would the Paracoussi make the Frenchmen his enemies? Is their anger nothing? Is their power not a thing to be feared?"

"And what is the Paracoussi Olata Ovae Utina? Hath he not many thousand warriors? The crane that rises in the east in the morning, though he flies all day, compasses not the land at sunset, which belongs to my dominions. East and west my people whoop like the crane, and hear no birds that answer but their own. Let my pale brother hush, for he speaks a foolish thing of his warriors. Did I dream, or did any runners tell me that the bones of the Frenchmen break through the skin, lacking food, and their sinews are so shrunken that they can never more strive in battle? Who shall fear them? I had pity on my brother when I heard these things. I sent him food, and bade my people say—'take this food which thou needest; the great Paracoussi asks for nothing in recompense, but thy guns, thy swords, and thy lances; weapons which they tell me thou hast strength to use no longer."

"Did they tell thee so, Utina? But thou shalt, see. Once

more, my brother, I implore thee to give us of thy abundance, and we will cheerfully impart to thee from our store of knives, reap-hooks, hatchets, mirrors, and lovely beads, such as will delight thy women. Here, behold,—this is some of the treasure which I have brought thee for the purposes of barter."

The lordly chieftain deigned not a single glance to the European wares, which, at a word from Laudonniere, one of the French soldiers laid at his feet. The French captain, as if loth to proceed to extremities, continued to entreat; while every new appeal was only answered, on the part of the savage prince, with a new speech of scorn, and new gestures of contempt. At length, Laudonniere's patience was exhausted, and he gave the signal which had been agreed upon with his lieutenant. In the next moment, the quick grasp of Alphonse D'Erlach was laid upon the Paracoussi's shoulders. He attempted to rise, and to grasp, at the same time, the macana which lay at his feet. But D'Erlach kept him down with his hands, while his foot was struck down upon the macana. In that moment, the war-conch was sounded at the entrance by several Indians who had been in waiting. It was caught up and echoed by the bugles of D'Erlach; the blast of which had scarcely been heard throughout the village, before it had been replied to, four several times, from as many different points where the French force had been stationed, ten soldiers in each. One desperate personal struggle which the Paracoussi made, proved fruitless to extricate him from the grasp of his captor; and he then sat quietly, without a word, coldly looking his enemies in the face.

CHAPTER II.

The captive Paracoussi lost none of his dignity in his captivity. He scorned entreaty. He betrayed no symptom of fear. That he felt the disgrace which had been put upon him, was evident in the close compression of his lips ; but he was sustained by the secret conviction that his warriors were gathering, and that they would rescue him from his captors by the overwhelming force of their numbers. At first his stoicism was shared by his family and attendants; but when Laudonniere declared his purpose to remove his prisoner to the boats, then the clamors of women, not less eloquent in the wigwam of the savage, than in the household of the pale faces, became equally wild and general. The Paracoussi had but one wife, foregoing, in this respect, some of his princely privileges, to which the customs of the red-men afforded a sufficient sanction. But there were many females in the royal dwelling, all of whom echoed the tumultuous cries o' of its mistress. This devoted woman, with her attendants. accompanied the captive to the boats, where, following the precautions adopted by D'Erlach, the Frenchmen arrived in safety. The warriors of the red-men had not yet time to gather and array themselves. Laudonniere gave the women and immediate companions of the Paracoussi to understand that his purpose was not to do his captive any injury. The French were hungry and must have food. When a sufficient supply was brought them, Olata Utina should be set free.

But these assurances they did not believe. They themselves, seldom set free their captives. Ordinarily, they slew all their male prisoners taken by surprise or in war, reserving the young females only. They naturally supposed, that what was the custom with them, founded upon sufficient reasons, at once of fear and superstition, must be the custom with the white men also. Accordingly, the queen of Utina, was not to be comforted. She followed him to the river banks, clinging to him to the last, and stood there ringing her hands and filling the air with her shrieks, while the people of Laudonniere lifted him into the bark, and pushed out to the middle of the river. It was well for them that this precaution was taken. The warriors of the Paracoussi were already gathering in great numbers. More than five hundred of them showed themselves on the banks of the river, entreating of Laudonniere to draw nigh that they might behold their prince. They brought tidings that, taking advantage of his captivity, the inveterate Potanou had suddenly invaded his chief village, had sacked and fired it, destroying all the persons whom he encountered. But Laudonniere was properly suspicious, and soon discovered, that, while five hundred archers showed themselves to him as suppliants, the shores were lined with thrice five hundred in snug ambush, lying close for the signal of attack. Failing to beguile the Frenchmen to the land, a few of them, in small canoes, ventured out to the bark in which their king was a prisoner, bringing him food—meal and peas, and their favorite beverage, the cassina tea. Small supplies were brought to the Frenchmen also; but without softening their hearts. Laudonniere had put his price upon the head of his captive, and would 'bate nothing of his ransom.

But it so happened, that the Indians were quite as suspicious and inflexible as the Frenchmen. They believed that Laudonniere only aimed to draw from them their stores, and then destroy their sovereign. A singular circumstance, illustrative of the terrible relations in which all savage tribes must stand toward each other, even when they dwell together in near neighborhood, occurred at this time, and increased the doubts and fears of the people of Utina. As soon as it was rumored about that this mighty potentate, whom they all so much dreaded, was a prisoner to the white man, the chiefs of the hostile tribes gathered to the place of his captivity, as the inhabitant of the city goes to behold in the menagerie the great lion of Sahara, the lord of the desert, of whom, when free in his wild ranges, it shook their hearts only to hear the roar. With head erect, though with chains about his limbs,—with heart haughty, though with hope humbled to the dust—the proud Paracoussi sate unmoved while they gathered, gazing upon him with a greedy malice that declared a long history of scorn and tyranny on the one hand, and hate and painful submission on the other. They walked around the lordly savage, scarcely believing their eyes, and still with a secret fear, lest, in some unlucky moment, he should break loose from his captivity, and resume his weapon for the purposes of vengeance. Eagerly and earnestly did they plead with Laudonniere either to put him to death, or to deliver him to their tender mercies. Among those who came to see and triumph over his ancient enemy, and, if possible, to get him into his power, was the Paracoussi Satouriova, one of Laudonniere's first acquaintances, whose power, perhaps, along the territories of May River, was only next to that of Utina. He, as well as the rest of the chiefs, brought bribes of maize and beans, withheld before, in order to persuade Laudonniere to yield to their desires. In this way he procured supplies, much beyond those which were furnished by the people of the prisoner, though still greatly disproportioned to his wants. The people of Utina, meanwhile, persuaded that their monarch could not escape the sacrifice, and aware of the several and strong influences brought to bear upon his captors, proceeded to do that which was likely to defeat all the hopes and calculations of the French. Their chiefs assembled in the Council House, assuming that Utina was dead already, and elected another for their sovereign, from among his sons. The measure was a hasty one, ill considered, and promised to lead to consequences the most injurious to the nation. The new prince immediately took possession of the royal wigwam, and began the full assertion of his authority. Parties were instantly formed among the tribes, from among the many who were dissatisfied with this assumption, and, but for the great efforts of the nobles of the country, the chiefs, the affair would have found its finish in a bloody social war; since, already had one of the near kinsmen of Olato Utina set up a rival claim to the dominion of his people.

But, it was sufficient that the election of the son of their captive, to the throne of his father, rendered unavailing the bold experiment of the Frenchmen, and threatened to defeat all the hopes which they had founded on the securing his person. The savages had adopted the most simple of all processes, and the most satisfactory, by which to baffle the invaders. Olata Utina was an old man, destined, in the ordinary course of nature, to give way in a short time to the very successor they had chosen. Why should they make any sacrifices to procure the freedom of one whom they did not need. Their reverence for royalty in exile was hardly much greater than it is found to-day in civilized Europe; and they resigned themselves to the absence of Olata Utina with a philosophy duly proportioned to the quantities of corn and peas which they should save by the happy thought which had already found a successor to his sway. In due degree with their resignation to the chapter of accidents, however, was the mortification of our Frenchmen, who thus found themselves cut off from all the hopes which they had built upon their bold proceeding. They had made open enemies of a powerful race, without reaping those fruits of their offence, which might have reconciled them to its penalties. Still they suffered in camp as well as in garrison, from want of food, and were allowed to entertain no expectations from the anxieties of the savages in regard to the fate of the captive monarch. His importance naturally declined in the elevation of his successor. Whether governed by policy or indifference, his people betrayed but little sympathy in his condition; and though keeping him still in close custody, treating him with kindness the while, Laudonniere was compelled to seek elsewhere for provisions. Apprised by certain Indians that, in the higher lands above, but along the river, there were some fields of maize newly ripening, he took a detachment of his men in boats and proceeded thither. Coming to a village called Enecaque, he was hospitably entertained by the sister of Utina, by whom it was governed. She gave him good cheer, a supper of mil, beans, and fish, with gourds of savory tea, made of cassina. Here it was found that the maize was indeed ripe: but the hungry Frenchmen suffered by the discovery and their own rapacity. They fastened upon it in its fresh state, without waiting for the slow process of cooking, to disarm it of its hurtful juices, and they became sick accordingly. Yet how could men be reproached for excess, who had scarcely eaten for four days, and for whom a portion of the food that silenced hunger during this time, consisted of a dish of young puppies newly whelped.

While on this expedition, it occurred to Laudonniere to revenge upon the lord of Edelano, the cruel murder of his soldier, Peter Gambier, whose story has been given in previous pages.

He was now drawing nigh to that beautiful island; and after leaving Enecaque, he turned his prows in search of its sweet retreats. But, with all his caution, the bird had flown. The lord of Edelano had been advised of what he had to fear, and, at the approach of the Frenchmen he disappeared, crossing the stream between, to the opposite forests, and leaving his village at the mercy of the enemy. Baffled of their revenge upon the offender, the Frenchmen vented their fury upon his empty dwellings. The torch was applied to the village, which was soon consumed. Returning to Enecaque, Laudonniere swept its fields of all their grain, with which he hastened back to his starving people at La Caroline. These, famishing still, "seeing me afar off coming, ranne to that side of the river where they thought I would come on land; for hunger so pinched them to the heart, that they could not stay until the victuals were brought them to the fort. And that they well showed as soon as I was come, and had distributed that little maize among them which I had given to each man, before I came out of the barke; for they eate it before they had taken it out of the huske."

The necessity of the garrison continued as great as ever. The wretched fields of the red-men afforded very scanty supplies. Other villages were sought and ransacked, those of Athoré, swayed by King Emola, and those of a Queen named Nia Cubacani. In ravaging the fields of the former, two of the Frenchmen were slain. But the provisions got from Queen Nia Cubacani, were all free gifts. The pale faces seem to have been favorites with the female sovereigns wherever they went. In the adventures of the Huguenots, as in those of the Spaniards under Hernan de Soto and other chiefs, the smiles of the Apalachian women seemed to have been bestowed as freely as were the darts and arrows of their lords and masters. In this way was the path of enterprise stripped of many of its thorns, and he whose arm was ever lifted against the savage man, seldom found the heart of the savage woman shut against his approach. This is a curious history, but it seems to mark usually the fortunes of the superior, invading the abodes of the inferior people. The women of a race are always most capable of appreciating the social morals of a superior

The Paracoussi Olata Utina, now made an effort to obtain his liberty. The hopes of the Frenchmen, in respect to his ransom, had failed. His people had shown a stubbornness, which, to do the Indian monarch justice, had not been greater than his own. He saw the poverty and distress which prevailed among his captors, in spite of all their attempts at concealment. He saw that the lean and hungry famine was still preying upon their hearts. He said to Laudonniere—

"Of what avail is it to you or to me, that you hold me here a captive? Take me to my people. The maize is probably ripened in my fields. One of these shall be set aside for your use wholly, with all its store of corn and beans, if you will set me free in my own country."

Laudonniere consulted with his chief men. They concurred in granting the petition of the Paracoussi. The two barks were accordingly fitted out, and, with a select detachment, Laudonniere proceeded with his captive to a place called Patica, some eight or nine leagues distant from the village of Utina. The redmen fled at their approach, seeking cover in the forests, though their king, himself, cried to them to await his coming. To pursue them was impossible. To trust the king out of their possession, without any equivalent, was impolitic. Another plan was pursued. One of the sons of the Paracoussi, a mere boy, had been taken with his father. It was now determined to dismiss this boy to the village, accompanied by one of the Frenchmen, who had been thither before, and who knew the character and condition of the country. His instructions were to restore the boy to his mother and his kindred, and to say that his father should be delivered also, if an adequate supply of provisions was brought to the vessel. The ancient chronicle, briefly, but very touchingly, describes the welcome which was given to the enfranchised child. All were delighted to behold him, the humblest making as much of him as if he had been the nearest kindred, and each man thinking himself never so happy as when permitted to touch him with his hand. The wife of Utina, with her father, came to the barks of the Frenchmen, bringing bread for the present wants of the company; but the policy of the Indians did not suffer the pleadings of the woman to prevail. The parties could not agree about the terms of ransom; the red-men, meanwhile, practised all their arts to delay the departure of the vessels. It was discovered that they were busy with their forest strategy, seeking rather to entrap the captain of the French, than to bargain for the recovery of their own chieftain. Laudonniere was compelled finally to return with his prisoner to La Caroline, as hungry as ever, and with no hopes of the future.

Here, a new danger awaited the captive. Furious at their disappointment, the starving Frenchmen, as soon as the failure of the enterprise was known, armed themselves, and with sword and matchlock assailed the little cavalcade which had the chief in custody, as they were about to disembark. With gaunt visages and staring eyes, that betrayed terribly the cruel famine under which they were perishing, and cries of such terrible wrath, as left but little doubt of the direst purpose, they darted upon their prey. But Laudonniere manfully interposed himself, surrounded by his best men, between their rage and his victim. Captain La Vasseur and Ensign D'Erlach, each seized upon a mutineer whom they held ready to slay at a stroke given; and other good men and true, coming to the rescue, the famishing mutineers were shamed and frightened into forbearance. But bitterly did they complain of the lack of wisdom in their captain, who had released the son, the precious hope of the nation, retaining the sire, for whom, having a new king, the savages cared nothing. Their murmurs drove Laudonniere forth once more. Taking the Paracoussi with him, after a brief delay, he proceeded to explore other villages along the river. The red-men planted two crops during the growing season. Their maize ripened gradually, and fields that yielded nothing during one month, were in full grain in that ensuing. For fifteen days the French commandant continued his explorations with small success; when the Paracoussi, whom nothing had daunted, of his proper and haughty firmness, during all his captivity, once more appealed to his captors:

"That my people did not supply you with maize and beanes when you sought them last, was because they were not ripe. I spake to you then as a foolish young man, anxious to set foot once more among my people. I should have known that the grain could not be ready then for gathering. But the season is now It is ripened everywhere, and, in the present abundance of my people, they will gladly yield to your demands, and give full ransom for their king. Take me thither then, once more, and my people will not stick to give you ample victual."

• The necessities of the French were too great to make them hesitate at a renewal of the attempt, where all others had proved so profitless; particularly when the old king, with some solemnity, placing his hand upon the wrist of the French captain, said to him—

"Brother, doubt me not—doubt not my people. If they answer thee not to thy expectations as well as mine, bring me back to thy people, and let them do with me even as they please?"

Again was the Paracoussi brought into the presence of his subjects. They assembled to meet him on the banks of a little river, which emptied into the main stream, and to which Laudonniere had penetrated in his vessels. They appeared with considerable supplies of bread, fish and beans, which they shared among the Frenchmen. They put on the appearance of great good feeling and friendship, and entered into the negotiations for the release of their king, with equal frankness and eagerness. But in all this they exhibited only the consummate hypocrisy of their race;—a hypocrisy not to be wondered at or complained of, as it is the only natural defence which a barbarous people can ever possibly oppose to the superior power of civilization. Their effort was simply still so to beguile the Frenchmen, as to ensnare their leader,—get *him* within their power, and then compel an exchange with his people of chief for chief. For this purpose they prolonged the negotiations. Small supplies of food, enough to provoke expectation, without satisfying demand, were brought daily to their visitors. But, in the meantime, their warriors began to accumulate along the shores, covered in the neighboring thickets, or crouching in patient watch along the reedy tracts that fringed the river. The vigilant eye of Alphonse D'Erlach soon detected the ambush; and at length, finding Laudonniere preparing to leave them, still keeping their king a captive, the savages resumed their negotiations with more activity, and withdrew their archers from the neighborhood.

It must not be supposed that théir love for their monarch was small, because they showed themselves so slow in bringing the humble ransom of corn and beans, which the French demanded. To them, that ransom was by no means insignificant. It swept their granaries. It took the food from their children. It drove them into the woods in winter without supplies, leaving them to the rigors of the season, the uncertainties of the chase, and with no other dependence than the common mast of the forest. It deprived them of the very seed from which future harvests were to be gathered. The drain for the supply of the hungry mouths at La Caroline, seemed to them perpetual, and Laudonniere aimed now not only to meet the wants of the present, but to store ships and fort against future necessities. It was of the last importance to the people of Olata Utina, that they should recover their king without subjecting their people to the horrors of such a famine as was preying upon the vitals of the Frenchmen.

They over-reached Laudonniere at last. They persuaded him that the presence of the king, among his people, was necessary to compel each man to bring in his subsidy;—that they must see him, in his former abodes, freed entirely from bonds, before they would recognize his authority;—that they feared, when they should have brought their grain, that the French would still retain their captive;—and, in short, insisted so much upon the freedom of Utina, as the *sine quâ non*, that the doubts of Laudonniere were overcome. It was agreed that two chiefs should become hostages for Olata Utina, and, in guaranty of the fulfilment of his pledges.

We are not told of the exact amount of ransom required for

the surrender of their king. It was probably enormous, according to the equal standards of Indian and Frenchmen, in this period and region. Willingly came the two chiefs to take the place of Olata Utina. They were admitted on board the bark, where he was kept in chains. They were warriors, and as they approached him, they broke their bows and arrows across, and threw them before him : Then, as they beheld his bonds, they rushed to his feet, lifted up and kissed his chains, and supported them, while the Frenchmen unlocked them from the one captive to transfer them to the hands and feet of those who came to take his place. These looked not upon the bonds as they were riveted about their limbs. They only watched the movements of their king with eyes that declared a well-satisfied delight. He rose from his place, and shook himself slowly, as a lion might be supposed to do, rousing himself after sleep. Never was head so erect, or carriage so like one who feels all his recovered greatness. He waved his hand in signal to the shore, where hundreds of his people were assembled to greet his deliverance.

The signal was understood, a mantle of fringed and gorgeously-dyed cotton was brought him by one of his sons. His macana, or war-club, and a mighty bow from which he could deliver a shaft more than five English feet in length, were also brought him. Over his shoulder the mantle was thrown by one of his attendants. The war-club was carried before him by a page. But, before he left the vessel, he bent his bow, fixed one of the shafts upon the deer sinews, which formed the cord, and drawing it to its head, sent it high in air, until it disappeared for a few seconds from the sight. This was a signal to his people. Their king, like the arrow, was freed from its confinement. It had gone like a bird of mighty wing, into the unchained atmosphere. A cloud of arrows from the shore followed that of their sovereign. To this succeeded a great shout of thanks and deliverance— "He! He! yo-he-wah! He—he—yo-he-wah." The echo of which continued to ring through the vaulted fórests, long after the Paracoussi had disappeared within their green recesses.

CHAPTER III.

THE Paracoussi, on parting with Laudonniere, renewed his assurances of good will, and repeated the promises which had been given to ensure his deliverance from captivity. The engagement required that a certain number of days should be allowed him, in which to gather supplies in sufficient quantity to discharge his ransom. Laudonniere left his lieutenants, Ottigny and D'Erlach, with the two hostages, in one of the barks, to receive the provisions which Utina was to furnish, while he himself returned to La Caroline. The lieutenants moored their vessel within a little creek which emptied into the May, and adopted all necessary precautions against savage artifice. The vigilance of Alphonse D'Erlach, in particular, was sleepless. He knew, more certainly than his superior, the necessities and dangers of the French, and the subtlety of the Indians. By day and night they lurked in the contiguous thickets, watchful of every opportunity for assault. An arquebuse presented in wantonness against the ledge which skirted the river, would frequently expel a group of shrieking warriors, well armed and covered with the war paint; and, with the dawn of morning, the first thing to salute the eyes of our Frenchmen would be long strings of arrows, planted in the earth, their barbs of flint turned upwards, from which long hairs shreds from heads which had been shorn for war, were to be seen waving in the wind. These were signs, too well understood by previous experience, of a threatened and sleepless hostility

It was soon found that the Paracoussi either could not or would not comply with his engagements. He sent a small supply of grain to the lieutenant, but said that more could not be provided except by a surrender of the hostages. The Frenchmen were required to bring the captives to the village, when and where they should be furnished with the full amount of the promised ransom Satisfied that all this was mere pretence, indicating purposes of treachery, the Frenchmen were yet too much straitened by want to forego any enterprise which promised them provisions. They, accordingly, set forth for the place appointed, in two separate bodies, marching so that they might support each other promptly, under the several leads of D'Erlach and Ottigny. The former held the advance. The village of Utina was six French leagues from the river where they left their barque, and the route which they were compelled to pursue was such as exposed them frequently to the perils of ambuscade. But so vigilant was their watch, so ready were they with matches lighted, and so close was the custody in which they kept their hostages, that the Indians, whom they beheld constantly flitting through the thickets, dared never make any attempt upon them. They reached the village in safety, and immediately proceeded to the dwelling-house of Olata Utina, raised, as before described, upon an artificial eminence. Here they found assembled all the chiefs of the nation; but the Paracoussi was not among them. He kept aloof, and was not to be seen at present by the Frenchmen. His chiefs received their visitors with smiles and great professions; but, as their own proverb recites, when the enemy smiles your scalp is in danger.

They pointed to great sacks of mil and beans which had already been accumulated, and still they showed the Frenchmen where hourly came other of their subjects adding still more to the pile.

"But wherefore," they demanded, "wherefore come our white brethren, with the fire burning in their harquebuses? See they not that it causes our women to be afraid, and our children to tremble in their terror. Let our brethren put out this fire, which makes them dread to come nigh with their peace-offerings, and know us for a friend, under whose tongue there is no serpent."

To this D'Erlach replied—"Our red brothers do themselves wrong. They do not fear the fire in our harquebuses. They know not its danger. The Frenchmen have always forborne to show them the power that might make them afraid. But this power is employed only against our enemies. Let the chiefs of the people of the Paracoussi Utina show themselves friends, and the thunder which we carry shall only send its fearful bolts among the foes of Utina, the people of Potanou, and the warriors of the great mountain of Apalatchy.

"If we are thus friends of the Frenchmen, why do they keep our beloved men in bondage? Are these the ornaments proper to a warrior and a great chief among his people?"

They pointed as they spoke to the fetters which embraced the legs and arms of the hostages, who sat in one corner of the council-house.

"Our red brothers have but to speak, and these chains fall from the limbs of their well beloved chiefs."

"Heh!—We speak!—Let them fall!"

"Speak to your people that these piles be complete," pointing to the grain.

"They have heard. See you not they come?"

"But very slowly;—and hearken to us now, brothers of the red-men, while we ask,—do the skies that pavilion the territories of the Paracoussi Utina rain down such things as these."

Here D'Erlach showed them a bunch of the arrows which they had found planted by the wayside as they came. The thin lips of the savages parted into slight smiles as they beheld them.

"These grow not by nature," continued D'Arlach; "they fall not from heaven in the heavy showers. They are sown by the red-men along the path which the white man travels. What is the fruit which is to grow from such seed as this?"

The chiefs were silent. The youth proceeded:

"Brothers, we are calm;—we are not angry, though we well know what these arrows mean. We are patient, for we know our own strength. The Paracoussi has promised us supplies of grain, and hither we have come. Four days shall we remain in waiting for it. Till that time, these well-beloved men shall remain in our keeping. When we receive the supplies which have been promised us, they shall be yours. We have spoken."

Thus ended the first conference. That night the French lieutenants found their way to the presence of the Paracoussi. He was kept concealed in a small wigwam, deeply embowered in the woods, but in near and convenient neighborhood to the village. He himself had sent for them, and one of his sons had shown the way. They found the old monarch still maintaining the state of a prince, but he was evidently humbled. His captivity had lessened his authority; and his anxiety to comply with the engagements made with the French had in some degree impaired his influence over his people. They had resolved to destroy the pale-faces, as insolent invaders of their territory, consumers of its substance and enemies of its peace. It was this hostility and this determination that had interposed all the obstacles in the way of procuring the supplies promised.

"They resist me, their Paracoussi," said Utina bitterly, "and have resolved on fighting with you! They will wage war against you to the last. See you not the planted arrows that marked your pathway to my village? These arrows are planted from the territories of Utina, by every pathway, to the very gates of La Caroline. They will meet your eyes wherever you shall return to the fortress. They mean nothing less than war, and such warfare as admits of no peace. Go you, therefore, go you with all speed to your vessels, and make what haste you can to the garrison. The woods swarm with my warriors, and they no longer heed my voice. They will hunt you to your vessel. They mean to throw trees athwart the creek so that her escape may be cut off, while they do you to death with their arrows, and I cannot be there to say to my people—'stay your shafts, these be our friends and allies.' They no longer hearken to my voice. I am a Paracoussi without subjects, a ruler without obedience,—a shadow, where I only used to be the substance."

The despondency of the king was without hypocrisy. It sensibly impressed our Frenchmen. They felt that he spoke the truth. He was then, in fact, excluded from the house of council, as incurring the suspicion of the red-men as fatally friendly to the whites. While they still conversed, they were alarmed by violent shrieks, as of one in mortal terror.

"That scream issues from a French throat!" exclaimed D'Erlach, as he rushed forth. He was followed by Lieutenant Ottigny and another. The Paracoussi never left his seat. The screams guided them into a neighboring thicket, into which they hurried, arriving there not a moment too soon. A Frenchman struggled in the grasp of five stalwart savages, who had him down and were preparing to cut his throat. He had been beguiled from the place which had been assigned him as a watch, and was about to pay the penalty of his folly with his life. In an instant the gallant Alphonse D'Erlach had sprung among them, his sword passing clear through the back of the most prominent in the group of assailants. His body, falling upon that of the captive, prevented the blows which the rest were showering upon him. They started in sudden terror at this interruption. Their own and the clamors of the Frenchman had kept them from all knowledge of the approaching rescue. In an instant they were gone. They waited for no second stroke from a weapon whose first address was so sharp and sudden. They left their captive, bruised and groaning, but without serious injury to life or limb.

The warnings and assurances of the Paracoussi were sufficiently enforced by this instance of the hostility of the red-men. But the necessity of securing all the supplies they might possibly procure from the natives, either through their own artifices or because of the apprehension for their chiefs, caused our Frenchmen to linger at the village of Utina. They were determined to wait the full period of four days which they had assigned themselves. In this period they saw the Paracoussi more than once. At each interview his admonitions were delivered with increased solemnity. They found his chiefs less and less accommodating at every interview. The piles of grain at the council-house increased slowly. Occasionally an Indian might be seen to enter and cast the contents of his little basket among the rest. The Frenchmen endeavored to persuade the chiefs to furnish men to carry the grain to their vessel, but this was flatly denied. Resolved, finally, to depart, each soldier was required to load himself with a sack as well filled as it was consistent with his strength to bear. This was slung across his shoulder, and, in this way, burdened with food for other mouths as well as their own, and carrying their matchlocks besides, the Frenchmen prepared to depart, on the morning of the 27th July, 1565, from the village of Utina to the bark which they had left. It was a memorable day for our adventurers. In groups, scornfully smiling as they beheld the soldiers staggering beneath their burdens, the chiefs assembled to see them depart from the village. Alphonse D'Erlach beheld the malignant triumph which sparkled in their eyes.

"We shall not be suffered to reach the bark in quiet;" was his remark to Ottigny. "Let me have the advance, Monsieur, if you please; I have dealt with the dogs before."

To this Ottigny consented; and leading one of the divisons of the detachment, as at coming, D'Erlach prepared to take the initiate in a progress, every part of which was destined to be marked with strife. The immediate entrance to the village of the Paracoussi, the only path, indeed, by which our Frenchmen could emerge, lay, for nearly half a mile, through a noble avenue, the sides of which were densely occupied by a most ample and umbrageous forest. The trees were at once great and lofty, and the space beneath was closed up with a luxuriant undergrowth which spread away like a wall of green on either hand. D'Erlach remembered this entrance.

"Here," said he to Ottigny, "Here, at the very opening of the path, our trouble is likely to begin. Let your men be prepared with matches lighted, and see that your fire is delivered only in squads, so that, at no time, shall all of your pieces be entirely empty."

Ottigny prepared to follow this counsel. His men were all
13

apprised of what they had to expect; and were told, at the first sign of danger, to cast down their corn bags, and betake themselves to their weapons wholly. The grain might be lost—probably would be—but better this, than, in a vain endeavor to preserve it, lose life and grain together. Thus prepared, D'Erlach began the march. He was followed, at a short interval, by Ottigny, with the rest of the detachment; a small force of eight arquebusiers 'excepted, who, under charge of a sergeant, were sent to the left of the thicket which bounded the avenue on one hand, with instructions to scour the woods in that quarter, yet without passing beyond reach of help from the main body.

All fell out as had been anticipated. D'Erlach was encountered as he emerged from the avenue, by a force of three hundred Indians. They poured in a cloud of arrows, but fortunately at such a distance as to do little mischief. With the first assault the Frenchmen dispossessed themselves of their burdens, and prepared themselves for fight. The savages came on more boldly, throwing in fresh flights of arrows as they pushed forward, and rending the forests with their cries. D'Erlach preserved all his steadiness and coolness. He saw that the arrows were yet comparatively ineffectual.

"Do not answer them yet, my good fellows," he cried, "but stoop ye, every man, and break the arrows, as many as ye can, that fall about ye."

He had seen that the savages, having delivered a few fires, were wont to rush forward and gather up the spent shafts, which, thus recovered, afforded them an inexhaustible armory, upon which it is their custom to rely. When his assailants beheld how his men were engaged, they rushed forward with loud shouts of fury, and delivering another storm of darts, they made demonstrations of a desire for close conflict, with their stone hatchets and macanas. At this show, D'Erlach spoke to his men in subdued accents.

"Make ye still as if ye would stoop for the fallen arrows, ye of the first rank; but blow ye your matches even as ye do so, and falling upon your knees deliver then your fire; while the second rank will cover you as ye do so, and while ye charge anew your pieces."

The command was obeyed with coolness; and, as the Indians darted forward, coming in close packed squadrons into the gorge of the avenue, the soldiers delivered their fire with great precision. Dreadful was the howl which followed it, for more than thirteen of the savages had fallen, mortally hurt, and two of their chief warriors had been made to bite the dust. Seizing the bodies of their slain and wounded comrades, the survivors immediately hurried into cover, and D'Erlach at once pushed forward with his command. But he had not advanced more than four hundred paces, when the assault was renewed, the air suddenly being darkened with the flight of bearded shafts, while the forest rang with the yells of savage fury. They were still too far for serious mischief, and were besides covered with the woods; so, giving the assailants little heed, except to observe that they came not too nigh, or too suddenly upon him, D'Erlach continued to push forward, doing as he had done before with the hostile arrows whenever they lay in the pathway. But the courage of the red-men increased as they warmed in the struggle, and they grew bolder because of the very forbearance of the Frenchmen Besides, their forces had been increased by other bodies, each approaching in turn to the assault, so as to keep their enemies constantly busy. In parties of two or three hundred, they darted from their several ambushes, and having discharged their arrows and met with repulse, retired rapidly to other favorite places of concealment to renew the conflict as it continued to advance. By this time, the whole body of the Frenchmen had become engaged in the fight. The force under Ottigny, following the example of that led by D'Erlach, had succeeded in pressing forward, though not without loss, while making great havoc with the red-men. These people fought, never men more bravely; and, but for the happy thought, that of destroying their arrows as fast as they fell, it is probable that the detachment had never reached La Caroline. They hovered thus about the march of the Frenchmen all the day, encouraging each other with shouts of vengeance and delight, and sending shaft upon shaft, with an aim, which, had they not been too greatly sensible of the danger of the arquebuse, to come sufficiently nigh, would have been always fatal. Yet well did the savage succeed, so long as they remained unintoxicated by their rage, in dodging the aim of the weapon. As Laudonniere writes—" All the while they had their eye and foot so quicke and readie, that as soone as ever they saw the harquebuse raised to the cheeke, so soon were they on the ground, and eftsoone to answer with their bowes, and to flie their way, if by chance they perceived that we were about to take them."

This conflict lasted from nine o'clock in the morning until night. It only ceased when the darkness separated the combatants. Even then, but for the deficiency of their arrows, they probably would not have withdrawn from the field. It was late in the night when the Frenchmen reached their boats, weary and exhausted, their grain wrested from them, their hostages rescued, and twenty-four of their number killed and wounded. The Floridians had shown themselves warriors of equal spirit and capacity. The determined exclusion of their Paracoussi from counsels which it was feared that he would dishonor, their manly resistance to the white invaders, their scornful ridicule of their necessities, their proud defiance of their power, and the fierce and unrelenting hostility with which they had chased their adversaries, remind us irresistibly of the degradation of Montezuma by his subjects, their prolonged warfare with the Spaniards, their sleepless hostility, and that bloody struggle which first drove them over the causeways of Tenochtitlan. The inferior state and wealth of the Paracoussi, Olata Ouvae Utina, constitutes no such sufficient element of difference, as to lessen the force of the parallel between himself and people, and those of the Atzec sovereign.

XX.

IRACANA,

OR THE EDEN OF THE FLORIDIAN.

THE disasters which befel his detachment, brought Laudonniere to his knees. He had now been humbled severely by the dispensations of Providence—punished for that disregard of the things most important to the colonization of a new country, which, in his insane pursuit of the precious metals, had marred his administration. His misfortunes reminded him of his religion.

"Seeing, therefore, mine hope frustrate on that side, I made my prayer unto God, and thanked him of his grace which he had showed unto my poore souldiers which were escaped."

But his prayers did not detain him long. The necessities of the colony continued as pressing as ever. "Afterward, I thought upon new meanes to obtaine victuals, as well for our returne into France, as to drive out the time untill our embarking." These were meditations of considerable difficulty. The petty fields of the natives, never contemplated with reference to more than a temporary supply of food;—never planted with reference to providing for a whole year, were really inadequate to the wants of such a body of men, unless by grievously distressing their proprietors. The people of Olata Utina had been moved to rage in all probability, quite as much because of their grain crops, about to be torn from them, as with any feeling of indignation in consequence of the detention of their Paracoussi. In the sacks of corn which the Frenchmen bore away upon their shoulders, they beheld the sole provisions upon which, for several months, their women and children had relied to feed; and their quick imaginations were goaded to desperation, as they depicted the vivid horrors of a summer consumed in vain search after crude roots and indigestible berries, through the forests. No wonder the wild wretches fought to avert such a danger; as little may we wonder that they fought successfully The Frenchmen, compelled to cast down their sacks of grain, to use their weapons, the red-men soon repossessed themselves of all their treasure. When Laudonniere reviewed his harrassed soldiers on their return from this expedition, "all the mill that he found among his company came but to two men's burdens." To attempt to recover the provisions thus wrested from them, or to revenge themselves for the indignity and injury they had undergone, were equally out of the question. The people of the Paracoussi could number their thousands; and, buried in their deep fortresses of forest, they could defy pursuit. Laudonniere was compelled to look elsewhere for the resources which should keep his company from want.

Two leagues distant from La Caroline, on the opposite side of May River, stood the Indian village of Saravahi. Not far from this might be seen the smokes of another village, named Emoloa. The Frenchmen, wandering through the woods in search of game, had alighted suddenly upon these primitive communities. Here they had been received with gentleness and love. The natives were lively and benevolent. They had never felt the wrath of the white man, nor been made to suffer because of his improvidence and necessities. His thunderbolts had never hurled among their columns, and mown them down as with a fiery scythe from heaven. The Frenchmen did not fail to remark that they were provident tribes, with corn-fields much more ample than were common among the Indians. These, they now concluded, must be covered with golden grain, in the season of harvest, and thither, accordingly, Laudonniere dispatched his boats. A judicious officer conducted the detachment, and stores of European merchandize were confided to him for the purposes of traffic. He was not disappointed in his expectations. His soldiers were received with open arms; and a " good store of mil," speaking comparatively, was readily procured from the abundance of the Indians.

But, in preparation for the return to France, other and larger supplies were necessary. The boats were again made ready, and confided to La Vasseur and D'Erlach. They proceeded to the river to which the French had given their name of Somme, now known as the Satilla, but which was then called among the Indians, the Iracana, after their own beautiful queen. Of this queen our Frenchmen had frequently been told. She had been described to them as the fairest creature, in the shape of woman, that the country had beheld: nor was the region over which she swayed, regarded with less admiration. This was spoken of as a sort of terrestrial paradise. Here, the vales were more lovely; the waters more cool and pellucid than in any other of the territories of earth. Here, the earth produced more abundantly than elsewhere; the trees were more stately and magnificent, the flowers more beautiful and gay, and the vines more heavily laden with grapes of the most delicious flavor. Sweetest inlets rose along the shore over which the moon seemed to linger with a greater fondness, and soft breezes played ever in the capacious forests, always kindling to emotions of pleasure, the soft beatings of the delighted heart. The influences of scene and climate were felt for good amongst the people who were represented at once as the most generous and gentle of all the Floridian natives. They had no wild passions, and coveted no fierce delights. Under the sway of a woman, at once young and beautiful, the daughter of their most favorite monarch, their souls had become attuned to sympathies which greatly tended to subdue and to soothe the savage nature. Their lives were spent in sports and dances. No rebukes or restraints of duty, no sordid cares or purposes, impaired the dream of youth and rapture which prevailed everywhere in the hearts of the people. Gay assemblages were ever to be found among the villages in the forests; singing their own delights and imploring the stranger to be happy also. They had a thousand songs and sports of youth and pleasure, which made life a perpetual round of ever freshening felicity. Innocent as wild, no eye of the ascetic could rebuke enjoyments which violated no cherished laws of experience and thought, and their glad and sprightly dances, in the deep shadows of the wood, to the lively clatter of Indian gourds and tambourines, were quite as significant of harmless fancies as of thoughtless lives. Happy was the lonely voyager, speeding along the coast, in his frail canoe, when, suddenly darting out from the forests of Iracana, a slight but lovely creature, with flowing tunic of whit cotton, stood upon the head land, waving her branch of palm or myrtle, entreating his approach, and imploring him to delay his journey, while he shared in the sweet festivities of love and youth, for a season, upon the shore,—crying with a sweet chant,—

"Love you me not, oh, lonely voyager—love you me not? Lo! am I not lovely; I who serve the beautiful queen of Iracana? will you not come to me, for a while!—come, hide the canoe among the reeds, along the shore, and make merry with the damsels of Iracana. I give to thee the palm and the myrtle, in token of a welcome of peace and love. Come hither, oh! lonely voyager, and be happy for a season!"

And seldom were these persuasions unavailing. The lonely voyager was commonly won, as was he who, sailing by Scylla and Charybdis, refused to seal his ears with wax against the song of the Syren. But our charmers, along the banks of the Satilla, entreated to no evil, laid no snares for the unwary, meditating their destruction. They sought only to share the pleasures which they themselves enjoyed. The benevolence of that love which holds its treasure as of little value, unless its delights may be bestowed on others, was the distinguishing moral in the Indian Eden of Iracana; and he who came with love, never departed without a sorrow, such as made him linger as he went, and soon return, when this were possible, to a region, which, among our Floridians, realized that period of the Classic Fable, which has always been designated, par excellence, as the "age of gold."

Our Frenchmen, under the conduct of La Vasseur and D'Erlach, reached the frontiers of Iracana, at an auspicious period. The season of harvest, among all primitive and simple nations, is commonly a season of great rejoicing. Among a people like those of Iracana, habitually accustomed to rejoice, it is one in which delight becomes exultation, and when in the supreme felicity of good fortune, the happy heart surpasses itself in the extraordinary expression of its joy. Here were assembled to the harvest, all the great lords of the surrounding country. Here was Athoree, the gigantic son of Satouriova, a very Anak, among the Floridians. Here were Apalou, a famous chieftain,— Tacadocorou, and many others, whom our Frenchmen had met and known before;—some of whom indeed, they had known in fierce conflict, and a strife which had never been healed by any of the gentle offices of peace.

But Iracana was the special territory of peace. It was not permitted, among the Floridians, to approach this realm with angry purpose. Here war and strife were tabooed things,—shut, out, denied and banished, and peace and love, and rapture, were alone permitted exercise in abodes which were too grateful to all parties, to be desecrated by hostile passions. When, therefore, our Frenchmen, beholding those only with whom they had so lately fought, were fain to betake themselves to their weapons, the chiefs themselves, with whom they had done battle, came forward to embrace them, with open arms.

"Brothers, all—brothers here, in Iracana;" was the common speech. "Be happy here, brothers, no fight, no scalp, nothing but love in Iracana,—nothing but dance and be happy."

Even had not this assurance sufficed with our Frenchmen, the charms of the lovely Queen herself, her grace and sweetness, not unmixed with a dignity which declared her habitual rule, must have stifled every feeling of distrust in their bosoms, and effectually exorcised that of war. She came to meet the strangers with a mingled ease and state, a sweetness and a majesty, which were inexpressibly attractive. She took a hand of La Vasseur and of D'Erlach, with each of her own. A bright, happy smile lightened in her eye, and warmed her slightly dusky features with a glow. Rich in hue, yet delicately thin, her lips parted with a pleasure, as she spoke to them, which no art could simulate She bade them welcome, joined their hands with those of the great warriors by whom she was attended, and led them away among her damsels, of whom a numerous array were assembled, all habited in the richest garments of their scanty wardrobes.

The robes of the Queen herself were ample. The skirts of her dress fell below her knees, a thing very uncommon with the women of Florida. Over this, she wore a tunic of crimson, which descended below her hips. A slight cincture embraced, without confining, her waist. Long strings of sea-shell, of the smallest size, but of colors and tints the most various and delicate, drooped across her shoulders, and were strung, in loops and droplets, to the skirts of her dress and her symar. Similar strings encircled her head, from which the hair hung free behind, almost to the ground, a raven-like stream, of the deepest and most glossy sable. Her form was equally stately and graceful—her carriage betrayed a freedom, which was at once native and the fruit of habitual exercise. Nothing could have been more gracious than the sweetness of her welcome; nothing more utterly unshadowed than the sunshine which beamed in her countenance. She led her guests among the crowd, and soon released La Vasseur to one of the loveliest girls who came about her. Alphonse D'Erlach she kept to herself. She was evidently struck with the singula. union of delicacy and youth with sagacity and character, which declared itself in his features and deportment.

Very soon were all the parties engaged in the mazes of the Indian dance of Iracana,—a movement which, unlike the waltz of the Spaniards, less stately perhaps, and less imposing—yet requires all its flexibility and freedom, and possesses all its seductive and voluptuous attractions. Half the night was consumed with dancing; then gay parties could be seen gliding into canoes and darting across the stream to other villages and places of abode. Anon, might be perceived a silent couple gliding away to sacred thickets; and with the sound of a mighty conch, which strangely broke the silence of the forest, the Queen herself reired with her attendants, having first assigned to certain of her chiefs the task of providing for the Frenchmen. Of these she had already shown herself sufficiently heedful and solicitous. Not sparing of her regards to La Vasseur, she had particularly devoted herself to D'Erlach, and, while they danced together, if the truth could be spoken of her simple heart, great had been its pleasure at those moments, when the spirit of the dance required that she should yield herself to his grasp, and die away languidly in his embrace.

"Ah! handsome Frenchman," she said to her companion,— "You please me so much."

His companions were similarly entertained. Captain La Vasseur was soon satisfied that he too was greatly pleasing to the fair and lovely savage who had been assigned him; and not one of the Frenchmen, but had his share of the delights and endearments which made the business of life in Iracana. The soldiers had each a fair creature, with whom he waltzed and wandered; and fond discourse, everywhere in the great shadows of the wood, between sympathizing spirits, opened a new idea of existence to the poor Huguenots who, hitherto, had only known the land of Florida by its privations and its gold. The dusky damsels, alike sweet and artless, brought back to our poor adventurers precious recollections of youthful fancies along the banks of the Garonne and the Loire, and it is not improbable, that, under the excitement of new emotions, had Laudonniere proposed to transfer La Caroline to the Satilla, or Somme, instead of May River, they might have been ready to waive, for a season at least, their impatient desire to return to France.

Night was at length subdued to silence on the banks of the Satilla. The sounds of revelry had ceased. All slept, and the transition from night to day passed, sweetly and insensibly, almost without the consciousness of the parties. But, with the sunrise, the great conch sounded in the forest. The Eden of the Floridian did not imply a life of mere repose. The people were gathered to their harvesting, and the labors of the day, under the auspices of a gracious rule, were made to seem a pleasure. Hand in hand, the Queen Iracana, with her maidens, and her guests, followed to the maize fields. Already had she found D'Erlach, and her slender fingers, without any sense of shame, had taken possession of his hand, which she pressed at moments very tenderly. He had already informed her of the wants and the sufferings of his garrison, and she smiled with a new feeling of happiness, as she eagerly assured him that his people should receive abundance. She bent with her own hands the towering stalks; and, detaching the ears, flung to the ground a few in all these places, on which it was meant that the heaps should be accumulated. "Give these to our friends, the Frenchmen," she said, indicating with a sweep of the hand, a large tract of the field, through which they went. D'Erlach felt this liberality. He squeezed her fingers fondly in return,—saying words of compliment which, possibly, in her ear, meant something more than compliment.

Then followed the morning feast; then walks in the woods; then sports upon the river in their canoes; and snaring the fish in weirs, in which the Indians were very expert. Evening brought with it a renewal of the dance, which again continued late in the night. Again did Alphonse D'Erlach dance with Iracana; but it was now seen that her eyes saddened with the overfulness of her heart. Love is not so much a joy as a care. It is so vast a treasure, that the heart, possessed of the fullest consciousness of its value, is for ever dreading its loss. The happiness of the Floridian Eden had been of a sort which never absorbed the soul. It lacked the intensity of a fervent passion. It was the life of childhood—a thing of sport and play, of dance and dream—not that eager and avaricious passion which knows never content, and is never sure, even when most happy, from the anxieties and doubts which beset all mortal felicity. Already did our Queen begin to calculate the hours between the present, and that which should witness the departure of the pleasant Frenchmen.

"You will go from me," said she to D'Erlach, as they went apart from the rest, wandering along the banks of the river and looking out upon the sea. "You will go from me, and I shall never see you any more."

"I will come again, noble Queen, believe me," was the assurance.

"Ah! come soon," she said, "come soon, for you please me very much, *Aphon.*"

Such was the soft Indian corruption of his christened name. No doubt, she too gave pleasure to 'Aphon.' How could it be otherwise? How could he prove insensible to the tender and fervid interest which she so innocently betrayed in him? He did not. He was not insensible; and vague fancies were quickening in his mind as respects the future. He was opposed to the plan of returning to France. He was for carrying out the purposes of Coligny, and fulfilling the destinies of the colony. He had warned Laudonniere against the policy he pursued, had foreseen all the evils resulting from his unwise counsels, and there was that in his bosom which urged the glorious results to France, of a vigorous and just administration of a settlement in the western hemisphere, in which he was to participate, with his energy and forethought, without having these perpetually baffled by the imbecility and folly of an incapable superior. In such an event, how sweetly did his fancy mingle with his own fortunes those of the gentle and loving creature who stood beside him. He told her not his thoughts—they were indeed, fancies, rather than thoughts—but his arm gently encircled her waist, and while her head drooped upon her bosom, he pressed her hand with a tender earnestness, which spoke much more loudly than any language to her heart.

The hour of separation came at length. Three days had elapsed in the delights of the Floridian Eden. Our Frenchmen were compelled to tear themselves away. The objects for which they came had been gratified. The bounty of the lovely Iracana had filled with grain their boats. Her subjects had gladly borne the burdens from the fields to the vessels, while the strangers revelled with the noble and the lovely. But their revels were now to end. The garrison at La Caroline, it was felt, waited with hunger, as well as hope and anxiety for their return, and they dared to delay no longer. The parting was more difficult than they themselves had fancied. All had been well entertained, and all made happy by their entertainment. If Alphonse D'Erlach had been favored with the sweet attentions of a queen, Captain La Vasseur had been rendered no less happy by the smiles of the loveliest among her subjects. He had touched her heart also, quite as sensibly as had the former that of Iracana.

Similarly fortunate had been their followers. Authority had ceased to restrain in a region where there was no danger of insubordination, and our Frenchmen, each in turn, from the sergeant to the sentinel, had been honored by regards of beauty, such as made him forgetful, for the time, of precious memories in France. Nor had these favors, bestowed upon the Frenchmen, provoked the jealousy of the numerous Indian chieftains who were present, and who shared in these festivities. It joyed them the rather to see how frankly the white men could unbend themselves to unwonted pleasures, throwing aside that jealous state, that suspicious vigilance, which, hitherto, had distinguished their bearing in all their intercourse with the Indians.

"Women of Iracana too sweet," said the gigantic son of Satouriova, Athore, to Captain La Vasseur, as the parties, each with a light and laughing damsel in his grasp, whirled beside each other in the mystic maze of the dance.

"I much love these women of Iracana," said Apalou, as fierce a warrior in battle, as ever swore by the altars of the Indian Moloch. "I glad you love them too, like me. Iracana woman good for too much love! They make great warrior forget his enemies."

"Ha!" said one addressing D'Erlach, "You have beautiful women in your country, like Iracana, the Queen?"

But, we need not pursue these details. The hour of separation had arrived. Our Frenchmen had brought with them a variety of commodities grateful to the Indian eye, with which they designed to traffic ; but the bounty of Iracana, which had anticipated all their wants, had asked for nothing in return. The treasures of the Frenchmen were accordingly distributed in gifts among the noble men and women of the place. Some of these

Iracana condescended to take from the hands of Aphon. Her tears fell upon his offering. She gave him in return two small mats, woven of the finer straws of the country, with her own hands—wrought, indeed, while D'Erlach sat beside her in the shade of a great oak by the river bank—and " so artificially wrought," in the language of the chronicle, " as it was impossible to make it better." The poor Queen had few words—

"You will come to me, *Aphon*—you will? you will? I too much want you! Come soon, *Aphon*. Iracana will dance never no more till *Aphon* be come."

"*Aphon*" felt, at that moment, that he could come without sorrow. He promised that he would. Perhaps he meant to keep his promise; but we shall see. The word was given to be aboard, and the trumpet rang, recalling the soldier who still lingered in the forest'shadows, with some dusky damsel for companion. All were at length assembled, and with a last squeeze of her hand, D'Erlach took leave of his sorrowful queen. She turned away into the woods, but soon came forth again, unable to deny herself another last look.

But the Frenchmen were delayed. One of their men was missing. Where was Louis Bourdon? There was no answer to his name. The boats were searched, the banks of the river, the neighboring woods, the fields, the Indian village, and all in vain. The Frenchmen observed that the natives exhibited no eagerness in the search. They saw that many faces were clothed with smiles, when their efforts resulted fruitlessly. They could not suppose that any harm had befallen the absent soldier. They could not doubt the innocence of that hospitality, which had shown itself so fond. They conjectured rightly when they supposed that Louis Bourdon, a mere youth of twenty, had gone off with one of the damsels of Iracana, whose seductions he had found it impossible to withstand. D'Erlach spoke to the Queen upon the subject She gave him no encouragement. She professed to know nothing, and probably did not, and she would promise nothing. She unhesitatingly declared her belief that he was in the forest, with some one that " he so much loved :" but she assured D'Erlach that to hunt them up would be an impossibility.

"Why you not stay with me, Aphon, as your soldier stay with the woman he so much love? It is good to stay. Iracana will love you too much more than other woman. Ah ! you love not much the poor Iracana."

"Nay, Iracana, I love you greatly. I will come to you again. I find it hard to tear myself away. But my people—"

"Ah ! you stay with Iracana, and much love Iracana, and you have all these people. They will plant for you many fields of corn ; you shall no more want ; and we will dance when the evening comes, and we shall be so happy, Aphon and Iracana, to live together ; Aphon the great Paracoussi, and Iracana to be Queen no more."

It was not easy to resist these pleadings. But time pressed. Captain La Vasseur was growing impatient. The search after Louis Bourdon was abandoned, and the soldiers were again ordered on board. The anxieties of La Vasseur being now awakened, lest others of his people should be spirited away. Of this the danger was considerable. The Frenchman was a more flexible being than either the Englishman or Spaniard. It was much easier for him to assimilate with the simple Indian ; and our Huguenot soldiers, who had very much forgotten their religion in their diseased thirst after gold, now, in the disappointment of the one appetite were not indifferent to the consolations afforded by a life of ease and sport, and the charms which addressed them in forms so persuasive as those of the damsels of Iracana. La Vasseur began to tremble for his command, as he beheld the reluctance of his soldiers to depart. He gave the signal hurriedly to Alphonso D'Erlach, and with another sweet single pressure of the hand, he left the lovely Queen to her own melancholy musings. She followed with her eyes the departing boats till they were clean gone from sight, then buried herself in the deepest thickets where she might weep in security.

Other eyes than hers pursued the retiring barks of the Frenchmen, with quite as much anxiety; and long after she had ceased to see them. On a little headland jutting out upon the river below, in the shade of innumerable vines and flowers, crouching in suspense, was the renegade, Louis Bourdon. By his side sat the dusky damsel who had beguiled him from his duties. While his comrades danced, he was flying through the thickets. The nation were, many of them, conscious of his flight; but they held his offence to be venial, and they encouraged him to proceed. They lent him help in crossing the river, at a point below; the father of the woman with whom he fled providing the canoe with which to transport him beyond the danger of pursuit. Little did our Frenchmen, as the boats descended, dream who watched them from the headland beneath which they passed. Many were the doubts, frequent the changes, in the feelings of the capricious renegade, as he saw his countrymen approaching him, and felt that he might soon be separated from them and home forever, by the ocean walls of the Atlantic. Whether it was that his Indian beauty detected in his face the fluctuations of his thoughts, and feared that, on the near approach of the boats, he would change his purpose and abandon her for his people, cannot be said; but just then she wound herself about within his arms, and looked up in his face, while her falling hair enmeshed his hands, and contributed, perhaps, still more firmly to ensnare his affections. His heart had been in his mouth; he could scarcely have kept from crying out to his comrades as the boats drew nigh to the cliff; but the dusky beauties beneath his gaze, the soft and delicate form within his embrace, silenced all the rising sympathies of brotherhood in more ravishing emotions. In a moment their boats had gone by; in a little while they had disappeared from sight, and the arms of the Indian woman, wrapped about her captive, declared her delight and rapture in the triumph which she now regarded as secure. Louis Bourdon little knew how much he had escaped, in thus becoming a dweller in the Floridian Eden.

XXI.

HISTORICAL SUMMARY.

The glowing accounts of the delights of the Floridian Eden which were brought by our returning voyagers, were not sufficient to persuade the garrison to forego their anxious desire to return to France. The home-sickness under which they labored had now reached such a height as to suffer no appeal or opposition. Nothing but the stern decree of authority could have silenced the discontents; and the authority lay neither in the will nor in the numbers under the control of Laudonniere. To such a degree of impatience had this passion for their European homes arisen, that, when it was found that the building of the vessel for their deportation would be delayed beyond the designated period, in consequence of the death, in battle with the savages, of two of the carpenters, the multitude rose in mutiny setting upon Jean de Hais, the master-carpenter,—who had innocently declared the impossibility of doing the work within the given time,—with such ferocity, as to make it scarcely possible to save his life. With this spirit prevailing among his garrison, Laudonniere was compelled to abandon the idea, altogether, of building the ship; and to address all his energies to the repair, for the desired purpose, of the old brigantine, which had been brought back to La Caroline, by the returning pirates. To work, with this object, all parties were now set with the utmost expedition. The houses which had been built without the fort were torn down, in order that the timber should be converted into coal for the uses of the forge; this being a labor much easier than that of using the axe upon the trees of the forest. The palisade which conducted from the fort to the river was torn down also by the soldiery, for the same purpose, in spite of the objections of Laudonniere. It was their policy to make their determination to depart inevitable, by rendering the place no longer habitable. The fort, itself, it was determined to destroy, when they were ready to sail, "lest some new-come guest should have enjoyed and possessed it." Our Frenchmen were very jealous of the designs of the English queen. They well knew that the haughty and courageous Elizabeth was meditating a British settlement in the New World; and though, after their own voluntary abandonment of the country, they had no right to complain that another should occupy the waste places, yet their jealousy was too greatly that of the dog in the manger, to behold, with pleased eye, the possession by another of the things which they themselves had been unable to enjoy. "In the meanwhile," says Laudonniere—seeking to excuse his own unwise management and feeble policy—"In the meanwhile, there was none of us to whome it was not an extreme griefe to leave a country wherein wee had endured so greate travailes and necessities, to discover that which wee must forsake through our owne countrymen's default. For if wee had beene succoured in time and place, and according to the promise that was made unto us, the war which was between us and Utina had not fallen out, neither should wee have had occasion to offend the Indians, which, with all paines in the world, I entertained in good amitie, as well with merchandize and apparel, as with promise of greater matters ; and with whome I so behaved myself, that although sometimes I was constrained to take victuals in some few villages, yet I lost not the alliance of eight kings and lords, my neighbours, which continually succoured and ayded me with whatever they were able to afford. Yea, this was the principal scope of all my purposes, to winne and entertaine them, knowing how greatly their amitie might advance our enterprise, and principally while I discovered the commodities of the country, and sought to strengthen myself therein. I leave it to your cogitation to think how neare it went to our hearts to leave a place abounding in riches (as we were thoroughly enformed thereof) in coming whereunto, and doing service unto our prince, we lefte our owne countrey, wives, children, parents and friends, and passed the perils of the sea, and were therein arrived as in a plentiful treasure of all our heart's desire."

It was while distressing himself with these cogitations that Laudonniere, on the 3d of August, 1565, took a walk, "as was his custom of an afternoon," to the top of a little eminence, in the neighborhood of the fort, which afforded a distant prospect of the sea. Here, looking forth with yearning to that watery waste which he was preparing to traverse, he was suddenly excited, as he beheld four sail of approaching vessels. At first, the tidings made the soldiers of the garrison to leap for joy. The vessels were naturally supposed to be those of their own countrymen; and such was the gladness inspired by this supposition, that "one would have thought them to be out of their wittes, to see them laugh and leap." But, something in the behavior of the strange ships, after a while, rendered our Frenchmen a little doubtful of their character. Instead of boldly approaching, they were seen to cast anchor and to send out one of their boats. A prudent fear of the Spaniards made Laudonniere get his soldiers in readiness, while Captain La Vasseur, with a select party, advanced to the river side to meet the visitors. They proved to be Englishmen— a fleet under the command of the celebrated John Hawkins ; and had on board one Martin Atinas, of Dieppe ; a Frenchman, who had been one of the colonists of Fort Charles,—one of those who returning to France, had been taken up at sea and carried into England. He had guided the English admiral along the coast, and his information had contributed to prompt the voyage of exploration which Hawkins had in hand. But the object of the British admiral was quite pacific, and his conduct exceedingly generous and noble. His ostensible purpose in putting into May River was to procure fresh water. Laudonniere permitted him to do so. Hawkins, perceiving the distressed condition of the Frenchmen, relieved them with liberal supplies of bread, wine and provisions. Apprised of their desire to return to France, he, with greater liberality and a wiser policy, offered to transport the whole colony. But Laudonniere was still jealous of the Englishman, and was apprehensive that, while he carried off the one colony, he would instantly plant another in its place. He declined the generous offer, but bargained with him for one of his vessels, for which Laudonniere chiefly paid by the furniture of the fortress, —the cannon, &c.,—viz.: "two bastards, two mynions, one thousand of iron (balls), and one thousand (pounds) of powder." These items included only a portion of the purchase consideration, in earnest of the treaty. Moved with pity at the wretched condition of the Frenchmen, the generous Englishman offered supplies for which he accepted Laudonniere's bills. These the subsequent misfortunes of the latter never permitted him to satisfy In this way our colonists procured " twenty barrels of meale, six pipes of beanes, one hogshead of salt, and a hundred (cwt.?) of waxe to make candles. Moreover, forasmuch as hee saw my souldiers goe barefoote, hee offered me besides fifty paires of shoes, which I accepted." "He did more than this," says Laudonniere. "He bestowed upon myselfe a great jarre of oyle, a jarre of vinegar, a barell of olives, a great quantitie of rice, and a baroll of white biscuit. Besides, he gave divers presents to the principal officers of my company according to their qualities: so that, I may say, that we received as many courtesies of the Generall as was possible to receive of any man living."

Here, we are fortunately in possession of the narrative of Hawkins himself, and his report of the encounter with our Frenchmen. It affords a good commentary upon the bad management of Laudonniere, and the worthless character of his followers; the sturdy Englishmen seeing, at a glance, where all the evils of the colony lay. He describes their first settlement as gathered from their own lips; their numbers, the period they had remained in the country, their frequent want, and the modes resorted to for escaping famine. His details comprise all the facts of our history, as already given. Of their discontents and rebels, he speaks as of a class, "who would not take the paines so much as to fishe in the river before their doores, but would have all thinges put in their mouthes. They did rebell against the Captaine, taking away first his armour, and afterwards imprisoning him, &c." The narrative of Hawkins gives the subsequent history of the rebels, their piracy, capture and fate. He mentions one particular, which we do not gather from Laudonniere, showing the sagacity of the Floridian warriors. Finding that the Frenchmen, in battle, were protected by their coats of mail, or escaupil, and the bucklers in familiar use at the time, they directed their arrows at the faces and the legs of their enemies, which were the parts in which they were mostly wounded. At the close of this war, according to our Englishmen, Laudonniere had not forty soldiers left unhurt. After detailing the supplies accorded to the colonists from his stores, he adds, " notwithstanding the great want that the Frenchmen had, the ground doth yield victuals sufficient, if they would have taken paines to get the same; *but they being souldiers, desired to live by the sweat of other men's browes."* Here speaks the jealous scorn of the sailor. " The ground yieldeth naturally great store of grapes, for in the time the Frenchmen were there they made twenty hogsheads of wine." Our poor Huguenots could seek gold and manufacture wine, but could not raise provisions. They were of too haughty a stomach to toil for any but the luxuries of life. " Also," says Hawkins, " it (the earth) yieldeth roots passing good, deere marvellous store, with divers other beastes and fowle serviceable to man. These be things wherewith a man may live, having corne or maize wherewith to make bread, for maize maketh good savory bread, and cakes as fine as flowre; also, it maketh good meale, beaten and sodden with water, and nourishable, which the Frenchmen did use to drink of in the morning, and it assuageth their thirst, so that they have no need to drink all the day after. And this maize was the greatest lack they had, because they had no labourers to sowe the same; and therefore, to them that should inhabit the land, it were requisite to have labourers to till and sowe the ground; for they, having victuals of their owne, whereby they neither spoil nor rob the inhabitants, may live not only quietly with them, *who naturally are more desirous of peace than of warre,* but also shall have abundance of victuals proffered them for nothing, &c." The testimony of Hawkins is as conclusive in behalf of the Floridians as it is unfavorable to our Frenchmen. He speaks in the highest terms of the qualities and resources of the country, as abounding in commodities unknown to men, and equal to those of any region in the world. He tells us of the gold procured by the Huguenot colonists, one mass of two pounds weight being taken by them from the Indians, without equivalent. The latter he describes as having some estimation of the precious metals; "for it is wrought flat and graven, which they wear about their necks, &c." The Frenchmen eat snakes in the sight of our Englishmen, to their "no little admiration;" and affirm the same to be a delicate meat. Laudonniere tells Hawkins some curious snake stories, which could not well be improved upon, even in the "Hunter's Camp," on a "Lying Saturday." "I heard a miracle of one of these adders,"—snakes a yard and a half long,—" upon the which a faulcon (hawk) seizing, the sayd adder did claspe her taile about her; which, the French captaine seeing, came to the rescue of the faulcon, and took her,—slaying the adder." There is no improbability in this story; but we shall be slow to give our testimony in behalf of that which follows: "And the Captaine of the Frenchmen saw also a serpent with three heads and foure feet, of the bignesse of a great spaniel, which, for want of a harquebuse, he durst not attempt to slay." Laudonniere had evidently some appreciation of the marvellous; but only *four* feet to *three* heads was a monstrous disproportion. The account which Hawkins gives of the abundance of fish in the neighborhood of the garrison, is no exaggeration, and only adds to the surprise that we feel at the wretched indolence and imbecility of the colonists, who, with this resource "at their doores," depended for their supply upon the Floridians.

Hawkins's account of the coast and characteristics of Florida is copious and full of interest, but belongs not to this narrative. He left the Huguenots, on the 28th July, 1565, making all preparations to follow in his wake; and on the fifteenth of August Laudonniere was prepared to depart also. The biscuit was made for the voyage, the goods and chattels of the soldiers were taken on board, and most of the water;—nothing delayed their sailing but head-winds;—when the whole proceeding was arrested by the sudden appearance of Ribault, with the long-promised supplies from France. The approach of Ribault was exceedingly cautious; so circumspect, indeed, that fears were entertained by the garrison that his ships were those of the Spaniards. The guns of the fortress were already trained to bear upon them when the strangers discovered themselves. The reasons for their mysterious deportment, as subsequently given, arose from certain false reports which had reached France, of the conduct of Laudonniere. He had been described, by letters from some of his malcontents in the colony, as affecting a sort of regal state—as preparing to shake off his dependence upon the mother-country—and setting up for himself, as the sovereign lord of the Floridas. Poor Laudonniere! living on vipers, crude berries and bitter roots, mocked by the savages on one hand, fettered and flouted by his own runagates and rebels on the other,—defied in his authority, and starving in all his state, was in no mood to affect royalty upon the River May. He was, no doubt, a vain and ostentatious person; but, whatever may have been his absurdities and vanities, at first, they had been sufficiently schooled by his necessities, we should think, to cure him of any such idle affectations. He had been subdued and humbled by defeat,—the failure of his plans, and the evident contempt into which he had sunk among his people. Yet of all this, the King of France and Monsieur de Coligny could have known nothing; and when we recollect that the colony was made up of Huguenots only, a people of whose fidelity the former might reasonably doubt, the suspicions of the Catholic monarch may not be supposed entirely unreasonable. At all events, Ribault was sent to supersede the usurping commander, and bore imperative orders for his recall. The armament confided to Ribault consisted of seven vessels, and a military force corresponding with such a fleet. We are also made aware that, on this occasion, the force which he command ed was no longer made up of Huguenots exclusively, as in the previous armament. A large sprinkling of Catholic soldiers accompanied the expedition, and the temporary peace throughout the realm enabled a great number of gentlemen and officers to employ themselves in the search after adventure in the New World. They accordingly swelled the forces of Ribault, and showed conclusively that the colonial establishment in Florida had grown into some importance at home. That Laudonniere should become a prince there, was calculated to exaggerate the greatness of the principality; and the jealousy of the French monarch, in all probability, for the first time, awakened his sympathy for the settlement. The same accounts which had borne the tidings of Laudonniere's ambition, may have exaggerated the resources and discoveries of the country; and possibly some specimens of gold —the mass of two pounds described by Hawkins—had dazzled the eyes and excited the avarice of court and people. Enough that Laudonniere was to be sent home for trial, and that Ribault was to succeed him in the government.

The approach of Ribault with his fleet was exceedingly slow. Head-winds and storms baffled his progress, and as he reached the coast of Florida he loitered along its bays and rivers, seeking to obtain from the Indians all possible tidings of the colony, before venturing upon an encounter with the supposed usurper of the sovereignty of the country. When, at length, he drew nigh to La Caroline, so suspiciously did he approach, that he drew upon him the fire of Laudonniere's men, and, but for the distance, and the seasonable outcry which was made by his followers, announcing who they were, a conflict might have ensued between the parties. To the great relief of Ribault, Laudonniere received him with submission. The former apprised him frankly of the reports in France to his discredit, and delivered him the letters of Coligny to the same effect. Laudonniere soon succeeded in convincing his successor that he had been greatly slandered—that he was entirely innocent of royalty, and almost of state, of any kind—that, however unfortunate he may have been—however incompetent to the duties he had undertaken, he was certainly not guilty of the extreme follies, the presumption, or the cruelty, which constituted the several points in the indictment urged against him. Ribault strove to persuade him to remain in the colony, and to leave his justification to himself. But this Laudonniere declined to do, resolving to return to France;—a resolution which, as we shall see hereafter, was only delayed too long,—to the further increase of the misfortunes of our captain. Meanwhile he fell sick of a fever, and the authority passed into the hands of Jean Ribault, whose return was welcomed by crowds of Indian chiefs, who came to the fortress to inquire after the newly-arrived strangers. They soon recognised the chief by whose hands the stone pillar had been reared, which stood conspicuous at the entrance of the river. He was easily distinguished, by many of them, by reason of the massy beard which he wore. They embraced him with signs of a greater cordiality than they were disposed to show to his immediate predecessor. The

Kings Homoloa, Seravahi, Alimacani, Malica, and Casti, were among the first to recall the ties of their former friendship, and to brighten the ancient chain of union, by fresh pledges. They brought to Ribault, among other gifts, large pieces of gold, which, in their language, is called "sieroa pira," literally "red metal,"—which, upon being assayed by the refiner, proved to be "perfect golde." They renewed their offers to conduct him to the Mountains of Apalachia, where this precious metal was to be had for the gathering. Ribault was not more inaccessible to this attractive showing than Laudonniere had been; but before he could project the desired enterprise, in search of the mountains which held such glorious possessions, new events were in progress, involving such dangers as superseded the hopes of gain among the adventurers, by necessities which made them doubtful of their safety The Spaniards, of whom they had long been apprehensive, were at length discovered upon the coast

XXII.

THE FATE OF LA CAROLINE.

CHAPTER I.

THE fleet of Ribault consisted of seven vessels. The *three* smallest of these had ascended the river to the fortress. The *four* larger, which were men of war, remained in the open roadstead. Here they were joined on the fourth of September by six Spanish vessels of large size and armament. These came to anchor, and, at their first coming, gave assurance of amity to the Frenchmen. But Ribault had been warned, prior to his departure from France, that the Spaniards were to be suspected. The crowns of France and Spain, it is true, were at peace, but the Spaniards themselves contemplated settlements in Florida, to which they laid claim, by right of previous discovery, including, under this general title, territories of the most indefinite extent. Philip the Second, that cold, malignant and jealous despot, freed by the amnesty with France from the cares of war in that quarter, now addressed his strength and employed his leisure in extending equally his sway, with that of the Catholic faith, among the red-men of America. Prior to the settlements of Coligny, he had begun his preparations for this object. The charge of the expedition was confided to Don Pedro Melendez de Avilez, an officer particularly famous among his countrymen for his deeds of heroism in the New World He himself, bore a considerable portion of the expense of the enterprise, and this was a consideration sufficiently imposing in the eyes of his sovereign, to secure for him the dignity of a Spanish Adelantado, with the hereditary government of all the Floridas. It was while engaged in the preparations for this expedition that tidings were received by the Spaniards of the settlements which had been begun by the Huguenots. The enterprise of Don Pedro de Melendez now assumed an aspect of more dignity. It became a crusade, and the eager impulse of ambition was stimulated by all the usual arguments in favor of a holy war. To extirpate heresy was an object equally grateful to both the legitimates of France and Spain; and the heartless monarch of France, Charles the Ninth, in the spirit which subsequently gave birth to the horrible massacre of St Bartholomew, it is reported—though the act may have been that of the Queen Mother—cheerfully yielded up his Protestant subjects in Florida, to the tender mercies of the Spanish propagandist. There is little doubt that the French monarch had signified to his Spanish brother, that he should resent none of the wrongs done to the colonies of Coligny; he himself being, at this very time, busied in the labor which was preparing for the destruction of their patron and brethren at home. Coligny well knew how little was the real sympathy entertained by the monarch for this class of his subjects, and he felt that there were sufficient reasons to fear, and to be watchful of, the Spaniards. He had some better authority than mere suspicion for his fear. Just as Ribault was about to take his departure from France, the Lord Admiral wrote him as follows, in a hasty postscript:—" As I was closing this letter, I received certain advices that Don Pedro Melendez departeth from Spain to go to the coast of New France, (Florida,) see that you suffer him not to encroach upon you, no more than you will suffer yourself to encroach on him."

The preparations of Melendez began to assume an aspect of great and imposing magnificence. Clergy and laity crowded to his service. Nearly twenty vessels, some of very considerable force, were provided; and three thousand adventurers assembled under his command. But Heaven did not seem at first to smile upon the enterprise His fleet was encountered by tempests as had been the "Grand Armada," and the number of his vessels before he reached Porto Rico had been reduced nearly two thirds. Some doubt now arose in the minds of the Spanish captains, whether they were in sufficient force to encounter Ribault. The bigotry and enthusiasm of Melendez rejected the doubt with indignation. His fanaticism furnished an argument in behalf of his policy, imposing enough to the superstitious mind, and which his followers were sufficiently willing to accept. "The Almighty," said the Adelantado, "has reduced our armament, only that his own arm might achieve the holy work."

The warning of danger contained in the letter of the Lord Admiral to Ribault did not fall upon unheeding senses. Still, the French captain was quite unprepared for the rapidity of the progress made by the Spaniards. When, with six large vessels, they suddenly appeared in the roadstead of May River, Ribault was at La Caroline. His officers had been apprised of the propriety of distrusting their neighbors, and accordingly showed themselves suspicious as they drew nigh. It was well they did so. In the absence of Ribault, with three of the ships at La Caroline, they were inferior in force to the armament of Melendez, and were thus doubly required to oppose vigilance to fraud and force. Fortunately, the Spaniards did not reach the road till near evening, when they had too little time for efficient operations. Hence the civility of their deportment, and the pacific character of their assurances. They lowered sail, cast anchor, and forbore all offensive demonstrations. But one circumstance confirmed the apprehensions of the Frenchmen. In the brief conversation which ensued between the parties, after the arrival of the Spaniards, the latter inquired after the chief captains and leaders of the French fleet, calling them by their names and surnames, and betraying an intimate knowledge of matters, which had been judiciously kept as secret as possible in France. This showed, conclusively, that, before Melendez left Spain, he was thoroughly informed by those who knew, in France, of the condition, conduct, and strength of Ribault's armament. And why should he be informed of these particulars, unless there were some designs for acting upon this information? The French captains compared notes that night, in respect to these communications, and concurred in the belief that they stood in danger of assault. They prepared themselves accordingly, to cut and run, with the first appearance of dawn, or danger. With the break of day, the Spaniards began to draw nigh to our Frenchmen; but the sails of these were already hoisted to the breeze. Their cables were severed, at the first sign of hostility, and the chase begun within the greatest animation. But, if the ships of the Huguenots were deficient in force, they had the advantage of their enemies in speed. They showed the Spaniards a clean pair of heels, and suffered nothing from the distant cannonade with which their pursuers sought to cripple their flight. The chase was continued through the day. With the approach of evening, the Spaniards tacked ship and stood for the River Seloy, or Selooe, called by the French, the River of Dolphins; a distance, overland, of but eight or ten leagues from La Caroline. Finding that they had the advantage of their enemies in fleetness, the French vessels came about also, and followed them at a respectful distance Having made all the discoveries which were possible, they returned to May River, when Ribault came aboard. They reported to him that the great ship of the Spaniards, called " The Trinity," still kept the sea; that three other ships had entered the River of Dolphins; that three others remained at its mouth; and that the Spaniards had evidently employed themselves in putting soldiers, with arms, munition, and provisions, upon shore. These, and further facts, reached him from other quarters. Emoloa, one of the Indian kings in amity with the French, sent them word that the Spaniards had gone on shore at Seloy in great numbers—that they had dispossessed the natives of their houses at that village; had put their " negro slaves, whom they had brought to labor," in possession of them; and were already busy in entrenching themselves in the place, making it a regular encampment.

Not doubting that they meant to assail and harrass the settlement of La Caroline from this point, with the view to expelling the colonists from the country, Ribault boldly conceived the idea of taking the initiate in the war. He first called a council of his chief captains. They assembled in the chamber of Laudonniere, that person being sick. Here Ribault commenced by showing the relative condition of their own and the enemy's strength. His conclusion, from his array of all the facts, was, that the true policy required that he should embark with all his forces, and seek the fleet of the Spaniards, particularly at a moment when it was somewhat scattered; when one great ship only kept the seas; when the rest were in no situation to support each other in the event of sudden assault, and when the troops of the Adelantado, partly on the shore, and partly in his vessels, were, very probably, not in proper order to be used successfully. His argument was not deficient in force or propriety. Certainly, with his own seven ships, all brought together, and all his strength in compact order and fit for service, he might reasonably hope to fall successfully upon the divided forces and scattered squadrons of his enemy, and sweep them equally from sea and land.

But Laudonniere had his argument also, and it was not without its significance. He opposed the scheme of Ribault entirely; representing the defenceless condition of the fortress, and the danger to the fleet at sea, and upon the coast, during a season proverbially distinguished by storms and hurricanes. His counsel was approved of by other captains; but Ribault, an old soldier and sea captain, was too eager to engage the enemy to listen to arguments that seemed to partake of the pusillanimous. It was very evident that he did not regard Laudonniere as the best of advisers in the work of war. He took his own head accordingly, and commanded all soldiers that belonged to his command to go on board their vessels. Not satisfied with this force, he lessened the strength of the garrison by taking a detachment of its best men, leaving few to keep the post but the invalids, who, like Laudonniere, were suffering, or but just recovering, from the diseases of the climate in midsummer. Laudonniere expostulated, but in vain, against this appropriation of his garrison. On the eighth of September, Ribault left the roadstead in pursuit of the Spaniards, and Laudonniere never beheld him again. That very day the skies were swallowed up in tempests. Such tempests were never beheld before upon the coast. The storms prevailed for several days, at the end of which time, apprehending the worst, Laudonniere mustered his command, and proceeded to put the fortress in the best possible condition of defence. To repair the portions of the wall which had been thrown down, to restore the palisades stretching from the fortress to the river, was a work of equal necessity and difficulty ; which, with all the diligence of the Frenchmen, advanced slowly, in consequence of the violence and long continuance of the stormy weather. The whole force left in the garrison consisted of but eighty-six persons supposed to be capable of bearing arms. Of their doubtful efficiency we may boldly infer from these facts. Several of them were mere boys, with sinews yet unhardened into manhood. Some were old men, completely *hors de combat* from the general exhaustion of their energies ; many were still suffering from green wounds, got in the war with Olata Utina, and others again were wholly unprovided with weapons. Relying upon the assumption that he should find his enemy at sea and in force, Ribault had stripped the garrison of its real manhood. His vessels being better sailers than those of the Spaniards, he took for granted that he should be able to interpose, at any moment, for the safety of La Caroline, should any demonstration be made against it. This was assuming quite too much. It allowed nothing for the caprices of wind and wave ; for the sudden rising of gales and tempests ; and accorded too little to the cool prudence, and calculating generalship of Pedro Melendez, one of the most shrewd, circumspect and successful of the Spanish generals of the period : nor, waiving these considerations, was the policy of Ribault to be defended, when it is remembered that he had been specially counselled that the Spaniards had made their lodgments in force upon the shores of Florida, not many leagues, by land, from the endangered fortress. His single virtue of courage blinded him to the danger from the former. He calculated first to destroy the fleet of the enemy, thus cutting off all resource and all escape, and then to descend upon the troops on land, before they could fortify their camp, and overwhelm them with his superior and unembarrassed forces. We shall see, hereafter, the issue of all these calculations. In all probability his decision was influenced quite as much by his fanaticism as his courage. He hated the Spaniards as Catholics, quite as much as they hated him and his flock as heretics. This rage blinded the judgment of the veteran soldier, upon whom fortune was not disposed to smile.

The condition of things at La Caroline, when Ribault took his departure, deplorable enough as we have seen, was rendered still worse by another deficiency, the fruit of this decision of the commander. The supplies of food which were originally brought out for the garrison, were mostly appropriated for the uses of the fleet, allowing for its possibly prolonged absence upon the seas. This absorbed the better portion of the store which was necessary for the daily consumption at La Caroline. A survey of the quantity in the granary of the fortress, made immediately after the departure of the fleet, led to the necessity of stinting the daily allowance of the garrison. Thus, then, with provisions short, with Laudonniere sick, and otherwise incompetent,—with the men equally few and feeble, improvident hitherto, and now spiritless,—the labors of defence and preparation at La Caroline went forward slowly; and its watch was maintained with very doubtful vigilance. We have seen enough, in the previous difficulties of the commandant with his people, to form a just judgment of the small subordination which he usually maintained. His government was by no means improved with the obvious necessity before him, and the hourly increase of peril. Alarmed, at first, by the condition in which he had been left, Laudonniere, as has been stated, proceeded with the *show* of diligence, rather than its actual working, to repair the fortress, and put himself in order for defence. But, with the appearance of bad weather, his exertions relaxed; his people, accustomed to wait upon Providence and the Indians,—praying little to the One and preying much upon the others—very soon discontinued their unfamiliar and disagreeable exertions. They could not suppose—averse themselves to bad weather—that the Spaniards could possibly expose themselves to chills and fevers during an equinoctial tempest, under any idle impulses of enterprise and duty; and their watch was maintained with very doubtful vigilance. On the night of the nineteenth of September, Monsieur de La Vigne was appointed to keep guard with his company. But Monsieur de La Vigne had a tender heart, and felt for his soldiers in bad weather. Seeing the rain continue and increase, " he pitied the sentinels, so much moyled and wet; and thinking the Spaniards would not have come in such a strange time, he let them depart, and, to say the truth, hee went himself into his lodging." But the Spaniards appear to have been men of inferior tastes, and of a delicacy less sympathising and scrupulous than Monsieur de La Vigne. Bad weather appeared to agree with them, and we shall see that they somewhat enjoyed the very showers, from the annoyance of which our French sentinels were so pleasantly relieved. We shall hear of these things hereafter. In the meanwhile, let us look in upon the Adelantado of Florida, Pedro Melendez, a strong, true man, in spite of a savage nature and a maddening fanaticism,—let us see him and the progress of his fortunes, where he plants the broad banner of Spain, with its castellated towers, upon the lonely Indian waters of the Selooe, that river which our Huguenots had previously dignified with the title of " the Dolphin."

CHAPTER II.

RIBAULT'S FORTUNES AT SELOOE.

It was on the twenty-eighth of August, the day on which the Spaniards celebrated the festival of St. Augustine, that the Adelantado entered the mouth of the Selooe or Dolphin River. He was attracted by the aspect of the place, and here resolved to establish a settlement and fortress. He gave the name of the Saint to the settlement. Having landed a portion of his forces, he found himself welcomed by the savages, whom he treated with kindness and who requited him with assurances of friendship From them he learned something of the French settlements, and of their vessels at the mouth of the May River, and he resolved to attempt the surprise of his enemies. We have seen the failure of this attempt. Disappointed in his first desire, like the tiger who returns to crouch again within the jungle from which he has unsuccessfully sprung, Melendez made his way back to the waters of the Selooe, where he proposed to plant his settlement, and which his troops were already beginning to entrench. Here he employed himself in taking formal possession in the name of the King of Spain, and having celebrated the Divine mysteries in a manner at once solemn and ostentatious, he swore his officers to fidelity in the prosecution of the expedition, upon the Holy Sacrament.

It was while most busy with his preparations, that the fleet of Ribault made its appearance at the mouth of the river. The two heaviest of the Spanish vessels, being relieved of their armament and troops, which had been transferred to the land, had been despatched, on the approach of the threatened danger, with all haste to Hispaniola. The two other vessels, at the bar or entrance of the harbor, were unequal to the conflict with the superior squadron of Ribault. Melendez was embarked in one of them, and the three lighter vessels of the French, built especially for penetrating shallow waters, were pressing forward to the certain capture of their prey, for which there seemed no possibility of escape. Melendez felt all his danger, but he had prepared himself for a deadly struggle, and was especially confident in the enthusiastic conviction that himself and his design were equally the concern of Providence. It would seem that fortune was solicitous to justify the convictions of so much self-esteem. Ribault's extreme caution in sounding the bar to which his vessels were approaching, lost him two precious hours; but for which his conquest must have been certain. There was no hope, else, unless in some such miraculous protection as that upon which the Spanish general seemed to count. Had these two vessels been taken and Melendez a prisoner, the descent upon the dismayed troops on shore, not yet entrenched, and in no preparation for the conflict with an equal or superior enemy, and the annihilation of the settlement must have ensued. The consequence of such an event might have changed the whole destinies of Florida, might have established the Huguenot colonies firmly upon the soil, and given to the French such a firm possession of the land, as might have kept the *fleur-de-lis* waving from its summits to this very day. But the miracle was not wanting which the Spanish Adelantado expected. In the very moment when the hands of Ribault, were stretched to seize his prizes, the sudden roar of the hurricane came booming along the deep. The sea rose between the assailant and his prey,—the storm parted them, and while the feebler vessels of Melendez, partially under the security of the land, swept back towards the settlement which he had made on shore, the brigantines and bateaux of Ribault were forced to rejoin their greater vessels, and they all bore away to sea before the gale. Under the wild norther that rushed down upon his squadron, Ribault with a groan of rage and disappointment, abandoned the conquest which seemed already in his grasp.

Melendez promptly availed himself of the Providential event, to insist among his people upon the efficiency of his prayers. They had previously been desponding. They felt their isolation, and exaggerated its danger. The departure of their ships for Hispaniola, their frequent previous disasters, the dispersion of nearly two thirds of the squadron with which they had left the port of Cadiz, but three months before; the labors and privations which already began to press upon them with a novel force; all conspired to dispirit them, and made them despair of a progress in which they were likely to suffer the buffetings only, without any of the rewards of fortune;—and when they beheld the approaching squadron of the French, in force so superior as to leave no doubt of the capture of their only remaining vessels, they yielded themselves up to a feeling of utter self-abandonment, to which the stern, grave self-reliance of Melendez afforded no encouragement. But when, with broad sweep of arm, he pointed to the awful rising of the great billows of the sea, the wild raging of cloud and storm in the heavens, the scudding flight of the trembling ships of Ribault, their white wings gradually disappearing in distance and darkness like feeble birds borne recklessly forward in the wild fury of the tempest, he could, with wonderful potency, appeal to his people to acknowledge the wonders that the Lord had done for them that day.

"Call you this the cause of our king only, in which we are

engaged my brethren? Oh! shallow vanity! And yet, you say rightly. It is the cause of our king—the greatest of all kings—the king of kings; and he will make it triumphant in all lands, even though the base and the timid shall despair equally of themselves and of Him! We shall never, my brethren, abandon this cause to which we have sworn our souls, in life and death, without incurring the eternal malediction of the Most High God, forever blessed be his name! We are surrounded by enemies, my friends; we are few and we are feeble; but what is our might, when the tempest rises like a wall between us and our foes, and in our greatest extremity, the hand of God stretches forth from the cloud, and plucks us safely from the danger. Be of good heart, then; put on a fearless courage; believe that the cause is holy in which ye strive, and the God of Battles will most surely range himself upon our side!"

Loud cries of exultation from his people answered this address A thousand voices renewed their vows of fidelity, and pledged themselves to follow blindly wherever he should lead. He commanded that a solemn mass of the Holy Spirit should be said that night, and that all the army should be present. He vouchsafed no farther words. Nothing, he well knew, that he could say, could possibly add to the miraculous event that had saved their vessels, before their own eyes, in the very moment of destruction. "Our prayers, our faith, my brethren; to these we owe the saving mercies of the Blessed Jesus!"

CHAPTER III.

MELENDEZ AT SELOOE.

But the enthusiasm excited by the dispersion of Ribault's vessels, and the escape of their own, was of short-lived duration among the Spaniards at Selooe. Human nature may obey a grateful impulse, and, while it lasts, will be insensible to common dangers and common necessities; but the enthusiasm which excites and strengthens for a season, is one also which finally exhausts; and when the enervation which succeeds to a high-strung exultation, is followed by great physical trials, and the continued pressure of untoward events, the creature nature is quite too apt to triumph over that nobler spirit whose very intensity is fatal to its length of life. The sign of providential favor which they had beheld wrought visibly in their behalf, the inspiriting language of their stern and solemn leader, the offices of religion, meant to evoke the presence of the Deity, and to secure, by appropriate rites, his farther protection, of which they had recently witnessed so wonderful a manifestation; these wore away in their effects upon our Spaniards, and in the toils and sufferings which they were subsequently to endure.

Perhaps nothing more greatly depresses the ordinary nature than an abode in strange and savage regions during a prevalence of cheerless, unfriendly weather. The soul recoils as it were upon itself, under the ungenial pressure from without, and looking entirely within, finds nothing but wants which it is impossible to satisfy. Memory then studiously recals, as if for the purposes of torture and annoyance, the aspects of the beloved ones who are far from us in foreign lands. The joys which we have had with old and loving associates. the sweets of dear homes, and the sounds of friendly voices, these are the treasures which she conjures up at such periods, in mournful contrast with present privations and all manner of denial. But if, in addition to these, we are conscious of accumulating dangers; if the storm and savage howl without; if hunger craves without being answered, and thirst raves for the drop of moisture to cool its tongue, in vain, we must not wonder if the ordinary nature sinks under its sorrows and apprehension, and loses all the elastic courage which would prompt endeavor and conduct to triumph. The master mind alone, may find itself strong under these circumstances—the man of inexorable will, great faith, and a far-sighted appreciation of the future and its compensations. But it is the master mind only which bears up thus greatly. The common herd is made of very different materials, and in quite another mould.

Don Pedro de Melendez was one of the few minds thus extraordinarily endowed. His prudence, keeping due pace with his religious fanaticism, approved him a peculiar character; a man of rare energies, extraordinary foresight and indomitable will. Resolute for the destruction of the heretics of La Caroline, he was yet one of that class of persons—how few—who can forego the premature attempt to gratify a raging appetite, in recognition of those embarrassing circumstances, which if left unregarded, would only operate for its defeat. He could wait the season, with all patience, when desire might be crowned with fruition. Yet was his thirst a raging one—a master passion—absorbing every other in his soul. All that had taken place on land and sea, had been certainly foreseen by him. Thus had he dispatched his ships seasonably to Hispaniola, as well for their security, as to afford him succor. If he doubted for the safety of those which remained to him, on the approach of Ribault, he was relieved of his doubts by his faith in the interposition of the Deity, and went forth to the encounter, himself heading the forlorn hope, as it were, without any misgivings of the result. He *knew* that the Deity would, in some manner, make himself manifest in succor for the true believer, even then engaged in the maintenance of His cause. He had foreseen the threatening aspects of the heavens, the wild tumults of the sea, the sullen and angry caprices of the winds. He *felt* that storm and terror were in prospect, and that they were meant as his defences against his enemy! But this did not prevent him from adopting all proper human precautions. He did not peril his prows beyond the shoals which environed the entrance to his harborage. He did not trust them beyond the natural bars at the mouth of the Selooe, leaving them to the unrestrained fury of the demon winds that sweep the blue waters of the gulf. Nor, assuming the bare possibility that the protection of the Deity might be withheld from the true believer, as much for the trial of his valor as his faith, in the moment of encounter with the heretic, was the Adelantado neglectful of the means for further struggle, should the assailants, successful with his shipping, approach the shores of Selooe in the endeavor to destroy his army. This he sought to protect by the best possible defences. His troops were under arms in order for battle. Every possible advantage of trench and picket was employed for giving them additional securities. His people had already taken possession of the Indian village, from whence the savages had been expelled; and their dwellings were converted into temporary fortresses, each garrisoned with its selected band. It is wonderful, how the veteran chieftain toiled, in the endeavor to secure his position. While he felt how little the Deity needed the strength of man, in working out the purposes of destiny, he well knew how necessary it was that man should show himself worthy, by his prudence and preparations, of the intervention and the care of Deity.

We have seen the issue of the unfortunate attempt of Ribault upon his enemy; with the absence of immediate danger, the first tumults of exultation on the part of the Spaniards, subsided into a sullen and humiliating repose. As night came on, they momently began to feel the increasing annoyances of their situation. That they were in temporary security from the heretic French, left them free to consider, and to feel, the insecurity and the unfriendly solitude of their situation. The frail palm covered huts of the Floridian savages, on the banks of their now raging river, with the tempest roaring among the affrighted forest trees, afforded but a sorry shelter to their numerous hosts. Darkness and thick night closed in upon them in their dreary and comfortless abodes, and their hearts sunk appalled beneath the terrific bursts of thunder that seemed to rock the very earth upon which they stood. They were not the tried veterans of Spain. Many among them wore weapons for the first time, and all were totally inexperienced in that foreign hemisphere, in which the elements wore aspects of terror which had never before entered their imaginations. Their officers were mostly able men and good soldiers, but even these had enjoyed but small experience in the new world. The levies of Melendez had been hurriedly made, with the view to anticipate the progress of Ribault. They were not such as that iron-hearted leader would have chosen for the terrible warfare which he had in view. Chilled by the ungenial atmosphere, confounded with torrents such as they had never before beheld, and which seemed to threaten the return of the deluge, they exaggerated the evils of their situation and
15

feared the worst. They were not ill-advised upon the subject of their own strength and resources, and whatever they might hope in respect to the probable ill-fortunes of Ribault and his fleet, they knew him to be an experienced soldier, and that his armament was superior, while his numbers were quite equal to their own. They now knew that they were the objects of his search and hate, as he had been of theirs, and they still looked with dread to his reappearance, suddenly, and the coming of a conflict which should add new terrors to the storm. They could not conceive the extent of the securities which they enjoyed, and fancied that with a far better acquaintance with the country than they possessed, he would reappear among them at the moment when least expected, and that they should perish beneath the fury of his fierce assault.

While thus they brooded over their situation, officers and men cowering in the frail habitations of the Indians, through which the rushing torrents descended without impediment, extinguishing their fires, and leaving them with no light but that fitful one, the fierce flashes from the clouds, which threatened them with destruction while illuminating the pale faces of each weary watcher;—Pedro Melendez, strengthened by higher if not a holier support, disdained the miserable shelter of the hovels where they crouched together. He trod the shore and forest pathways without sign of fear or shows of disquiet or annoyance. He smiled at the sufferings which he yet strove to alleviate. He opened his stores for the relief of his people, yet partook of none himself. He gave them food and wine of his own, even while he smiled scornfully to see them eat and drink. His solicitude equally provided against their dangers and their fears. He placed the necessary guards against the one, and soothed or mocked the other. He alone appeared unmoved amidst the storm, and might be seen with unhelmed head, passing from cot to cot, and from watch to watch, urging vigilance, providing relief, and encouraging the desponding with a voice of cheer His eye took in without shrinking, all the aspects of the storm. He gazed with uplifted spirit as the wild red flashes cleft the great black clouds which enveloped the forests in a shroud. " Ay !" he exclaimed, " verily, O Lord! thou hast taken this work into thine own hands!" And thus he went to and fro, without complaint, or suffering, or fatigue, till his lieutenants with shame beheld the example of the veteran whom they had not soul or strength to emulate. His deportment was no less a marvel than a reproach to his people. They could not account for that seemingly unseasonable delight which was apparent in his face, in the exulting tones of his voice, and the eager impulse of his action. That a glow-like inspiration should lighten up his features, and give richness and power to his voice, while they cowered from the storm and darkness in fear and trembling, seemed to them indications rather of madness than of wisdom. But in truth, it was inspiration. Melendez had been visited by one of those sudden flashes of thought which open the pathway to a great performance. A brave design filled his soul; a sudden bright conception, to the proper utterance of which he hurried with a due delight. He summoned his chief leaders to consultation in the great council house of the tribe of Selooe, a round fabric of mixed earth and logs, with a frail palm leaf thatch, fragments of which, the fierce efforts of the tempest momently tore away. The rain rushed through the rents of ruin, the wind shrieked through the numerous breaches in the walls, but Melendez stood in the midst, heedless of these annoyances, or only heedful of them so far as to esteem them services and blessings. He knew the people with whom he had to deal, their fears, their weaknesses, and discontents, the base nature of many of their desires, and the utter incapacity of all to realize the intense enthusiasm which shone within his soul. He could scorn them, but he had to use them. He despised their imbecility, but felt how necessary it was too temporize with their moods, and make them rather forgetful of their infirmities, than openly to denounce and mock them. His eye was fastened upon certain of his chiefs in especial, whose weaknesses were more likely to endanger his objects than those of the rest, since these were associated with a certain degree of pretension arising from their occupance of place. But there is no one in more complete possession of the subtleties of the politician, than the fanatic of intense will. All his powers are concentrated upon the single object, and he values this too highly to endanger it by any rashness. He can make allowances for the weaker among the brethren, so long as they have the power to yield service; he only cuts them down ruthlessly, when, like the tree bringing forth no fruit, the question naturally occurs to the politician, " Why cumbereth it the ground ?" Melendez was prepared to act the politician amidst all his fanaticism. For this reason, though his resolution was inexorably taken, he summoned his officers to a solemn deliberation—a council of war—to determine upon what should be done in the circumstances in which they stood.

CHAPTER IV.

THE COUNCIL OF WAR AT SELOOE.

It was midnight when the assemblage of the Spanish captains took place in the great council house of the savages of Selooe. Already, that night, had the place been consecrated by the performance of a solemn mass in honor of the Holy Spirit. The purposes of the present gathering were, in the opinion of Melendez, not less honorable to the Deity. Rude logs strewn about the building, even as they had been employed by the red-men, furnished seats for the Spanish officers. They surrounded a great fire of resinous pine, which now blazed brightly in the centre of the apartment. In this respect the scene had rather the appearance of savage rites than of Christian council. In silence, the nobles of Castile, of Biscay and the Asturias took their places. Their eyes were vacant, and their hearts were depressed. They caught nothing of that exulting blaze which lightened up the features of Melendez.

"Oh! ye of little faith!" he exclaimed, rising in their midst, "is it thus that ye give acknowlegment to God for the blessings ye have received at his hands, and for that care of the Guardian Shepherd, to which ye, thus far, owe your safety? Have ye already lost the memory of that wondrous sign wrought this day for your deliverance,—when your eyes beheld a wall of storm and thunder pass between your captain and his little barques, and the overwhelming squadron of the heretic Ribault? Was this manifestation of his guardian providence made for us in vain ? Said it not, plainly as the voice of Heaven might say, that our mission was not ended—that there was other work to be wrought by our hands, and that he was with us, to help us in the great achievement of his purposes. Lo! you now, the very storm, that rages about us, and beneath the terrors of which ye tremble, is but a further proof of his guardianship. Under cover of the rages of the tempest, shall we press on to the complete achievement of our work. We shall march to the conquest of La Caroline,—we shall destroy these arch-heretics—these enemies of God, in the very fortress of their strength—in the very place which they have set apart, in the vain hope of security, as their home of refuge!"

Audible murmurs here arrested the speaker.

"What is it that ye fear, my children?" continued Melendez.

Then some among them cried out—"What madness is it that we hear? Shall we, thus enfeebled as we are, with our great ships speeding to Hispaniola, here, left as we are on the wild shores of the savage, not yet entrenched, shall we divide our strength, in the hope to conquer La Caroline, leaving to the heretic Ribault to fall upon our camp when we depart, to pursue us as we tread the great forests of the Floridian, and to destroy us between the power which he brings and that which awaits us at La Caroline?"

"Oh! my brethren! would ye could see with my vision! Ribault will not trouble our camp, neither will he pursue us in our absence. He speeds before the terrors of the tempest. He flies from the destruction which will scarcely suffer him to escape. A voice cries to me that he already perishes beneath the engulphing waters of the Mexican sea; or is cast upon the bleak and treacherous shores and islands which guard the domain of the Floridian. Even if he should escape these dangers, weeks must pass before he can return to these waters of Selooe, the heathen empire of which we have consecrated with the name and confided to the holy keeping of the blessed St. Augustine! This tempest is no summer gale, subsiding as rapidly as it begins. It will rage thus for many days. In that time, encouraged by the Lord, we shall pass the forest wastes that lie between us and La Caroline. With five hundred men, and a host of these red warriors, we shall penetrate in less than four days to the fortress of the heretics—and while they dream that they sleep securely under the shadows of the tempest, we shall rush upon their slumbers, and give them to sleep eternally. My valiant comrades, this is the resolution which I have taken; but I would hear your counsel. I would not that ye should not cheerfully adopt the resolve which is assuredly a dictate from Heaven itself. For, if we destroy not these heretics, they will destroy us. If we cut off the people of La Caroline ere Ribault shall return, his fortress is ours, the cannon of which we shall turn upon him. It is a war *a l'outrance* between us. They will give us no quarter: they shall have none. This tempest gives us the assurance that we shall have no danger from Ribault, if we seize the precious moments for our enterprise, when he is vainly striving with the tempests of the deep, and vainly striving against the winds that bear him away hourly still farther from the scene of our achievements."

We need not pursue the deliberations of the Spanish council. It is enough if we report the result. In the speeches of Melendez, already made, we see the full force of his argument, which was sound and sensible, and could only be opposed by the fears of those who sought to avoid exposure, who dreaded the elements, the unknown in their condition, and who shrunk from enterprises which promised nothing but hard blows, and which tasked their hardihood beyond all their past experience in war. There were arguments and pleas put in by the over-cautious and the timid, to all of which the Adelantado listened patiently, but to all of which he opposed his arguments, based at once upon the obvious policy natural to their circumstances, and to the equally obvious requisitions of the Deity, as shown by an interposition in their favor, which they were all prepared to acknowledge as fervently as Melendez. His quiet but inflexible will prevailed; the council gradually became of his mind. The unsatisfied were at least silenced, while those whom he convinced were clamorous in their plaudits of a scheme which they ascribed, as Melendez did himself, to the immediate revelation of Heaven.

"I thank you, noble gentlemen," were the words of the Adelantado, as they separated for the night. "That our opinions so well correspond increases my confidence in our plan. Not that I had doubts before. I had thy assurance, oh! Lord! that this adventure had thy heavenly sanction. *In te Domine speravi,*—let us never be confounded! And now, my comrades, let us separate. With the dawn, though the storm rages still, as I hope and believe it will, we must prepare for this enterprise. We shall choose five hundred of our best soldiers, carry with us provisions for eight days, and in that time our work will be done. Our force will be divided into six companies, each with its flag and captain, and a select body of pioneers, armed with axes, shall be sent before to open a pathway through the forest. That we have no guide is a misfortune; but God will provide so that we fail not. Fortunately we know in what quarter lies La Caroline—the distance is known also, and we shall not go wide, if we are only resolved to seek and to destroy the heretics with firm and valiant hearts, filled with a proper faith in heaven."

Even as he concluded, one at the entrance of the council-house entreated entrance. It proved to be a priest, the Reverend

Father Salvandi, who brought with him a strange man, overgrown with beard, and partly in the costume of a mariner.

"My son," said the priest, "here is the very man you want. This is one Francis Jean, a Frenchman,—once a heretic, but now, conscious of his errors, and repentant in the hands of Holy Church. He hath recanted of his sins, and hath come back willingly to the folds of Christ. He hath fled from La Caroline, from the cruelties of Laudonniere, the heretic, and will report what he knows, touching the condition of the Lutheran fortress and the people thereof."

"Said I not, my comrades, that God would provide!" cried Melendez in exultation. "This is the very man whom we want. What art thou?"—to the Frenchman.

"I was a heretic, my lord,—I am now a Christian. I was beaten by Laudonniere, and I fled from him, taking off one of his barques. He hath sworn my life; I would take his. I know the route to La Caroline. I will show the way to your soldiers."

"Ah! Laudonniere will hang you, if he gets you into his power."

"For that reason, my lord, I would have you get him in yours."

"You shall have your wish. The Lord hath indeed spoken! Your name?"

"Francis Jean!"

"Be faithful—guide my people to this fortress of the heretics, and you shall be rewarded. But, if treacherous, Francis Jean, you shall hang to the first tree of the forest!"

"Doubt me not, my lord. I will do you good service!"

"Be it so! My comrades—the Lord hath provided. Señor Martin de Ochoa, take this man into thy keeping. Do him no hurt,—let him be well entreated, but let him not escape from thy sight."

The Reverend Father Salvandi bestowed his benediction upon the kneeling circle, and they separated for the night. And still the storm roared without, and still the rains descended, but the heart of Melendez rejoiced in the tempest, as it were an angel sent by Heaven to his succor.

CHAPTER V.

THE DINNER-PARTY OF MELENDEZ.

BUT the consolations of Melendez were not those of his people, nor did they arrive at his conclusions. It was soon bruited abroad that he was to march through the tempest upon La Caroline, and his soldiers spoke the open language of sedition. Their clamors reached the ears of Melendez, but he was one of those wonderful politicians who know what an error it is, at times, to be too quick of sight and hearing. The discontents of the *canaille* gave him little concern; yet he watched them without seeming to do so; and employed processes of his own for inducing their quiet, without showing himself either apprehensive or angry. Some of his officers were guilty of seditious speeches also—some of those whom his will had silenced in council, rather than his arguments convinced. He took his measures with these in a simple manner, without allowing his preparations to be arrested for a moment. One of these officers, named St. Vincent, positively declared his purpose not to go upon an expedition where they would only get their throats cut; and that if Melendez persisted in his mad design, he would embark with all those left at St. Augustine, and take his route back to Hispaniola. This same person, with the Señors Francis Recalde and Diego de Maya, openly and boldly remonstrated with the Adelantado against the enterprise. He answered them by inviting them, and all other of his officers who had been of the council, to a great dinner which he prepared for them that day. Here he gave them quite a splendid entertainment, and in the midst of their hilarity he said—

"That it was with very great surprise he discovered that the secret councils of the last night had been improperly revealed to all the world—councils of war," said he, "my comrades, are matters the value of which depend wholly upon their secrecy. It would be my duty to find out and punish the authors of this wretched infidelity; but I am too well persuaded of the mercies of God to myself and to all of us, not to be indulgent to the faults of our people. This offence, accordingly, is forgiven, no matter who shall have been the offender. But, hereafter, I may say that all future seditions among the soldiers shall be punished in the officers. It is from the officers only that the soldiers are led into insubordination. They shall answer for their men. Let it be known, however, that all who lose heart, who tremble at this enterprise, to which God himself has summoned us, are at liberty to remain. I am satisfied, however, that the greater number are prepared to depart with me the moment I give the signal, under the proper example of their captains. Still, I am willing to hear counsel from you touching this expedition. I am not mulish enough to adhere to a resolution when better counsels are given against it Speak freely your minds, therefore, if you think otherwise than myself; remembering this only, that our resolution, once taken, if there shall be one so bold as to oppose words where he should do his duty, he shall be cashiered upon the spot. And now, my comrades, this wine of Xeres is not amiss. Let us drink. We are of one mind, I perceive, in council; let our unanimity extend to our drink. I drink to the speedy overthrow of heresy, and the spread of the true faith; both certain where the sword of valor is always ready to obey the voice of God!"

The toast was drank with enthusiasm. The discontents were silenced. How should it be otherwise where the authority was so generous, conveying its suggestions through the generous wines of Xeres, and only hinting at the possibility of disgrace and punishment, in the occurrence of events scarcely possible to those who claimed to draw the sword of valor in the service of the Deity. The Adelantado gave no farther heed to the factions of his army. He probably adopted the best precautions. It is true that St. Vincent still mouthed threats of disobedience, but the policy of Melendez had no ears in his quarter; and the preparations went on, without interruption, for the march against La Caroline!

CHAPTER VI.

THE STORMING OF LA CAROLINE.

THE preparations for departure were complete. The Adelantado himself marched at the head of his vanguard, the immediate command of which was confided to Señor Martin de Ochoa, with a troop of Biscayans and Asturians, armed with axes, for clearing their pathway through the forest. With these went the traitor, Francis Jean, who had abandoned his religion and La Caroline together. He was watched closely, but proved faithful to his new masters. Dreary, indeed, was the progress of Melendez. The storm prevailed all the time. The rain soaked their garments, and it was with difficulty they could protect their ammunition and provisions. The fourth day of the march they were within five miles of La Caroline, but arrested by an immense tract of swamp, in passing which the water was up to their middles. The whole country was flooded, and the *freshet* momently increased, in consequence of the continued rains. These had become more terrible in volume than ever. The windows of heaven seemed again opened for another deluge. The hearts of the Spaniards sunk, as their toils and sufferings increased. More than a hundred slunk away, fell off on the route, and made their way over the ground which they had trodden, reporting the worst of disasters to their comrades, defeat and destruction, by way of excusing their cowardice. But the indomitable courage and unbending will of the adelantado, his presence and voice of command in every quarter, still prevailed to bring his remaining battalions forward. It was in vain that his troops muttered curses upon his head. Fernan Perez, an ensign of the company of St. Vincent, was bold enough to say, that " he could not comprehend how so many brave gentlemen should let themselves be led by a wretched Asturian mountaineer—a fellow who knew no more about carrying on war on land than a horse !"

The ensign had a great deal more to say of the same sort, of which Melendez was not ignorant, but of which he took no notice. He was a sage dissimulator who answered discontent with policy, and strengthened his people's hearts by divine revelation. He called another council of his officers. He told them of his prayers to and consultations of Heaven, seeking to know the will of God only in the performance of his work,—persuaded that each of them had made like prayers all night; that they were accordingly in the very mood of mind to resolve what was to be done in their extremity. He made this to appear as bad as possible, describing them as "harrassed with fatigue, shorn of strength, without bread, munitions or any human resource."

Some one counselled their retreat to St. Augustine before the Huguenots should discover them.

"Very good advice," quoth Melendez, "but suffer me still another word. The prospect is undoubtedly a gloomy one, but look you, there are the portals of La Caroline. Now, it may be just as well to see how affairs stand with our enemies. According to all appearances they are not in force. We may not have the power to take the place, but it is well to see whether the place can be taken. If we retreat now, we are not sure that we shall do so securely. They will probably hunt us through the forest, at every step of the way, encouraged by our show of weakness and timidity. It is not improbable that we may surprise this fort. Men seldom look either for friends or enemies in bad weather. I doubt if they can sustain a bold assault; but if they do, and we fail, we have the consolation at least of having done all that was possible for men."

The assault was agreed upon; and in a transport of joy, the Adelantado sunk upon his knees, in the mire where he stood, and called upon his troops to do likewise, imploring the succor of the God of battles.

He gave his orders with rapid resolution and according to a fixed design already entertained. Taking with him Francis Jean, the renegade, he put himself at the head of one division of his troops, and gave other bodies to the Captains Martin de Ochoa, Francis Recalde, Andres Lopez Patino and others, and, covered by the midnight darkness from observation—with all sounds of drum and trumpet stilled—with the echoes of their advancing squadrons hushed in the fall of torrents and the roar of sweeping winds—the assailants made their way, slowly and painfully but without staggering, toward the silent bastions of La Caroline.

Under the guidance of the renegade Frenchman the Spanish captains made a complete reconnoissance of the fortress. A portion of it was still unrepaired, and this they penetrated without difficulty. We have seen, in a previous chapter, with what doubtful vigilance the lieutenants of Laudonniere performed their duties. It will not be forgotten that, on the night of the 19th September, the charge of the watch lay with Captain de la Vigne; nor will it be forgotten with what pity that amiable captain regarded the condition of his sentinels, exposed to such unchristian weather. We left the fortress of La Caroline in most excellent repose; the storm prevailing without, and the garrison asleep within. It was while they slept that Don Pedro de Melendez was praying to heaven that he might be permitted to assist them in their slumbers, changing the temporary into an eternal sleep. Thus passed the night of the 19th September over La Caroline. The dawn of the 20th found the Spaniards, in several divisions, about to penetrate the fortress. Two of their leaders, Martin de Ochoa and the master of the camp had already done so. They had examined the place at their leisure, passing through an unrepaired breach of one of the walls. Returning, with the view to making their report, they had mistaken one pathway for another, and encountered a drowsy Frenchman, who, starting at their approach, demanded " *Qui vive?*" Ochoa promptly answered, " France," and the man approached them only to receive a stunning blow upon the head. The Frenchman recovered himself instantly, drew his sword, and made at the assailant, but the master of the camp seconded the blow of Ochoa, and the Frenchman was brought to the ground. The sword of the Spaniard was planted at his throat, and he was forbidden to speak under pain of death. He had cried aloud, but had failed to give the alarm, and this pointed suggestion silenced him from farther attempts. He was conducted to Melendez, who, determined to see nothing but good auguries, cried out, without caring to hear the report—" My friends, God is with us! We are already in possession of the fort." At these words the assault was given. The captive Frenchman was slain, as the most easy method of relieving his captors of their charge, and the Spaniards darted pell-mell into the fort, the fierce Adelantado still leading in the charge, with the cry—" Follow me, comrades, God is for us!" Two Frenchmen, half-naked, rushed across his path. One of them he slew, and Don Andres Patino the other. They had no time allowed them to give the alarm; but just at this moment a soldier of the garrison who was less drowsy than the rest, or more apprehensive of his duty, had sauntered forth from the shelter of his quarters and stood upon the ramparts, looking forth in the direction of a little " sandie knappe," or hill, down which a column of the Spaniards were rushing in order of battle. This vision brought him to the full possession of all his faculties. He gave the *cri de guerre*, the signal of battle, but as he wheeled about to procure his weapons, he beheld other detachments of the Spaniards making their way through the unrepaired and undefended breaches in the wall. Still he cried aloud, even as he fled, and Laudonniere started from his slumbers only to hear the startling cry—" To arms! to arms! The enemy is upon us!"

The warning came too late. The amiable weakness which

withdrew the sentinels from the walls because of the weather, was not now to be repaired by any energy or courage. The garrison was aroused, but not permitted to rally or embody themselves. Melendez with his troop had reached the *corps de garde* quite as soon as Laudonniere. The latter—lately supposed to have usurped royal honors—was very soon convinced that the only object before him was the safety of his own life. With the first alarm, he caught up sword and buckler, and rushed valiantly enough into the court. But he only appeared to be made painfully conscious that everything was lost. His appeals to his soldiers only brought his enemies about him, who butchered his men as they approached their guns, and who now appeared in numbers on every side, in full possession of the fortress. The magazines were already in their hands, and a desperate effort of Laudonniere's artillerists to recover them, was followed only by their own destruction. The most vigorous resistance, hand to hand, was made on the southwest side of the fort. Here the Frenchmen opposed themselves with cool and determined courage, to the entrance of the enemy Hither Laudonniere hurried, crying aloud to his men in the language of encouragement, and doing his utmost, by the most headlong valor, to repair the mischiefs of his feeble rule and most unhappy remissness of authority. Verily, to those who saw how well he carried himself in this the moment of his worst despair, the past errors of the unhappy Laudonniere had been forgiven if not forgotten. But the struggle, on the part of any valor, was utterly in vain. The Spaniards had won a footing already too secure for dispossession. Led on by Pedro Melendez, with ever and anon his fanatic war-cry—" God is with us, my comrades," ringing in their ears, now thoroughly excited by the earnest of success which they enjoyed, in overwhelming numbers and in the full faith that they fought the battles of Holy Church, the Spaniards were irresistible. They mocked the tardy valor of our Huguenots, their feeble force, and purposeless attempts. At length the party led by Melendez confronted Laudonniere. The Spanish chieftain knew not the person of his enemy. But the renegade Frenchman, Francis Jean, discovered his ancient leader, and the desire for revenge, which had led to his treachery, filled his heart with exultation at the prospect of the gratification of his passion. He cried to Melendez:

"That is he! That is the captain of the heretics—that is Laudonniere!"

"Ah, traitor! Is it thou?" cried Laudonniere. "Let me but live to slay thee, and I care nothing for the rest."

With these words he sprang upon the traitor guide, and would have slain him at a stroke, but for the interposition of Melendez. He thrust back the renegade, and confronted the captain of the Huguenots. But Laudonniere shrank from the conflict, for Melendez was followed by his troop; and, saving one man, a stout soldier named Bartholomew, who fought manfully with a heavy partizan, he stood utterly alone and unsupported. He gave back, or rather was drawn back by Bartholomew; but now that Melendez and his people had seen the particular prey whom they had been seeking, they rushed with fiercer appetite than ever to make him captive. The efforts of the Spaniards were then redoubled. The fierce bigot Pedro Melendez himself—a stalwart warrior, clad in heavy black armor of woven mail, with a great white cross upon his breast—made the most desperate efforts to bring Laudonniere to the last passage at arms; and for a time the Frenchman, though quite too light and enfeebled by sickness for the contest with such a champion, was eager to indulge him. He struggled with the friendly arm which perforce drew him away, and great was his rage, though impotent, when the rush of a number of his own fugitives passing between at this moment, hurried him onward as by the downward rush of a torrent, to the safety of his life if not to the increase of his honor. At that moment Laudonniere had gladly redeemed by a glorious death, at the hands of the fierce Asturian, the errors and the failures of his life. But this was denied him, and, vainly struggling against the tide of fugitives, he was swept with them in the direction of the *corps de garde.* Laudonniere yielded in this manner only foot by foot, striking at the foe and at his own runagates alike, and receiving upon his shield, with the dexterity of an accomplished cavalier, the assault of a score of pikes which pressed beyond the heavy blade of Melendez. When at length the retreating Frenchmen had reached the court of the fortress, they scattered headlong, finding themselves confronted by new and consolidated masses of the enemy, and each of them sought incontinently his own method of escape. "*Sauve qui peut !*" was the cry, and the crowd by which Laudonniere had hitherto been borne unwillingly along, now melted away on every hand, leaving him again almost alone in the presence of the Spaniard. And still the faithful fellow, Bartholomew, clung to his superior, saving him from the rashness which would only have flung away his own life without an object. He hurried along his unhappy and now reckless captain, taking his way into the yard of Laudonniere's lodging. Thither they were closely pursued, and, but for a tent that happened to be standing in the place, they must have been taken. But, passing behind this tent, while the Spaniards were busied in groping within it, or cutting away the cords,

"Hither, now, Monsieur René," cried Bartholomew, grasping

the commandant by the wrist and drawing him along; "follow me now and we shall surely escape. They have left the breach open by the west, near to the lodging of Monsieur D'Erlach, and by that route shall we gain the thickets."

"Ah!" cried Laudonniere, long and grateful recollections of a tried fidelity, to which he had not always done justice, extorting from him a groan; "Ah! this had never happened had Jean Ribault left me Alphonse!"

And the tears gushed from his eyes, and he paused and thrust the point of his sword into the earth with vexation and despair.

"We have not a moment, Monsieur René," cried the soldier with impatience; "the tent is down; the Spaniards are foiled for a moment only. They will be sure to seek you in the breach."

"There! there! indeed!" cried the commandant bitterly, "there should they have found me at first; but now!—Lead on! lead on! my good fellow. As thou wilt!"

Soon our fugitives had cleared the breach, and were now without the walls. The misty shroud which covered the face of nature, and enveloped as with a sea the thickets to which they were making, favored their escape. The unhappy Laudonniere found himself temporarily safe in the forests; but if remote from present danger, they were not so far from the fortress as to be insensible to the work of death and horror which was in progress there, the evidence of which came to their ears in the shrieks of women for mercy, and the groans and cries of tortured men.

"Slay! slay! Smite and spare not!" was the dreadful command of Melendez. "The groans of the heretic make music in the ears of Heaven!"

Laudonniere shut his ears, and with his companion plunged deeper into the forests. Here he found other fugitives like himself, and others subsequently joined him; some were wounded even unto death, others slightly; all were terror-stricken, shuddering with horror, incapable from woe and agony. What had they beheld, what endured, and what was the prospect before them but of massacre? A hasty council was convened among the party, and the advice of Laudonniere—he could command no longer—was, that they should bury themselves among the reeds and within the marshes which lay along the river, out of sight, until they could make their small vessels, by which the mouth of the river was still guarded, aware of their situation. But this council was agreeable to a part only, of that bewildered company. Another portion preferred to push for one of the Indian villages, at some little distance in the forests, where, hitherto, they had found a friendly reception. They persevered in this purpose, leaving Laudonniere and a few others in the marshes. Hither, then, these hapless fugitives sped, till they could go no farther; and until their commandant himself, still unrecovered from the chill and fever which had seized him at the first coming on of autumn, declared his inability to go deeper into the thicket, though it promised him the safety which he sought. He was already up to his neck in water, and such was his weakness, that he was about to yield to his fate But for the faithful and unwearied support of one of his soldiers, Jean du Chemin, who held him above the water when he would have sunk, and who stuck by him all the rest of that day, and through the long and dreary night which followed, he must have perished. Meanwhile, two of his soldiers swam off in the direction of the vessels. Fortunately for those swimmers, those in the vessels had been already apprized of the taking of the fort by Jean de Hais, the master carpenter, who had made his escape the first, by dropping down the river in a shallop. The boats of the vessels were immediately pushed up the stream, and succeeded in picking up the swimmers, and, finally, when Laudonniere and his faithful companions were both about to sink, in extricating them from their marshy place of refuge. Eighteen or twenty of the fugitives (among whom was the celebrated painter, Jaques le Moyne de Morgues, to whom we owe mostly the illustrations of Floridian scenery, costume, and lineaments preserved in De Bry and other collections) were rescued in this manner, and conveyed on board the ships. These, with Laudonniere, subsequently made their way, after many disasters, perils of the sea and land, a detention in England, where they were again indebted to the humanity of the English for succor and sympathy. An artful attempt was made by Melendez to obtain possession of these vessels, but he was baffled. They sailed from the river of May on the 25th September, 1565, thus abandoning forever the design of planting themselves and their religion permanently in Florida. Let us now look to the farther proceedings of the conquerors in possession of their prize!

CHAPTER VII.

VÆ VICTIS.

AND now, it falls to our lot to record the most cruel passage in all this history; to relate the mournful and terrible fate which befel the wretched Huguenots taken at the capture of La Caroline, and the sanguinary deed by which the Spanish chief, through a gloomy fanaticism, stained foully the honorable fame which his skill and courage in arms might have ensured to his memory All resistance having ceased on the part of the Huguenots of La Caroline, the standard of Castile was unrolled from its battlements, instead of the white folds and the smiling lilies of France. The name of the fortress was solemnly changed to San Matheo, the day on which they found themselves in its possession being that which was dedicated to the honor of that saint. The arms of France and of Coligny, which surmounted the gateways of the place, were erased and those of Spain were graven there instead, and the keeping of the fortress was assigned to a garrison of three hundred men, under the command of Gonzalo de Villaroël. These duties occupied but little time, and did not interfere with other performances of the Adelantado, which he thought not the less conspicuous among the duties required at his hands. His prisoners were brought before him. These were, perhaps, not so numerous, though forming a fair proportion of the number left by Ribault in the garrison. It is perhaps fortunate that no greater number had been left, since, in all probability, the same want of watch and caution by which the fortress had been lost, would have equally been shown, with any numbers, under such an easy commandant as Laudonniere, and in the particular circumstances which had taken place. Of these prisoners many were women and children. We have seen that Laudonniere succeeded in rescuing some twenty persons. Several had fled to the forests and taken shelter with the tribes of neighboring Indians. In some few instances, the red-men protected them with fidelity. But in the greater number of cases, terrified by the sudden appearance and the strength of the Spaniards, they had yielded up the fugitives at the fierce demand of the Adelantado. Others of the miserable Huguenots, warned by the Indians that they could no longer harbor, were shot down by the pursuing Spaniards, as they fled in terror through the forests. Twenty perished in this manner, offering no resistance, and long after the struggle in La Caroline had ended.

The surviving prisoners were then brought before the conqueror. They were manacled, and presented a spectacle which must have moved the sympathies of any ordinary nature. But Pedro de Melendez was not of an ordinary nature. The natural sympathies had given way to a morbid passion amounting to insanity, by which his judgment was confounded. The sight of weeping, and trembling women and children; of captives naked, worn, exhausted, enfeebled by years, by disease, by cruel wounds—all pleading for his mercy—only seemed to strengthen him in the most cruel resolution. "The groans of the heretic, are music in the ears of heaven!" Upon this maxim he designed an appropriate commentary.

"Separate these women from the other prisoners."

It was done.

"Now detach from these last, all children under fifteen years."

His command was obeyed. The women and children thus set apart were consigned to slavery. Of their farther fate the historian knows nothing. The young and tender were probably persuaded to the Roman Catholic altars, and thus finally achieved their deliverance. The more stubborn, we may reasonably assume, perished in their bonds, passing from one condition of degradation to another. Of the rest the history is terribly definite. Fixing his cold, dark eye upon the male captives upon whose fate he had yet said nothing, he demanded—

"Is there among ye any who profess the faith of the Holy Catholic Church?"

Two of the prisoners answered in the affirmative.

"Take these Christians away, and let their bonds be removed. The Holy Father, Salvandi, will examine them in the faith of Mother Church. For the rest, are there any among ye, who, seeing the error of your ways, will renounce the heresy of Luther, and seek once more communion with the only true church?"

A drear silence followed. The captives looked mournfully at each other, and at the Adelantado; but in his face there was no encouragement, and nothing but despair was expressed in the aspects of their fellows.

"Be warned!" continued the Adelantado. "To those who seek the blessings of the true church, she generously openeth her arms. To those who turn away, indifferently or in scorn, she decrees death temporal and death eternal. Hear ye!—and now say."

The silence was unbroken.

"Are ye obdurate? or do ye not comprehend that your lives rest upon your speech? Either ye embrace the safety which the church offers, by an instant renunciation of that of the foul heretic Luther, or ye die by the halter!"

One sturdy soldier advanced from the group—a bold, high-souled fellow—his brows lifted proudly with the conscious impulse which worked within his soul.

"Pedro de Melendez, we are in your power. You are master of our mortal bodies, but with the death before us that you threaten, know that we are members of the reformed Church of Christ, which ye name to be of Luther—that, holding it good to live in this faith, we deem it one in which it will not be amiss to die!"

And the speaker looked round him, into the faces of his fellows, and they lightened up with a glow of cheerfulness and pride, though no word was spoken.

"Speaks this man for the rest of ye?" demanded Melendez.

For a moment there was silence. At length a matelit advanced—a common sailor—a man before the mast.

"Ay! ay! captain! what he says we say! and there's no use for more palaver. Let there be an end of it. We are of the church of Messer Luther, and no other; if death's the word, we're ready. We're not the men, at the end of the reckoning, to belie the whole voyage!"

"Be it it even as ye say!" answered Melendez coldly, but sternly, and without change of accent or show of passion: "Take them forth, and let them be hung to yonder tree!"

Then rose the shrieks of women and the cries of children; women seeking to embrace their husbands and children clinging to the knees of their doomed sires. But these produced no relentings. The parties were separated by the strong hand, and the unhappy men were hurrried to the fatal tree. The priest stood ready to receive their recantations. His exhortations were not spared; but soldier and sailor had equally spoken for the resolute martyrdom of the whole. The reverend father preached to them, and promised them in vain. Amidst cries and curses, the victims were run up to the wide-spreading branches of a mighty oak, dishonored in its employment for such a purpose, and perished in their fidelity to the faith which they professed. Their bodies were left hanging in the sun and wind, destined equally as trophies of the victor, and warnings to the heretic. A monument was instantly raised beneath the tree, upon which was printed in largo characters—

> "These do not suffer thus as Frenchmen, but as Heretics and Enemies to God!"

XXIII.

THE FORTUNES OF RIBAULT.

CHAPTER I.

HAVING thus rendered himself master of La Caroline, effectually displacing the Huguenots from the region which they had acquired, and maintained so long through so many vicissitudes, Melendez prepared to hurry back to his camp on the banks of the Selooe. He but lingered to review the force of the garrison, and with his own hands, fresh reeking with the blood of his slaughtered victims, to lay the foundations of a church dedicated to the God of Mercy, when he set forth with the small body of troops, which he reserved to himself from the number that accompanied his expedition, scarcely a hundred men, impatient for return, lest Ribault, escaping from the storm, should visit upon his settlement at St. Augustine the same wrath which had lighted upon La Caroline. The heavy torrents from which he had already suffered so much continued to descend as before, and the whole face of the country was inundated; his people suffered inconceivably upon the march, but the Adelantado was superior to the sense of suffering. He felt himself too much the especial favorite of God, to suffer himself to doubt that the toils and inconveniences of such a progress as that before him, were anything but tests of his fidelity, and the means by which the Deity designed to prepare him properly for the holy service which was expected at his hands. He reached his camp in safety. His arrival was the source of a great triumph and an unexpected joy. Here he had been reported as having perished, with all his army, at the hands of the French The deserters, who had abandoned him on the route, in certain anticipation of this fate, had not scrupled to spread this report by way of excusing their own inconstancy and fears. His people accordingly passed instantly from the extremity of terror to that of joy and triumph. They marched out, *en masse*, at his approach, to welcome him as the vanquisher of the heretics; the priests at their head, bearing the cross of Christ, the conqueror, and chanting *Te Deum*, in exultation at the twofold conquest which he had won, at the expense equally of their own, and the enemies of the church.

His triumphs were not without some serious qualifications. In the midst of their joy, an incendiary, as he supposed, had reduced to ashes the remaining vessels in the harbor. A portion of his garrison, a little after, showed themselves in mutiny against their officers, this spirit having been manifested before his departure for La Caroline. He was apprised also of a mishap to one of his greater ships, the San Pelayo, which had been sent to Hispaniola, filled with captive Frenchmen taken at different periods, and who were destined to suffer the question as heretics in the Inquisition of the mother country. These had risen upon the crew, overpowered them, captured the vessel, and carried her safely into Denmark.

While meditating, and seeking to repair some of these mishaps, Melendez received intelligence of Ribault and his fleet, which caused him some inquietude. His own shipping being destroyed, his future safety depended wholly upon the condition of Ribault's armament, since, with their small vessels, his harborage might be entered at any moment, and his sole means of defence lay with his troops upon the land, where his entrenchments were not yet sufficiently advanced to offer much, if any obstacle, to a vigorous assailant. But farther advices, brought him by the savages, relieved him measurably from any apprehensions from the shipping of his enemy. In this respect the condition of the French was no better than his own. The unfortunate Ribault, driven before the hurricane, had been wrecked with all his squadron, upon the bleak and unfriendly shores of Cape Cannaverel; his troops were saved, with the exception of the crew and armament of one vessel, containing a detachment under the Sieur de la Grange, all of whom perished but the captain. Dividing his troops into two or more bodies, Ribault advanced along the shore, proceeding northerly, in the direction of La Caroline, and one of his detachments had reached the inlet of Matanzas, when Melendez was first advised of their approach. He was told by the Indians that about four leagues distant, a large body of white men were embarrassed in their progress by a bay, over which they had no means to pass. Upon this intelligence, the Adelantado, taking with him forty picked soldiers, proceeded with all despatch to the designated place. His proceedings were marked by subtlety and caution. With such a force, he could hope to do nothing in open warfare against the numbers of Ribault, which, after all casualties, were probably six or seven hundred men. But nobody knew better than Melendez how to supply the deficiencies of the lion with the arts of the fox. He concealed his troop in the woods that bordered the inlet, and from the top of a tree surveyed the scattered groups of Frenchmen on the opposite shore. They were two hundred in number, and some of them had been engaged in the construction of a raft with which to effect their passage. But the roughness of the waters, and the strength of the current forbade their reliance upon so frail a conveyance, and while they were bewildered with doubt and difficulties, Melendez showed himself alone upon the banks of the river. When he was seen from the opposite shore, a bold Gascon of Saint Jean de Luz plunged fearlessly into the stream, and succeeded in making the passage.

"Who are these people?" demanded Melendez.

"We are Frenchmen, all, who have suffered shipwreck."

"What Frenchmen?"

"The people of M. Ribault, Captain-General of Florida, under commission of the king of France."

"I know no right to Florida, on the part of France or Frenchmen. I am here, the true master of the country, on behalf of my sovereign, the Catholic king, Philip the Second. I am Pedro Melendez, adelantado of all this Florida, and of the isles thereof. Go back to your general with my answer, and say to him, that I am here, followed by my army, as I had intelligence that he too was here, invading the country in my charge."

The Gascon returned with the speech, and soon after was persuaded again to swim the stream, with a request for a safe conduct from the Spanish general, on behalf of four gentlemen of the French, who desired to treat with him. It was requested that a batteau which Melendez had brought along shore with his provisions, and which was now safely moored beside the eastern banks, might be sent to bring them over. To all this Melendez readily consented. The arrangement suited him exactly. His troop was still in reserve, covered rather than concealed within the forest, and so disposed as to seem at a distance to consist of overwhelming numbers. But six men were suffered to accompany the Spanish commander. These, well armed, were quite equal to the four to whom he accorded the interview. These soon made their appearance. Their leader told the story of their melancholy shipwreck, the privations they had borne, the wants under which they suffered, and implored his assistance to regain a fortress called La Caroline, which the king, his master, held at a distance of some twenty leagues.

Melendez replied—

"Señor, I have made myself the master of your fort. I have laid strong hands upon the garrison. I have slain them all, sparing none but the women, and such children as were under fifteen years."

The Frenchmen looked incredulous.

"If you doubt," he continued, "I can soon convince you. I have brought hither with me the only two soldiers whom I have admitted to mercy. I spared them, because they claimed to be of the Catholic faith. You shall see them, and hear the truth from their own lips. In all probability you know them, and will recognise their persons. Rest you here, while I send you something to eat. You shall see your compatriots, with some of the spoils taken at La Caroline. These shall prove to you the truth of what I say."

With these words he disappeared. Soon after, refreshments were brought to our Frenchmen, and when they had eaten, the two captives at La Caroline, who had been spared on account of their faith, were allowed to commune with them, and to repeat all the facts in the cruel history of La Caroline. Nothing of that terrible tragedy was concealed. Melendez had a policy too refined for concealment, when the revelation of his atrocities was to be the means for their renewal. To strike the hearts of the

Frenchmen with such terror, as to have them at his mercy, was a profound secret of success in dealing with the wretched, suffering, and already desponding outcasts in his presence.

After an hour's absence he returned.

"Are you satisfied," he asked? "of the truth of the things which I have told you."

"We can doubt no longer;" was the reply; "but this does not lessen our claim upon your humanity as men, and your consideration as Frenchmen. Our people are at peace, there is amity and alliance between our sovereigns. You cannot deny us assistance, and the vessels necessary for our return to France."

"Surely not, if you are Catholics, and if I had the means of helping you to ships. But you are not Catholics. The alliance between our kings is an alliance of members of the true Church, both sworn against heretics."

"We are members of the Reformed Church," was the reply of the officers; "but we are men; human; made equally in the image of the Deity, and serve the same God, if not at the same altars. Suffer us, at least, to remain with you for a season, till we can find the means for returning to our own country."

"Señor, it cannot be. As for sheltering heretics, that is impossible. I have sworn on the holy sacrament, to root out and to extirpate heresy, wherever I encounter it—by sea or land—to wage against the damnable heresy which you profess a war to the utterance, as vindictive as possible, to the death and to the torture; and in this resolution I conceive myself to be serving equally the king of France as the king, my sovereign. I am here in Florida for the express purpose of establishing the Holy Roman Catholic Faith! I will assist no heretic to remain in the country."

"Assist us to leave it, señor: that is in truth what we demand."

"Demand nothing of me. Yield yourselves to my mercy—at discretion—deliver up your arms and ensigns, and I will do with you as God shall inspire me. Consent to this—these are my only terms—or do what pleases you. But you must hope nothing at my hands—neither truce nor friendship."

With this cruel ultimatum, he quitted them, giving them opportunity to return and report to their comrades. In two hours they reappeared, and made him an offer from the two hundred men gathered on the opposite banks, of twenty thousand ducats, only to be assured of their lives. The answer was as prompt as it was characteristic.

"Though but a poor soldier, señor, I am not capable of governing myself, in the performance of my duties, by any regard to selfish interests. If I am moved to do an act of grace, it will be done from pure generosity. But do not let these words deceive you. I tell you as a gentleman, and an officer holding a high commission from the king of Spain, that, though the heavens and the earth may mingle before my eyes, the resolution which I once make, I never change!"

It will scarcely be thought possible that any body of men, having arms in their hands, and still in possession of physical powers sufficient for their use, would, under such circumstances, listen to such a demand. But the forces of Ribault had been terribly demoralized by disaster and disappointment. Privation had humbled their souls, and the utter exhaustion of their spirits made them give credence to vain hopes of mercy at the hands of their enemy, which at another period they could never have entertained. The report of their envoy found them ready to make any concessions. It required but half an hour to determine their submission. The returning batteau brought over with four officers all their ensigns, sixty-six arquebuses, twenty pistols, a large number of swords and bucklers, casques and cuirasses, their whole complement of munitions, and a surrender of the entire body at discretion. Melendez gladly seized upon these spoils. He embarked twenty of his soldiers in his batteau, with orders to bring over the Frenchmen, in small divisions, and to offer them no insult; but, as they severally arrived on the eastern side of the bay, they were conducted out of sight, and under the guns of his arquebusiers. They were then given to eat, and when the repast was ended, they were asked if any among them were Catholics. There were but eight of the whole number who replied in the affirmative. These were set apart, to be conducted to St. Augustine. The rest frankly avowed themselves to be good Christians of the Reformed Church. These were immediately seized, their arms tied behind their backs, and in little squads of six, were conducted to a spot in the background, where Melendez had traced, with his cane, a line upon the sand. Here they were butchered to a man, each succeeding body sharing the same fate, without knowing, till too late, that of their comrades. There was no pause, no mercy, no relentings in behalf of any. All perished, to the number of two hundred; and Pedro Melendez returned to his camp at St. Augustine, again to be welcomed with *Te Deum*, and the acclamation for good Christian service, from a Christian people.

CHAPTER II.

The congratulations of his people were yet resounding in his ears, when the savages brought him further intelligence of Frenchmen gathered upon the borders of that bay which had arrested the progress of the previous detachment. They were represented to be more numerous than the first, and Melendez did not doubt that they constituted the bulk of Ribault's force under the immediate command of that leader. He proceeded to encounter him as he had done the other party, but on this occasion he increased his own detachment to one hundred and fifty men. These he ranged, in good order during the night, along the banks of the river, which the Huguenots had begun their preparations to pass. They had been at work upon the radeau or raft which had been begun by the preceding party, but their progress had been unsatisfactory, and the prospect of the passage, in such a vessel, over such an arm of the sea, was quite as discouraging as to their predecessors. With the dawn, and when they discovered the force of Melendez on the opposite shore, the drums sounded the alarm, the royal standard of France was advanced, and the troops were ranged in order of battle. Poor Ribault still observed the externals of the veteran, if only to conceal the real infirmities which impaired the moral of his command.

Seeing this display of determination, Melendez, with proper policy, commanded his people to proceed to breakfast without any show of excitement or emotion. He himself promenaded the banks of the river, accompanied only by his admiral and two other officers, as indifferently as if there had been no person on the opposite side. With this, the clamors of the French tambours ceased—the fifes were allowed to take breath—and in place of the warlike standard of their country, the commander of the Huguenots displayed a white flag as sign of peace, and his trumpets sounded for a parley. A response from the Spanish side of the river, in similar spirit, caused one of the Frenchmen to advance within speaking distance, upon the raft, who requested that somebody might be sent them, as their radeau could not contend against the current. A pirogue was finally sent by the Spaniard, which brought over the sergeant-major of Ribault. This man related briefly the necessities and desires of his commander. He was totally ignorant of all that had taken place. He had been wrecked, and had lost all his vessels ; that he had with him three hundred and fifty soldiers ; that he was desirous of reaching his fortress, twenty leagues distant ; and prayed the assistance of the Spaniards, to enable him to do so. At the close, he desired to know with whom he was conferring.

Melendez answered as directly as he had done in the previous instance, when dealing with the first detachment. He did not scruple to add to the narrative of the capture of La Caroline, and the cruel murder of its garrison, the farther history of the party whom he had encountered in the same place with themselves.

" I have punished all these with death ;" he continued ; and, still further to assure the officer of Ribault of the truth of what he said, he took him to the spot where lay in a heap the exposed, the bleached and decaying bodies of his slaughtered companions. The Frenchman looked steadily at the miserable spectacle, and so far commanded his nerves as to betray no emotion. He continued his commission without faltering ; and obtained from Melandez a surety in behalf of Ribault, with four or six of his men, to cross the river for the purpose of conference, with the privilege of returning to his forces at his leisure. But the adelantado positively refused to let the Frenchmen have his shallop or bateau. The pirogue, alone, was at their service. With this, the French general could pass the strait without risk; and he was compelled to content himself with this. The policy of Melendez was not willing to place any larger vessel in his power.

Ribault crossed to the conference, accompanied by eight of his officers. They were well received by the adelantado, and a collation spread for them. He showed them afterwards the bodies of their slain companions. He gave them the full history of the taking of La Caroline, and the treatment of the garrison, and brought forward the two Frenchmen, claiming to be Catholics, whose lives had been spared when the rest were massacred. There was something absolutely satanic in the conduct of the Spaniard, by which Ribault was confounded. He was not willing to believe the facts that he could not question.

"Monsieur," said he to Laudonniere, "I will not believe that you design us evil. Our kings are friends and brothers, and in the name of this alliance between them, I conjure you to furnish us with a vessel for returning to our country. We have suffered enough in this: we will leave it in your hands entirely. Help us to the means necessary for our departure."

To this Melendez replied in the very same language which he had used to the preceding detachment:

"Our kings are Catholics both; they hold terms with one another, but not with heretics. I will make no terms with you. I will hold no bonds with heretics anywhere. You have heard what I have done with your comrades. You hear what has been the fate of La Caroline. You behold the corses of those who but a few days ago followed your banner; and now I say to you that you must yield to my discretion, leaving it to me to do with you as God shall determine me!"

Aghast and confounded, Ribault declared his purpose to return and consult with his people. In a case so extreme, particularly as he had with him many gentlemen of family, he could not undertake to decide without their participation. Melendez approved this determination, and the general of the French re-crossed the river.

For three hours was the consultation carried on in the camp of our Huguenots. Ribault fully revealed the terrible history of what had passed, of what he had heard and seen in the camp of the Spaniards. The cold and cruel decision of Melendez in their case, as in that of the previous troops, was unfolded without reserve. There were no concealments, and, for a time, a dull, deep and dreary silence overspread the assembly. But all had not been crushed by misfortune into imbecility. There were some noble and fierce spirits whose hearts rose in all their strength of resolution, as they listened to the horrible narrative and the insolent exaction.

"Better perish a thousand deaths, in the actual conflict with a thousand enemies, than thus submit to perish in cold blood from the stroke of the cowardly assassin!"

Such was the manly resolution of many. Others, again, like Ribault, were disposed to hope against all experience. The fact that Melendez had treated them so civilly, that he had placed food and drink before them, and that his manners were respectful and his tones were mild, were assumed by them to be conclusive they were not to suffer as their predecessors had done.

"They were beguiled with the same arguments," said young Alphonse D'Erlach; "arguments which appealed to their hunger their thirst, their exhaustion, and their spiritless hearts—arguments against truth, and common sense and their own eyes. He who listens to such arguments will merit to fall by the hands of the assassin."

We need not pursue the debate which continued for three hours. At the end of this time, Ribault returned to the landing.

"A portion of my people," he said, "but not the greater number, are prepared to surrender themselves to you at discretion."

"They are their own masters," replied Melendez; "they must do as they please; to me it is quite indifferent what decision they make."

Ribault continued:

"Those who are thus prepared to yield themselves have instructed me to offer you twenty thousand ducats for their ransom; but the others will give even a greater sum, for they include among them many persons of great wealth and family;—nay, they desire further, if you will suffer it, to remain still in the country."

"I shall certainly need some succors," replied Melendez, "in order to execute properly the commands of the king, my master, which are to conquer the country and to people it, establishing here the Holy Evangel;—and I should grieve to forego any assistance."

This evasive answer was construed by Ribault according to his desires. He requested permission to return and deliberate with his people, in order to communicate this last response. He readily obtained what he asked, and the night was consumed among the Huguenots in consultation. It brought no unanimity to their counsels.

"I will sooner trust the incarnate devil himself, than this Melendez," was the resolution of Alphonse D'Erlach to his elder brother. "Go not, *mon frére*, yield not: the savage Floridian has no heart so utterly stony as that of this Spaniard. I will peril anything with the savage, ere I trust to his doubtful mercy."

And such was the resolve of many others, but it was not that of Ribault.

"What!" exclaimed one of his friendly counsellors—"he has shown you our slain comrades, butchered under the very arrangement which he accords to us, and yet you trust to him?"

The infatuated leader, broken in spirit, and utterly exhausted in the struggle with fate, replied:

"That he has freely shown me what he has done, is no proof that he designs any such deeds hereafter. His fury is satiated. It is impossible that he will commit a like crime of this nature It is his pride that would have us wholly in his power."

"He hath fed on blood until he craves it," cried Alphonse D'Erlach. "You go to your death, Monsieur Ribault. The tiger invites you to a banquet where the guest brings the repast."

He was unheard, at least by the Huguenot general.

"We will leave this man, my friends," cried Alphonse D'Erlach, the strong will and great heart naturally rising to command in the moment of extremity. "We will leave this man. *Quem Deus vult perdere prius dementat.* He goes to the sacrifice!"

And when Ribault prepared in the morning to lead his people across the bay, he found but an hundred and fifty of all the force that he commanded during the previous day. Two hundred had disappeared in the night under the guidance of D'Erlach.

CHAPTER III.

The fates had the blinded Ribault in their keeping. He was ferried across the stream for the last time, by the grim ferryman vouchsafed him; and the trophies which he first laid at the feet of the adelantado consisted of his own armor, a dagger, a casque of gold, curiously and beautifully wrought; his buckler, his pistolet, and a secret commission which he had received at the hands of Admiral Coligny himself. The standards of France and of the Admiral were then lowered at the feet of the Spaniard, then the banners of companies, and finally the sword of the Huguenot general. Never was submission more complete and shameful. The spirit of the veteran was utterly broken and gone. But this degradation was not thus to end. Melendez gave orders that he and the companions he had brought with him, eight in number, should be tied with their hands behind their backs. The indignity brought the blush with tenfold warmth into the cheeks of the old warrior. He foresaw the inevitable doom before him, but he felt the shame only.

"Have I lived for this? Is it thus, Monsieur Melendez, that you treat a warrior and a Christian?"

"God forbid that I should treat a Christian after this fashion. But *are* you a Christian, señor?"

"Of the Reformed Church, I am!" was the reply.

"I do not hold yours, señor, to be a church of Christ, but of Satan. Bind him, my comrades, and take him hence."

A significant wave of the fatal staff, which had prescribed the line upon the spot of earth selected as the chosen place of sacrifice—the scene of a new *auto-da-fé* as fearful as the preceding—

finished his instructions, and as the guards led the veteran away, he commenced, in the well-known spirit of the time, to sing aloud the psalm " *Domine, memento mei,* &c.," in that fearful moment well conceiving that there was left him now but one source of consolation, and none of present hope. He addressed no words of expostulation to his murderer; but as they led him away, he calmly remarked—" From the earth we came, to the earth we must return; soon or late, it is all the same; such must have been the fate. It is not what we would, but what we must."

He renewed his psalm, the sounds of which grated offensively on the bigot ears of Melendez, falling from such lips, and he impatiently made the signal to his men to expedite the affair. The Huguenot general was led off singing. One of the accounts before us—for there is a Spanish and a French version of the history, differing in several minute, but really unimportant particulars —describes the last scene of Ribault's career, in a brief but striking manner. The eight which constituted this party had each his assassin assigned him. Among the companions of Ribault at the moment of execution, was Lieutenant Ottigny, of whom we have heard more than once before in the history of La Caroline. They were led into the woods, out of sight and hearing of the French on the opposite side of the bay, all of whom were to be brought over, ten by ten, to the same place of sacrifice. The soldier to whom Ribault had been confided, when they had reached the spot strewn thickly with the corses of his murdered people, said to him—

" Señor, you are the general of the French?"

" I am!"

" You have always been accustomed to exact obedience, without question, from all the people under your command?"

"Without doubt!" replied Ribault, somewhat wondering at the question.

"Deem it not strange, then, señor," continued the soldier, "that I execute faithfully the orders I have received from my commandant!"

And, speaking these words, he drove his poignard into the heart of the victim, who fell upon his face, in death, without uttering a groan. Ottigny and the others perished in like manner, and with no farther preliminaries. Why pursue the details with the rest? In this mannner each unconscious band of the Huguenots, thus surrendering to the clemency of Melendez, was simply ferried across the river to execution. And still the boat returned for and with its little compliment of ten—it was only a proper precaution that denied that more should be brought—and the succeeding voyagers dreamed not, even as they sped, their comrades were sinking one by one under the hands of their butchers. More than a hundred perished on this occasion, but four of the number avowing themselves to be of the Roman Catholic Church, and being spared accordingly.

CHAPTER IV.

OF THOSE WHO REFUSED TO FOLLOW THE FORTUNES OF RIBAULT.

WE have seen that two hundred of the followers of Ribault had refused to submit to the arrangement, by which that unhappy commander had sacrificed himself and all those who accompanied him into the camp of Melendez. These two hundred had been counselled to the more manly course which they had taken, by the youthful but sagacious lieutenant, Alphonse D'Erlach. This young man well understood their enemy. His counsel, if followed by Ribault, would probably have resulted in conquest rather than misfortune.

"We are strong,"—said D'Erlach to his companions—"strong enough to maintain ourselves in any position, which we may take and hold with steadfastness. We have three hundred and fifty soldiers, all with arms in their hands, and it requires only that we shall use our arms and maintain our independence. Why treat at all with the Spaniards? They may assist us across this strait, but why cross it at all? To gain La Caroline? That, according to his own showing, is already in his hands. Indeed, of this, you tell us, there can be no question. What then? Of what avail to seek the post which he has garrisoned, and which, properly fortified, is beyond our utmost strength. It is evident that, fortifying La Caroline and his new post on the banks of the Salooe, he has no available force with which he dares assail us. In the meantime, let us leave this position. Let us retire further to the south, regain the coast upon which our vessels were wrecked, rebuild them, or one at least, in which, if your desire is to return to France, we can re-embark; or, as I would counsel, retire to a remoter settlement, where we may fortify ourselves, and establish the colony anew, for which we first came to Florida. Why abandon the country, when we are in sufficient strength to keep it? Why forego the enterprises which offer us gold and silver in abundance, a genial climate, a fertile soil, a boundless domain, in which our fortunes and our faith may be made equally secure. As for the savages of Florida, I know them and I fear them not. They are terrible only to the timid and the improvident. With due precautions, a proper courage, and arms in our hands, we shall mock at their wandering bands, whose attacks are inconstant, and upon whom the caprice of the seasons is forever working such evil as will prevent them always from bringing large numbers together, or keeping them long in one organization. But, hold the savages to be as terrible as you may, they are surely less to be feared, are less faithless and less hostile, than these sanguinary Spaniards. Do not, at all events, deliver yourselves, bound hand and foot, in petty numbers, to be butchered in detail, by this monstrous cutthroat!"

His counsels prevailed with the greater number. They left the camp of Ribault at midnight, and commenced their silent march along the coast, making for the bleak shores which had seen their vessels stranded. Here they arrived after much toil and privation, and, cheered by the manly courage of D'Erlach, they proceeded at once to build themselves a vessel which should suffice for their escape from the country, or enable them to penetrate without difficulty to regions not yet under the control of the Spaniards. For the work before them they possessed the proper facilities. The fragments of their shattered navy were within their reach. The expedition had been properly provided with carpenters and laborers; and in that day every mariner was something of a mechanic. They advanced rapidly with their work, but at the end of three weeks the clouds gathered once more about their heads. Once more the haughty banners of the Spaniard were beheld, the vindictive enemy being resolved to give them no respite, to allow of no refuge upon the soil, to afford them no prospect of escape from the country.

Advised by the Indians that the surviving Frenchmen were at work at Carnaverel, building themselves both fortresses and vessels, Melendez sent an express to the Governor of San Matheo, late La Caroline, with orders to send him instantly one hundred and fifty of his men. These arrived at St. Augustine on the 23d of October, under the conduct of Don Andres Lopez Patiño, and of Don Jean Velez de Medrano. To these troops Melendez added a like number from his own garrison, and on the 26th or the month, they commenced their march to the south, on foot. His provisions and munitions were sent in two shallops along the shore, and each night they came to anchor opposite his camp. On the first day of November, they came in sight of the French. These, immediately abandoned their work, and seizing their arms retired to a small sandy elevation which they had previously selected as a place of refuge against attack, and which they had strengthened by some slight defences. Here they prepared for a desperate and deadly struggle. The force of their assailants was one-third stronger than their own. They had the advantage, also, of supplies and munitions, in which the Frenchmen were deficient; but a sense of desperation increased their courage, and they showed no disposition to entreat or parley. But Melendez had no desire to compel them to a struggle in which even success would probably be fatal ultimately to himself. His main strength was with him, but should he suffer greatly in the assault, as it was very evident he must, the French being in a good position, and showing the most determined front, his army would be too greatly weakened, perhaps, even for their safe return to St. Augustine, through a country filled with hostile Indians, whom, as yet, he had neither conquered nor conciliated. Having reconnoitred the position taken by the Frenchmen, he generously made them overtures of safety. He proposed not only to spare their lives, but promised to receive as many of them as thought proper, into his own ranks as soldiers.

This offer led to a long and almost angry conference among the French. Their councils were divided. Many of their leaders were men wholly ignorant of the country, and disheartened by the cruel vicissitudes and dangers through which they had passed. Many of them were persons of wealth and family, who were anxious once more to find themselves in a position which demanded no farther struggle, and which might facilitate their return to the haunts of civilization. Others, again, were Catholics, whose sympathies were not active in behalf of the Huguenots with whom they now found themselves in doubtful connection. Others were jealous of the sudden spring to authority, which, in those moments of peril when all others trembled, had been made by the young adventurer, Alphonse D'Erlach. It was in vain that he counselled them against giving faith to the Spaniards.

"What is your security, my friends? His word? His pledge of mercy to you, when he showed none to your brethren? Look at the hand which he stretches out to you; it is yet dripping with the blood of your people, butchered, in cold blood, at La Caroline, and the Bay of Matanzas. Trust him not, if you would prosper—if ye would not perish likewise. Believe none of his assurances, even though he should swear upon the Holy Evangel."

"But what are we to do, Monsieur D'Erlach? We have small provisions here. He hath environed us with his troops."

"We may break through his troops. We have arms in our hands, and if we have but the heart to use them, like men, we may not only save ourselves, but avenge our butchered comrades."

His entreaties and arguments were unavailing. It was sufficient for our broken-spirited exiles that Melendez had volunteered to them those guaranties of safety which he had denied to their brethren. They prepared to yield.

"Go not thou with these people, my brother," said Alphonse D'Erlach, to that elder brother whom we have seen, with himself, a trusted lieutenant of Laudonniere. He flung himself tenderly upon the bosom of the other, as he prayed, and the moisture gathered in his eyes. The elder was touched, but his inclinations led him with the rest.

"He hath sworn to us, Alphonse, that life shall be spared us, and that we shall be free to enter his service or return to France."

"Would you place life at his mercy?"

"It is so now!"

"No! never! while the hand may grasp the weapon. If we would defy him as men, we should rather have his life at ours. Oh! would that we were men. Enter his service! Dost thou think of this? Wouldst thou receive commands from the lips of him who hath murdered thy old commander!"

"No! surely, I shall never serve Melendez. I seek this only as the mean whereby to return to France."

"And wherefore return to France? What hath France in reserve for us but the shot, the torture, and the scourge. Here, brother, here, with the wild Floridian, let us make our home. Let us rather put on the untamed habits of the savage, his garments torn from bear and panther; let us anoint our bodies with oil; let us stain our cheeks with ocre; and taking bond with the Apalachian and Floridian, let us haunt the footsteps of the Spaniard with death and eternal hatred, till we leave not one of

17

them living for the pollution of the soil. This is my purpose, brother, though I go forth into the wilderness alone!"

"Thou shalt not go alone, Alphonse. We will live and die together."

The brothers embraced. The bond was knit between them, whatever might be the event; and when, at morning, the main body of the Frenchmen surrendered themselves to the Spanish adelantado, the Erlachs were not among them. They, with twenty others, all Huguenots, who detested equally the power and feared the savage fanaticism of Melendez, had disappeared silently in the night, leaving as a message for the Spanish chief, that they preferred infinitely to be devoured by the savages, than to receive his mercy. Melendez looked anxiously to the dark forests in which they had shrouded themselves from his pursuit. He would gladly have penetrated their depths of shadow and their secret glooms, in search of victims, whom he certainly never would have spared if caught; but the object was too small for the peril which it involved; and having destroyed the fort and shipping which they had been building, content with having broken up the power of the French in the country, he returned with his captives to St. Augustine. He kept his faith with them. Many of them joined themselves to his troops, and accompanied his expeditions, and others who were Huguenots found new favor with him by undergoing conversion to his faith. With this chapter fairly ends the history of the Huguenot colonies of Coligny in Florida; but other histories followed which will require other chapters.

XXIV.

ALPHONSE D'ERLACH.

THE dawn of the morning after the separation of D'Erlach with his few companions from the great body of the French, found the former emerging from a dense thicket which they had traversed through the night. They were still but a few miles from their late encampment. A bright and generous sun, almost the first that had shone for several weeks in unclouded heavens, seemed to smile upon their desperate enterprise. The cries of wild fowl awaking in the forests, with occasionally the merry chaunt of some native warbler, arousing to the day, spake also in the language of encouragement. On the borders of a little lake, they found some wild ducks feeding, which they approached without alarming them, and the fire of a couple of arquebuses gave them sufficient food for the day. A small supply of maize, prepared after the Indian fashion, was borne by each of the party, but this was carefully preserved for use in a moment of necessity. Assuming the possibility of their being pursued, the youthful leader urged their progress until noon, when they halted for repose, in a dense thicket, which promised to give them shelter. Here, having himself undertaken the watch, Alphonse D'Erlach counselled his people to seek for a renewal of their strength in slumber. They followed his counsel without scruple, though not without a struggle on the part of his brother, and others among them, to share his watch. This he would not permit, alleging his inability to sleep, but promising, when he felt thus disposed, to devolve his present duty upon others. Long and sweet was the slumbers which they enjoyed, and unbroken by any alarm. When they awakened, the sun had sloped greatly in the western heavens, and but two or three marching hours remained of the day. These they employed with earnestness and vigor. The night found them on the edge of a great basin, or lake, thickly fenced in with great trees, and a dense and bewildering thicket. As the day closed, immense flocks of wild fowl, geese, ducks, and cranes, alighted within the waters of the lake, and again did the arquebusiers, with a few shot, provide ample food for the ensuing day. Here they built themselves a fire, around which the whole party crouched, a couple only of their number being posted as sentinels on the hill side, from which alone was it reasonable to suppose that an enemy would appear. Again did they sleep without disturbance, arising with the dawn, again to resume their progress. But before they commenced their journey, a solemn council was held as to the course which they should pursue. On this subject the mind of their youthful leader had already adopted a leading idea. His experience in the country, as well as that of his brother, during frequent progresses, had enabled them to form a very correct notion of the topography of the region. Besides, several of their followers, were of the first colonies of Ribault, and had accompanied Laudonniere, Ottigny, and both the Erlachs on various expeditions among the Indians.

"We are now upon the great promontory of the Floridian," said

Alphonse, "a region full of dense thickets and impenetrable swamps. These we should labor to avoid, as well as any approach in the direction of the Spaniards. By pursuing a course inclining to the north-west for a while, we shall be enabled to do so, and this done, gradually steering for the north-east, we shall be enabled to reach the great mountains of the Apalachia. This is a region where, as we know, the red-men are more mild and gentle, more laborious, with larger fields of grain, and more hospitably given than those which inhabit the coasts. It may be that having sufficiently ascended the country, it will be our policy to leave the mountains on our left, following at their feet, until we shall have passed the territories in the immediate possession of the Spaniard. Then it will be easy to speed downwards to the eastern coasts, where the people always received us with welcome and affection. We may thus renew our intercouse with the tribes that skirt the bay of St. Helena—the tribes of Audusta, Ouade, Maccou and others of which ye wot. But, whether we take this direction or not, our present course should be as I have described it. When we have reached the country where the land greatly rises, it will be with us to choose our farther progress. There is gold, as we know, in abundance in these mountains of the Apalachian; and it may be our good hap even to attain to the great city of the mountains of which Potanou and others have spoken, and to which certain travellers have given the name of the Grand Copal, of the existence of which I nothing doubt. This, they report as but fifteen or twenty days' march from St. Helena, north-westward. It will, follow, if this description be true, that we are quite as near to this place, as to St. Helena. Here is adventure and a marvellous discovery open to us, my comrades and we shall, perhaps, in future days, bless the cruelty of the Spaniards which hath thus driven us on the road to fortune. At least, we should have reason to rejoice that we are here, when our comrades lie stark and bleeding on the shores of Cannaverel. We are few, but we are true; we have health and vigor; we have arms in our hands, and are quite equal to any of the small bands of Indians that infest the country. We shall seek to avoid encounters with them, but shall not fear them if we meet; and all that I have seen of the red-man inclines me to the faith, that they who deal with him justly will mostly find justice, nay, even reverence in return. What remains, but that we steadily pursue our progress, heedful where we set our feet, keeping our minds in patience, never hurrying forward blindly, and never being too eager in the attainment of our object. Our best strength will lie in our patience This will save us when our strength shall fail."

This counsel found no opposition. There was much discussion of details, and the leading suggestion of his mind being adopted, Erlach readily yielded much of the minutiæ to others. We shall not follow the daily progress of our adventurers. Enough that for twenty-seven days they travelled without suffering disaster. There were small ailments of the party—some grew faint and feeble, others became slightly lamed; and occasionally all hearts drooped; but on such occasions the troop went into camp, chose out some secure thicket, built themselves a goodly fire, and while the invalids lay around it, the more vigorous hunted and brought in game. Wild turkeys were in abundance. Sometimes they roosted at night upon the very trees under which our Frenchmen slept. On such occasions the hunters rose at dawn, and with well-aimed arquebuses shot down two or more; the very fatness of the birds being such, as made them split open as they struck the earth. Anon, a wandering deer crossed their path, and fell a victim to their shot. In this way they gradually advanced into the hilly country. Very seldom had they met with any of the red-men, and never in any numbers. These treated them with great forbearance, were civil, shared with them their slender stock of provisions, and received a return in trinkets, knives, or rings of copper, and little bells, a small store of which had been providentally brought by persons of the party. Sometimes, these Indians travelled with them, camped with them at night, and behaved themselves like good Christians. From these, too, they gathered vague intelligence of the great city which lay among the mountains. This was described to them, in language often heard before, as containing a wealth of gold, and other treasures in the shape of precious gems, which, assuming the truth of the description given by the red-men, our Frenchmen assumed to be nothing less than diamonds, rubies and crystals. But they were told that this country was in possession of a very powerful people, fierce and warlike, who were very jealous of the appearance of strangers. The city of Grand Copal was described as very populous and rich, a walled town, which it would be difficult to penetrate.

These descriptions contributed greatly to warm the imaginations of our Frenchmen, but as the several informants differed in regard to the direction in which this great city lay, it so happened that parties began to be formed in respect to the route which should be pursued. Opinion was nearly equally divided among them. Alphonse D'Erlach was for pursuing a more easterly course than was desired by some ten or more of the party. He was influenced by information previously derived from the Indians, when he went into the territories of Olata Utina, and beyond. But the more recent testimony was in favor of the west, and this he was disposed to disregard. For a time, the discussion led to nothing decisive. His authority was still deferred to and the course continued upon which he had begun. But as the winter began to press more severely upon the company, and as their usual supplies of game began to diminish from the moment that they left the lakes, and great swampy river margin of the flat country, from that moment, as if justified by suffering, the Frenchmen lessened in their deference to a leader who was at once so youthful and so imperative. Alphonse D'Erlach beheld these symptoms with apprehension and misgiving. He well knew how frail was the tenure by which he held his authority, from the moment that self-esteem began to be active in the formation of opinion. He felt that a power for coercion was wanting to his authority, and resorted to all those politic arts by which wise men maintain a sway without asserting it. He would say to them:

"My comrades, there are but twenty-two of us in a world of savages. Hitherto, for more than thirty days, we have traversed the wildernesses in safety. This is solely due to the fact that we have suffered no differences to prevail among us. If you feel that I have counselled and led you in safety, you may also admit that I have led you rightly; for safety has been our first object. We are as fresh and vigorous now, as when we left the dreary plains of Cannaverel. Not one has perished. We have not suffered from want of food, though frequently delayed in obtaining it. Methinks, that you have no reason to complain of me. But if there be dissatisfaction with my authority, choose another leader. Him will I obey with good will; but do not suffer yourselves to disagree, lest ye separate, and all parties perish."

This rebuke was felt and had its effect for a season; but when, after a week of farther and seemingly unprofitable wandering—when they had attained no special point—when they rather continued to skirt the mountains, pressing to the northward, than to ascend them—the spirit of discontent was re-awakened. The circumstance which rather gratified Alphonse D'Erlach, for the present, that they had met so few of the natives, none in large numbers, and had succeeded mostly in avoiding their villages, was the circumstance that led to dissatisfaction among his followers. They were eager to have their hopes fortified by daily or nightly reports from those who might be supposed to know; they desired, above all, to gather constant tidings of the great city of the mountains—to receive intimations of its proximity; and this, they began to assert, was impossible, so long as they should forbear to penetrate the mountains themselves. Against this desire their young leader strove for many reasons. It is not improbable that he himself doubted the existence of the marvellous city of Grand Copal. At all events, he well knew that to penetrate the mountains, during winter, which already promised to be one of intense rigor, would subject his party to great suffering, and, should food fail them even partially in the unfriendly solitudes, would terminate in the destruction of the whole. By following the mountains, along the east for a certain distance, he knew he should finally arrive at the heads of the streams descending to the sea in the neighborhood of the first settlements made by the Huguenots; that he should there find friendly and familiar nations, and perhaps secure a home for his people, and found a new community in the happy territories of Iracana, the Eden of the Indians, of the beautiful and loving Queen, whereof, he began to have the tenderest recollections. He also knew that, only by pursuing his way along the mountains, aiming at this object, could he be secure from the Spaniards in the possession of La Caroline, as well as St. Augustine, who, he did not doubt, were already preparing for exploration of the golden territories of which they had heard, as well as the French.

But his arguments failed to influence the impatient people under his control. Sharp words and a warm controversy, one night, took place over the camp-fires, and led to a division of the party in nearly equal numbers. It was in vain that Alphonse D'Erlach and his brother employed all their arguments, and used every appeal, in order to persuade his people to cling together as the only means of safety. One Le Caille, a sergeant, who was greatly endowed, in his own regards, as a leader among men, and who had enjoyed some experience in Indian adventure under Laudonniere, set himself in direct opposition to the two brothers. "We are leaving the route, entirely, to the great city. We are speeding from it rather than towards. It lies back of us already, according to all the accounts given us, and as we march now, we seek nothing. There is our path, pointing to the great blue summist in the north-west, and thither should we turn, if we seek for the Grand Copal."

He found believers and followers. So warm had grown the controversy, that the two parties separated that very night, and camped apart, each having its own fires. The greater number, no less than thirteen, went with Le Caille, leaving but nine to D'Erlach, including himself and brother. The young leader brooder over the disaster, for such he regarded it, in silence. He found that it was in vain that he should argue, solely on the strength of his own conjectures, against any course which they should take, when his own course, though maintaining them in health and safety, had failed to bring them to any of the ends which they most desired. They were now wearied of wandering—they craved a haven where they might rest for a season;

and were quite willing to listen to any one who could speak with boldness and seeming certainty of any such place. Thus it was that they followed Le Caille.

"Let us at least separate in peace and good-fellowship, *mes camarades*," said Alphonse D'Erlach, passing over, with the dawn, to that side of the thicket where the others had made their camp. They embraced and parted, taking separate courses, like a stream that having long journeyed through a wild empire, divides at last, only to lose themselves both more rapidly in the embracing sea.

For more than two hours had they gone upon their different routes, the one party moving straight for the mountains, the other still pursuing the route along their bases, in the direction of the east, when Alphonse D'Erlach said to his brother :

"It grieves me that these men should perish : they will perish of cold and hunger, and by violence among the savages. This man Le Caille will fight bravely, but he is a sorry dolt to have the conduct of brave men. Besides, we shall all perish if we do not keep together. Perhaps it is better that we should err in our progress—go wide from the proper track—than that we should break in twain. Let us retrace our steps—let us follow them, and unite with them for a season, at least, until their eyes open upon the truth."

He spoke to willing listeners. His followers obeyed him through habit; they acknowledged the authority of a greater will and a stronger genius ; but they had not been satisfied. They, too, hungered secretly for the great city and the place of rest, and were impatient of the wearisome progress, day by day, without any ultimate object in their eyes. Cheerfully, and with renewal of their strength, did they turn at the direction of their leader, and push forward to re-unite with their comrades. They had a wearisome distance of four hours to overcome, but they had hopes to regain their brethren by night, as they knew that they would rest two hours at noon for the noonday meal, which, it was resolved, should not, on this occasion, delay their progress, and by moving with greater speed than usual, it was calculated that the lost ground might be recovered.

Meanwhile, the party of Le Caille had crossed a little river which they had to wade. The depth was not great, reaching only to their waists, but it was very cold and it chilled them through. They halted accordingly on the opposite side, and built themselves a fire. Here the rest taken and the delay were unusually long, and contributed somewhat to the efforts made by D'Erlach's party to overtake them. When, after a pause of two hours, the troop of Le Caille was prepared again to move, it was considerably past the time of noon. As they gathered up their traps, one of their party who had gone aside from the rest, was suddenly confounded to behold a red-man start up from the bushes where he had been crouching, in long and curious watch over their proceedings. The Frenchman, who was named Rotrou, was quite delighted at the apparition, since they eagerly sought to gather from the Indians the directions for their future progress, and none had been seen for many days. Rotrou called to the Indian in words of good-nature and encouragement, but the latter, slapping his naked sides with an air of defiance, started off towards the mountains. Rotrou again shouted; the savage turned for a moment and paused, then waving his hand with a significant gesture, he responded with the war-whoop, and once more bounded away in flight. The rash and wanton Frenchman immediately lifted his arquebuse, and fired upon the fugitive. He was seen to stagger and fall upon his knee, but immediately recovering himself, he set off almost at as full speed as ever, making for a little thicket that spread itself out upon the right. The party of Le Caille by this time came up. They penetrated the covert where the red-man had been seen to shelter himself, and for a while they tracked him by his blood. But at length they came to a spot where he had evidently crouched and bound up his hurts. They found a little puddle of blood upon the spot, and some fragments of tow, moss, and cotton cloth, some of which had been used for the purpose. Here all traces of the wounded man failed them; and they resumed their route, greatly regretting that he should have escaped, but greatly encouraged, as they fancied that they were approaching some of the settlements of the natives.

It was probably an hour after this event when D'Erlach and his party reached the same neighborhood, and found the proof of the rest and repast which that of Le Caille had taken on the banks of the little river. This sight urged them to new efforts, and though chilled also very greatly by the passage of the stream, they did not pause in their pursuit, but pressed forward without delay, having the fresh tracks of their brethren before their eyes, for the guidance of their footsteps. It was well they did so. In little more than an hour after this, while still urging the forced march which they had begun, they were suddenly arrested by a wild and fearful cry in the forests beyond, the character of which they but too well knew, from frequent and fierce experience. It was the yell of the savage, the terrible war-whoop of the Apalachian, that sounded suddenly from the ambush, as the rattle of the snake is heard from the copse in which he makes his retreat. Then followed the discharge of several arquebuses, four or five in number, all at once, and soon after one or two dropping shots.

"Onward!" cried Alphonse D'Erlach; "we have not a moment to lose. Our comrades are in danger! On! Fools! they have delivered nearly or quite all their pieces; and if the savage be not fled in terror, they are at the mercy of his arrows. Onward, my brave Gascons! Let us save our brethren."

The young captain led the advance, but though pushing forward with all industry, he did not forego the proper precautions His men were already taught to scatter themselves, Indian fashion, through the forests, and at little intervals to pursue a parallel course to each other, so as to lessen the chances of surprise, and to offer as small a mark as possible to the shafts of the enemy. The shouts and clamor increased. They could distinguish the cries of the savages from those of the Frenchmen. Of the latter, they fancied they could tell particular voices of individuals. They could hear the flight of arrows, and sometimes the dull, heavy sounds of blows as from a macana or a clubbed arquebuse ; and a few moments sufficed to show them the savages darting from tree to tree, and here and there a Frenchman apparently bewildered with the number and agile movements of his foes, but still resolute to seek his victim. At this moment Alphonse D'Erlach stumbled upon a wounded man. He looked down. It was the Sergeant, Le Caille himself. He was stuck full of arrows; more than a dozen having penetrated his body, and one was yet quivering in his cheek just below his eye. Still he lived, but his eyes were glazing. They took in the form of D'Erlach. The lips parted.

"Le Grand Copal, Monsieur—eh!" was all he said, when the death-rattle followed. He gasped, turned over with a single convulsion, and his concern ceased wholly for that golden city, in the search for which he had forgotten every other. D'Erlach gave but a moment's heed to the dying man, then pushed forward for the rescue of those who might be living. They were surrounded by more than fifty savages, and among these were scattered groups of women and even children. In fact, Le Caille, in his pursuit of the Indian wounded by Rotrou, had happened upon a village of the Apalachians.

It was fortunate for D'Erlach that the savages were quite too busy with the first, to be conscious of the second party. . They had been brought on quietly, and, scattered as they had been in the approach, they were enabled to deliver their fire from an extensive range of front. It appalled the Indians, even as a thunder burst from heaven. They had gathered around the few Frenchmen surviving of Le Caille's party, and were prepared to finish their work with hand-javelins and stone hatchets. The Frenchmen were not suffered to reload their pieces, and were reduced to the necessity of using them as clubs. They were about to be overwhelmed when the timely fire of the nine pieces of D'Erlach's party, the shout and the rush which followed it, struck death and consternation into the souls of their assailants, and drove them from their prey. With howls of fright and fury the red-men fled to deeper thickets, till they should ascertain the nature and number of their new enemies, and provide themselves with fresh weapons. But D'Erlach was not disposed to afford them respite. His pieces were reloaded ; those of the Frenchmen of Le Caille—all indeed who were able—joined themselves to his party, and the Indians were pressed through the thicket and upon their village. To this they fled as to a place of refuge. Our Frenchmen stormed it, fired it over the heads of the inmates, and terrible was the slaughter which followed. The object of D'Erlach was obtained. He had struck such a panic into the souls of the savages, that he was permitted to draw off his people without molestation ; but the inspection of the fatal field into which the rashness of Le Caille had led his party, left D'Erlach with few objects of consolation. Seven of them were slain outright, or mortally wounded; three others were slightly wounded, and but three remained unhurt. The survivors were brought off in safety, greatly rejoicing in a rescue so totally undeserved. The party that night encamped in a close wood, in a spot so chosen as to be easily guarded. Two of the persons mortally wounded in the conflict died that night; the third, next day at noon. They were not abandoned till their cares and sufferings were at an end, and their comrades buried them, piling huge stones about their corses. Repose was greatly wanting to the party; but they were conscious that the Indians were about them. D'Erlach knew too well the customs of the Apalachian race to doubt that the runners had already sped, east and west, bearing *le baton rouge*—the painted club of red, which summons the tribe to which it is carried to send its young vultures to the gathering about the prey.

He sped away accordingly, re-crossing the little river where the party of Le Caille had encountered the Indian spy, and pressing forward upon the route which he had been before pursuing. Day and night he travelled with little intermission, in the endeavor to put as great a space as possible between his band and their enemies. But the toil had become too severe for his people. They began to falter, and were finally compelled to halt for a rest of two or more days, in a snug and pleasant valley, such as they could easily defend. Here they suffered several disasters. One of his men, drying some gunpowder before the fire, it exploded, and he was so dreadfully burnt that he survived but a day, and expired in great agony. Another, who went out after game, never returned. He probably fell a victim to his own imprudence, or sunk under the arrows of some prowling savage. The camp was broken up in haste and apprehension, and the march resumed. Their force was now reduced to thirteen men, and these were destined to still further reduction. The cold had become excessive. The feet of the Frenchmen grew sore from constant exercise ; and at length, despairing of the long progress still before them before they could reach the sea, Alphonse D'Erlach yielded to the growing desire of his people to ascend the mountains and seek a nearer spot of refuge, or at least of temporary repose. He began to give ear more earnestly to the story of the great city of the mountains ; or, he seemed to do so. At all events,—such was the suggestion—'we can shelter ourselves for the winter in some close valley of the hills ; here we can build log dwellings, and supply ourselves with game as hunters.' The Frenchmen had acquired sufficient experience of Indian habits to resort to their modes of meeting the exigencies of the season. They knew what were the roots which might be bruised, macerated, and made into bread ; and they had been fed on acorns more than once by the Floridian savages. They began the painful ascent, accordingly, which carried them up the heights of Apalachia, that mighty chain of towers which divide the continent from north to south. They had probably reached the region which now forms the upper country of Georgia and South Carolina.

It was in the toilsome ascent of these precipitous heights that they encountered one of those dangers which D'Erlach had striven so earnestly to elude. This was a meeting with the Indians, in any force. A body of more than forty of them were met descending one of the gorges up which the Frenchmen were painfully making their way. The meeting was the signal for the strife. The war-whoop was given almost in the moment when the parties discovered each other. The Indians had the superiority as well in position as in numbers; being on an elevation considerably above that of the Frenchmen. They were a large, fine-limbed race of savages, clad in skins, and armed with bows and stone-hatchets. They had probably never beheld the white man before, and knew nothing of his fearful weapons. They were astounded by the explosion of the arquebuse, and when their chief tumbled from the cliff on which he stood, stricken by an invisible bolt, they fled in terror, leaving the field to the Frenchmen. But, three of the latter were slain in the conflict, and three others wounded. The path was free for their progress, but they went forward with diminished numbers, and sinking hearts. The survivors were now but ten, and these were hurt and suffering from sore, if not fatal, injuries. The cold increased. The savages seemed to have housed themselves from the fury of the winds, that rushed and howled along the bleak terraces to which the Frenchmen had arisen. They buried themselves in a valley that offered them partial protection, built their fires, raised a miserable hovel of poles and bushes for their covering, and sent out their hunters. Two parties, one of two, the other of three men, went forth in pursuit of a bear whose tracks they had detected; leaving five to keep the camp, three of whom were wounded men. Of these two parties, one returned at night, bringing home a turkey. They had failed to discover the hiding-place of the bear. The other did not reappear all night. Trumpets were sounded and guns fired from the camp to guide their footsteps, but without success; and with the dawn Alphonse D'Erlach set forth with his brother and another, one Philip le Borne, to seek the fugitives. Their tracks were found and followed for a weary distance; lost and again found. Pursued over ridge and valley, in a zigzag and ill-directed progress, showing that the lost party had been distracted by their apprehensions. This pursuit led the hunters greatly from the camp; but D'Erlach had made his observations carefully at every step, and knew well that he could regain the spot. He had provided himself well with such food as they possessed, and his little party was well armed. He refused to discontinue the search, particularly as they still recovered the tracks of the missing men. For two days they searched without ceasing, camping by night, and crouching in the shelter of some friendly rock that kept off the wind, and building themselves fires which guarded their slumbers from the assaults of wolf and panther; the howls of the one, and the screams of the other, sounding ever and anon within their ears, from the bald rocks which overhung the camp. On the morning of the third day the fugitives were found, close together, and stiffened in death. They had evidently perished from the cold.

Very sadly did the D'Erlachs return with their one companion to the camp where they had left their comrades. But their gloom and grief were not to suffer diminution. What was their horror to find the spot wholly deserted. The ashes were cold where they had made their fires: the probability was that the place had been fully a day and night abandoned. No traces of the Frenchmen were left—not a clue afforded to their brethren of what had taken place. Alphonse D'Erlach, however, discovered the track of an Indian moccasin in the ashes, but he carefully obliterated it before it was beheld by his companions. It was apparent to him that his people had suffered themselves to be surprised; but whether they had been butchered or led into captivity was beyond his conjecture. His hope that they still lived was based upon the absence of all proofs of struggle or of sacrifice.

To linger in that spot was impossible; but whither should they direct their steps

"We are but three, now, my comrades," said the younger D'Erlach,—"we must on no account separate. We must sleep and hunt together, and suffer no persuasions to part us. Let us descend from this inhospitable mountain, and, crossing the stretch of valley which spreads below, attempt the heights opposite. We may there find more certain food, and better protection from these bleak winds."

"Better that we had perished with our comrades, under the knife of Melendez," was the gloomy speech of the elder D'Erlach.

"It is always soon enough to die," replied the younger. "For shame, my brother!—it is but death, at the worst, which awaits us. Let us on!"

And he led the way down the rugged heights, the others following passively and in moody silence.

They crossed the valley, through which a river went foaming and flashing over huge rocks and boulders, great fractured masses from the overhanging cliffs, that seemed the ruins of an ancient world. The stream was shallow though wild; and crossing from rock to rock they made their way over without much trouble or any accident. The ascent of the steep heights beyond was not so easy. Three days were consumed in making a circuit, and finding a tolerable way for clambering up the mountain. Cold and weary, hungry and sick at heart, the elder D'Erlach and Philip le Borne, were ready to lie down and yield the struggle. Despair had set its paralyzing grasp upon their hearts; but the considerate care, the cheerful courage, the invigorating suggestion, of the younger D'Erlach, still sufficed to strengthen them for renewed effort, when they were about to yield to fate. He adopted the legend of the great city. These rocks were a fitting portal to such a world of empire and treasure. He dwelt with emotion upon its supposed wonders, and found reasons of great significance for assuming it to be near at hand. And they toiled after him up the terrible heights, momently expecting to hear him cry aloud from the summit for which they toiled—" Eureka ! Here is the Grand Copal !" In this progress the younger D'Erlach was always the leader; Philip le Borne struggled after him, though at a long distance, and, more feeble than either, the elder D'Erlach brought up the rear. Alphonse had nearly reached the bald height to which he was climbing, when a fearful cry assailed him from behind. He looked about instantly, only in time to see the form of le Borne disappear from the cliff, plunging headlong into the chasm a thousand feet below. The victim was too terrified to cry. Life was probably extinguished long before his limbs were crushed out of all humanity amongst the jagged masses of the fractured rocks which received them. The cry was from the elder D'Erlach. He saw the dreadful spectacle at full; beheld his companion shoot suddenly down beside him, with outstretched arms, as if imploring the succor for which he had no voice to cry. He saw, and, overcome with horror, sank down in a convulsion upon the narrow ledge which barely sufficed to sustain his person. Alphonse D'Erlach darted down to his succor, and clung to him till he had revived.

" Where is Philip ?" demanded the elder brother.

" We are all that remain, my brother," was the reply.

The other covered his eyes with his hands, as if to shut out thought; and it was some time before he could be persuaded to re-attempt the ascent. Alphonse clung to his side as he did so , never suffered him to be beyond reach of his arm, and, after several hours of the greatest toil, succeeded in placing him safely upon the broad summit of the mountain. And what a prospect had they obtained—what a world of wonder, of beauty and sublimity—fertile realms of forest; boundless valleys of verdure; illimitable seas of mountain range, their billowy tops rolling onward and onward, till the eye lost them in the misty vapors of the sea of sky beyond.

But the eyes of our adventurers were not sensible to the sublimity and beauty of the scene. They beheld nothing but its wildness, its stillness, its coldness, its loneliness, its dread and dreary solitude.

"We are but two, my brother, two of all," said the elder D'Erlach. "Let us die together, my brother."

"If fate so pleases," was the reply—"well! But let us hope that we may live together yet."

"I am done with hope. I am too weary for hope. My heart is frozen. I see nothing but death, and in death I see something very sweet in the slumber which it promises. Why should we live? It is but a prolongation of the struggle. Let us die. Oh! Alphonse, your life is not less precious to me than mine own. I would freely give mine, at any moment, to render yours more safe; yet, if you agree, my hand shall strike the dagger into your heart, if yours will do for mine the same friendly office."

"No more, my brother! Let us not speak or think after this fashion. Our frail and feeble bodies are forever grudgeful of the authority which our souls exercise upon them. If they are weary, they would escape from weariness, at sacrifices of which they know not the extent; would they sleep, they are not unwilling that the sleep should be death, so that they may have respite from toil. My brother, I will not suffer my body so to sway my soul if I can help it. I will still live, and still toil, and still struggle onward, and when I perish it shall be with my foot advanced, my hand raised, and my eye guiding, in the progress onward—forever onward. It will be time enough to think of death when death grapples us and there is no help. But, till that moment, I mock and defy the tempter, who would persuade me to rest before my limbs are weary and my strength is gone."

"But, Alphonse, my limbs are weary, and my strength is gone."

"Let your heart be strong; keep your soul from weariness, and your limbs will receive strength. Sleep, brother, under the shelter of this great rock, while I kindle fire at your feet, and prepare something for you to eat."

And while the elder brother slept, the other watched and warmed him, and some shreds of meat dried in the sun, and a slender supply of meal corns, parched by the fire, with a vessel of water, was prepared and ready for him at awakening.

But he awakened in no better hope than when he had laid down. He ate and was not strengthened. The hope had gone out from his heart, the fire from his eye, his soul lacked the cheerful vigor necessary to exertion, and his physical strength was nearly exhausted.

"Would that I had not awakened!" was his mournful exclamation, as his eyes opened once more to the dreary prospect from the bald eminence of that desolate mountain-tower. "Would that I might close mine eyes and sleep, my brother, sleep ever, or awake to consciousness only in a better world."

"This world is ours, my brother," responded the younger, impetuously; and, if we are men, if we had no misgivings—if we could feel only as we might—that the weariness of this day would find a wing to-morrow; we should conquer it, and be worthy of better worlds hereafter. But he who gives himself up to weariness, will neither find nor deserve a wing. Thou hast eaten—thou hast drunken,—thou shouldst be refreshed. I have neither eaten nor drunken, since we set off at dawn this morning for our progress across the valley."

"Reproach me not, Alphonse," replied the other; "thou hast a strength and a courage both denied to me."

"Believe it not; be resolute in thy courage, and thy strength will follow. It is the heart, verily, that is the first to fail."

"Mine is dead within me!"

"Yet another effort, *mon frére*,—yet one more effort! The valley below us looks soft and inviting. There shall we find shelter from the bleak winds that sweep these bald summits."

"It is cold! and my limbs stiffen beneath me," answered the other, as he rose slowly to resume a march which was more painful to his thoughts than any which he had of death. But for his deference to the superior will of the younger brother, he had surely never risen from the spot. But he rose, and wearily followed after the bold Alphonse, who was already picking his way down the steep sides of the mountain.

We need not follow the brothers through the painful details of a progress which had few varieties to break its monotony, and nothing to relieve its gloom. Two days have made a wonderful difference in the appearance of both. Wild, stern and wretched enough before in aspect, there was now a grim, gaunt, wolf-like expression in the features of Alphonse D'Erlach, which showed that privation and labor were working fearfully upon the mind as well as the body. He was emaciated—his eyes sunken and glossy, staring intensely yet without expression—his hair matted upon his brows, and his movements rather convulsive than energetic. His soul was as strong as ever—his will as inflexible; but the tension of the mind had been too great, and nature was beginning to fail in the support of this rigor. He now strove but little in the work of soothing and cheering his less courageous brother. He had no longer a voice of encouragement, and he evidently began to think that the death for which the other had so much yearned would perhaps be no unwelcome visitor. Still, as if the maxims which we have heard him utter were a portion of his real nature, his cry was forever " On," and still his hand was outstretched towards blue summits that seemed to hide another world in the gulfs beyond them.

" I can go no farther, Alphonse. I will go no farther. The struggle is worse than any death. I feel that I must sleep. I feel that sleep would be sweeter than anything you can promise."

" If you sleep, you die."

" I shall rejoice!"

" You must not, brother. I will help you. I will carry you."

He made the effort as he spoke—for a moment raised up the failing form of his brother—staggered forward, and sank himself beneath the burden.

" Ha! ha!" he laughed hoarsely; " that we should fail with the Golden Copal in sight! But if we rest, we shall recover. Let us rest. Let us kindle here a fire, my brother, for my limbs feel cold also."

" It is death, Alphonse."

" Death! Pshaw! We cannot fail now; now that we are

nearly at the summit. I tell you, brother, we are almost at the portals of that wondrous city. Once I doubted there were such city, but I have seen glimpses of towers, and methought but now I beheld the window in a turret from which a fair woman was looking forth. See now! Look you to the right—there where you see the mountain sink as it were, then suddenly rise again, the slopes leading gently up to a tower and a wall. The evening sunlight rests upon it. You see it is of a dusky white, and the window shows clearly through the stone, and some one moves within it. Dost thou see, my brother?"

" I see nothing but the sky and ocean. It is the waters that roll about us."

" It is the winds that you hear, as they sweep down from yonder mountains. But where I point your eyes is certainly a tower, a great castle—no doubt one that commands the ascent to the mountains."

" Brother, this is so sweet!"

" What?"

" Ah! what a blessed fortune! Escaped from the bloody Spaniard, afar from the inhospitable land of the Floridian, to see once more these sweet waters and the well-known places."

" What waters? What places?"

" Do you know them not—our own Seine and the cottage, Alphonse? Ha! ha! there they are! I knew they would come forth. Old Ulrich leads them; and Bertha is there, and brings little Etienne by the hand. And, ah! ha! ha! Joy, mother, we are come again!"

" He dreams! he dreams! If thus he dies, with such a dream, there can be no pain in it. Let him dream! let him dream!"

And Alphonse D'Erlach hastened to kindle the flames, and he

tore from his own body the garment to warm his dying brother; and he clasped his hands convulsively as he listened to the faint and broken words that fell from his lips, subsiding at last into,

"Mother, we are come!"

And then he lay speechless. The younger brother turned away, and looked yearningly to the mountains.

"If I can only reach yon castle, he should be saved. It is not so far! but this valley to cross—but that low range of rocks to overcome. It shall be done. I will but cover him warmly with leaves and throw fresh brands upon the fire, and before night I shall return with help."

And he did as he said. He threw fresh brands upon the fire; he wrapped the senseless form of his brother in leaves and moss; and, stooping down, grasped his hand and printed a long, last kiss upon his lips. The eyes of the dying man opened, but they were fixed and glassy. But Alphonse saw not the look. His own eyes were upon the castellated mountain. He sped away, feebly but eagerly, and as he descended into the valley, he looked back ever and anon; and as he looked, his voice, almost in whispers, would repeat the words—"Keep in heart, brother. I will bring you help;" and thus he sped from the scene.

The day waned rapidly, but still the young Alphonse sped upon his mission. He crossed the plain; he urged his progress up the ridgy masses that formed the foreground to the great cliffs from which the castled towers still appeared to loom forth upon his sight. He cast a momentary glance upon the sun, wan, sinking with a misty halo among the tops of the great sea-like mountains that rolled their blue and billowy summits in the east, circumscribing his vision, and he murmured—

"I shall be in time. Do not despair, my brother. I will soon be with you and bring you succor."

And thus he ascended the stony ridges, height upon height gradually ascending, till he came to a sudden gorge—a chasm rent by earthquake and convulsion from the bosom of the great mountain for which he sped. He looked down upon the gorge, and as he descended, he turned his eye to the lone plateau upon which his brother had been laid to dream, and cried:

"I go from your eyes, my brother, but I go to bring you help."

And he passed with tottering steps, and a feebleness still increasing, but which his sovereign will was loth to acknowledge, down into the chasm, and was suddenly lost from sight.

Scarcely had he thus passed into the great shadow of the gorge, when the howl of wolves awakened the echoes of the valley over which he had gone. And soon they appeared, five in number, trotting over the ground which he had traversed, and, with their noses momently set to earth, sending up an occasional cry which announced the satisfaction of their scent. Now they ascend the stony ridges. For a moment they halt and gather upon the verge of the great chasm; then they scramble down into its hollows, and howling as they go and jostling in the narrow gorges, they too pass from sight into the obscurity of the mountain shadows.

Another spectacle follows in their place. Sudden, along the rocky ledges of the high precipices which overhang the gorge, darts forth a graceful and commanding form. It is a woman that appears, young and majestic, lofty in carriage, yet winning in aspect. She belongs to the red races of the Apalachian, but she is fairest among her people. The skin of a panther forms her mantle, and her garments are of cotton, richly stained. She carries a bow in her hand, and a quiver at her back. Her brows are encircled by a tiara of crimson cotton, from which arise the long white plumes of the heron. She claps her hands, and cries aloud to others still in the shadows of the mountain. They dart out to join her, a group of graceful-looking women and of lofty and vigorous men. She points to the gorge beyond, and fits an arrow to her bow. The warriors do likewise, and her shaft speeds upon its mission of death, shot down amidst the shadows of the gorge. A cry of pain from the wolf,—another and another, as the several shafts of the warriors speed in the same direction. Then one of the warriors hurls a blazing torch into the abyss, and the wounded wolves speed back through the gorges, and the hunters dart after them with shafts, and blazing torches, and keen pursuit. Meanwhile, the Apalachian princess descends the precipice with footsteps wondrous sure and fast. Her damsels follow her with cries of eagerness, and soon they disappear—all save the hunters, who pursue the wolves with well-aimed darts, till they fall howling one by one, and perish in their tracks. Then the warriors scalp their prey and turn back, pass through the gorge, and follow in the footsteps of their princess. The sun sinks, the night closes upon the valley, and all is silent.

XXV.

DOMINIQUE DE GOURGUES.

1.—EARLY HISTORY OF GOURGUES.

THE tidings of the fearful massacre of the Huguenots in Florida, as well in Spanish, as in French accounts, at length reached France. Deep was the feeling of horror and indignation which they everywhere excited among the people. Catholics, not less than Protestants, felt how terrible was the cruelty thus inflicted upon humanity, how insolent the scorn thus put upon the flag of the country. Wild and bitter was the cry of anguish sent up by the thousand bereaved widows and orphans of the murdered men. But this cry, this feeling, this sense of suffering and shame, awakened no sympathies in the court of France. The king, Charles IX., heard the "supplication" of the wives and children of the sufferers, without according any answer to their prayer. The blood of nearly nine hundred victims cried equally to earth and heaven for vengeance, and cried in vain to the earthly sovereign. He had no ear for the sorrows and the wrongs of heresy; and the plaint of humanity was stifled in the supposed interests of religion. Charles was most regally indifferent to a crime which relieved him of so many troublesome subjects; and was at that very time, meditating the most summary processes for still farther diminishing their numbers. He was yet to provide an appropriate finish to such a history of massacre in the bloody tragedy of St. Bartholomew. The wrong done to the honor of his flag and nation, by a rival power, was not felt. We have already hinted the strong conjecture, urged by historians, that the Spanish expedition, under Melendez, was planned with the full privity and concurrence of the king of France. His conduct, at this period, would seem fully to justify the suspicion. His existing relations with his brother of Spain were not of a sort to be periled now by the exhibition of his sympathies with a cause, and on behalf of a sect, which both monarchs had reason to hate and fear, and were preparing to extirpate.

But, if the Court of France demanded no redress for the massacre of its people, and that of Spain offered none, either redress or apology, there was yet a deep and intense passion dwelling in the heart of the one nation, and yearning for revenge upon that of the other. There was still a chivalrous feeling in France which showed itself superior to the exactions of sect or party, and which brooded with terrible intensity over the bloody fortunes of the French in Florida. This moody meditation at length found its fitting exponent. The sentiment that stirs earnestly in the popular heart will always, sooner or later, obtain a fitting voice; and where it burns justifiably for vengeance, it will not long be wanting in a weapon. The avenger arose in due season to satisfy the demands of justice!

The Chevalier, Dominique de Gourgues, was a Gascon gentleman, born at Mont de Marsan, in the County of Cominges. His family was one of considerable distinction. It had always been devotedly attached to the Catholic religion, nor had he ever for a moment faltered in the same faith. His career had been a remarkable one, signalized by great valor, and the most extreme vicissitudes of fortune. He had served in the armies of France during the long and capricious struggles in Italy, which had been the chief arena for conflict in the reigns of Charles the Eighth, of Louis XII., of Francis the First, and down to the present period. Here he had associated, under the command of Brissac and others, with that valiant brother Gascon, Blaize de Montluc, who, in his commentaries, would probably have told us much about the prowess of Gourgues, if he had not been so greatly occupied with the narrative of his own.* But the forbearance of Montluc has not deprived us of all the testimony which belongs to the fame

* The Chevalier de Gourgues is only twice mentioned, but both times with favor, in the chronicles of Montluc. The instances occur in Italy, in 1556; one of which describes the capture of Gourgues, the other his rescue from captivity. "*La il fut prius douze ou quatorze chevaux legers de ma compagnie, dont le Capitaine Gourgues, qui estoit à la suite de Strassi, estoit du nombre,*" &c. Montluc was not the Gascon to leave his people in captivity. He prepares to scale the fort in which they are confined, and, his attempt begun, Gourgues was Gascon enough to help himself. The Spaniards had a guard of eighteen or twenty men over their prisoners, who were sixty or eighty in number, the latter being tied in pairs, to make them more secure. As soon as the prisoners heard the cry of "*France, France!*" from their friends without, they began the struggle within—"*ils commencerent à se secouer les uns et les autres, et mesmes le Capitaine Gourgues, qui se deslia le premier,*" etc. The prisoners, led by Gourgues, assail their guards with naked arms, wrest from them their weapons, and where these are wanting, employ paving stones, actually killing the greater number, and taking the rest captive. Such was the success of the surprise, and the spirit which they displayed.

of the chevalier. Of all the subaltern officers of his time, no one achieved a more brilliant reputation. Among the Gascons, confessedly distinguished above all others by their reckless daring, and headlong eagerness after glory in battle, the courage of Gourgues was such as raised him to the rank of a hero of romance. His youthful eyes had opened upon the latest fields of that race of heroes of whom Bayard was the superior and perhaps the last. He was one of the Sampsons of that wondrous band, whose wars, according to Trivulcio—one not the least remarkable among them, —were those of the giants;—the Swiss, in the fullest vigor of their martial fame, and at the height of their insolence;—the Spaniards, with Hernan de Cordova, the great captain, at their head, and crowning the career of Charles V. with a power and a lustre which his own merits did not deserve;—the Italians, under the sway of, and deriving their spirit from, the fierce martial pontiff, Julius II., and the French, boasting of a cavalry, headed by Bayard, La Palisse and others, worthy of such associates, and such as the armies of Europe had never beheld before. Montluc, who had been trained in part in the same house with Bayard, and Boiteres, who, as a page of the knight *sans peur et sans reproche*, makes a famous figure in the chronicles of *le loyal serviteur*, being among the leaders whom the Chevalier de Gourgues followed into battle. He partook of their spirit, and proved himself worthy to sustain the declining honors of chivalry. But his fortunes were as adverse as his merits were distinguished. With thirty men, near Sienna, in Tuscany, he sustained, for a long time, the shock of a large division of the Spanish army. He saw, at length, every man of his command fall around him, and was made a prisoner The captive of the Spaniard, in that day, when the emperor of the country and his favorite generals showed themselves utterly and equally insensible to good faith and generosity, was to be a slave. They conducted war with little regard to the rules that prevailed among civilized nations. The valor that Gorgues displayed, instead of commending him to their admiration and favor, only provoked their fury; and they punished, with shameful bonds, those brave actions which the noble heart prefers to applause and honor. Gourgues was transferred in chains to the gallies. In this degrading condition, chained to the oar, he was captured by the Turks off the coast of Sicily; the Turks then being in alliance, to the shame of Christendom, with the French monarch, and against the Spaniards. He was conducted by his new captors to Rhodes and thence to Constantinople. Sent once more to sea, under his new master, he was retaken by a Maltese galley, and thus recovered his liberty. But his latter adventures had given him a taste for the sea. His progresses brought him to the coast of Africa, to Brazil, and, according to Lescarbot, though the point is doubted, to the Pacific Ocean. The details of this career are not given to us, but the results seem to have been equally creditable to the fame, and of benefit to the fortunes of our chevalier. He returned to Mont de Marsan, with the reputation of being one of the most able and hardy of all the navigators of his time. He had scarcely established himself fairly in his ancient home, where he had invested all the fruits of his toils and enterprise, when the tidings came of the capture of La Caroline, and the massacre of the French in Florida by Melendez. He felt for the honor of France, for the grief of the widows and orphans thus cruelly bereaved, and was keenly reminded of that brutal nature of the Spaniard, under which he had himself suffered so long, and in a condition so humiliating to a noble spirit. He had his own wrongs and those of his country to avenge. He brooded over the necessity before him, with a passion that acquired new strength from contemplation, and finally resolved never to give himself rest till he had exacted full atonement, in the blood of the usurpers in Florida, for the crime of which they had been guilty to his people and himself.

II.

BLAIZE DE MONTLUC.

THIS sublime purpose—sublime by reason of the intense individuality which it betrayed—the proud, strong and defiant will, which took no counsel from the natural fears of the subject, and was totally unrebuked by the placid indifference of the sovereign to his own duties—was not, however, to be indulged openly; but was compelled, by force of circumstances; the better to effect its object—to subdue itself to the eye, to cloak its real purposes, to suffer not the nearest or best friend to conceive the intense design which was working in the soul of the hero. We have seen that the Marechal, Blaize de Montluc, a very celebrated warrior, a very brave fellow, an accomplished leader and a good man, though a monstrous braggart—the very embodiment of Gascon self-esteem, had long been a personal friend of the Chevalier de Gourgues. Montluc was the king's lieutenant in Guyenne, and to him De Gourgues proceeded to obtain his commission for sailing upon the high seas. Montluc, like himself, was a Catholic; but, unlike de Gourgues, was a bitter hater of the Huguenots. Our chevalier had been too long a prisoner with Spaniard and Turk—too long a cruiser upon lonely oceans, confined to a little world which knew and cared nothing for sects and parties, to feel very acutely as a politician in matters of religion. Such a life as that which he had so long led, was well calculated to conduce to toleration. "Vengeance is mine:" saith the Lord; and he was very willing to believe that in his own good time, the Lord will do himself justice upon the offender. He was no hater of Calvin or the Protestants—was quite willing that they should pray and preach after the desires of their own hearts; and did by no means sympathise with his friend, Montluc, in regard to the heretics whom he denounced. But he said nothing of this to the Marechal He knew that nothing could be said safely, in relation to this vexing struggle, which tore the bowels of the nation with perpetual strifes. He had been taught policy by painful experience; and, though boiling with intense excitement, could conceal the secret flame with an exterior of snow, such as shrouds the top of the burning Orizaba. He found the old knight in the enjoyment of a degree of repose, which was no ways desirable to one of his character. The man of whom the epitaph records—written by himself:—

"Cy dessous reposent les os
De Montluc, qui n'eut onc repos.'

was not the person to feel grateful in the possession of an office which gave no exercise to his restless and martial propensities.

"We are shelved, *mon ami*," he said with a grim smile to De Gourgues, as they sat together in the warm chamber of the speaker:—"We are shelved. We are under petticoat government. Lords and rulers are now made by the pretty women of the Court, and an old soldier like myself, who has saved the monarchy, as you know, a dozen times, has nothing now to do but to hang up his armor, and watch it while it falls to pieces with the rust. But I have made myself a name which is famous throughout Europe, and for the opportunity to do this, I must needs be grateful to my king. I have the lieutenancy of Guyenne, but how long I am to have it is the question. There are others who hunger after the shoes I wear; but whether they will fit so well upon the feet of Monsieur, the Marquis de Villars, must be for other eyes to determine. All I know, is, that I am laid up forever. Strength fails, and favor fails, and I chafe at my own lack of strength. I shall never be happy so long as my knees refuse to bend as I would mount horse, yet bend even too freely when I would speed on foot. But what is this expedition for which you desire the royal seal? Certainly, we Gascons are the most restless of all God's creatures. Here now are you but just arrived at home, and beginning to make merry with your friends, and here you are, all at once, impatient to be upon the seas again. Well, you have won a great fame upon the ocean, and naturally desire to win still more. I' faith, I feel a great desire to keep you company. I would be at work to the last, still doing, still conquering, and dying in the greatest of my victories. What says the Italian—'*Un bel mourir, tutta la vita onora!*' Did this adventure of yours, Monsieur, but promise a great battle, verily, I should like to share it with you."

"Ah! Monsieur, my friend, your passion is no longer mine, though I am too much of the Gascon still, to fail, at the sound of the trumpet, to prick mine ears. But this adventure tells for fortune rather than fame. I find no fame a specific against famine. I would seek now after those wordly goods which neither of us looked to find in the wars with the Spaniard. And for which reason, failing to find, we are in danger now of being put aside by ladies' minions, and the feathered creatures of the Court. There is great gain now to be won by a visit to the Coast of

Benin, in Africa, whence we carry the negro cannibal, that he may be made a Christian by proper labor under Christian rule."

And De Gourgues proceeded to unfold the history of the traffic in slaves, as it was carried on by all nations at that period; its marvellous profit and no less marvellous benefits to the untutored and miserable heathen. The Marechal listened with great edification.

"Ah! Monsieur, were I now what you knew me when we fought in Tuscany, now nearly thirty years ago! But it is too late. I must ever remain what I am, a poor Gascon, as my sovereign hath ever known me; too heedful of his fortune ever to give proper tendance to my own!"

III.

GOURGUES AT SEA.

The Chevalier de Gourgues received his commission, and his preparations for the expedition were at once begun. He converted his goods and chattels into money—his lands and moveables. He sold everything that he possessed. Nor did he rest here. He borrowed of friends and neighbors. His credit was good—his reputation great—himself beloved. It was easy to inspire confidence in the ostensible objects of his expedition. The world then conceived very differently of the morals of such an enterprise, than it does at present. The moneys thus realized were employed in arming two *roberges*, or brigantines,—ships of light burthen, resembling the Spanish caravels; and one *patache*, or tender, a vessel modelled after the frigate of the Levant, and designed for penetrating shallow harbors. One hundred and fifty soldiers, and eighty sailors, formed his complement of men, of whom one hundred were armed with the cross-bow. There were many gentlemen, volunteers, in the expedition; and De Gourgues had taken the precaution to secure the services of one who had been a trumpeter under Laudonniere, and had made his escape with that commander. Provisions for a year were laid in; and every preparation having been made, and every precaution taken, as well with the view to secrecy, as to the prosecution of the object, the squadron sailed for Bordeaux, on the second day of August, 1567, just two years after the flight of Laudonniere from Florida. But the fates, at first, did not seem to smile upon the enterprise. Baffled by contrary winds, our chevalier was at length driven for shelter into the Charente, where he lay till the twenty-second, when he put to sea, only to encounter new disappointments. His ships were separated by a severe tempest, and some time elapsed before they were re-united. He had provided against this event by ordering his rendezvous at the mouth of the *Rio del Oro*, upon the coast of Africa. From this point he ranged the coast down to Cape Blanco, where, instigated by the Portuguese, he was assailed by three African chiefs, with their naked savages, whom he beat off in two actions. He then proceeded and continued in safety upon his route, until he reached Cape Verd, when he turned his prows suddenly in the direction of America. The first land which he made in this progress was Dominica, one of the smaller Antilles; thence he drew on to Porto Rico, and next to Mona; the cacique of which place supplied him liberally with fresh provisions. Stretching away for the continent, he encountered a tempest, which constrained him to seek shelter in the port of San Nicholas, on the west side of Hispaniola, where he repaired his vessels, greatly shattered by the storm, but where he vainly endeavored to lay in new supplies of bread; his biscuit having been mostly damaged by the same cause;—the Spaniards, with great inhospitality, refusing him all supplies of food. Scarcely had he left San Nicholas, when he was encountered by a hurricane, which drove him upon the coast, exposing him to the most imminent peril, and from the danger of which he escaped with great difficulty; he gained, after many hardships, the west side of the Island of Cuba, and found temporary respite at Cape San Antonio, where he went on shore for a season.

IV.

GOURGUES DECLARES HIS PURPOSE TO HIS FOLLOWERS, IN A SPEECH.

His worst dangers of the sea were over. He was now within two hundred leagues of Florida, his prows looking, with unobstructed vision, directly towards the enemies he sought. And now, for the first time, he deemed it proper to unfold to his people the true object of the expedition. He assembled together all his followers:

"Friends and comrades," he said, "I have hitherto deceived you as to my objects. They were of a sort to require, in the distracted condition of our country, the utmost secrecy. It so happens that France, torn by rival religious factions, is not properly sensible of what is due to her honor and her people. I have chosen you, as persons whom I mostly know, as persons who know me, and have confidence in my courage, my honor, and my judgment. I have chosen you to achieve a great work for the honor of the French name, and for the safety of the French people

Though we quarrel and fight among ourselves at home, yet should it be a common cause, without distinction of party, to protect our people against the foreign enemy, and to avenge the cruelties they have been made to suffer. It is for a purpose of this nature, that I have brought you hither. I have heard many of you speak with tears and rage of the great crime of which the Spaniards, under Melendez, have been guilty, in butchering our unhappy countrymen in Florida; nine hundred widows and orphans have cried in vain for vengeance upon the cruel murderers. You know all this terrible history—you are Frenchmen and brethren of these unfortunate victims. You know the crime of our enemies, the Spaniards; always our enemies, and never more so than when they profess peace to us, and speak with smiles. What should be our crime, if we suffer them to escape just punishment for their butchery; if, with the means of vengeance in our hands, and our enemies before us, we longer delay the hour of retribution? We must avenge the murder of our countrymen; we must make the Spaniards of Florida atone, in blood, for the shame and affront which they have put upon the lilies of France! If you feel as I do, the day of vengeance and just judgment is at hand. That I am resolute in this object—that it fills my whole soul with but one feeling—my whole mind with but one thought—you may know, when you see that I have sold all my wordly goods, all the possessions that I have on earth, in order to obtain the means for the destruction of these Spaniards of Florida. I take for granted that you feel with me, that you are as jealous of the honor of your country as myself, and that you are prepared for any sacrifice—life itself—in this cause, at once so glorious, and so necessary to the fame and safety of our people. If our Frenchmen are to be butchered without a cause, and find no avenger, there is an end of the French name, and honor, and well-being; they will find no refuge on the face of the earth. Speak, then, my comrades. Let me hear that you feel and think and will resolve with me. I ask you to do nothing, and to peril nothing, beyond myself I have already staked all my worldly fortunes on this one object. I now offer to march at your head, to give you the first example of self-sacrifice. Is there one of you who will refuse to follow?"

A speech so utterly unexpected, at first took his followers by surprise; but the appeal was too grateful to their real sympathies, their commander too much beloved, and the infusion of genuine Gascons too large among the adventurers, to make them hesitate in their decision. They felt the justice of the appeal; were warmed to indignation by the sense of injury and discredit cast upon the honor and the arms of France; and, soon recovering from their astonishment, they eagerly pledged themselves to follow wherever he should lead. With cries of enthusiasm they declared themselves ready for the work of vengeance; and, taking them in the humor which he had inspired, De Gourgues suffered not a moment's unnecessary delay to interfere with his progress. Crowding all sail upon his vessels, he rapidly crossed the straits of Bahama, and stretched, with easy course, along the low shores of the Floridian.

V.

GOURGUES WELCOMED BY THE FLORIDIANS.

IT was not very long before his vessels drew in sight of one of the Forts of the Spaniards, situated at the entrance of May River. So little did they apprehend the approach of any French armament, that they saluted that of De Gourgues, as if they had been ships of their own nation, mistaking them as such. Our chevalier encouraged their mistake. He answered their salute, gun for gun; but he passed onward without any intercourse, and the night following entered the river, called by the Indians Tacatacourou, but to which the French had given the name of the Seine, some fifteen leagues distant.

Here, confounding the strangers with the Spaniards, a formidable host of Indians were prepared to give them battle. The red-men had by this time fully experienced the tender mercies of their brutal and bigoted neighbors; and had learned to contrast them unfavorably with what they remembered of the Frenchmen under Ribault and Laudonniere. With all the faults of the latter, they knew him really as a gentle and moderate commander; by no means blood-thirsty, and doing nothing in mere lust of power, wantonly, and with a spirit of malicious provocation only. There were also other influences at work among them, by which to impress them favorably towards the French, and make them bitterly hostile to the usurpers by whom they had been destroyed. It needed, therefore, only that Gourgues should make himself known to the natives, to discover their hostility. He employed for this purpose his trumpeter, who had served under Laudonniere, and was well known to the king, Satouriova, whose province lay along the waters of the Tacatacourou, and with whose tribe it was the good fortune of our Frenchmen to encounter. Satouriova, knew the trumpeter at once, and received him graciously. He soon revealed the existing relations between the red-men and the Spaniards, and was delighted when assured that the Frenchmen had come to renew and brighten the ancient chain of friendship which had bound the red-men in amity with the people of La

Caroline. The interview was full of compliment and good feeling on both sides. The next day was designated for a grand conference between Satouriova and Gourgues. The interview opened with a wild and picturesque display, which, on the part of the Indians, loses nothing of its dignity because of its rudeness. The stern and simple manners of the red-men, their deliberation, their forbearance, the calm which overspreads their assemblies, the stately solemnity with which the orator rises to address them, their patient attention; these are ordinary characteristics, which make the spectator forgetful of their poverty, their rude condition, the inferiority of their weapons, and the ridiculous simplicity of their ornaments. Satouriova anticipated the objects of Gourgues. Before the latter could detail his designs, the savage declared his deadly hatred of the Spaniards. He was already assembling his people for their destruction. They should have no foothold on his territories!

All this was spoken with great vivacity; and he proceeded to give a long history of the wrongs done to his people by the usurpers. He recurred, then, to the terrible destruction of the Frenchmen at La Caroline, and at the Bay of Matanzas; and voluntarily pledged himself, with all his powers, to aid Gourgues in the contemplated work of vengeance.

The response of our chevalier was easy. He accepted the pledges of Satouriova with delight. He had not come, he said, with any present design to assail the Spaniards, but rather with the view to renew the ancient alliance of the Frenchmen with the Floridians; and, should he find them in the proper temper to rise against the usurpers, then, to bring with him an armament sufficiently powerful to rid the country of the intruders. But, as he found Satouriova in such excellent spirit, and filled with so brave a resolution, he was determined, even with the small force at his command, to second the chief in his desires to rid himself of his bad neighbors.

"Do you but join your forces to mine,—bring all your strength —put forth all your resolution—show your best valor, and be faithful to your pledges, and I promise you that we will destroy the Spaniards, and root them out of your country!"

The Cassique was charmed with this discourse, and a league, offensive and defensive, was readily agreed upon between the parties. Satouriova, at the close of the conference, brought forward and presented to Gourgues a French boy, named Pierre de Bré, who had sought refuge with him when La Caroline was taken, and whom he had preserved with care, as his own son, in spite of all the efforts of the Spaniards to get him into their power. The boy was a grateful gift to Gourgues; useful as an interpreter, but particularly grateful as one of the first fruits of his mission. That night Satouriova despatched a score or more of emissaries, in as many different directions, to the tribes of the interior. These, each, bore in his hands the war-macana, *le Baton Rouge*, the painted red-club, which announces to the young warriors the will of their superior. The runner speeds with this sign of blood to the distant village, strikes the war-post in its centre, waves his potent sign to the people, declares the place of gathering, and darts away to spread still more the tidings. When he faints, the emblem is seized by another, who continues on the route. In this way, the whole nation is aroused, as by the sudden flaming of a thousand mountain beacons. A single night will suffice to alarm and assemble the people of an immense territory. The Indian runner, day by day, will out-travel any horse. The result of this expedition was visible next day, to Gourgues and his people.

The chiefs of a score of scattered tribes, with all their best warriors, were assembled with Satouriova, to welcome the Frenchmen to the land.

VI.

OLOTOCARA.

SATOURIOVA, surrounded by his kinsmen, his allies, and subordinate chiefs, appeared in all his state on the banks of the river, almost with the rising of the sun. There were, in immediate attendance, the Paracoussies or Cassiques. Tacatacourou—whose tribe, living along its banks for the time, gave the name to the river—Helmacana, Athoree, Harpaha, Helmacapé, Helicopilé, Mollova, and a great many others. We preserve these names with the hope that they may help to conduct the future antiquary to the places of their habitation. Being all assembled, all in their dignities, each with his little band of warriors, numbering from ten to two hundred men, they despatched a special message to the vessels of Gourgues, inviting him to appear among them. By a precautionary arrangement the escort of our chevalier appeared without their weapons, those of the red-men being likewise removed from their persons, and concealed in the neighboring woods. Gourgues yielded himself without scruple to the arrangements of his tawny host. He was conducted by a deferential escort to the mossy wood where the chiefs had assembled, and placed at the right hand of Satouriova. The weeds and brambles had been carefully pulled away from the spot—the place had been made very clean, and the seat provided for Gourgues was raised, like that of Satouriova, and nicely strewn, in the same manner, with a mossy covering. With his trumpeter and Pierre de Bré, the captain of the French found no embarrassment in pursuing the conference. It was protracted for some time, as is usually the case with Indian treaties, and involved many considerations highly important to the en terprise; the number of the Spaniards, the condition of their fortresses, their vigilance, and all points essential to be known, before venturing to assail them. Much time was consumed in mutual courtesies. Gifts were exchanged between the parties; De Gourgues receiving from Satouriova, among other things, a chain of silver, which the red chief graciously and with regal air cast about the neck of the chevalier.

It was while the conference thus proceeded, that a cry without was heard from among the great body of the tribes assembled. Shouts full of enthusiasm announced the approach of a favorite; and soon the Frenchmen distinguished the words, " Holata Cara !" " Holata Cara !"* which we may translate, " Beloved Chief or

* The name is usually written Olotocara; but, to persons familiar with the singular degree of carelessness with which the Indian names were taken down by the old voyagers and chroniclers, and the different modes employed by French, Spanish and English in spelling the same words, there should be nothing arbitrary in their orthography; nothing to induce us to surrender our privilege of seeking to reconcile these names with well-known analogies. My opinion is, that Olotocara was a compound of two words, the one signifying chief or ruler, the other indicative of the degree of esteem or affection with which he was regarded, or as significant of his qualities. Olata, or Holata, was a frequent title of distinction among the Floridians, and Holata Cara, or Beloved Chief or Warrior, is probably the true orthography of the words compounded into Olotocara or Olocotora It may have been Olata Tacara, and there may have been some identification of this chief with him from whom the river Tacatacourou took its name. Charlevoix writes it Olocotora; Hakluyt, Olotocara. It will be seen that our method of writing the name makes it easy to reconcile it with that of Hakluyt—Olotocara—Holata Cara—and with that of the title

Captain," and which preceded the sudden entrance of a warrior, the appearance of whom caused an instantaneous emotion of surprise in the minds of the Frenchmen.

The stranger was fair enough to be a Frenchman himself. His complexion was wonderfully in contrast with that of the other chiefs, and there was a something in his bearing and carriage, and the expression of his countenance, which irresistibly impressed De Gourgues with the conviction that he was gazing upon one of his own countrymen. The features of the stranger were smooth as well as fair, and in this, indeed, he rather resembled the race of red than of white men. But he was evidently very young, yet of a grave, saturnine cast of face, such as would denote equally middle age and much experience, and yet was evidently the result of temperament. His hair, the portion that was seen, was short, as if kept carefully clipped; but he wore around his brows several thick folds of crimson cotton, in fashion not greatly unlike that of the Turk. There were many of the chiefs who wore a similar head-dress, though whence the manufacture came, our Frenchmen had no way to determine. A cotton shirt, with a falling cape and fringe reaching below to his knees, belted about the waist with a strip of crimson, like that which bound his head, formed the chief items of his costume. Like the warriors generally, he wore well-tanned buckskin leggings, terminating in moccasins of the same material. He carried a lance in his grasp, while a light macana was suspended from his shoulders.

---

familiar to the Floridian usage, past and present. Thus Olata Utina occurs before in this very chronicle; and no prefix is more common in modern times, among the Seminoles, than that of Holata; thus, Holata Amathla, Holata Fiscico, Holata Mico. It is also used as an appendage; thus, Wokse Holata, as we write *Esquire* after the name.

"Holata Cara!" said Satouriova, as if introducing the stranger to the Frenchmen, the moment that he appeared, and the young chief was motioned to a seat. In a whisper to the trumpeter, Gourgues asked if he knew anything about this warrior; but the trumpeter looked bewildered.

"Such a chief was not known to us," said he, "in the time of Laudonniere."

"He looks for all the world like a Frenchman," murmured Gourgues.

"He reminds me," continued the trumpeter, "of a face that I have seen and know, Monsieur; but, I cannot say. If that turban were off now, and the paint. This is the first time I have ever heard the name. But the boy, Pierre, may know him."

Gourgues whispered the boy:

"Who is this chief? Have you ever seen him before? Do you know him?"

"No, Monsieur; I have never seen him. I have heard of him. He is the adopted son of the Great Chief, adopted from another tribe, I hear. But he is as white as I am, almost, and looks a little like a Frenchman. I can't say, Monsieur, but I could swear I knew the face. I have seen one very much like it, I think, among our own people."

"Who?"

"I can't say, Monsieur, I can't; and the more I look, the more I am uncertain."

Something more was said in an equally unsatisfactory manner, and, in the meantime, the stranger took his seat in the assembly without seeming concern. He betrayed no curiosity when his eye rested upon the Frenchmen. When it was agreed that two persons should be sent, one of the French and one of the red chiefs to make a *reconnaissance* of the Spanish fortress, he rose quietly, looked towards Satouriova, and, striking his breast slightly, with his right hand, simply repeated his own name,—

" Holata Cara !"

" It is well," said the chief, with an approving smile ; and Holata Cara, on the part of the Indians, and Monsieur d'Estampes, a gentleman of Comminges, on the part of the Frenchmen, were sent to explore the country under the control of the Spanish usurpers. Holata Cara immediately disappeared from the assembly A few moments after he was buried in the deepest of the neighboring thickets, while a beautiful young savage—a female—who might have been a princess, and wore, like one, a fillet about her brow, and carried herself loftily as became a queen, stood beside him, with her hand resting upon his shoulder, and her eye looking tenderly up into his ; while she said, in her own language :

" I will follow you, but not to be seen ; and our people shall be nigh to watch, lest there be danger from the Spaniard."

The chief smiled, as if, in the solicitous speech to which he listened, he detected some sweet deceit; but he said nothing but words of parting, and these were kind and affectionate. It was not long before Holata Cara joined Monsieur d'Estampes, the boy Pierre de Bré being sent along with them, on the *reconnaissance* which the allies had agreed was to be made. In the meantime, the better to assure Gourgues of the safety of D'Estampes, Satouriova gave his son and the best beloved of all his wives, into the custody of the French as hostages, and they were immediately conveyed to the safe-keeping of the ships.

VII

FIRST FRUITS OF THE ADVENTURE

The reconnaissance was completed. The report of Holata Cara and D'Etampes showed that the Spanish fortress of San Matheo, formerly La Caroline, was in good order, and with a strong garrison. Two other forts which the Spaniards had raised in the neighborhood, commanding both sides of the river, and nearer to its mouth, were also surveyed, and were found to be well manned and in proper condition for defence. In these three forts, the garrison was found to consist of four hundred soldiers, unequally distributed, but with a force in each sufficient for the post. Thus advised, the allies proceeded severally to array their troops for the business of assault. But, before marching, a solemn festival was appointed on the banks of the Salina Cani—by the French called the Somme—which was the place appointed for the rendezvous. Here the red-men drank copious draughts of their cassine, or apalachine, a bitter but favorite beverage, the reported nature of which is that it takes away all hunger and thirst for the space of twenty-four hours, from those that employ it. Though long used to all sorts of trial and endurance, Gourgues found it not so easy to undergo this draught. Still, he made such a show of drinking, as to satisfy his confederates; and this done, the allied chiefs, lifting hands and eyes, made solemn oath of their fidelity in the sight of heaven. The march was then begun, the red-men leading the way, and moving, in desultory manner, through the woods, Holata Cara at their head; while, pursuing another route, but under good guidance, and keeping his force compactly together, our chevalier conducted his Frenchmen to the same point of destination. This was the river Caraba, or Salinacani, named by Ribault the Somme, which was at length reached, but not without great difficulty, the streams being overflowed by frequent and severe rains, and the marshy and low tracts all under water. Food was wanting also to our Frenchmen, the bark appointed to follow them with provisions, under Monsieur Bourdelois not having arrived.

They were now but two leagues distant from the two smaller forts which the Spaniards had established and fortified, in addition to that of La Caroline, on the banks of the May, or, as they had newly christened it, the San Matheo. While bewildered with doubts as to the manner of reaching these forts—the waters everywhere between being swollen almost beyond the possibility of passage—the red-men were consulted, and the chief, Helicopilé, was chosen to guide our Frenchmen by a more easy and less obvious route. Making a circuit through the woods, the whole party at length reached a point where they could behold one of the forts; but a deep creek lay between, the water of which rose above their waists. Gourgues, however, now that his object was in sight, was not to be discouraged by inferior obstacles ; and, giving instructions to his people to fasten their powder flasks to their morions and to carry their swords and their calivers in their hands above their heads, he effected the passage at a point which enabled them to cover themselves from sight of the Spaniards by a thick tract of forest which lay between the fort and the river. It was sore fording for our Frenchmen ; for the bed of the creek was paved with great oysters, the shells of which inflicted sharp wounds upon their legs and feet; and many of them lost their shoes in the passage. As soon as they had crossed, they prepared themselves for the assault. Up to this moment, so well had the red-men guarded all the passages, and so rapid had been their march, with that of Gourgues and his party, that the Spaniards had no notion that there were any Frenchmen in the country. Still, they were on the alert; and so active did they show themselves, in and about the fort, that our chevalier feared that his approach had been discovered.

But no time was to be lost. Giving twenty arquebusiers to his Lieutenant Casenove, and half that number of mariners, armed with pots and balls of wild fire, designed to burn the gate of the fort, he took a like force under his own command, with the view to making simultaneous assaults in opposite quarters. The two parties were scarcely in motion, before Gourgues found the chief Holata Cara at his side, followed by a small party of the red-men; the rest had been carefully concealed in the woods, in order to pursue the combat after their primitive fashion. Holata Cara was armed only with a long spear, which he bore with great dexterity, and a macana which now hung by his side. a flattened club, the two edges of which were fitted with the teeth of the shark, or with great flints, ground down to the sharpness of a knife. This was his substitute for a sword, and was a weapon capable of inflicting the most terrible wounds. The spear which he carried was headed also with a massive dart of flint, curiously and finely set in the wood, and exhibiting a rare instance of Indian ingenuity, in its excellence as a weapon of offence, and its rare and elaborate ornament Gourgues examined it with much interest. The instrument was antique. It might have been in use an hundred years or more. The heavy but elastic wood, almost blackened by age and oil, was polished like a mirror by repeated friction. The grasp was carved with curious ability, and exhibited the wings of birds with eyes wrought among the feathers, in the sockets of which great pearls were set, the carving of the feathers forming a bushy brow above, and a shield all about them, so that, grasp the weapon as you would, the pearls were secure from injury. Gourgues examined the owner of the spear with as much curiosity as he did the weapon. But without satisfaction. The features of the other were immoveable. But the signals being all made, Holata Cara waved his hand with some impatience to the fort, and Gourgues had no leisure to ask the questions which that moment arose in his mind.

"It was," says the venerable chronicle, "the Sunday eve next after Easter-day, April, 1568," when the signal for the assault was given. Gourgues made a brief speech to his followers before they began the attack, recounting the cruel treachery and the bloody deeds of the Spaniards done upon their brethren at La Caroline and Matanzas Bay. Holata Cara, resting with his spear head thrust in the earth, listened in silence to this speech. The moment it was ended, he led the way for the rest, from the thicket which concealed them. As soon as the two parties had emerged from cover, they were descried by the watchful Spaniards.

" To arms! to arms!" was the cry of their sentinels. " To arms! these be Frenchmen!"

To the war-cry of "Castile" and "Santiago!" that of "France!" and "Saint-Denis for France," was cheerily sent up by the assailants; and it was observed that no shout was louder or clearer than that of Holata Cara, as he hurried forward.

When the assailants were within two hundred paces of the fort, the artillery of the garrison opened upon them from a culverin taken at La Caroline, which the Spaniards succeeded in discharging twice, with some effect, while the Frenchmen were approaching. A third time was this piece about to be turned upon the assailants, when Holata Cara, rushing forwards planted his spear in the ground, and swinging from it, with a mighty spring, succeeded, at a bound, in reaching the platform. The gunner was blowing his match, and about to apply it to the piece, when the spear of the Indian chief was driven clean through his body, and the next moment the slain man was thrust headlong down into the fort Stung by this noble example, Gourgues hurried forward, and the assault being made successfully on the opposite side at the same instant, the Spaniards fled from the defences. A considerable slaughter ensued within, when they rushed desperately from the enclosure.

But they were encountered on every side. Escape was vain Of the whole garrison, consisting of threescore men, all were slain, with the exception of fifteen, who were reserved for a more deliberate punishment.

Meanwhile the fortress on the opposite side of the river opened upon the assailants, and was answered by the four pieces which had been found within the captured place. The Frenchmen were more annoyed than injured by this distant cannonade, and immediately prepared to cross the river for the conquest of this new enemy. Fortunately, the *patache*, bringing their supplies, had ascended the stream, and, under cover from the guns of the Spaniard, lay in waiting just below. Gourgues, with fourscore soldiers, crossed the stream in her; the Indians not waiting for this slow conveyance, but swimming the river, carrying their bows and arrows with one hand above their heads.

The Frenchmen at once threw themselves into the woods which covered the space between this second fort and La Caroline, the latter being only a league distant. The Spaniards, apprised of the movement of the patache, beholding shore and forest lined with the multitudes of red-men, and hearing their frightful cries on every hand, were seized with an irresistible panic, and, in an evil moment abandoned their stronghold, in the hope of making their way through the woods, to the greater fortress of La Caroline. But they were too late in the attempt. The woods were occupied by enemies. Charged by the advancing Frenchmen, they rushed into the arms of the savages, and, with the exception of another fifteen, were all butchered as they fought or fled. Holata Cara was again found the foremost, and the most terrible agent in this work of vengeance.

VIII.

THE CONQUEST OF LA CAROLINE.

The Chevalier de Gourgues now proposed temporarily to rest from his labors, and give himself a reasonable time before attempting the superior fortress of La Caroline, in ascertaining its strength, and the difficulties in the way of its capture. The captives taken at the second fort were transferred to the first, and set apart with their comrades for future judgment. From one of these he learned that the garrison of La Caroline consisted of near three hundred men, under command of a brave and efficient governor. His prisoners he closely examined for information. Having ascertained the height of the platform, the extent of the fortifications, and the nature of the approaches, he prepared scaling ladders, and made all the necessary provisions for a regular assault. The Indians, meanwhile, had been ordered to environ the fortress, and so to cover the whole face of the country, as to make it impossible that the garrison should obtain help, convey intelligence of their situation to their friends in St. Augustine, or escape from the beleagured station.

While these preparations were in progress, the Spanish governor at La Caroline, now fully apprised of his danger, and of the capture of the two smaller forts, sent out one of his most trusty scouts, disguised as an Indian, to spy out the condition of the French, their strength and objects. But Holata Cara, who had taken charge of the forces of the red-men, had too well occupied all the passages to suffer this excellent design to prove successful. He made the scout a prisoner, and readily saw through all his disguises. Thus detected, the Spaniard revealed all that he knew of the strength and resources of the garrison. He described them as in very great panic, having been assured that the French numbered no less than two thousand men. Gourgues determined to assail them in the moment of their greatest alarm, and before they should recover from it, or be undeceived with regard to his strength. The red-men were counselled to maintain their ambush in the thickets skirting the river on both sides, and leaving his standard-bearer and a captain with fifteen chosen men in charge of the captured forts and prisoners, Gourgues set forth on his third adventure. He took with him the Spanish scout and another captive Spaniard, a sergeant, as guides, fast fettered, and duly warned that any attempt at deception, or escape, would only bring down instant and condign punishment upon their heads. His ensign, Monsieur de Mesmes, with twenty arquebusiers, was left to guard the mouth of the river, and, with the red-men covering the face of the country, and provided with all the implements necessary to storm the defences, Gourgues began his march against La Caroline.

It was late in the day when the little band set forth, and evening began to approach as they drew within sight of the fortress. The Don in command at La Caroline was vigilant enough, and soon espied the advancing columns. His cannon and his culverins, commanding the river thoroughly, began to play with great spirit upon our Frenchmen, who were compelled to cover themselves in the woods, taking shelter behind a slight eminence within sight of the fortress. This wood afforded them sufficient cover for their approaches almost to the foot of the fortress—the precautions of the Spaniard not having extended to the removal of the forest growth by which the place was surrounded, and by help of which the designs of an enemy could be so much facilitated. It was under the shelter of this very wood, and by this very route—so Gourgues learned from his prisoners—that the Spaniards had successfully surprised and assaulted the fortress two years before.

Here, then, our chevalier determined to lie perdu until the next morning, the hour being too late and the enemy too watchful, at that moment, to attempt anything. Besides, Gourgues desired a little time to see how the land lay, and how his approaches should be made. On that side of the fortress which fronted the hill, behind which our Frenchmen harbored, he discovered that the trench seemed to be insufficiently flanked for the defence of the curtains.

While meditating in what way to take advantage of this weakness, he was agreeably surprised by the commission of an error, on the part of the garrison, which materially abridged his difficulties. The Spanish governor, either with a nervous anxiety to anticipate events, or with a fool-hardiness which fancied that they might be controlled by a wholesome audacity, ordered a sortié, and Gourgues with delight beheld a detachment of threescore soldiers, deliberately passing the trenches and marching steadily into the very jaws of ruin.

Holata Cara, as if aware by instinct, was at once at the side of our chevalier, with his spear pointing to the fated detachment. In a moment, the warrior sped with the commands of Gourgues, to his lieutenant, Cazenove, who, with twenty arquebusiers, covered by the wood, contrived to throw himself between the fortress and the advancing party, cutting off all their chances of escape. Then it was that, with wild cries of "France! France!" the chevalier rose from his place of hiding, with all his band, and rushed out upon his prey, reserving his fire until sufficiently near to render every shot certain. The Spaniards recoiled from the assault; but, as they fled, were encountered in the rear by the squad under Cazenove. The battle cry of the French, resounding at once in front and rear, completed their panic, and they offered but a feeble resistance to enemies who neither asked nor offered quarter. It was a massacre rather than a fight; and still, as the French paused in the work of death, a shrill deathcry in their midst aroused them anew, and they could behold the lithe form of the red chief, Holata Cara, speeding from foe to foe, with his macana only, smiting with fearful edge—a single stroke at each several victim, followed ever by the agonizing yell of death! Not a Spaniard escaped of all that passed through the trenches on that miserable sortie!

Terrified by this disaster, so sudden and so complete, the garrison were no longer capable of defence. They no longer hearkened to the commands or the encouragements of their governor. They left, or leaped, the walls; they threw wide the gates, and rushed wildly into the neighboring thickets, in the vain hope to find security in their dark recesses, and under cover of the night. But they knew not well how the woods were occupied. At once a torrent of yells, of torture and of triumph, startled the echoes on every side. The swift arrow, the sharp javelin, the long spear, the stone hatchet, each found an unresisting victim; and the miserable fugitives, maddened with terror, darted back upon the fortress, which was already in the possession of the French. They had seized the opportunity, and in the moment when the insubordinate garrison threw wide the gates, and leaped blindly from the parapets, they had swiftly occupied their places. The fugitive Spaniards, recoiling from the savages, only changed one form of death for another. They suffered on all hands—were mercilessly shot down as they fled, or stabbed as they surrendered; those only excepted who were chosen to expiate, more solemnly and terribly, the great crime of which they had been guilty!

IX.

THE SACRIFICE OF THE VICTIMS.

The captured fortress was won with a singular facility, and with so little loss to the assailants, as to confirm them in the conviction that the service was acceptable to God. HE had strengthened their hearts and arms—HE had hung his shield of protection over them—HE had made, through the sting of conscience, the souls of the murderous Spaniards to quake in fear at the very sight of the avengers! The fortress of La Caroline was found to have been as well supplied with all necessaries for defence, as it had been amply garrisoned. It was defended by five double *culverins*, by four *minions*, and divers other cannon of smaller calibre suitable for such a forest fortress. "Eighteen great cakes of gunpowder," (it would seem that this combustible was put up in those days moistened, and in a different form from the present, and hence the frequent necessity for drying it, of which we read,) and every variety of weapon proper to the keeping of the fortress, had been supplied to the Spaniards; so that, but for the unaccountable error of the sortie, and but for the panic which possessed them, and which may reasonably be ascribed to the natural terrors of a guilty conscience, it was scarcely possible that the Chevalier de Gourgues, with all his prowess, could have succeeded in the assault. He transferred all the arms to his vessels, but the gunpowder took fire from the carelessness of one of the savages, who, ignorant of its qualities, proceeded to seethe his fish in the neighborhood of a train, which took fire, and blew up the store-house with all its moveables, destroying all the houses within its sweep! The poor savage himself seems to have been the only human victim. The fortress was then razed to the ground, Gourgues having no purpose to reestablish a colony which he had not the power to maintain.

But his vengeance was not complete. The final act of expiation was yet to take place; and, bringing all his prisoners together, he had them conducted to the fatal tree upon which the Spaniards had done to death their Huguenot captives! This was at a short distance from the fortress.

Mournful was the spectacle that met the eyes of the French men as they reached the spot. There still hung the withered and wasted skeletons of their brethren, naked, bare of flesh, bleached, and rattling against the branches of the thrice-accursed tree! The tempest had beaten wildly against their wasted forms—the obscene birds had preyed upon their carcasses—some had fallen and lay in undistinguished heaps upon the earth; but the entire skeletons of many, unbroken, still waved in the unconscious breezes of heaven! For two weary years had they been thus tossed and shaken in the tempest. For two years had they thus waved, ghastly, white, and terrible, in mockery of the blessed sunshine! And now, in the genial breezes of April, they still shook aloft in horrible contrast with the green leaves, and the purple blossoms of the spring around them! But they were now decreed to take their shame from the suffering eyes of day! A solemn service was said over the wretched remains, which were taken down with cautious hands, as considerately as if they were still accessible to hurt, and buried in one common grave! The red-men looked on wondering, and in grave silence; and Holata Cara, leaning upon his spear, might almost be thought to weep at the cruel spectacle.

But his aspect changed when the Spanish captives were brought forth. They were ranged, manacled in pairs, beneath the same tree of sacrifice. Briefly, and in stern accents, did Gourgues recite the crime of which they had been guilty, and which they were now to expiate by a sufferance of the same fate which they had decreed to their victims! Prayers and pleadings were alike in vain. The priest who had performed the solemn rites for the dead, now performed the last duties for the living judged! He heard their confessions. One of the wretched victims confessed that the judgment under which he was about to suffer was a just one; that he himself, with his own hands, had hung no less than five of the wretched Huguenots. With such a confession ringing in their ears, it was not possible for the French to be merciful! At a given signal, the victims were run up to the deadly branches, which they themselves had accursed by such employment; and even while their suspended forms writhed and quivered with the last fruitless efforts of expiring consciousness, the chieftain Holata Cara looked upon them with a cold, hard eye, stern and tearless, as if he felt the dreadful propriety of this wild and unrelenting justice! The deed done—the expiation made—Gourgues then procured a huge plank of pine, upon which he caused to be branded, with a searing iron, in rude, but large, intelligible characters, these words, corresponding to that inscription put by the Spaniards over the Huguenots, and as a fitting commentary upon it:—

"These are not hung as Spaniards,
nor as Mariners, but as
Traitors, Robbers, and
Murderers!"

How long they hung thus, bleaching in storm and sunshine; how long this terrible inscription remained as a record of their crime and of this history, the chronicle does not show, nor is it needful. The record is inscribed in pages that survive storm, and wreck, and fire;—more indelibly written than on pillars of brass and marble! It hangs on high forever, where the eyes of the criminal may read how certainly will the vengeance of heaven alight, or soon or late, upon the offender, who wantonly exults in the moment of security in the commission of great crimes done upon suffering humanity.

XI.

THE CHIEFS OF THE LILY AND THE TOTEM EMBRACE AND PART.

"SAN AUGUSTINE!"

Such were the words spoken to Gourgues by Holata Cara at the close of this terrible scene of vengeance, and his spear was at once turned in the direction of the remaining Spanish fortress. Gourgues readily understood the suggestion, but he shook his head regretfully—

"I am too feeble! We have not the force necessary to such an effort!"

The red chief made no reply in words, but he turned away and waved his spear over the circuit which was covered by the thousand savages who had collected to the conflict, even as the birds of prey gather to the field of battle.

But Gourgues again shook his head. He had no faith in the alliance with the red-men. He knew their caprice of character, their instability of purpose, and the sudden fluctuations of their moods, which readily discovered the enemy of the morrow in the friend of to-day. Besides, his contemplated task was ended. He had achieved the terrible work of vengeance which he had proposed to himself and followers, and his preparations did not extend to any longer delay in the country. He had neither means nor provisions.

He collected the tribes around him. All the kings and princes of the Floridian gathered at his summons, on the banks of the Tacatacorou, or Seine, where he had left his vessels, some fifteen leagues from La Caroline. Thither he marched by land in battle array, having sent all his captured munitions and arms with his artillerists by sea, in the patache.

The red-men hailed him with songs and dances, as the Israelites hailed Saul and David returning with the spoils of the Philistines.

" Now let me die," cried one old woman, " now that I behold the Spaniards driven out, and the Frenchmen once more in the country."

Gourgues quieted them with promises. It may be that he really hoped that his sovereign would sanction his enterprise, and avail himself of what had been done to establish a French colony again in Florida ; and he promised the Floridians that in twelve months they should again behold his vessels.

The moment arrived for the embarkation, but where was Holata Cara ? The Frenchman inquired after him in vain. Satouriova only replied to his earnest inquiries,—

" Holata Cara is a great chief of the Apalachian ! He hath gone among his people."

A curious smile lurked upon the lips of the Paracoussi as he made this answer ; but the inquiries of Gourgues could extract nothing from him further.

They embraced—our chevalier and his Indian allies—and the Frenchmen embarked, weighed anchor, and, with favoring winds, were shortly out of sight. Even as they stretched away for the east, the eyes of Holata Cara watched their departure from a distant headland where he stood embowered among the trees. The graceful figure of an Indian princess stood beside his own, one hand shading her eyes, and the other resting on his shoulder At length he turned from gazing on the dusky sea.

" They are gone !" she exclaimed.

"Gone!" he answered, in her own dialect. "Gone! Let us depart also!" And thus speaking, they joined their tawny followers who awaited them in the neighboring thicket, within the shadows of which they soon disappeared from sight.

XI.

MORALS OF REVENGE.

HISTORIANS have been divided in opinion with regard to the propriety of that wild justice which Dominique de Gourgues inflicted upon the murderers of his countrymen at La Caroline. One class of writers hath preached from the text, " Vengeance is mine saith the Lord ;" another from that which, permissive rather than mandatory, declares that " Whoso sheddeth man's blood, by man shall his blood be shed."

Charlevoix regrets that so remarkable an achievement as that of Gourgues, so honorable to the nation, and so glorious for himself, should not have been terminated by an act of clemency, which, sparing the survivors of the Spanish forts, should have contrasted beautifully with the brutal behavior of the Spaniards under the like circumstances ; as if the enterprise itself had anything but revenge for its object ; as if the butcheries which accompanied the several attacks upon the Spanish forts, and the butcheries which followed them—where the victims were trembling and flying men —were any whit more justifiable than the single, terrible act of massacre which appropriately furnished the catastrophe to the whole drama !

If the Spaniards were to be spared at all, why the enterprise at all? No wrong was then in progress, to be defeated by interposition ; no design of recovering French territory or re-establishing the French colony was in contemplation, making the enterprise necessary to success hereafter. The entire purpose of the expedition was massacre only, and a bloody vengeance!

It is objected to this expedition of Gourgues, that reprisals are rarely possible without working some injustice. This would be an argument against all law and every social government. But it is said that revenge does not always find out the right victim, particularly in such a case as the present, and that the innocent is frequently made to suffer for the guilty.

Gourgues could not, it would seem, have greatly mistaken his victims, when we find one of them confessing to the murder of five of the Huguenots by his own hand, and none of them disclaiming a participation in the crime. But there is a better answer even than this instance affords, and it conveys one of those warning lessons to society, the neglect of which too frequently results in its discomfiture or ruin.

That society or nation which is unable or unwilling to prevent or punish the offender within its own sphere and province, must incur his penalties; and this principle once recognized, it becomes imperative with every citizen to take heed of the public conduct of his fellow, and the proper exercise of right and justice on the part of his ruler. There are, no doubt, difficulties in the way of doing this always; but what if it were commonly understood and felt that each citizen had thus at heart the wholesome administration of exact justice on the part of the society in which he lived, and the Government which can exist only by the sympathies of the people? How prompt would be the remedy furnished by the ruler to the suffering party! how slow the impulse to wrong on the part of the criminal!

The suggestion that magnanimity and mercy shown to the

Spaniards by Gourgues, after his victory, would have had such a beautiful effect upon the consciences of those guilty wretches, is altogether ridiculous. The idea exhibits a gross ignorance of the nature of the Spaniards at the time. Gourgues knew them thoroughly. A more base, faithless, treacherous and murderous character never prevailed among civilized nations, and never could prevail among any nation of *warlike* barbarians. We do not mean to justify Gorgues; but may say that it is well, perhaps, for humanity, that heroism sometimes puts on the terrors of the avenger, and visits the enormous crime, which men would otherwise fail to reach, with penalties somewhat corresponding with the degree and character of the offence! There are sometimes criminals whom it is a mere tempting of Providence to leave only to the judgments of eternity and their own seared, cold, and wicked hearts. The murderer whose hands you cannot bind, you must cut off; not because you thirst for his blood, but because he thirsts for yours! But ours is not the field for discussion, and we may well leave the question for decision to the instincts of humanity. The vengeance which moves the nations to clap hands with rejoicing has, perhaps, a much higher guaranty and sanction than the common law of morals can afford.

XII.

THE CHEVALIER AT HOME—MONTLUC COUNSELS GOURGUES FROM HIS COMMENTARIES.

HAVING taken his farewell of the Floridians, and embarked with all his people, it was on board of his vessels, with their wings spread to the breeze, that the Chevalier De Gourgues offered up solemn acknowledgments to Heaven, for the special sanction which he had found in its favor for the enterprise achieved. It was with a heart full of gratitude, that he bowed down on the deck of his little bark, and offered up his prayer to the God of Battles for the succor afforded him in his extremity. It was with a light heart that he meditated upon the sanguinary justice done upon the cruel enemies of his people ; the honor of his country's flag redeemed by a poor soldier of fortune, when disgraced and deserted by the monarch and the court, who derived all their distinction from its venerable and protecting folds. It was with a just and honorable pride that he felt how certainly he had made the record of his name in the pages of history, by an action grateful to the fame of the soldier, and still more grateful to the fears and sympathies of outraged humanity. The acclamations of the wild Floridian—their praises and songs of victory, however wild and rude—were but a foretaste of those which he had a right to expect from the lips of his countrymen in *la Belle France !* Alas! the hand of power covered the lips of rejoicing ! The despotism of the land shook a heavy rod over the people, silencing the voice of praise, and chilling the heart of sympathy. But let us not anticipate.

The Chevalier De Gourgues sailed from the mouth of the Tacatacorou, on the third of May, 1568. For seventeen days the voyage was prosperous, and his vessels ran eleven hundred leagues ; and on the sixth of June, thirty-four days after leaving the coast of Florida, he arrived at Rochelle. The latter half of his voyage had been far different from the first. As at his departure from France, he suffered severely from head winds and angry tempests. His provisions were nearly exhausted, and his people began to suffer from famine. His consorts separated from him in the storm, one of them, the *patache*, being lost with its whole complement of eight men; the other not reaching port for a month after himself. His escape was equally narrow from other and less merciful enemies than hunger and shipwreck. The bruit of his adventure, to his great surprise, had reached the country before him. The Spanish court, well served, in that day, by its emissaries, had been advised of his progress, and that he had appeared at Rochelle. A fleet of eighteen sail, led by one large vessel, was instantly despatched in pursuit of him.

Received with good cheer and great applause by the people of Rochelle, it was fortunate that he did not linger there. He set forth with his vessel for Bordeaux; there he went to render an account to his friend, the Marechal Blaize de Montluc, of his adventures. This timely movement saved him. The pursuing Spaniards reached Che-de-Bois the very day that he had left it, and continued the chase as far as Blaze. He reached Bordeaux in safety, and made his report to the king's lieutenant.

Montluc was one of those glorious Gascons who would always much prefer to fight than eat. He was proud of the chevalier as a Gascon, and he loved him as a friend. But the approbation that he expressed in private, he did not venture openly to speak.

"You have done a famous thing, Monsieur De Gourgues, you have saved the honor of France, and won immortal glory for yourself; but the king's lieutenant must not say this to the king's people. I praise God that you are a Gascon like myself, and no race, I think, Monsieur De Gourgues, was ever quite so valiant as our own; but my friend, I fear they do not love us any the better that they have not the soul to rival us. I fear that the glory thou hast won will bring thee to the halter only. Hearken, my friend, Dominique, dost thou know that, at this very moment, thy vessel is pursued by a host of Spanish caravels? the winds rend and the seas sink them to perdition! Thou knowest, how I hate, and scorn, and spit upon the cut-throat scoundrels! Well! That is not all. I tell thee, Dominique, my friend, there is a courier already on his way to the ambassador of Spain, who will demand thy head from our sovereign, that it may give pleasure to his sovereign, the black-hearted and venomous Philip What would he with thy head, my friend? I tell thee, it is his wretched selfishness that would take thy head—not that it may be useful to him, but that it shall no longer be of use to thee! Was there ever such a fool and monster! Thou shouldst keep thy head, my friend, so long as thou hast a use for it thyself, even though it ache thee many times after an unnecessary bottle!"

"Think'st thou, Montluc, that there is any danger that the court of France will give ear to the king of Spain?"

"Give ear! Ay, give both ears, my friend! Our head is in the lap of Spain already. She hath the shears with which she shall clip the hair by which our strength is shorn; and, if she will, me thinks, she may clip head as well as hair, when the humor suits. It is not now, my friend, as when we fought against the bloody dogs at Sienna, remembering only to outdo the famous deeds of the stout men-at-arms that followed Bayard and La Palisse in the generation gone before. Ah! *Monsieur*, thou wast with me in those days. Thou rememberest, I trow, the famous skirmish which we had before the little town of Sêve. But I will read thee from my commentaries, which I have been writing in imitation of Roman Cæsar, of the wonderful wars and sieges in which I have fought, and in which I have evermore found most delight."

And he drew forth from his cabinet, as he spoke, the great

volume of manuscripts, afterwards destined to become the famous depository of his deeds.

"I have written like a Gascon, Monsieur De Gourgues, but let none complain who is not able to do battle like a Gascon! He who fights well, my friend, may surely be allowed the privilege of showing how goodly were his deeds. I will read thee but a passage from that famous skirmish at Sève; not merely that thou shouldst see the spirit of what I have written, and bear witness to the truth, but that thou mayst find for thyself a fitting lesson for thy own conduct in the straight which is before thee."

Having found the passage, Montluc read as follows:

"As the Signior Francisco Bernardin and myself, who, for that time were the Marshals of the camp, drew nigh to the place, and were beginning to lodge the army, there sallied forth from fort, and church, and trench, a matter of two or three hundred men, who charged upon us with the greatest fury. I had with me at that time, but the Captain Charry—a most brave captain, whom thou must well remember—"

Gourgues nodded assent—

"——with fifty arquebusiers and a small body of horse Knowing this my weakness, the Baron de Chissy, our campmaster, sent me a reinforcement of one hundred arquebusiers. But my peril was such, that I sent to him straightway for other help, telling him that we were already at it, and close upon the encounter. At this very moment, Monsieur de Bonnivet, returning post from court, and hearing of the fighting, said to the Baron de Chissy, without alighting from his horse—

"'Do thou halt here till the Maréchal shall arrive, and, meanwhile, I will go and succor Monsieur de Montluc.'

"He was followed by certain captains and arquebusiers on

horseback. We had but an instant for embrace when he arrived, for the enemy were already charging our men.

"'You are welcome, Monsieur de Bonnivet,' I said to him quickly; 'but alight, and let us set upon these people, and beat them back again into their fortress.'

"Whereupon, he and his followers instantly alighted, and he said to me, 'do you charge directly upon those, who would recover the fort.'

"Which said, he clapped his buckler upon his arm, while I caught up an halbert, for I ever (as thou knowest) loved to play with that sort of cudgel. Then I said to Signior Francisco Bernardin—

"'Comrade, whilst we charge, do you continue to provide the quarters.'

"But to this he answered—

"'And is that all the reckoning you make of the employment the Marechal hath entrusted to our charge? If it must be that you will fight thus—I will be a fool for company, and, once in my life, play Gascon also.'

"So he alighted and went with me to the charge. He was armed with very heavy weapons, and had, moreover, become unwieldy from weight of years. This kept him from making such speed as I. At such banquets, my body methought did not weigh an ounce. I felt not that I touched the ground; and, for the pain of my hip (greatly hurt as thou knowest by a fall at the taking of Quiers) that was forgotten! I thus charged straightway upon those by the trench upon one side, and Monsieur de Bonnivet did as much upon his quarter; so that we thundered the rogues back with such a vengeance, that I passed over the trench, pell-mell. amidst the route, pursuing, smiting and slaying, all the way, till
20

we reached the church! I never so laid about me before, or did so much execution at any one time. Those within the church, seeing their people in such disorder, and so miserably cut to pieces, in a great terror, fled from the place, taking, in flight, a little pathway that led along the rocky ledges of the mountain, down into the town. In this route, one of my men caught hold upon him who carried their ensign; but the fellow nimbly and very bravely disengaged himself from him, and leapt into the path; making for the town as fast as he could speed. I ran after him also, but he was too quick even for me, as well he might be,—*for he had fear in both his heels!*"

Here Montluc paused, and closed the volume.

"It is enough that I have read; for thou wilt see the counsel that I design for thee. It is not easy for thee to take it, being a Gascon; but such it is, borrowed from the wisdom of that same ensign. Thou sawest him scamper, for thou wert on that very chase;—now, if thou wouldst save thy head from the affections of the king of Spain, *take fear in both thy heels*, and run as nimbly as that ensign."

"Verily, it is not easy, Monsieur de Montluc, seeing that I am conscious of no wrong, but rather of a great service done to my country; and if my own king deliver me not up, wherefore should I fear him of Spain."

"That is it, my friend! Our king will, not from his own nature, but from that of others, who love not this service to thy country. The Queen-mother will deliver thee up, the Princes of Lorraine will deliver thee up, and the devil will deliver thee up—all having a great affection for the king of Spain—if thou trust not the counsel of thy friends, and wilfully put thy head in one direction where the wisdom of thy heels would show thee quite another. Hast thou forgotten that good proverb of the Italians, which we heard so much read from their lips and honored in their actions,—' *No te fidar, et no serai inganato?*' Above all, *mon ami*, trust nothing to thy hope, when it builds upon thy service done to kings. It is a hope that has hung a thousand good fellows who might be living to this day. Now, in counselling thee to flight and secrecy, I counsel thee against my own pride and pleasure. It would be a great delight to me to have thee near me, while I read thee all mine history;—the beginning, even to the end thereof;—the thousand sieges, battles and achievements, in which I have shown good example to the young valor of France, and made the Gascon name famous throughout the world."

The heart of the Chevalier Gourgues was not persuaded. He could not believe that his good deeds for his country's good and honor, would meet with ill-return and disgrace.

" The king will do me justice."

" Verily, should he even give thee to him of Spain, or hang thee himself, they will call it by no other name," answered the other drily.

" But the baseness and the cowardice of flight! This confiding one's courage and counsel to one's heels, Montluc!"

" Is wisdom, as thou shouldst know from the story of Achilles. Verily, it requires that the secret meaning of this vulnerableness of the heel on the part of the son of Thetis, is neither more nor less than that he was a monstrous coward --that he would have been the bravest man of the world, but for the weakness that always made him fly from danger. It was in the form of allegory that the satirical poet stigmatised a man in authority. You see nothing in the treatment of Hector by Achilles, but what will confirm this opinion. He will not fight with him himself, but makes his myrmidons do so. What is this, but the case of one of our own plumed and scented nobles, who procures his foe, whom he fears, to be murdered by the Biscayan bully whom he buys?—But, let me read thee a passage from my commentaries bearing very much upon this history."

XIII.

FALL OF THE CURTAIN.

We need not listen to this passage. The reader will find it, with other good things, in the huge tome of the braggart, and garrulous, but very shrewd and valiant old Gascon. Enough to say, that this counsel did not prevail with his friend. Gourgues determined to persevere in his original intention of presenting himself at court. His reasons for this resolution were probably not altogether shown to Montluc. Gourgues was a bankrupt, and needed employment. His expedition had absorbed his little fortune, and left him a debtor, without the means of repayment. With the highest reputation as a captain, by land and sea,—and with his name honored by the sentiment of the nation, which was not permitted to applaud,—he still fondly hoped that his friend had mistaken his position, and that he should be honored and welcomed to the favor and service of his sovereign. He was one of those to hope against hope.

"As thou wilt! Unbolt the door for the man who is wilful. If thy resolution be taken, I say no more. But thou shalt have letters to the Court, and if the words of an old friend and brother in arms may do thee good, thou shalt have the sign-manual of Montluc, to as many missives as it shall please thee to despatch."

The letters were written; and, with a full narrative of his expedition prepared, the Chevalier de Gourgues made his appearance at court. He had anticipated the ambassador of Spain; but he was received coldly. The Queen Mother, and the Princes of Lorraine, with all who worshipped at their altars, turned their backs upon the heroic enthusiast. The king forebore to smile. In his secret heart, he really rejoiced in the vengeance taken by his subject upon the Spaniards, but he was not in a situation to declare his true sentiments. Meanwhile, the Spanish ambassador demanded the offender, and set a price upon his head. The Queen Mother and her associates denounced him. A process was initiated to hold him responsible, in his life, for an enterprise undertaken without authority against the subjects of a monarch in alliance with France; and our chevalier was compelled to hide from the storm which he dared not openly encounter. For a long time he lay concealed in Rouën, at the house of the President de Marigny, and with other ancient friends. In this situation, the Queen of England, Elizabeth, made him overtures, and offered him employment in her service; but the tardy grace of his own monarch, at length, enabled him to decline the appointments of another and a hostile sovereign. But, nevertheless, though admitted to mercy by the king of France, he was left without employment. Fortune, in the end, appeared to smile. Don Antonio, of Portugal, offered him the command of a fleet which he had armed with the view to sustaining his right to the crown of that country, which Philip of Spain was preparing to usurp. Gourgues embraced the offer with delight. It promised him employment in a familiar field, and against the enemy whom he regarded with an immortal hate; but the Fates forbade that he should longer listen to the plea of revenge. While preparing to render himself to the Portuguese prince, he fell ill at Tours, where he died, universally regretted, and with the reputation of being one of the most valiant and able captains of the day— equally capable as a commander of an army and a fleet. We cannot qualify our praise of this remarkable man by giving heed to the moral doubts which would seek to impair the glory, not only of the most remarkable event of his life, but of the century in which he lived. We owe it to his memory to write upon his monument, that his crimes, if his warfare upon the Spaniards shall be so considered, were committed in the cause of humanity!

Our chronicle is ended. The expedition of Dominique de Gourgues concludes the history of the colonies of France in the forests of the Floridian.

APPENDIX.

ORIGINALLY, it was the design of the Author, to write a religious narrative poem on the subject of the preceding history The following sections, however, were all that were written

I.

THE VOICE.

A midnight voice from Heaven! It smote his ear,
That stern old Christian warrior, who had stood,
Fearless, with front erect and spirit high,
Between his trembling flock and tyranny,
Worse than Egyptian! It awakened him
To other thoughts than combat. "Dost thou see;"—
Thus ran the utterance of that voice from Heaven,—
" The sorrows of thy people? Dost thou hear
Their groans, that mingle with the old man's prayer,
And the child's prattle, and the mother's hymn?
Vain help thy cannon brings them, and the sword,
Unprofitably drunk with martyr blood,
Maintains the Christian argument no more.
Arouse thee for new labors. Gird thy loins
For toils and perils better overcome

By patience, than the sword. Thou shalt put on
Humility as armor; and set forth,
Leading thy flock, whom the gaunt wolf pursues,
To other lands and pastures. 'T is no home
For the pure heart in France! There, Tyranny
Hath wed with Superstition; and the fruit—
The foul, but natural issue of their lusts,
Is murder!—which, hot-hunting fresher feasts,
Knows never satiation;—raging still,
Where'er a pure heart-victim may be found
In these fair regions. It will lay them waste,
Leaving no field of peace,—leaving no spot
Where virtue may find refuge from her foes,
Permitted to forbear defensive blows,
Most painful, though most needful to her cause!
"The brave shall perish, and the fearful bend,
Till unmixed evil, rioting in waste,
Wallows in crime and carnage unrebuked!
Vain is thy wisdom,—and the hollow league,
That tempts thee to forbearance, worse than vain.
Flight be thy refuge now. Thou shalt shake off
The dust upon thy sandals, and go forth
To a far foreign land;—a wild, strange realm,
That were a savage empire, most unmeet
For Christian footstep, and the peaceful mood,
But that it is a refuge shown by God
For shelter of his people. Thither, then,
Betake thee in thy flight. Let not thy cheek
Flush at the seeming shame. It is no shame
To fly from shameless foes. This truth is taught

APPENDIX.

By him, the venerable sire who led
His people from the Egyptians. Lead thou thine.
Forbear the soldier's fury. I would rouse
The Prophet and the Patriarch in thy breast,
And make thee better seek the peaceful march,
Than the fierce, deadly struggle. Thou shouldst guide,
With pastoral hand of meekness, not of blood,
The tribes that still have followed thee, and still,
Demand thy care. Far o'er the western deeps
Have I prepared thy dwelling ! A new world,
Full of all fruits and lovely to the eye,—
Various in mount and valley, sweet in stream,
Cool in recesses of the ample wood,
With climate bland, air vigorous, sky as pure
As is the love that proffers it to faith—
Await thee; and the seas have favoring gales
To waft thee on thy path ! Delay and die !"

II.

COLIGNY'S RESOLVE

" And, if I perish !" the gray warrior said,—
" I perish still in France ! If cruel foes
Beleaguer and ensare me to my fate,
The blow will fall upon me in the land
Which was my birth-place. Better there to die
The victim for my people, than to fly
Inglorious, from the struggle set for us
By the most cruel fortunes ! Not for me
The hope of refuge in a foreign clime,

While that which cradled me lies desolate
In blood and ashes! It is better here
To strive against the ruin and misrule,
Than basely yield the empire to the foe,
Whose sway we might withstand; and whose abuse,
Unchecked, were but the fruitful argument
For thousand years of woe! I would not lay
These aged bones to sleep in distant lands,
Though pure and peaceful; but would close mine eye
Upon the same sweet skies—by tempests now
Torn and disclouded—upon which gladly first
They opened with delight in infancy.
This fondnesss, it may be, is but a weakness
Becoming not my manhood. Be it so!
I know that I *am* weak; but there's a passion,
That glows with loyal anger in my heart,
And shows like virtue. It forbids my flight;
And, for my country's glory, and the safety
Of our distracted and diminished flock,
Declares how much more grateful were the strife—
That proud defiance which I still have given
To those fierce enemies, whose sleepless hate
Hath shamed and struck at both. I deem it better
To struggle with injustice than submit;
For still submission of the innocent
Makes evident the guilty; and the good,
Who yield, but multiply the herd of foes,
That ravin when the retribution sleeps!
What hope were there for sad humanity,
If still, when came the danger, fled the brave?

Fled only to beguile, in fierce pursuit,
The wolfish spoiler, leaving refuge none,
In heart or homestead ? Not for me to fly—
Not though, I hear, Eternal Sire ! thy voice
Still speaking with deep utterance in my soul,
Commending my obedience. All in vain,
I strive to serve thee with submission meet,
And move to do thy will. The earth grows up,
Around me ; and the aspects of my home,
Enclose me like the mountains and the sea,
Forbidding me to fly them. Natural ties,
That are as God's, upon the mortal heart,
Fetter me still to France ! and yet thou knowest,
How reverent and unselfish were my toils,
In this our people's cause. I have not spared
Day or night labor ; and my blood hath flowed,
Unstinted, in the strife that we have waged.
The sword hath hacked these limbs—the poisoned cup
Hung at these lips. The ignominous death,
From the uplifted scaffold, look'd upon me,
Craving its victim ; the assassin's steel,
Turned from my ribs, with narrowest graze avoiding
The imperil'd life ! Yet never have I shrunk,
Because of these flesh-dangers from the work
Whereto my hand was set. Let me not now
Turn from the field in flight, though still to lead
The flock that I must die for ! *This* I know !
I cannot *always* 'scape. The blow *will* come !
Not always will the poisonous draught be spill'd,
Or the sharp steel be foil'd, or turn'd aside ;—

And to the many martyrs in this cause,
Already made, my yearning spirit feels,
Its sworn alliance. I will die like them,
But cannot fly their graves! I *dare* not fly,
Though death awaits me here, and, soft, afar,
Sits safety in the cloud and beckons me."

III.

THE VOYAGE.

" And leave thy flock to perish ?"—Thus the **voice**.
Reproachful to the patriarch.—" No," he cried,
" They shall partake the sweet security,
Of the far home of refuge thou assign'st.
They shall go forth from bondage and from death:
The path made free to them, their feet shall take;
My counsels shall direct them, and my soul
Still struggle in their service. Those who fly,
Best moved by fond obedience,—with few ties
To fasten the devoted heart to earth,
And looking but to heaven;—and those who still,
With that fond passion of home which fetters me,
Prefer to look upon their graves in France,—
Shall equally command my care and toil,
Though not alike my presence. They who go forth
To the far land of promise which awaits them,
Mine eye shall watch across the mighty deep,
And still my succors reach them, while the power
Is mine for human providence; and still,
Even from the fearful eminence of death,

APPENDIX.

My spirit, parting from its shrouding clay,
Survey them with the thought of one who loves,
Glad in the safety which it could not share!"

Even as he said,—a little band went forth
Still resolute for God;—having no home.
But that made holy by his privilege:
Their prayers unchecked, their pure rites undisturbed,
They bending at high altars, with no dread,
Lest other eyes than the elect should see,
Their secret smokes arise.
     To a wild shore,
Most wild, but lovely,—o'er the deeps they came
Propitious winds at beck, and God in heaven,
Looking from bluest skies. From the broad sea,
Sudden, the grey lines of the wooing land,
Stretched out its sheltering haven, and afar,
Implored them, with its smiles, through gayest green,
That to the heart of the lone voyagers,
Spoke of their homes in France.
     "And here," they cried,
"Cast anchor! We will build our temples here!
This solitude is still security,
And freedom shall compensate all the loss
Known first in loss of home! Yet naught is lost,—
All rather gained, that human hearts have found
Most dear to hope and its immunities,
If that we win *that* freedom of the soul,
It never knew before! Here should we find
Our native land,—the native land of soul,

Where conscience may take speech,—where truth take root,
And spread its living branches, till all earth
Grows lovely with their heritage. From the wild
Our pray'rs shall rise to heaven; nor shall we build
Our altars in the gloomy caves of earth,
Dreading each moment lest the accusing smoke,
That from our reeking censers may arise,
Shall show the imperial murderer where we hide "

www.ingramcontent.com/pod-product-compliance
Lightning Source LLC
Chambersburg PA
CBHW051855300426
44117CB00006B/407